Readings in Development
Microeconomics, volume 1

Readings in Development Microeconomics
Volume 1: Micro-Theory

Edited by Pranab Bardhan
and Christopher Udry

The MIT Press
Cambridge, Massachusetts
London, England

This book was set in Palatino on '3B2' by Asco Typesetters, Hong Kong, and was printed and bound in the United States of America.

Library of Congress Cataloging-in-Publication Data

Readings in development microeconomics / edited by Pranab Bardhan and Christopher Udry.
    p.   cm.
  Includes bibliographical references and index.
  Contents: v. 1. Micro-theory. — v. 2. Empirical microeconomics.
  ISBN 0-262-02484-5 (hc. : vol. 1) — ISBN 0-262-52282-9 (pbk. : vol. 1) —
ISBN 0-262-02485-3 (hc. : vol. 2) — ISBN 0-262-52283-7 (pbk. : vol. 2)
  1. Development economics. 2. Microeconomics. I. Bardhan, Pranab K.
II. Udry, Christopher.
HD75.R398   2000
338.5—dc21   00-041571

Contents

Introduction

After being written off in a number of premature obituaries, the field of development economics has been rejuvenated in recent years. This has been particularly the case in applications of theories of imperfect information, strategic interaction, endogenous mechanisms of growth and poverty traps, incentives and institutions, and also in careful econometric estimation of basic relationships on the basis of detailed household surveys and farm- and firm-level data. The literature is now so large and scattered in different journals that we felt it is necessary to try to bring some compact structure in a diffuse field,[1] keep some unifying theme and standard of rigor, and provide some major papers in one easily accessible source. In doing this we had to be necessarily selective and rather arbitrary in our choice of articles; for every article selected here we could think at least of two other superb ones in the same area that we could not include. So readers should look upon ours as merely an illustrative effort to bring some of the flavor of what is cooking at the frontier of the subject, not as one self-contained counter of one-stop shopping.

We start in chapter 1 with a broad historical overview of how some of the main ideas which have had considerable influence in recent advances in the general body of economics were originally conceived in the context of developing economies. As economic theory has turned more toward the study of information-based market failures, coordination failures, self-reinforcing mechanisms, multiple roles of prices and the general idea of the potential complexity of market interactions, it has inevitably turned to questions that have long exercised development economists.

Sharecropping, one of the ancient and yet current institutional arrangements in world agriculture, provided the context of the application of one of the first principal-agent models in economics. This began the process of a whole group of development economists probing the microeconomic rationale of informal agrarian institutional arrangements in poor countries in an environment of pervasive risks and information asymmetry. Chapter 2 surveys the theoretical literature on sharecropping with special emphasis on the roles of risk-sharing, incentive provision, wealth constraints and screening in such an environment. It tries to look for common threads in a diversity of models explaining different aspects of sharecropping.

Market fragmentation is one of the common characteristics of developing countries particularly in factor markets (like land, labor, credit, and insurance markets). In chapter 3 Basu and Bell provide a useful framework of "fragmented duopoly" where each seller has a captive segment and a contested (shared with the other seller) segment of customers in the market. The subgame perfect equilibrium of the model shows a method of analyzing familiar topics in development like interlinkage of implicit contracts (simultaneously in land, labor and credit markets, for example) and disguised unemployment.

In chapter 4 Banerjee and Newman trace the dynamic implications of credit market imperfections in terms of occupational decisions of the wealth-constrained. Initial wealth distributions have long-run effects. In high-inequality initial situations poor people unable to afford the collateral required to be self-employed entrepreneurs or employers crowd the labor market, depressing wages and thus the bequest they leave for children, leading to credit traps and inter-generational reproduction of poverty and inequality.

Poverty traps and persistent inequality are also the themes of chapter 5, but now in terms of investment in human capital. Ljung-qvist shows, in a model with increasing returns to educational investment and an imperfection in the credit market for such investment (as future increased earnings cannot be pledged as collateral for a loan), that the poor cannot afford to have education and skill formation. In equilibrium a poor country, even when it has the same technology and preferences as the richer countries with which it trades, will remain characterized by a high ratio of unskilled workers in the labor force and a large wage differential between skilled and unskilled workers.

One way out of credit traps is to get together with other borrowers and try to mitigate the information problems that are behind credit market failures. A major way to do so is to form a credit cooperative and provide peer monitoring. In chapter 6 Banerjee, Besley, and Guinnane build a model designed to provide incentives for such monitoring and test this with nineteenth century data on German cooperatives.

Postwar development economics started with Rosenstein-Rodan's idea of a backward economy making a big push into industrialization by coordinating investments across sectors: when domestic markets are small, a simultaneous expansion of many sectors can be self-sustaining through mutual demand support, even if by itself no sector can break even. The presumption is one of multiple equilibria, and the essential problem is to coordinate an escape from the low-level equilibrium trap to a higher-income equilibrium with industrialization. In chapter 7 Murphy, Shleifer, and Vishny formalize this idea in the context of an imperfectly competitive economy with large fixed costs and aggregate demand spillovers. They provide three examples: a firm adopting increasing returns must be shifting demand toward manufacturing goods, or redistributing demand toward the periods in which other firms sell, or paying part of the cost of the essential infrastructure, such as a railroad. In the first two cases industrialization of one sector raises the demand for other manufactures directly and so makes large-scale production in other sectors more attractive; in the third case industrialization in one sector increases the size of the market for railroad services used by other sectors and so renders the provision of these services more viable.

The literature on such complementarities arising as an outcome of equilibrium interaction in models of monopolistic competition has proliferated in recent years and Matsuyama in chapter 8 provides a useful survey of the common features of such models. In particular he shows the role of complementarities in generating regional clustering of industries, uneven development with international trade, and underdevelopment traps, and provides a careful assessment of the logic of coordination failures and of what Myrdal called the principle of cumulative causation.

In chapter 9 Lucas focuses on human capital accumulation as the main engine of growth and surveys some models of trade and growth in this context. He emphasizes that for the endogenous growth mechanism of learning by doing, particularly on-the-job learning, to occur in an economy on a sustained basis, it is necessary that workers and managers continue to take on tasks that are new to them, so as to move up the quality ladder in goods. This has interesting implications for evolving trade structures in the world economy and rapid productivity growth episodes in some parts of it.

In chapter 10 Puga and Venables look upon economic underdevelopment as a manifestation of the spatial pattern of agglomeration, in a model of increasing returns in manufacturing, backward and forward linkages among industries (emphasized by Hirschman in the early development literature), and transport costs and other trade barriers. Development occurs as this pattern changes, with industry spreading from existing concentrations to new ones. But this may not be a gradual process of convergence by all countries, but instead involve countries moving sequentially from the group of poor countries to the group of rich countries. The authors examine the role of trade policy in industrialization in this context.

The last two chapters deal with environmental issues in development, a subject of great interest to policy thinkers today. We focus on two primary issues, one relating to trade policy, and the other to incentive design and common property—both of these issues have given rise to some controversy in recent years. In chapter 11 Copeland and Taylor have a simple general-equilibrium model in which income-induced differences in environmental policy between a rich and a poor country create incentives to trade. In a framework that distinguishes between the scale, composition and technique effects of international trade on pollution, they show that openness to international markets fundamentally alters the way income effects determine pollution levels. Aggregate world pollution may rise with trade. The distribution of economic growth matters: growth in the rich country may increase this pollution level while growth in the poor country may lower it.

The distinguishing feature of environmental economics is, of course, the predominance of externalities and the various institutional ways of coping with them—much of the policy discussion is dominated by the institutional failures of the state or the market in this matter. In the sphere of local externalities arising from common resources (like forests, fishery, grazing lands, irrigation water) which are vital for the daily livelihood of the rural poor, an alternative institutional arrangement is for the local community organizations to collectively manage such resources. In chapter 12 Seabright discusses the strategic and incentive design issues in the management of con-

flicts in such an arrangement and the contrasts with the more familiar arrangements of private property rights or bureaucratic control.

Note

1. In a textbook (*Development Microeconomics*, [Oxford: Oxford University Press, 1999])
we have tried to provide such a compact structure. This text may be used (but not
necessarily) alongside these readings.

1   Economics of Development and the Development of Economics

Pranab Bardhan

In his ethnographic account of the Econ tribe, Axel Leijonhufvud (1973) comments on how the status relationships in this tribe are determined by skills in manufacturing certain types of implements, called "modls:"

> The priestly caste (the Math-Econ), for example, is a higher "field" than either Micro or Macro, while the Develops just as definitely rank lower.... The low rank of the Develops is due to the fact that this caste, in recent times, has not strictly enforced the taboos against association with the Polscis, Sociogs and other tribes. Other Econ look upon this with considerable apprehension as endangering the moral fiber of the tribe and suspect the Develops even of relinquishing modl-making.

Twenty years later, one can say that the situation has not basically changed, except that "modl-making" has increased even among the "Develops" and that intermixing with other tribes is now also common in some other, growing, fields (like institutional or industrial economics) which have moved away from pristine Walrasian economics (the latter described by Leijonhufvud as the making of "exquisite modls finely carved from bones of walras"). Leijonhufvud ends his story with a sad account of the decay of the Econ culture, marked particularly by the loss of a sense of history among the younger generations.

The vain purpose of this chapter is to try to restore some historical perspective with respect to the many contributions of development economics to *the rest of economics*, and to point to the younger generations, if they care to listen, how some of the glittering ideas they currently play with originally came from that now-neglected field, or how sometimes they have rediscovered, with great fanfare, insights that were well-known in the development literature, familiarity with which would have enriched their own work.

From the Center to the Periphery of Economics

The classical economists of the 17th, 18th and early 19th century were, of course, all development economists, as they were writing about a developing country (in most cases, Britain) going through a process of industrial transformation. Then, in the 100 years before World War II, development economics primarily took the form of protectionist arguments for industrialization in the rest of the world (List in Germany, Manoilescu in Eastern Europe, Ranade in India and the like). In the third decade of this century it briefly flourished in the Soviet Union, dwelling on the problems of capital accumulation in a dual economy and of surplus mobilization from agriculture, and on the characteristics of the equilibrium of the family farm: the best products of this period, the dual economy model of Preobrazhenski (1926 [1965]), the two-sector planning model of Feldman (1928 [1964]) and the peasant economy model of Chayanov (1925 [1966]) came to be regarded as landmarks in the post-World War II literature, after these works were translated into English.

But it is only after 1940 that the subject really took off, beginning with the famous paper of Rosenstein-Rodan (1943) and the book by Mandelbaum (1945)—both, incidentally, written about the development problems of southeastern Europe—and then the woks of Nurkse, Lewis, Mohalanobis, Hirschman, Scitovsky, Kuznets, Chenery and others.[1] Much of this literature originated in a clear perception of the limited usefulness, in understanding underdevelopment, of orthodox economics, particularly its standard Walrasian form with constant returns to scale, pure competition, perfect information, insignificant transaction costs and externalities, supposed institution-neutrality, price-sensitive adjustments in market clearing and so on. For many years development economics carried on its lonely and difficult struggle to escape the well-worn grooves of mainstream economics and got marginalized in the process. As is not uncommon in isolated marginal groups, some members turned to iconoclastic excesses (for example, indiscriminate state interventionism or autarkism and preoccupation with blanket market failures). As news of the failures and disasters of regulatory and autarkic states in developing countries reached academia and demoralization set in among this group, orthodox economists made successful inroads in partially recapturing this rebel territory and many a premature obituary of development economics was written.[2]

It is an irony of the recent history of economic thought that while this process of taming the unruly heretics and bringing them back to the orthodox faith was going on, the pillars of orthodox Walrasian economics were themselves crumbling at the onslaught of a whole generation of mainstream economists armed with their models of informational asymmetry, imperfect and incomplete markets, dynamic externalities and increasing returns to scale, multiple equilibria and self-reinforcing mechanisms of path dependence, models which development economists of yesteryear would have been comfortable with, even though some of these were beyond their own model-making capacity. While under the sponsorship of international agencies market fundamentalism was being rammed down the throat of the hapless debt-ridden countries in the so-called third (and now also the second) world, faith in it was being considerably shaken among mainstream economic theorists.

In this Reformation that economic theory has been undergoing I believe the contributions of the main concerns of development economics, those faint rumblings from the periphery, have not been insignificant. Stiglitz (1989) reminds us:

A study of LDC's is to economics what the study of pathology is to medicine; by understanding what happens when things do not work well, we gain insight into how they work when they do function as designed. The difference is that in economics, pathology is the rule: less than a quarter of mankind lives in the developed economies.

One may add that orthodox Walrasian economics has not fared very well in the diagnosis and treatment of even relatively healthy economies, and in the current revamping of the main body of economic analysis insights garnered over the years from the pathological cases have turned out to be quite useful. In the following discussion I shall, somewhat schematically, refer to several of these insights.

Efficiency Wage Theory

When in recent years high and persistent unemployment in developed countries became a focus of serious attention, macro and labor economists in search of micro-foundations of this disturbing phenomenon turned to issues which exercised many development economists in the 1950s and 1960s: how to explain the coexistence of a significant positive wage and massive unemployment and underemployment; the puzzle was particularly striking for densely populated agriculture of poor countries where trade unions are weak or non-existent and minimum wage legislation is hardly enforced. One of the theories—developed independently by Leibenstein (1957) and Mazumdar (1959)—built on the link between nutrition intake and work efficiency and explored the effects of this link on wages and involuntary unemployment: at too low a wage, the productivity of a worker may also be too low for the employer to be interested in hiring him or her. This is the now-famous efficiency wage theory, although its current interpretations have generalized the link between wage and efficiency in terms of incentives, morale and effort-intensity (see the papers in Akerlof and Yellen, 1986), and even this generalization was first recognized in the context of less developed countries by Stiglitz (1974).[3]

The models of Leibenstein and Mazumdar are, I believe, the first to illustrate the general principle that if the price of a factor or a good has functions other than simply the usual market-clearing one (for example, indicating something about the quality of the factor or the good), one essentially gets beyond the confines of the market-clearing Walrasian equilibrium, and, as Stiglitz has shown in several papers, many real-world phenomena like involuntary unemployment or credit rationing become analytically tractable as examples of this general principle. Another important corollary of the same models is that the usual separability of equity and efficiency of orthodox economics breaks down: a more egalitarian distribution of land, for example, by reducing the malnourishment of the currently unemployed, may lead to a rise in aggregate output in the economy (Dasgupta and Ray, 1986). The general principle involved here is now recognized in the literature on imperfect information and transaction costs: the terms and conditions of contracts in various transactions, which directly affect the efficiency of resource allocation, crucially depend on ownership structures and property relations. The idea that whether a market economy is or is not Pareto efficient depends on the distribution of wealth was generalized in Greenwald and Stiglitz (1986).

Dynamic Externalities

Apart from non-clearing labor markets, the other major preoccupation of early development theory was the large impact of positive externalities on the development process. Three or four decades later, the so-called new growth theory is trying to formalize this idea of how externalities generated by investment can explain divergence in growth outcomes across countries or regions. The old literature classified two major types of such externalities: technological and pecuniary. This distinction, originally due to Viner, was popularized by Scitovsky (1954).

Technological externalities relate to the spillovers from one firm's investment on the productivity of other firms in the same or other sectors. The recent growth literature—which starts with Romer (1986, 1990) and Lucas (1988)—has increased the consciousness of the profession about the importance of these external effects (particularly those flowing from investment in human capital). However, it tends to overlook (and thus fails to learn from) the earlier development literature which abounds with many examples of (and sophisticated debates on) these effects through learning, skill-formation, machine user-supplier interaction, networks of technology diffusion, and so on.

Formalization of dynamic externalities in the earlier literature was largely in the context of learning by doing, following Arrow's (1962) model. For example, the infant-industry argument,[4] the most popular argument for protection in developing countries, was modelled on those lines by Bardhan (1970) and Clemhout and Wan (1970). The acquired and sometimes policy-driven nature of dynamic comparative advantage, to which the East Asian challenge has awakened many developed-country trade theorists, has been a persistent theme in the trade and development literature for decades. In general, the literature on the microeconomics of technological progress has always emphasized the pervasiveness of externalities in the innovation process, in the transfer, absorption, development and adaptation of new technologies; and the problems posed by the catching-up process in the developing countries helped shape the directions of this literature.

Where the earlier development literature went astray—and in this respect the new aggregate endogenous growth models are not any more careful—is in underestimating the difficulty of identifying the few sectors and locations where the spillover effects may be large and particularly difficult to internalize.[5] Learning is often highly localized[6] and project-specific. Unique, gigantic, capital-intensive projects sometimes do not generate enough of diffuse externalities. The extent of spillovers also depends crucially on the nature of competition that the

policy environment promotes and of the physical and social infrastructure, including the level of education in the general population.

Development economists of the 1940s and 1950s made an especially impressive contribution in the case of "pecuniary" external
economies, in particular the case of what may be called economies of
market coordination. The insight is originally due to Young (1928)
and Rosenstein-Rodan (1943) and developed by many others, particularly Nurkse (1953), Scitovsky (1954) and Fleming (1955). When
domestic markets are small (and foreign trade is costly), simultaneous expansion of many sectors can be self-sustaining through mutual
demand support, even if by itself no sector can break even.[7] To capture the full flavor of the problem of strategic complementarity of
industries in terms of market size, one needs a full-scale model of
plant-level economies of scale in production which can be tapped
with large demand spillovers. This formalization was done in a recent
model by Murphy, Shleifer and Vishny (1989).[8]

The Rosenstein-Rodan idea must be one of the early examples in
the flowering of the general literature on coordination failures in
economics. As Krugman (1992) has pointed out, the basic idea has
also been fruitful in generating examples of multiple equilibria in
international trade (with increasing returns in the production of nontraded intermediate goods bringing about external economies at the
level of final goods), and the presence or absence of agglomeration
effects in regional economics and economic geography. Related ideas
have been used in the growth theory of Kaldor (1966) and Shleifer
(1986), and in the macroeconomics of unemployment in the models of
Cooper and John (1988), Hart (1982), Kiyotaki (1988) and Weitzman
(1982), based essentially on coordination failures in the face of
demand interlinkages.

The idea of how plant-level economies of scale get translated into
increasing returns at the aggregate level through "pecuniary" external economies, which was so central to the development economics
of the 1950s, lost much of its intellectual force in the subsequent
decades, not so much because it lacked, until recently, a firm anchor-
ing in a formal model using tools of imperfect markets equilibrium
analysis, as Krugman (1992) suggests, but more because at the policy
level the difficulties of aggregate coordination were underestimated
(particularly at the existing levels of administrative capacity and
political coherence in the developing countries) and the incentive and
organizational issues of micro-management of capital were under-
appreciated. The resulting government failures diverted the pro-

fession's attention from what nevertheless remains an important source of market failure discovered by early development economics.

Multiple Equilibria and Hysteresis

Growth models with increasing returns, macroeconomic models of unemployment equilibrium with imperfect competition, and game-theoretic models have generated a plethora of cases of multiple equilibria in the recent literature in economics. The 1950s development theory started with a presumption of multiple equilibria and posed the essential problem as one of escaping a "low-level equilibrium trap" to a better higher-income equilibrium. There were two quite distinct mechanisms involved in the models of that decade: one worked through the economic-demographic interactions of income, savings and endogenous population growth, so the problem was to escape a Malthusian trap with a "critical minimum effort"—as in the models of Buttrick (1958), Nelson (1956) and Leibenstein (1957); the other was based on the kind of increasing returns which generate strategic complementarities among sectors, through a process of "cumulative causation" (Myrdal, 1957), requiring a coordinated "big push" (Rosenstein-Rodan, 1943) for industrialization.

In the literature on multiple equilibria with underdevelopment traps, one can discuss two different dynamic processes of how a particular equilibrium actually gets established. The economic-demographic models, as well as models of learning and international specialization (where a poor country gets trapped in an historical pattern of specialization) or of unequalizing spirals in North-South interaction (Krugman, 1981, 1987), focus on the decisive role of history or initial conditions. The task of development policy here is to compensate for an historical handicap. On the other hand, big-push models like that of Rosenstein-Rodan emphasize the role of expectations (about investment by other firms) and self-fulfilling prophecy. The task of development policy is to coordinate expectations around high investment. This "history versus expectations" dichotomy has been further analyzed by Krugman (1991) and Matsuyama (1991), and the relative importance of the past and expected future is shown to depend on some parameters of the economy (like the discount rate and the speed of adjustment).

The importance of hysteresis in a model of multiple equilibria with increasing returns has now been highlighted in the work on path-dependence in technological development and industrial location in developed countries (Arthur, 1989; David, 1985) and in models of unemployment (Blanchard and Summers, 1987). Expectation-driven multiple equilibria are now a prominent feature in models of network externalities in technology adoption (Farrell and Saloner, 1986) and in macroeconomic models of search (Diamond and Fudenberg, 1987; Howitt and McAfee, 1988). In all these models, the desirability of adopting a particular course depends on how many others are expected to do the same, a general point which Rosenstein-Rodan, Scitovsky and others tried to drive home in development economics decades back.

Multiplicity of equilibria also creates more intellectual space for cultural, sociological and political factors in influencing the process of economic adjustment to an equilibrium. Early recognition of this may partly explain why the "Develops" in Leijonhufvud's Econ tribe were among the first to break the taboo against association with "Polscis," "Sociogs" and other tribes.

Persistence of Dysfunctional Institutions

The self-reinforcing mechanisms which bring about hysteresis and "lock-in" can also be used to explain the persistence of socially suboptimal institutions. Development economists, particularly those with a radical orientation, have never tired of pointing to many long-lasting institutions in poor countries which block economic progress. The property-rights school and the "new" institutional economists often implicitly or explicitly deny this: their account of how more efficient institutions and governance structures evolve in response to new benefit-cost possibilities often displays a certain ahistorical functionalism and even a kind of vulgar Darwinism about the survival of the fittest institution. The more recent literature on institutional economics, however, validates the insight of development economists about suboptimal institutions.

Transaction costs, which form the base of the new institutional economics, themselves can reduce pressures from any social selection process by raising barriers to entry and exit. Then there are the self-reinforcing forces, like increasing returns from adopting a particular institution locking in what may turn out to be an inferior institution in the long run or like a mutually sustaining network of social sanctions on deviants. Akerlof (1984), drawing partly upon the example of the Indian caste system, has built models to show how economically unprofitable or socially unpleasant customs may persist as Nash equilibria when each individual conforms out of fear of loss of reputation from disobedience. These equilibria are difficult to disturb by small shocks.

Principal-Agent Models and Missing Markets

Many of the existing suboptimal institutions may, nevertheless, be serving some real economic function under a set of informational constraints and missing markets (particularly of credit and insurance in the case of poor countries). In the 1970s and 1980s, when economic theory was going through a major overhaul to accommodate imperfect and asymmetric information and incomplete markets and jettisoning some of its fundamental theorems on the way, development economics was often at the forefront in this change-over, since those information problems are particularly acute in the context of development. Stiglitz provided the leadership to a whole group of development economists probing the microeconomic rationale of the formation of agrarian institutions in poor countries in an environment of pervasive risks, information asymmetry and moral hazard.[9] Stiglitz's (1974) model of share-cropping—viewing this ancient institution as a compromise between risk and work incentive effects—is one of the first fully worked out principal-agent models in economics; in this paper he explicitly points out that the agency problem of sharecropping is in some respects essentially the same as the problem of management within a corporation.[10] Some other problems in developing countries inspired work on adverse selection models: for example, Akerlof's famous "lemons" paper (1970) was motivated to a large extent by his experience in India (it says in its first paragraph: "This paper presents a struggling attempt to give structure to the statement, 'Business in underdeveloped countries is difficult'"); and Stiglitz's (1975) paper on education as a screening device—one of the early papers on screening and signalling—was explicitly in response to questions posed to him in Kenya about the role of higher education.

Development economists have always emphasized the crushing effects of capital market imperfections (or even non-existence), in terms of dictating smaller scale in production and risk-taking and of adoption of myopic policies. These problems are now better appreciated in the literature on credit rationing under imperfect information and imperfect enforcement, particularly as the agency costs in the credit market rise when the borrowers are poorer. The development literature has also pointed our attention to the conflict between the risk-pooling advantages of a large formal credit market and the monitoring advantages of local, informal, sometimes non-market, lending. Studies of successful schemes of traditional rotating credit associations and also group loans (as in the widely noted case of Grameen Bank in Bangladesh) in poor countries have focussed attention on the important idea of peer monitoring, which as Arnott and Stiglitz (1991) have argued, can be an important mechanism for controlling moral hazard in credit markets, labor markets and insurance markets in both developed and less-developed countries.

The Enforcement Problem in International Loan Contracts

A particularly important macroeconomic extension of the issues of credit market imperfections is in the international field. The debt crisis of the developing countries in the 1980s gave rise to a burgeoning literature on an analysis of the implications and consequences of "sovereign risk," the various deterrents to default and the credibility of sanctions—the leading references here are those of Eaton and Gersovitz (1981), Eaton, Gersovitz and Stiglitz (1986), Kletzer (1984), and Bulow and Rogoff (1989). (One might also look up the symposium in the Winter 1990 issue of this journal.) This has not merely filled a major lacuna in the field of international finance, but also opened up a significant line of research emphasizing the importance of enforcement problems in economic relationships, apart from providing an early formulation of the reputation model the idea of which subsequently received extensive application elsewhere.

Targeting in the Theory of Economic Policy

Various arguments indiscriminately used in support of protection in developing countries gave rise, in reaction, to the theory of economic policy under what are called "domestic distortions" in the literature on international trade theory. For example, popular arguments for protection (or even banning of some imports) with a view to curbing luxury consumption of the rich in poor countries, were countered quite early in the trade and development literature by the argument that a trade restriction is not the first-best policy for achieving this or other purely domestic objectives. For example, if curbing luxury consumption is the objective, the first-best policy is to have a consumption tax on luxuries; if reducing economic inequality is the objective, progressive income and wealth taxation may be better than tariffs on luxury imports.

Similarly, if an infant industry cannot get off the ground on account of an inability to raise credit to cover initial losses in an imperfect credit market, then the optimum policy may be to subsidize credit, not protection. In several papers in the 1960s by Ramaswami, Bhagwati, Srinivasan and Johnson, all synthesized later in a paper by Bhagwati (1971), the general principle of targeting in economic policy was developed: "distortions" or departures from the usual marginal conditions of Pareto-efficiency are best tackled by using policy instruments that act most directly on the relevant margin. Not merely is this the most general result available to this day in the theory of trade policy, it allowed liberal economists the leeway, in departure from the practice of classical economists, to be an interventionist on matters of domestic policy and at the same time to be a free-trader in the international arena.

One extension of this literature originating in the concerns of development policy came in the form of the well-known Diamond-Mirrlees (1971) result in the theory of public finance on the desirability of aggregate production efficiency, under certain conditions, even when the first-best optimum is not achievable (in the absence of lump-sum taxes to adjust consumer incomes). Again, intervention is to be directed as closely as possible to the source of the distortion, to be applied to the prices the consumers (not the producers) face.

Cost-Benefit Analysis

This part of applied welfare economics, which dates back to Dupuit (1844 [1952]), received a major impetus from the project evaluation literature in development economics in the 1960s and early 1970s. The most influential works in this field have been those of Tinbergen (1967), Little and Mirrlees (1974), and Dasgupta, Marglin and Sen for the UNIDO (1972). The analytical insights of this literature, particularly on the key shadow prices of labor, investment and foreign exchange—which combine ideas from trade theory, general-equilibrium public finance theory and development planning—have now become part of mainstream economics on the general principles of evaluation of public investment.

Beyond Utilitarianism

The literature on the economics of destitution and deprivation and peoples' ways of coping with such severe misfortunes and inequities made development economists more aware of the limitations of the metric of utilities. To quote Sen (1984): "Judging importance by the mental metric of happiness or desire-fulfillment can take a deeply biased form due to the fact that the mental reactions often reflect defeatist compromises with harsh reality induced by hopelessness. The insecure sharecropper, the exploited landless laborer, the over-worked domestic servant, the subordinate housewife, may all come to terms with their respective predicaments in such a way that griev-ance and discontent are submerged in cheerful endurance by the necessity of uneventful survival." This, among other things, has induced a whole group of economists and economic philosophers led by Sen to challenge the foundations of welfare economics and to suggest new measures of well-being, for example in terms of basic capabilities and functionings in human life.[11]

Other Spillovers from Development Economics

There are many other examples of how the results of the study of developing countries have spilled over the confines of its own field and enriched the general body of economics. The study of rent-seeking—as in Krueger (1974)—in connection with trade restrictions in developing countries has contributed to the general theory of public choice. The theory of commodity price stabilization has con-tributed to the more general literature on risk and saving. The dual economy models of development, based on the traditional-modern or formal-informal distinction, have been extended to the case of dualism between "primary" and "secondary" job markets in the labor economics of developed countries. The theory of interlinked contracts in land, labor, credit or output markets between the same parties in poor countries—see Bardhan (1989) for an overview of this literature—has added new dimensions to the general industrial eco-nomics literature on nonlinear pricing and tie-in sales, and the gen-eral theory of vertical relations based upon moral hazard.

This chapter has identified several areas where ideas which have had considerable influence in both microeconomics and macroeco-nomics, were first developed in the context of development economics. Sometimes recent theorists were driven by their own intellectual agenda to these ideas, oblivious of the pre-existing and quite rich development literature. In particular, as economic theory has turned more toward the study of information-based market failures, coordination failures, multiple roles of prices and the general idea of the potential complexity of market interactions, it has inevitably turned to questions that have long exercised development economists. The latter in turn are nowadays more aware of the healthy disciplining effects of market rivalry (even when markets work highly imperfectly) and of the pitfalls of reflexive interventionism.

There is, of course, no doubt that over the years development economics has benefitted a great deal from the concepts and tools pioneered in other fields. But it has not been a one-way traffic. While the problems of the world's poor remain as overwhelming as ever, studying them has generated enough analytical ideas and thrown up enough challenges to the dominant paradigm to make all of us in the profession somewhat wiser, and at least somewhat more conscious of the possibilities and limitations of our existing methods of analysis.

Notes

1. For an introduction to this formative period of development economics as well as a retrospective view by some of the pioneers themselves, see Meier and Seers (1984).

2. For example, see Hirschman (1982), Little (1982) and Lal (1983).

3. This paper influenced the subsequent literature in labor economics on the importance of labor turnover and the mechanisms (such as deferred compensation) intended to control it.

4. For many years one major critique of the infant-industry argument has been that the "infant," once protected, often refuses to grow into an adult and keeps on lobbying for prolongation of the "temporary" protection. The literature made clear that the commitment to remove the protection after some years was not binding. This is an early example in development economics of the issues of time consistency and credibility of policy, which now form the subject of a rapidly growing macroeconomic literature in the context of monetary and fiscal policy and business and electoral cycles. For a review of the latter literature, see Persson and Tabellini (1990).

5. For a brief but balanced account of this issue see Shleifer (1991).

6. Concern about "appropriate technology" in developing countries, about the applicability of improved methods of production localized around existing methods in developed countries, influenced the theory of localized technical progress by Atkinson and Stiglitz (1969).

7. This can be particularly important when jointly used infrastructure and other nontraded support services and inputs are indispensable for the production process.

8. An earlier formalization of the idea of gains from coordination in the process of industrialization drawing upon Rosenstein-Rodan and Nurkse is presented in the development textbook of Basu (1984) in terms of conjectural demand on the lines of non-Walrasian equilibrium analysis.

9. For an overview of this literature, see Bardhan (1984), Bardhan (1989) and Stiglitz (1988).

10. Even ignoring risk and incentive effects, the idea of share-cropping, where the marginal cost of employing labor is less than the average cost, thus lending an inherent bias toward expanding employment and output, influenced Weitzman's famous work on the share-economy (1984) in the context of macroeconomic stagflation.

11. The interested reader might begin with Sen (1985, 1987); see also Anand and Ravallion in the Winter 1993 issue of the *Journal of Economic Perspectives*.

References

Akerlof, G. A., "The Market for 'Lemons': Quality Uncertainty and the Market Mechanism," *Quarterly Journal of Economics*, August 1970, *84*:3, 488–500.

Akerlof, G. A., *An Economic Theorist's Book of Tales*. Cambridge: Cambridge University Press, 1984.

Akerlof, G. A., and J. Yellen, *Efficiency Wage Models of the Labor Market*. Cambridge: Cambridge University Press, 1986.

Anand, S., and M. Ravallion, "Human Development in Poor Countries: On the Role of Private Incomes and Public Services," *Journal of Economic Perspectives*, Winter 1993, *7*:1, 133–50.

Arnott, R., and J. E. Stiglitz, "Moral Hazard and Nonmarket Institutions: Dysfunctional Crowding Out or Peer Monitoring?," *American Economic Review*, March 1991, *81*:1, 179–90.

Atkinson, A. B., and J. E. Stiglitz, "A New View of Technological Change," *Economic Journal*, September 1969, *79*:315, 573–78.

Arrow, K. J., "The Economic Implications of Learning by Doing," *Review of Economic Studies*, June 1962, *29*, 155–73.

Arthur, W. B., "Competing Technologies, Increasing Returns, and Lock-in by Historical Events," *Economic Journal*, March 1989, *99*:394, 116–31.

Bardhan, P., *Economic Growth, Development and Foreign Trade: A Study in Pure Theory*. New York: Wiley-Interscience 1970.

Bardhan, P., *Land, Labor and Rural Poverty*. New York: Columbia University Press, 1984.

Bardhan, P., *The Economic Theory of Agrarian Institutions*. Oxford: Oxford University Press, 1989.

Bardhan, P., "A Note on Interlinked Rural Economic Arrangements," (1969). In Bardhan, P., ed., *The Economic Theory of Agrarian Institutions*. Oxford: Oxford University Press, [1989], 237–42.

Basu, K., *The Less Developed Economy*. Oxford: Basil Blackwell, 1984.

Bhagwati, J., "The Generalized Theory of Distortions and Welfare." In Bhagwati, J. et al., eds., *Trade, Balance of Payments and Growth: Essays in Honor of C. P. Kindleberger*. Amsterdam: North-Holland, 1971, 69–90.

Blanchard, O., and L. Summers, "Hysteresis in Unemployment," *European Economic Review*, February–March 1987, *31*:1/2, 288–95.

Bulow, J., and K. Rogoff, "A Constant Recontracting Model of Sovereign Debt," *Journal of Political Economy*, February 1989, *97*:1, 155–78.

Buttrick, J., "A Note on Professor Solow's Growth Model," *Quarterly Journal of Economics*, November 1958, 72, 633–36.

Chayanov, A. V., *The Theory of Peasant Economy*. (1925). Homewood: Irwin, [1966].

Clemhout, S., and H. Wan, "Learning-by-Doing and Infant Industry Protection," *Review of Economic Studies*, January 1970, *37*:1, 33–56.

Cooper, R., and A. John, "Coordinating Coordination Failures in Keynesian Models," *Quarterly Journal of Economics*, August 1988, *103*:3, 441–63.

Dasgupta, P., and D. Ray, "Inequality as a Determinant of Malnutrition and Unemployment: Theory," *Economic Journal*, December 1986, *96*:384, 1011–34.

David, P., "Clio and the Economics of QWERTY," *American Economic Review*, May 1985, *75*:2, 332–37.

Diamond, P., and J. A. Mirrlees, "Optimal Taxation and Public Production II: Tax Rules," *American Economic Review*, June 1971, *61*:3, 261–78.

Diamond, P., and D. Fudenberg, "Rational-Expectations Business Cycles in Search Equilibrium," mimeo, MIT, 1987.

Dupuit, J., "On the Measurement of the Utility of Public Works," (1844), *International Economic Papers*, no. 2. London: Macmillan, [1952].

Eaton, J., and M. Gersovitz, "Debt with Potential Repudiation: Theoretical and Empirical Analysis," *Review of Economic Studies*, April 1981, *48*:2, 289–309.

Eaton, J., M. Gersovitz, and J. E. Stiglitz, "The Pure Theory of Country Risk," *European Economic Review*, June 1986, *30*:3, 481–513.

Farrell, J., and G. Saloner, "Installed Base and Compatibility: Innovation, Product Preannouncements and Predation," *American Economic Review*, December 1986, *76*:5, 940–55.

Feldman, G. A., "On the Theory of Growth Rates of National Income," (1928). In Spulber, N., ed., *Foundations of Soviet Strategy for Economic Growth*. Indiana University Press, [1964], 1974–99, 304–31.

Fleming, J. M., "External Economies and the Doctrine of Balanced Growth," *Economic Journal*, June 1955, 65, 241–56.

Greenwald, B., and J. E. Stiglitz, "Externalities in Economies with Imperfect Information and Incomplete Markets," *Quarterly Journal of Economics*, May 1986, *101*:2, 229–64.

Hart, O., "A Model of Imperfect Competition with Keynesian Features," *Quarterly Journal of Economics*, February 1982, 97:1, 109–38.

Hirschman, A., "The Rise and Decline of Development Economics." In Gersovitz, M. et al., eds., *The Theory and Experience of Economic Development*. London: Allen and Unwin, 1982, 372–90.

Howitt, P., and R. P. McAffee, "Stability of Equilibria with Externalities," *Quarterly Journal of Economics*, May 1988, 103:2, 261–77.

Kaldor, N., *Causes of the Slow Rate of Economic Growth of the United Kingdom: An Inaugural Lecture*. Cambridge: Cambridge University Press, 1966.

Kiyotaki, N., "Multiple Expectational Equilibria under Monopolistic Competition," *Quarterly Journal of Economics*, November 1988, 103:4, 695–713.

Kletzer, K., "Asymmetries of Information and LDC Borrowing with Sovereign Risk," *Economic Journal*, June 1984, 94:374, 287–307.

Krueger, Anne, "The Political Economy of the Rent-Seeking Society," *American Economic Review*, June 1974, 64:3, 291–303.

Krugman, P., "Trade, Accumulation and Uneven Development," *Journal of Development Economics*, April 1981, 8:2, 149–61.

Krugman, P., "The Narrow Moving Band, the Dutch Disease, and the Competitive Consequences of Mrs. Thatcher," *Journal of Development Economics*, October 1987, 27:1/2, 41–55.

Krugman, P., "History versus Expectations," *Quarterly Journal of Economics*, May 1991, 106:2, 651–67.

Krugman, P., "Toward a Counter-Counterrevolution in Development Theory," mimeo, The World Bank, 1992.

Lal, D., *The Poverty of Development Economics*. London: Hobart Paperback, 1983.

Leibenstein, H., *Economic Backwardness and Economic Growth: Studies in the Theory of Economic Development*. New York: Wiley, 1957.

Leijonhufvud, A., "Life among the Econ," *Western Economic Journal*, September 1973, 11:3, 327–37.

Little, I. M. D., *Economic Development: Theory, Policy and International Relations*. New York: Basic Books, 1982.

Little, I. M. D., and J. A. Mirrlees, *Project Appraisal and Planning for Developing Countries*. London: Heinemann, 1974.

Lucas, R. E., "On the Mechanics of Economic Development," *Journal of Monetary Economics*, July 1988, 22:1, 3–42.

Mandelbaum, K., *The Industrialization of Backward Areas*. Oxford: Basil Blackwell, 1945.

Matsuyama, K., "Increasing Returns, Industrialization and Indeterminacy of Equilibrium," *Quarterly Journal of Economics*, May 1991, 106:2, 616–50.

Mazumdar, D., "The Marginal Productivity Theory of Wages and Disguised Unemployment," *Review of Economic Studies*, June 1959, 26, 190–97.

Meier, G. M., and D. Seers (eds.), *Pioneers in Development*. Washington, D.C.: World Bank, 1984.

Murphy, K., A. Shleifer, and R. Vishny, "Industrialization and the Big Push," *Journal of Political Economy*, October 1989, 97:5, 1003–26.

Myrdal, G., *Economic Theory and Underdeveloped Regions*. London: G. Duckworth, 1957.

Nelson, R., "A Theory of Low-Level Equilibrium Trap in Underdeveloped Economics," *American Economic Review*, December 1956, 46, 894–908.

Nurkse, R., *Problems of Capital Formation in Underdeveloped Countries*. Oxford: Basil Blackwell, 1953.

Persson, T., and G. Tabellini, *Macroeconomic Policy, Credibility and Politics*. New York: Harwood Academic Publishers, 1990.

Preobrazhenski, E., *The New Economics*. (1926), Oxford: Clarendon Press, [1965].

Romer, P., "Increasing Returns and Long-run Growth," *Journal of Political Economy*, October 1986, 94:5, 1002–37.

Romer, P., "Endogenous Technical Change," *Journal of Political Economy*, October 1990, 98:5, S71–S102.

Rosenstein-Rodan, P., "Problems of Industrialization of Eastern and Southeastern Europe," *Economic Journal*, June-September 1943, 53, 202–11.

Scitovsky T., "Two Concepts of External Economies," *Journal of Political Economy*, April 1954, 62, 143–51.

Sen, A. K., *Resources, Values and Development*. Oxford: Basil Blackwell, 1984.

Sen, A. K., *Commodities and Capabilities*. Amsterdam: North-Holland, 1985.

Sen, A. K., *On Ethics and Economics*. Oxford: Basil Blackwell, 1987.

Shleifer, A., "Implementation Cycles," *Journal of Political Economy*, December 1986, 94:6, 1163–90.

Shleifer, A., "Externalities and Economic Growth: Lessons from Recent Work," mimeo, Harvard University, 1991.

Stiglitz, J. E., "Incentives and Risk Sharing in Sharecropping," *Review of Economics Studies*, April 1974, 41:2, 219–55.

Stiglitz, J. E., "Alternative Theories of Wage Determination and Unemployment in LDC's: The Labor Turnover Model," *Quarterly Journal of Economics*, May 1974, 88:2, 194–227.

Stiglitz, J. E., "The Theory of 'Screening', Education and Distribution of Income," *American Economic Review*, June 1975, 65:3, 283–300.

Stiglitz, J. E., "Economic Organization, Information, and Development." In Chenery, H. B., and T. N. Srinivasan eds., *Handbook of Development Economics*, vol. I. Amsterdam: North-Holland, 1988, 94–160.

Stiglitz, J. E., "Rational Peasants, Efficient Institutions, and a Theory of Rural Organization: Methodological Remarks for Development Economics." In Bardhan, P. eds., *The*

Economic Theory of Agrarian Institutions. Oxford: Oxford University Press, 1989, 18–29.

Tinbergen, J., *Development Planning.* London: Weidenfield and Nicolson, 1967.

UNIDO, *Guidelines for Project Evaluation.* New York: United Nations [1972].

Wietzman, M., "Increasing Returns and the Foundations of Unemployment Theory," *Economic Journal,* December 1982, *92:*368, 787–804.

Weitzman, M., *The Share Economy.* Cambridge: Harvard University Press, 1984.

Young, A., "Increasing Returns and Economic Progress," *Economic Journal,* December 1928, *38,* 527–42.

2   Theories of Sharecropping

Nirvikar Singh

1 Introduction

This chapter is an attempt to examine some of the different explanations for the existence of sharecropping. I discuss the roles of risk-sharing, incentive provision, wealth constraints, and screening. A common feature of the different theories is an emphasis on uncertainty and on asymmetries in information. I attempt to evaluate as well as describe some models of tenancy where share contracts are a useful resource allocation device. The emphasis is on theoretical considerations, and I do not attempt a systematic treatment of the historical[1] or empirical[2] aspects. Neither do I provide a mountain-top survey, revealing broad patterns and hitherto unseen connections. Instead, I attempt to cut through some of the thickets of individual models enough to expose their essentials. As will be seen, no sweeping conclusions emerge.

Some of my interpretations and analyses are no doubt idiosyncratic. Still, in analysing the specific models presented here, I have benefited from many other surveys and syntheses. These include works by Newbery and Stiglitz (1979), Binswanger and Rosenzweig (1984), Jaynes (1984), Quibria and Rashid (1984), Richards (1986), and Mohan Rao (1986). I have tried to avoid going over the same ground as these studies, and hope there will be enough that is new here even for someone who has read all the above.[3] Finally, for anyone who has not, this piece is meant to be fairly self-contained.

The remainder of this chapter is organized as follows. In Section 2 it is argued that the Walrasian paradigm, where in all individuals behave as price-takers, has no place in explanations of sharecropping. The share in a share contract is not a price, of course. Furthermore, the Walrasian model makes sense only as an approximation to situations where someone sets prices. This approximation may not hold when asymmetries in information are the underlying rationale for sharecropping.

In Section 3, explanations for sharecropping based on risk-sharing are examined. In some cases, wage and fixed-rent contracts appropriately combined can do as well as share contracts in spreading risk. Sharecropping comes into its own only when there are multiple risks of some kinds, or indivisibilities, or incentive problems.

Incentive-based explanations are the focus of the models considered in Section 4. For share contracts to be better than fixed-rent contracts, which are efficient in terms of incentive provision for the tenant, there must be some other factor as well. Different possibilities are the need for risk-sharing, input provision by the landlord with its own incentive problems, and constraints on the tenant's ability always to make a fixed rent payment. Several diverse models are considered in this section, although they all have incentive problems as an underlying common thread. This is the longest section in the chapter, and reflects the importance of providing incentives for a tenant to make more efficient decisions. Also, some issues in modelling landlord monitoring of tenant decisions are considered, since monitoring is widespread in practice.

Section 5 considers explanations based on screening of potential tenants with heterogeneous abilities that cannot be observed by landlords. The screening explanation alone seems to be unsatisfactory, but, combined with imperfect credit markets and default possibilities, it is more convincing. The last category of explanation, in Section 6, is based on the sharing of input costs, which in turn results from capital market imperfections.

We may see that these classifications are somewhat arbitrary. I might have dealt with the explanation based on conflicts between insurance and incentive provision under "risk-sharing" in Section 3, rather than under "incentives" in Section 4. I might also have created a category of explanations based on credit/capital market imperfections, which would have included models from Sections 4, 5, and 6. I could have provided a wholly different categorization based on imperfections in markets for insurance, labour, credit, and capital. The virtue of my classifications is directness—I have tried to emphasize proximate or significant causes in the various multifaceted explanations of sharecropping.[4] Having gone through the various models in Sections 3–6, I do not "pick a winner." This is because I do not think that there is a single explanation, no matter how ingenious or complicated, of the existence of share contracts or sharecropping. Sharecropping has existed in various times and places in various forms. It has disappeared over time and reappeared. Sometimes the tenant's share is one-half; sometimes it is not. Sometimes the output share equals the cost share; sometimes it does not. Sometimes productivity is higher on sharecropped land than on other types of tenancy or with self-cultivation; sometimes it is not. Sometimes share-croppers are poor; sometimes they are prosperous. Sometimes sharecroppers produce risky cash crops; sometimes they produce for subsistence. I do not think a single theory can capture all of these aspects of sharecropping!

What will emerge from Sections 2–6, however, is that I think some approaches and some models are better than others. While sometimes these judgements are based on casual empiricism, mostly they rely on the internal logic and consistency of the models themselves. Hence I hope this piece will provide a basic sifting of theories of sharecropping.

2   The Nature of Share Contracts and Sharecropping Equilibrium

There are two points I wish to make in the section as a preliminary to discussing specific explanations of sharecropping. First, the output share in a share contract is not a price-like variable. Second, models of sharecropping where everyone is price-taker, especially in the market for land, do not seem to be logically satisfactory. Below, I expand on these observations and their implications for the nature of an equilibrium with sharecropping.

The first point—that the output share in a share contract is not a price-like variable, and should not therefore be treated as a given by individuals who are otherwise price-takers in a competitive model—has been made by Newbery (1974). He was commenting on Bardhan and Srinivasan's (1971) general equilibrium formalization of the mis-allocation arising from sharecropping, argued by Marshall in his famous footnote. Since then, numerous authors have made similar observations, and offered various solutions.[5]

The basic problem with the "Marshallian" model is that the tenant taking the share as given will demand land up to the point where its marginal product is zero, whatever the share.[6] In general, there will not be an equilibrium share that clears the market for land, since the landlord has a supply function for land that will be to the left of the demand function, unless land is unrealistically abundant.

There are ways around this problem that maintain the assumption that all individuals take the share as given. Jaynes (1982) provides an elegant solution that illustrates the problems with the usual model. To describe this, I introduce the following notation. The production function is $Q(L, T)$, with constant returns to scale, where L is labour input and T is the quantity of land. We may write it as $Tq(\lambda)$, where $\lambda = L/T$. Jaynes assumes that individuals are contract-takers, where a contract specifies a pair (λ, α), and α is the tenant's share of output. Hence this implies that everyone takes the share in share contracts as given. However, they also take as given the labour–land ratio associated with a contract: they do not choose how much they would like of the other input given their own input. Furthermore, if there are many contracts available, each with a different labour–land ratio, the corresponding output share may differ as well. This last is the crucial assumption, as Jaynes shows: if the tenant's share decreases as he uses more land with a given labour input, he will no longer demand land till its marginal product is zero. A similar constraint will apply to the landlord's demand for labour. Formally, Jaynes allows for a continuum of contracts, (λ, α), which, if indexed by λ, define the share as a function of $\lambda, \alpha = a(\lambda)$. The tenant and landlord's first-order conditions with respect to λ are, respectively,

$$a'(\lambda)q(\lambda) + a(\lambda)q'(\lambda) = a(\lambda)q(\lambda)/\lambda \tag{1}$$

and

$$\{1 - a(\lambda)\}q'(\lambda) = a'(\lambda)q(\lambda). \tag{2}$$

Together, these determine the equilibrium contract $(\lambda^*, a^*(\lambda^*))$. Note that $a^{*\prime}(\lambda^*) > 0$; otherwise neither equality can be satisfied since, in general, $0 < q'(\lambda) < q(\lambda)/\lambda$. Hence if $a'(\lambda) = 0$ there is no equilibrium: the point made by Newbery and others. On the other hand, Jaynes shows that, with a share that varies with the labour–land ratio, and usual assumptions on utility functions, the equilibrium is identical to a standard competitive (i.e. Walrasian) equilibrium, with markets for labour and land, and individual price-takers in each market. Hence there is no need for the array of share contracts if there are wage and rental rates determined by supply and demand. This is a result that carries over to the case of uncertainty, discussed in the next section. In any event, Jaynes's construct is not meant to provide a realistic solution to modelling the determination of equilibrium shares. His own explanation (Jaynes 1982, 1984) relies on a form of capital market imperfection[7] and does not assume that all individuals take the output share in share contracts as a given.

Another way round non-existence of equilibrium while maintaining the assumption of share-taking behaviour is that of Alston, Datta, and Nugent (1984), but this has its own problems.[8] A better alternative is to do away with the assumption of share-taking behaviour. This is what is normally done in models of sharecropping. I shall argue that it is more logical to assume that one side, typically the landlord,[9] sets the parameters of the contract. Furthermore, it is not really logical to assume that landlords who set the parameters of share contracts take wages and rental rates as given by the market. This is not to say that landlords can do whatever they like. They must be able to attract tenants at the terms they offer. And this may also depend on what other landlords offer.

The basis of the argument is as follows. In the usual competitive model where everyone is a price-taker—i.e. the Walrasian model— prices are set to clear markets by a fictional auctioneer. Of course, this is not taken as a literal description of the resource allocation process. Instead, the usual justification is that the Walrasian outcome is close to the equilibrium where some individuals actually set prices, and there are appropriately large numbers, so that no single individual has much aggregate influence. The latter formulation is usually that of a game where the individuals in the economy are the players, so that there is no need for a *deus ex machina* such as an auctioneer. There are rigorous demonstrations of approximation results and equivalence in the limit, as numbers become infinite.[10] However, these results are generally available for models without asymmetries of information. And the explanations that I shall present subsequently, especially in Sections 4 and 5, depend critically on imperfect or incomplete information. Hence, even if it is possible sensibly to assume price-taking behaviour—and for moral hazard models it may not be—it does not seem reasonable in such models.

As I have said, it is usual in models of sharecropping to assume that the landlord sets the share. For example, in cases where the landlord cannot observe the tenant's effort—treated in detail in Section 4—he chooses the tenant's share to provide appropriate incentives for effort. It is crucial that he recognizes the tenant's response to changes in the share: share-taking behaviour by the landlord will not give sensible results. However, such behaviour is sometimes combined with price-taking behaviour in a "competitive" rental market, that is, where an auctioneer determines the equilibrium fixed rent to land.[11] This does not seem plausible. Roughly, the landlord is behaving very differently towards two different contracts in the same market—land. More formally, a landlord offering a share contract may plausibly incorporate a fixed payment to or from the tenant. If $\tilde{Q}$ is the (random) output, α the tenant's share, and C the fixed payment, the share contract specifies that the tenant gets $\alpha\tilde{Q} + C$. For any such contract, we assume that the landlord anticipates the tenant's response to the contract parameters (α, C) and chooses these parameters to maximize his own expected benefit. This presumably includes share contracts with α very close to 1, and C negative. But if $\alpha = 1$, we have a fixed-rent contract. To say that in this case the landlord's assumption about the tenant's behaviour and his own decision process change drastically seems implausible. Instead, it seems more realistic to assume that, if the landlord agrees to a fixed-rent contract with the tenant, he will do so under the same sort of conditions as for a share contract, anticipating the tenant's labour input decision and contract acceptance conditions. A similar argument applies to wage contracts, where $\alpha = 0$ and C is positive.

In the above, for simplicity of exposition, I suppressed the quantity of land. One might tackle its determination in the usual way that firm size is determined in conventional microeconomic theory, by assuming initially increasing and then decreasing returns to farm size. This allows the endogenous determination of the quantity of land per tenant, and the number of tenants per landlord (or perhaps the number of landlords per tenant). With only decreasing, constant, or increasing returns, however, the issue of farm size is problematical, as it usually is in a competitive equilibrium.

Let us conclude this section with a simple example of what a competitive equilibrium will look like in our framework. General questions of the nature, existence of efficiency of equilibrium and the role of exclusivity of contracts are discussed in a series of papers by Arnott and Stiglitz.[12] I describe the model of Shetty (1988), considered in more detail in Section 4. There are more potential tenants than landlords. The optimal landlord–tenant ratio is 1. Each potential tenant has the same reservation expected utility, determined by some other opportunities. Tenants are divided into several classes, according to their wealth levels; otherwise they are identical. There is moral hazard, so landlords choose contract parameters anticipating the tenants' effort responses. Wealthier tenants are more desirable, because they are less likely to default on agreed payments, and because they work harder in equilibrium. Hence landlords compete for wealthier tenants. Now the individuals with the lowest wealth who actually become tenants compete for tenancy. Hence they receive only their reservation expected utility; otherwise a landlord could undercut and still get the same tenant. Landlords with such tenants obtain a certain expected utility—endogenously determined. Landlords with other, wealthier, tenants must get the same expected utility; otherwise the landlords with poorer tenants could profitably steal away the wealthier, more productive, ones. Hence the wealthier tenants obtain a higher equilibrium expected utility: they get the full benefit of their higher productivity. This model, therefore, shows what a competitive equilibrium looks like in a simple model. Moral hazard implies that landlords choose contract parameters. There is no role for price-taking behaviour, however: in particular, landlords do not take as given the rental rate for land. However, the wealthiest tenants get fixed-rent contracts, and the rental rate, while chosen by landlords, is determined in equilibrium by the return to landlords with the poorest tenants. Competition equalizes returns across landlords (and tenants with the same wealth), since differences in returns will lead to undercutting by some landlord through variation in the contract terms. This is competitive behaviour in the sense of monopolistic competition: each landlord assumes that what he does will have no effect on what other landlords do, presumably because he is small relative to the market. The behavioural assumptions are consistent in such a model, and we do not have to worry about how prices are actually determined, since they are chosen implicitly or explicitly by landlords, subject to competitive pressures. Hence this type of formulation seems a good way to approach formal modelling of a competitive equilibrium with share contracts.

3   Sharecropping and Risk-sharing

The idea that share contracts might have risk-sharing advantages over fixed-rent and wage contracts was suggested by Cheung (1968, 1969a, 1969b). The basis for the argument is that a fixed-rent contract causes the worker as tenant to bear all the production risk, in the absence of insurance markets or other means for diversifying risk. In a similar situation, the landlord would bear all the risk if he or she hired the worker at a fixed wage. Hence if both landlord and worker are risk-averse, neither arrangement is optimal in terms of risk-bearing. A share contract, on the other hand, assigns some risk to each of the contracting parties, and might be preferable. This analysis assumes that there is no incentive problem, so that inputs such as labour are observable and can be specified in the contract. With this assumption, however, the strongest form of the risk-sharing explanation does not hold. This was demonstrated by Reid (1976), and by Newbery and Stiglitz in a sequence of articles.[13] The most general statement of the critique of the risk-sharing explanation is in Newbery and Stiglitz (1979). They demonstrate that, if there are constant returns to scale in production, and no indivisibilities, there will be a mix of wage and fixed-rent contracts on two subplots that gives the same pattern of returns in every state of the world to the landlord and to the tenant as does a share contract for the whole plot. Their formalization is as follows.

Let α be the tenant's share in a share contract, r the rental rate, and w the wage rate. Let L and T be the agreed-on amounts of land and labour, and let $\tilde{Q}(L, T, \theta)$ be the production function, where θ is a random variable denoting the state of the world. Suppose that a fraction k of the land is rented out and the remainder is cultivated at a fixed wage. The worker/tenant's income will be

$$\tilde{Q}(kL, kT, \theta) - rkT + w(1 - k)L = k\tilde{Q}(L, T, \theta) - rkT + w(1 - k)L, \qquad (3)$$

by the assumption of constant returns to scale (CRS). Now, if k^* is chosen such that

$$rk^*T - w(1 - k^*)L = 0, \qquad (4)$$

then the worker/tenant's income is $k^*\tilde{Q}(L, T, \theta)$, which is what a sharecropper with share k^* would receive in each state of the world. Now suppose that there are markets for labour and land with the above prices, w and r. Would a share contract improve matters for the tenant? For this to be the case, it must be that $\alpha > k^*$. Now, however, if the same steps are repeated for the landlord, he will get $(1 - k^*)\tilde{Q}(L, T, \theta)$ with the specified mix of wage and fixed-rent contracts. He will prefer a share contract if $1 - \alpha > 1 - k^*$, or $\alpha < k^*$. Hence there is no share contract that would improve matters for both landlord and tenant over the specified mix of wage and rent contracts; the best they can do is replicate the pattern of returns with a share contract with $\alpha = k^*$. In other words, sharecropping does not provide superior risk-sharing.

The above analysis sidesteps the issue of precisely how the wage rate, rental rate, and share are determined. In that sense it is very general. However, it would be useful to clarify how w, r, and α come about, and also briefly to look at the interaction between risk-sharing and input allocation. Having done this, I shall offer some further interpretation of the results, and examine its scope.

One possible assumption, of course, is that landlords and tenants/workers are price-takers with respect to the wage and rental rates. In that case, Newbery (1977) has shown that the competitive equilibrium is constrained Pareto-efficent; that is, a central planner specifying labour and land inputs, base consumption levels, and output shares for all market participants[14] cannot achieve a Pareto improvement. Now if share contracts are also made available, whether both landlord and tenant take the share as given or the landlord offers a particular share, the previous argument still holds: the tenant will only accept a share $\alpha \geq k^*$, the landlord will only accept or offer a share $\alpha \leq k^*$. Hence only $\alpha = k^*$ can prevail in equilibrium, with no effect on resource allocation.

A similar argument may be given for the case where the landlord specifies land and labour inputs as well as the contract terms for his tenant, subject to providing the tenant with his reservation expected utility. We can generalize the result by allowing for side-payments in the share contract.[15] The contract-setting monopolist can do as well with a mix of fixed-rent and wage contracts as with a share contract—the latter is not needed.

As a final case, consider a monopolistic landlord who takes the wage rate as given, but chooses the rental rate based on the tenant's demand for land, $T_d(r)$; in other words, the tenant is a price-taker in the market for land. Now the resulting equilibrium will not even be constrained-efficient: there is the standard monopolistic misallocation.

In this case a share contract that achieves the competitive outcome, plus a side-payment, can make both sides better off. In some sense this is merely the result of a better input allocation. However, the point to be made is that here, while risk-sharing is partly the result of contractual choice given the input levels, the amount of risk depends on those inputs.[16] The two decisions are really intertwined. Thus the result on the irrelevance of sharecropping for risk-sharing must be interpreted as conditional in some contexts, where there are additional inefficiencies with wage and fixed-rent contracts alone.

Before we further consider the scope of the irrelevance result, a summary interpretation is in order. The essence of the argument is that any linear function of output will slope between 0 and 1 and constant term between $-rT$ and wL can be attained for the tenant through a mix of fixed-rent and wage contracts. Since share contracts are linear in output, in general, allowing share contracts does not expand the set of attainable returns. It may be noted that linear sharing rules are in general not optimal.[17] Hence a share contract with some nonlinearity might improve risk-sharing over a mix of wage and rent contracts. Subsistence constraints or tied provision of inputs might effectively introduce such nonlinearities, but there is no obvious evidence in this regard.

The assumption of constant returns to scale has been used in the analyses presented so far. Allen (1984) shows that in a sense this assumption is unnecessary. The point is simple. The arguments above assumed that production would be carried out separately for the two subplots given to fixed rent and wage cultivation. However, if the two plots can be cultivated together, output can be the same under the mixed wage and rent agreement as under sharecropping, even with economies of scale. Essentially, any share contract can be reinterpreted as assigning output from some fraction of land to the landlord and from the remainder to the tenant. There is a corresponding assignment of output from fractions of labour, so that there is an implicit exchange of land for labour, with an implicit relative price, the rent–wage ratio. Typically, this need not be a market price, and in the examples Allen presents[18] the worker or tenant did not usually have access to wage-earning opportunities at parametrically given rates. Still, these contracts specified an exchange of labour for land, and could be interpreted either as share contracts or as a combination of wage and rent contracts, with identical resource allocation patterns.[19]

A second, more important, limitation of the irrelevance result is that it assumes only that output is risky. If there are multiple sources of risk, share contracts can improve matters over a combination of fixed-rent and wage contracts. This is demonstrated by Newbery (1977) and Newbery and Stiglitz (1979). I outline their analysis below.

Suppose that the wage and rental rate are competitively determined; that is, everyone behaves as a price-taker with respect to the markets for labour and land. Suppose also that the wage rate is subject to some randomness.[20] This may be due partly to the same factors that affect output. However, there may be additional sources of uncertainty in the agricultural labour market, such as the demand for non-agricultural labour. Let $\tilde{w}$ be the random wage. Then the worker/tenant's income from mixing fixed rent and wage contracts in proportions $k : 1 - k$, with L units of labour and T units of land, will be

$$k\tilde{Q} - rkT + \tilde{w}(1 - k)L$$

There are now two random variables, and as long as $\tilde{Q}$ and $\tilde{w}$ are not perfectly correlated, this is a linear function of $\tilde{Q}$ only if $k = 1$. On the other hand, a share contract still specifies $\alpha\tilde{Q} + C$ for the tenant. Hence there are now patterns of returns with share contracts that cannot be achieved with a combination of wage and rent contracts.

The above argument assumes that the share tenant's opportunity cost of labour is not subject to randomness, but is just the disutility of his labour. If the sharecropper can sell his labour at $\tilde{w}$, or has to hire in workers at $\tilde{w}$, then his income will also be subject to the additional randomness arising from labour market uncertainty. Newbery and Stiglitz look at this more complicated case. They show that the share tenant will optimally combine four contracts: a fixed-rent contract, a share contract, a wage contract, and a fixed-rent contract with a share sublease. The income from the last of these involves no labour market randomness, which is why it is undertaken. It is shown that if $\tilde{Q}(L, T, \theta) = \theta Q(L, T)$, that is if production risk has a multiplicative form, then the above combination will lead to production efficiency and optimal risk-sharing.[21] On the other hand, this is not the result with only wage and rent contracts. The result that share contracts increase the set of contingent consumption possibilities is true even if production risk is non-multiplicative, only full efficiency is not then attained.

Another case where share contracts may improve risk-sharing is if there are non-tradable inputs. Examples in some circumstances are managerial and supervisory labour,[22] and the services of draft animals. The reason for absence of these markets may be moral hazard. Here we focus on the situation where a potential tenant has a fixed amount of a non-tradable input, so there is no explicit incentive problem. Pant (1983) has considered such a model, but without un-certainty; and fixed-rent contracts, which would then be optimal, are arbitrarily ruled out. Bell (1986) considers a world with uncertainty, and argues that risk-sharing might be improved with share contracts in addition to wage and fixed-rent arrangements. Suppose there are competitively determined wages and rental rates. In the absence of a market for the non-tradable input, the competitive equilibrium will not be constrained-efficient in general. The reason is that marginal products and implicit risk prices are not equated across individuals with different endowments of the non-tradable input. Then it turns out that, if there are households that would work only for wages in the presence of wage and fixed-rent contracts, one can find share contracts that will induce these households to choose some degree of share tenancy and at the same time are profitable for landlords. The intuition is that these households can now use their endowments of non-tradables, without being exposed to the greater risk of fixed-rent contracts. Bell demonstrates this explicitly in the context of a bar-gaining model.[23] The above analysis is in the presence of parametric rental and wage rates. As Bell points out, if the landlord chooses all contract parameters, subject to providing the tenant/worker with his reservation utility, he can anyway appropriate the imputed rents attributable to the non-tradable. In this case, if a mix of wage and fixed-rent contracts is offered, and the subplots are cultivated together, sharecropping offers no risk-sharing advantage (cf. Allen 1984 above.)

A final rationale for sharecropping in the context of risk-sharing relies on a different labour market imperfection from wage uncer-tainty. Suppose true labour input is not observable. Then wage con-tracts provide no incentives for effort. The above analyses have all assumed that the amount of land and labour could be specified in the contract and enforced. If this is not the case, a share contract will be the preferred risk-sharing arrangement, as it also provides uniform incentives—albeit imperfect ones—for effort. A mix of a fixed-rent and a wage contract would provide correct incentives on the part of the land that was rented out, but no incentives on the part cultivated with wage labour.[24] The focus is now equally if not more on incen-tives rather than risk-sharing, and these issues are dealt with in the next section.

4   Sharecropping and Input Incentives

In this section we shall concentrate on labour, probably the most important input,[25] and the subject of the most debate—going back to Adam Smith—about the link between sharecropping and incentives. The well-known[26] argument is that sharecropping leads to inefficient labour input decisions because the sharecropper receives only a fraction of his marginal product of labour. The efficient solution, it has been argued, is fixed-rent or wage contracts. The theories we shall examine here provide explanations of why sharecropping might be preferred to fixed-rent contracts or in some cases wage contracts. The common assumption is that labour input cannot be measured, and hence cannot be controlled by the landlord.[27] While hours worked may be observable, actual effort may not be; in any case, it is more difficult to measure. By labour input I mean the effective input, taking account of effort variation. Initially, I consider a set of models where labour input is not observable at all by the landlord. Later, I discuss models where the landlord can imperfectly monitor the input, but at a cost.[28] With one exception, the models are static, in that the input decision is made just once, resulting, subject to uncertainty, in an output—there has been no modelling (that I know of) of the various stages and types of labour inputs involved in agricultural production.

Non-observability of labour does not in itself imply a rationale for sharecropping; the incentive problem can be dealt with by fixed-rent contracts, which provide efficient incentives. This assumes that there are no other market imperfections. Hence the theories presented here involve various types of such imperfections. The first set assumes that the tenant is risk-averse and there is no insurance market. The landlord therefore plays a dual role, providing land and insurance, and the optimal contract from his or her perspective involves a trade-off between incentive provision and insurance provision. This model was introduced to the sharecropping literature by Stiglitz (1974a), but it is a special case of the pure moral hazard principal-agent framework that goes back to Ross (1973) and Mirrlees (1974).[29] The second theory is a formalization by Eswaran and Kotwal (1985c) of ideas in Reid (1976, 1977) and Bliss and Stern (1982). It is based on provision of labour inputs (interpreted as supervisory and managerial) by both landlord and tenant. Hence there is a two-sided incentive problem. The third group has two very different models, that of Hurwicz and Shapiro (1978) and that of Shetty (1988), which both rely on wealth constraints to explain sharecropping.[30] Hence the focus in these models is on capital market imperfections:[31] the tenant cannot borrow to cover bad years.

We begin with the incentives–insurance trade-off model. We assume for simplicity that the landlord is risk-neutral. This is not at all necessary. Other simplifying assumptions are as follows. There is only one landlord and one tenant. The latter has a utility function $U(Y) - L$, where Y is income and L is labour input. The tenant's reservation utility is K. The amount of land given on rent is fixed, so is suppressed in the model. The production function is $\tilde{Q}(L, \theta) = \theta Q(L)$, where θ is a random variable with mean 1, representing exogenous uncertainties that are typical of agricultural production. As usual, $Q' > 0$ and $Q'' < 0$. The tenant's income, Y, is a function of output, as determined by the contract offered by the landlord. For example, for a fixed-rent contract, $Y = \theta Q(L) - R$, where R is the rental payment to the landlord. For a pure share contract, $Y = \alpha \theta Q(L)$, where α is the tenant's share. If there is a side-payment as well, $Y = \alpha \theta Q(L) + C$. The general theory of such models demonstrates that the optimal contract need not be differentiable, and in fact can be almost anything, depending on the parameters of the model.[32] While contracts that involve linear functions of output may be optimal, there are no economically obvious assumptions that ensure this in the one-shot framework. However, Holmstrom and Milgrom (1987) have provided a dynamic analysis where linear contracts are always optimal, and we consider this and the relevance for sharecropping below. Otherwise, this literature on sharecropping just assumes that the set of possible contracts is restricted to the examples above: one can appeal to bounded rationality, perhaps, for justification.

One approach has been to compare fixed rent and "pure" share contracts (with no side-payment). While a fixed-rent contract is optimal if the tenant is risk-neutral,[33] it causes a risk-averse tenant to bear all the risk. The argument is then that a share contract provides some incentives, while at the same time reducing the tenant's risk. It is not clear, however, that the share contract *will* be better. For example, if the tenant is close to being risk-neutral, the landlord may not find it worthwhile to sacrifice incentives for labour input by using a share contract. It should be noted that the landlord cares about insuring the tenant because by doing so he can lessen the bite of the latter's reservation utility constraint. However, it may be less costly to do this by reducing the fixed rent and maintaining efficient incentive provision. This intuition suggests that sufficient risk aversion on the part of the tenant will tilt the scales in favour of a share contract. Newbery and Stiglitz (1979) analyze the resource allocation consequences of a pure share contract in this case. We shall concentrate on what seems a more appealing analysis, where the landlord chooses α and C for the optimal linear contract, $\alpha\theta Q(L) + C$. This includes the fixed rent and pure share contracts as special cases. This kind of analysis was done by Stiglitz (1974a), and has been extended in several directions by (for example) Braverman and Stiglitz (1982, 1986a).

Using the notation developed above, the landlord's problem in this framework is

$$\max_{\alpha,C,L} \; E_\theta\{(1-\alpha)\theta Q(L) - C\}$$

$$\text{s.t.} \quad E_\theta[U\{\alpha\theta Q(L) + C\}] - L \geq K$$

$$E_\theta[U'\{\alpha\theta Q(L) + C\}\alpha\theta Q'(L)] - 1 = 0. \tag{5}$$

The first constraint is the tenant's acceptance condition. The second constraint is the tenant's first-order condition for labour input choice given the contract parameters, and its presence is the crux of the incentive issue: the landlord cannot directly monitor or control labour input. We shall assume throughout that first-order conditions characterize the solution uniquely.[34]

Given the side payment, C, which may be negative, the landlord can drive the tenant down to his reservation utility level, K. Hence the two constraints may be solved for $L(\alpha, K)$ and $C(\alpha, K)$, and substituting these in the landlord's objective function, one obtains his first-order condition (omitting arguments and using subscripts for partial derivatives):

$$-Q + (1-\alpha)Q'L_\alpha - C_\alpha = 0, \tag{6}$$

or, rearranging,

$$\alpha = 1 - \frac{Q + C_\alpha}{Q'L_\alpha} \tag{7}$$

It is possible to show, from the constraints, that $C_\alpha = -QE(U'\theta)/E(U')$, which is negative and less than Q in magnitude with risk aversion.[35] Hence $Q + C_\alpha$ is positive, and whether α is less than 1, from the above formula, depends on the sign of L_α.[36] Now, intuitively, one would expect it to be the case that, since there is an incentive problem, in equilibrium increasing the share would increase effort. In that case $\alpha < 1$, and the model predicts that a share contract (usually with a side-payment) will be used. However, it is hard to establish $L_\alpha > 0$ in general, and I am not aware of a fully general result. Even $U''' < 0$,[37] which is in turn implied by decreasing absolute risk aversion (DARA), is not sufficient. DARA has been suggested by Arrow (1971) as a plausible condition.

I have given this issue some attention, because, while without side-payments α must lie between 0 and 1, it is not completely obvious in this case. Certainly $\alpha > 1$ could not be interpreted as a share contract. It may also be noted that the model gives no general prediction of the size of the share, in particular whether it is close to one-half, the most commonly observed value. In this respect its predictions are weak. The model also predicts that labour input will be lower than if it could be observed and controlled by the landlord, but this does *not* imply that there is a more efficient outcome given the lack of observability of labour input.

As noted, many of the above simplifying assumptions are unnecessary. Allowing for a risk-averse landlord, the choice of plot size by the landlord, competition among landlords, or more general utility or production functions does not change the character of the prediction that share contracts will be used. The assumption of possible side-payments deserves some comment. I have assumed it for logical theoretical reasons: an either–or choice of a fixed-rent or pure share contract by the landlord seems unduly restrictive. The empirical evidence is less clear-cut, since explicit side-payments are not often observed. However, one would expect them to be disguised if there are cost-sharing arrangements or production or consumption loans.[38]

We next turn to some more dynamic considerations in the context of this basic incentive model of sharecropping. In the sharecropping literature, there have been two points made in a multi-period context. First is the argument, going back at least to J. S. Mill (1848), that sharecropping involves inferior incentives for investment by the tenant. Second is Johnson's (1950) suggestion that the incentive problem described above in a static framework will be mitigated or dealt with entirely by offering short-term leases with renewal contingent on satisfactory overall performance. There is also a large general literature on repeated principal–agent relationships that is relevant for landlord–tenant contracts. Finally, there is the specific contribution of Holmstrom and Milgrom (1987) that looks at labour input and production as processes over time.

We begin with the general models of dynamic agency. The first such studies were those of Radner (1981) and Rubinstein (1979). Both show that, in an infinitely repeated version of the basic one-period model, the first-best solution (efficient insurance and incentives) can be achieved if there is no discounting of the future. There is a class of contracts that do this, by punishing the agent (tenant) for a period of time if aggregate output falls below expectations. The implication for explanations of sharecropping is that share contracts may not be inefficient in a repeated context: the incentive problem is fully dealt with. Note that fixed-rent contracts will still not be optimal. Also, the share contract in this framework must be supplemented by possible penalties based on the history of output.

It is interesting that recent work (e.g. Allen 1985b) shows that, if borrowing and lending is possible on perfect credit markets, then long-term contracts will be no better than a sequence of short-term contracts in the repeated model. In the models of Radner and others, however, borrowing and lending are not possible. In this sense, sharecropping and its durability are more explicable in agricultural contexts where credit markets are absent or imperfect, for there the incentive problem is efficiently handled, and so there is no cost to this institution.

The suggestion of Johnson that the incentive problem in share-cropping can be overcome by evicting tenants who do not perform satisfactorily over time may be looked at as an example of the above repeated models. However, there is a difference in that, if the relationship is not infinite, the conclusion of those models may not hold: there is a probability that the tenant may not be around to enjoy future good times. Also, severing the contractual relationship is a less efficient way of providing incentives than are monetary penalties, since the landlord gains nothing from the termination,[39] and it may reduce incentives for land-improving labour input.

Newbery (1975) has provided a partial formalization of Johnson's idea. He shows that, if the sharecropper has to provide an average return to the landlord comparable to the latter's opportunity cost, say, the return from a fixed-rent contract, he will choose an efficient amount of labour. The payment to the landlord still varies with output, so the tenant's risk is reduced from that in a fixed-rent contract. However, since this model does not explicitly model termination for poor performance, it is more in the spirit of the Radner-type models. An alternative formulation is that of Bardhan and Singh (see Bardhan 1984 Ch. 8). This is a two-period model with a pure share contract. Without side-payments, the landlord cannot in general drive the tenant to his reservation utility level. Hence there is a real loss to the tenant if he is evicted.[40] Furthermore, a contract that involves eviction if output is below a certain level provides increased incentives for effort. In this model, the conflict between static and dynamic incentives is also formalized. Some first-period labour is assumed to increase second-period output through land or other improvements. Setting the satisfactory performance level too high is costly in terms of reducing incentives for this kind of labour input.

I shall close the discussion of this set of models with a presentation of the work of Holmstrom and Milgrom (1987). This is based on Hart and Holmstrom's (1987) exposition, but it is couched in terms of landlord and tenant, and choice of rental contract.

Production and effort in his framework are modelled as processes over time. This seems especially descriptive of agriculture, where final output is the result of different stages and types of labour throughout the year. Furthermore, the landlord and tenant will be able to monitor the stages of growth of the crop from start to end. Specifically, the agent controls the drift rate μ of a one-dimensional Brownian motion $\{\tilde{Q}(t); t \in [0,1]\}$, which is the analog for stochastic processes of the normal distribution. Formally,

$$d\tilde{Q}(t) = L(t)\, dt + \sigma\, dB(t), \qquad t \in [0,1] \tag{8}$$

where B is standard Brownian motion (zero drift and unitary variance). Hence the instantaneous variance, $\sigma\, dt$, is assumed constant. $L(t)$ is here the rate of effort of the tenant, and $d\tilde{Q}(t)$ is the incremental output.

The tenant has a utility function with constant absolute risk aversion, that is, of the exponential form

$$U\left[Y(\tilde{Q}) - \int \delta\{L(t)\}\right] = -\exp\left\langle -a\left[Y(\tilde{Q}) - \int \delta\{L(t)\}\right]\right\rangle \tag{9}$$

where δ is the instantaneous cost of effort and a is the coefficient of absolute risk aversion. Here $Q = \tilde{Q}(1)$, the output at the end of the period, that is, the quantity harvested. The function $\delta(L)$ is assumed convex. The integral is with respect to time, to give the total cost of effort, measured in income-equivalent terms.

The key to the model is that the tenant can observe the growth of the crop, $\tilde{Q}(t)$, and adjust effort $L(t)$ appropriately, based on the entire path of this growth. It turns out that this large expansion of the tenant's choice set limits the landlord's options dramatically, and that the optimal rule is linear. Hence share contracts emerge naturally. For example, if the cost of effort is $L^2/2$, the optimal contract turns out to be $\alpha\tilde{Q} + C$, where

$$\alpha = \frac{1}{1 + a\sigma^2}. \tag{10}$$

Hence the prediction is that the tenant's share goes down as his aversion to risk increases, or as production uncertainty increases. If either of these factors is non-existent, then $\alpha = 1$: a fixed-rent contract is optimal.

This concludes discussion of the first group of models. I shall now describe a model where both landlord and tenant provide different types of labour inputs and these are not publicly observable.

The model is due to Eswaran and Kotwal (1985c). There is one landlord and one potential tenant. Each is risk-neutral, so insurance or risk-sharing do not enter. The plot size is fixed, so we may suppress the quantity of land in what follows. Eswaran and Kotwal allow for material inputs, purchased at a market price; but while these are relevant for the numerical simulations they carry out, their existence is not essential to the qualitative explanation, so we ignore them here. Hence we focus on labour inputs. Output is given by $\theta\hat{Q}(M, E)$, where M is managerial input, E is effective labour input, $\hat{Q}$ is expected output, and θ is a random variable with expected value 1. E is in turn given by

$$E = E(S, L; \varepsilon) \tag{11}$$

where S is supervisory input, L is the amount of labour hired, and ε is a parameter $(0 \le \varepsilon \le 1)$ that captures the relative importance of supervision in a unit of effective labour. If the technology of supervision improves, it becomes less important, so ε decreases. Substituting in for E, we obtain the production function

$$\theta Q(M, S, L; \varepsilon).$$

This is assumed concave in the inputs. It is assumed that L is easily observable, but managerial and supervisory effort are not. Furthermore, it is assumed that the landlord and tenant have differential abilities in providing these inputs. The landlord is better at management. One hour of the tenant's time devoted to management is equivalent to a fraction γ of the landlord's time so spent. Similarly, one hour of the landlord's time devoted to supervision is equivalent to a fraction δ of the tenant's time so spent. The justifications are that the landlord has better access to information, markets, and institutions, while the tenant is better able to supervise family labour, possibly a large component of L. The final assumptions about labour inputs M, S, and L are that they have constant opportunity costs v, u, and w $(w \leq u, v)$ and that the landlord and tenant each have a fixed amount of labour that can be allocated to M or S.

There are three contractual options considered. First, the landlord can self-cultivate by hiring (unskilled) labour at the wage w and providing management and supervision himself. Second, he can lease out the land to a tenant for a fixed rent; the tenant then hires labour L and provides M and S himself. Finally, the landlord and tenant can enter into a share contract in which the former provides M and the latter S. The share contract provides the opportunity for specialization in tasks where each person has an absolute advantage. However, there is an incentive problem for each, since M and S are unobservable, and neither receives its full marginal product. The analysis proceeds by calculating the expected net income of the landlord for each of the three types of contracts. The landlord will pick the contractual form that gives him the highest expected payoff.

The fixed-wage contract requires the landlord to solve

$$\max_{M, S, L} Q(M, \delta S, L) - wL + (1 - M - S)v \tag{12}$$

where output is the numeraire, his endowment of labour is scaled to be one unit, and M, S, and $M + S$ lie between 0 and 1.[41] Let this maximum be π^{lw}.

Under the fixed-rent contract, the tenant solves

$$\max_{M, S, L} Q(\gamma M, S, L) - wL + (1 - M - S)u - R \tag{13}$$

with constraints as above, and R the fixed-rent total. Let this maximum be π^{tr}. Assuming that this is greater than the tenant's opportunity cost, u, and that there is competition among potential tenants for land, the rental amount will be

$$R = \pi^{tr} - u. \tag{14}$$

Hence the landlord's expected payoff is

$$\pi^{lr} = R + v = \pi^{tr} + (v - u). \tag{15}$$

The share contract is more complicated. Eswaran and Kotwal model it as follows. Expected output net of the optimal hired labour cost is

$$\pi(M, S) = \max_{L} Q(M, S, L) - wL. \tag{16}$$

The share contract assigns on average $\alpha\pi(M, S) + C$ to the tenant and the remainder to the landlord. Given the share contract, the landlord and tenant non-cooperatively choose M and S respectively to solve

$$\max_{M}(1 - \alpha)\pi(M, S) + (1 - M)v - C \tag{17}$$

and

$$\max_{S} \alpha\pi(M, S) + (1 - S)u + C, \tag{18}$$

subject to the endowment constraints on M and S. The resulting Nash equilibrium[42] is $M^*(\alpha), S^*(\alpha)$. The landlord, given these functions of the share, α, chooses the parameters α and C[43] to solve

$$\max_{\alpha, C}(1 - \alpha)\pi\{M^*(\alpha), S^*(\alpha)\} + \{1 - M^*(\alpha)\}v - C, \tag{19}$$

subject to giving the tenant the latter's opportunity income, u. The landlord's resulting expected payoff is denoted π^{ls}.

Finally, the landlord compares π^{lw}, π^{lr}, and π^{ls}, and chooses the contract type that gives him the highest expected payoff. An explicit analytical solution is not possible, so Eswaran and Kotwal do numerical simulations, and see how varying the parameters affects contractual choice. For example, they find that, if both γ and δ are low, sharecropping is preferable to the landlord; if γ is high, a fixed-rent contract is best; if δ is high, a fixed-wage contract is best. This is all straightforward. The important point is that the numerical example establishes that all three contractual forms are possible for different parameter values. There are several other interesting comparative-statics exercises in the paper—readers are referred to it for details.

The final point I wish to bring out is that the numerical examples suggest that, when sharecropping is the preferred mode, the share will be around one-half. This may be roughly interpreted as reflecting the "partnership" nature of sharecropping in this model.

The chief virtue of the model is that it incorporates the observation that sharecropping is often associated with active participation by the landlord and with pooling of managerial skills or other non-marketable inputs. Since both sides supply such inputs, of which they have different effective endowments, neither a fixed-rent nor a wage contract may be optimal. Another useful prediction is that, with varying conditions, one contractual form or other may dominate. The model is also rich in other qualitative predictions, at least for the Cobb–Douglas production technology. A more detailed justification of the model is in the paper.

There are also several possible criticisms. First, the nature of the share contract is not clear. The tenant is assumed to have an absolute advantage in supervision because it is easier to supervise family labour. However, the cost of this labour is subtracted off before shares are calculated. Furthermore, this is also treated as a cost for the tenant, so presumably L is only outside labour. In any case, it is effectively assumed that there is full cost-sharing, i.e. in proportion to the output share.[44] This is perhaps not realistic. It is argued in the paper that the results would be similar with the more usual output-sharing. However, since the results are based on numerical calculations, this conclusion is not obviously justified. This problem extends to the model's prediction based on numerical calculations that the share will be around one-half. In spite of these strictures, however, Eswaran and Kotwal's approach is rich and worthy of extension.

The third set of models—those of Hurwicz and Shapiro (1978) and Shetty (1988)—are very different in other respects, but they share as their driving force the idea that there are wealth or income constraints on the tenant. This is certainly realistic. What it does is rule out fixed-rent contracts for tenants who are sufficiently constrained. Share contracts then play a role.

The Hurwicz–Shapiro framework is, in fact, very different from the other models in this section. There is no uncertainty in production, so risk is not a factor. A single landlord deals with a tenant whose disutility of effort is unobservable.[45] Hence, if Q is output, $Y(Q)$ the tenant's income as a function of output, and d the disutility of producing that output, the tenant's "indirect" utility function is of the form

$Y(Q) - d(Q;k)$

where k is some real-valued parameter known to the tenant but not to the landlord. For example, d may be quadratic, of the form

$$d(Q;k) = kQ^2. \tag{20}$$

The results of the published paper are for this case, but they are derived for any positive d with $d', d'' > 0, d''' \geq 0$ in unpublished work (Hurwicz and Shapiro 1977). Note that the so-called indirect utility function is obtained simply by inverting the production function $Q = Q(L)$, and substituting for labour L in the utility function. The landlord's payoff is $Q - Y(Q)$, so is also linear in income. The constraint on the tenant's reward function is that his income cannot be negative, so $Y(0) = 0$, $Y(Q) \geq 0$. This is what rules out a fixed-rent contract, since then $Y(Q) = Q - R$ is negative for $Q < R$, which will occur for some k.

It should be noted at this point that Hurwicz and Shapiro do not stress this feature or interpretation of the constraint on the tenant's reward function. However, if this constraint were not there, the asymmetric information would not matter since the landlord could attain efficiency by a fixed-rent contract. This has been pointed out by Allen (1985a).

A major departure from the usual literature in Hurwicz and Shapiro is in the objective of the landlord faced with incomplete information. He does not maximize expected utility in a Bayesian manner. Instead, he is assumed to minimize "regret." In this formulation, this amounts to choosing $Y(Q)$ to maximize

$$\min_k \{\pi(Y,k)/\hat{\pi}(k)\} \tag{21}$$

where $\hat{\pi}(k)$ is the best payoff for the landlord if he has complete information (essentially, the total surplus), and $\pi(Y,k)$ is his payoff given the payment rule $Y(Q)$ and parameter k, determined by the tenant maximizing $Y(Q) - d(Q;k)$ with respect to Q. The lower the ratio $\pi/\hat{\pi}$, the greater the landlord's "regret." Since he does not observe k, he chooses $Y(Q)$ to minimize the regret in the worst possible case, which is given by the minimum over k.

Hurwicz and Shapiro proceed to show, without further restrictions on $Y(Q)$,[46] that the unique solution is $Y(Q) = \frac{1}{2}Q$, i.e. a share contract with a 50–50 split! The proof of this result is long and involved, and the intuition is not obvious. Clearly, it depends on the special objective function of the landlord. Also, it depends on disutility of producing higher outputs increasing fast enough. A very rough explanation of the result is that the landlord is constrained to a linear payment rule by his lack of information plus his desire to avoid the worst. The share of one-half is not general, in fact, since if the tenant's utility of income is concave the landlord's optimal share is three-fourths.

To some extent, then, this model remains a curiosity, but it suggests an interesting alternative to dealing with situations of incomplete information, and, like Holmstrom and Milgrom's work, leads to linear sharing rules in a natural manner.

Shetty's (1988) model is along more familiar lines. His main goal is to provide an explanation for the tenancy ladder hypothesis.[47] He does this by showing that, in a model where tenants vary in wealth, where this wealth can be collateral for amounts due as rent, and where default on fixed-rent commitments is possible, richer tenants will get fixed-rent contracts and earn higher profits than poorer tenants who get share contracts.

The formal model involves risk-neutral landlords and tenants, so risk-sharing and insurance do not matter. Hence, if a tenant's wealth is enough to cover fixed-rent commitments even if output is low, he will get a fixed-rent contract. This is preferable to other contracts because effort cannot be observed, and only a fixed-rent contract provides efficient incentives for labour input. Neglecting other inputs,[48] and using the notation from the first model presented in this section, the nominal payment the tenant receives or retains is $\alpha\theta Q(L) + C$. However, this cannot be less than the negative of this wealth, W. Hence the tenant's effective income is

$$\max\{\alpha\theta Q(L) + C, -W\}. \tag{22}$$

In words, if $\alpha\theta Q(L) + C$ is negative, the tenant draws on his assets to pay the landlord. He can do this until the lower bound $-W$ is reached. Similarly, the landlord's effective income is

$$\min\{(1-\alpha)\theta Q(L) - C, \theta Q(L) + W\}. \tag{23}$$

It is easily seen that the total is always $\theta Q(L)$, the actual output. The effect of the possibility that the tenant cannot fully meet his obligations is that each party's income is no longer linear in output, but only piecewise linear. In fact, the tenant's return is convex and that of the landlord is concave.

As in the first model of this section, the landlord chooses α and C to maximize his expected income, given the tenant's utility-maximizing choice of labour input. (There is disutility of effort, as usual.) Shetty actually considers potential tenants with different wealth levels and identical reservation utilities. Wealth is observable, and landlords compete for wealthier tenants, whose expected return is higher. There is one plot per landlord, and plot size is fixed. Hence, while the tenant of marginal wealth level who is hired gets his reservation utility, the expected income of landlords from wealthier tenants is equated to that from poorer tenants. One may simply write this formally as maximizing the tenant's expected utility with respect to α and C subject to the constraints of the landlord's competitive expected income and the tenant's choice of labour input, the latter given the contract terms. The solution is mathematically similar. Of course, if W is high enough, then, as Shetty shows, fixed-rent contracts will be used; i.e., $\alpha = 1$, $R = -C < W$. In this case the bite of the incentive constraint is removed, and the efficient outcome is reached. If wealth is below the critical value, Shetty argues that sharecropping will emerge. The argument is that the optimal contract in this case will not simply involve reducing the fixed-rent payment, since a contract that involves no default can be improved on by a contract that involves increasing α and reducing C. (Note: C is negative if there is a fixed payment to the landlord.) Hence the optimal contracts for poorer tenants will involve default. Shetty also shows that the level of θ, say θ_1, at which the tenant cannot make the agreed-on payment, $(1 - \alpha)\theta Q - C$, to the landlord is decreasing in wealth.

While this reasoning establishes that a fixed-rent contract will not be used for tenants below a certain wealth level, it does not demonstrate that the actual contract will be a share contract, i.e. with α between 0 and 1.[49] To show this, consider the landlord's choice of contract, subject to providing the tenant with utility K^*—which, owing to competition for tenants, will be above reservation utility K for tenants with more wealth than the marginal tenant—and the tenant's labour input decision. This problem is

$$\max_{\alpha, C, L} E\{(1 - \alpha)\theta Q(L) - C | \theta \geq \theta_1\} + E\{\theta Q(L) + W | \theta < \theta_1\}$$

$$\text{s.t.} \quad E\{\alpha\theta Q(L) + C | \theta \geq \theta_1\} + E(-W | \theta < \theta_1) - L = K^*$$

$$E\{\alpha\theta Q'(L) | \theta \geq \theta_1\} - 1 = 0. \tag{24}$$

Now, as in the initial analysis of this section, the constraints may be solved for $L(\alpha), C(\alpha)$, which can then be substituted in the landlord's objective function. His first-order condition is thus

$$\{-Q + (1 - \alpha)Q'L_\alpha\}E(\theta|\theta \geq \theta_1)$$

$$- C_\alpha E(1|\theta \geq \theta_1) + Q'L_\alpha E(\theta|\theta < \theta_1) = 0.^{50} \tag{25}$$

Now from the tenant's utility constraint, and using his first-order condition for labour input,

$$E\{\theta Q(L) + C_\alpha|\theta \geq \theta_1\} = 0. \tag{26}$$

Substituting in (29) and using $E(\theta) = 1$, the landlord's choice of α is given by

$$Q'(L)L_\alpha\{1 - \alpha E(\theta|\theta \geq \theta_1)\} = 0. \tag{27}$$

But the first two terms are non-zero. Hence

$$\alpha = 1/E(\theta|\theta \geq \theta_1). \tag{28}$$

Since the denominator is greater than $E(\theta) = 1$,[51] the optimal α is less than 1. Hence we do have a share contract.

Thus Shetty's model predicts that poorer tenants who may default will receive share contracts. This is established in a model with wealth constraints and heterogeneous (in terms of wealth) tenants—both realistic assumptions—and with a characterization of the monopolistically competitive equilibrium. All of these are useful features.

I shall conclude this section with a discussion of costly monitoring of labour input. In all the models considered here, with the exception of Eswaran and Kotwal, it was assumed that the incentive problem arose from the non-observability of labour. One might interpret this as approximating the case where actually supervising the tenant's labour input is totally uneconomical. It is interesting to examine the implications of monitoring that is costly but worthwhile undertaking. This is because several analyses (e.g. Lucas 1979 and Alston, Datta, and Nugent 1984) have tried to provide explanations of sharecropping based on such costly monitoring. In essence, one might argue that the incentive problem is not fundamentally different if monitoring is imperfect, that is, if the landlord through his effort cannot tell precisely what the tenant or worker's effort is, but can only get a better estimate of that effort. This argument seems basically sound.

The focus here is therefore on the proper modelling of monitoring technology and costs.

The general approach to monitoring in moral hazard situations is that the landlord observes some noisy signal of the tenant's or worker's effort. Such a signal is in general informative—in fact, output itself can be thought of in this way—and the payment rule will be based on it.[52] Of course, when the landlord has this extra information, the tenant will work harder in equilibrium. It is not obvious what might correspond to this in the real world. An example might be the landlord saying that the tenant has not worked very hard, and reducing the latter's share as punishment. I do not know if anything like this occurs in practice. The special case of perfect monitoring is perhaps easier to interpret. Then the landlord can exactly observe labour input. He specifies the efficient level in the contract, and if it is not provided he punishes the tenant somehow. Thus the contract payment depends on labour input as well as output. Here, of course, there is no incentive problem as such.[53] Note that a risk-averse worker will receive a fixed wage, provided he supplies the agreed-upon labour input—any other contract imposes risk. In the literature on sharecropping, the assumption of perfect monitoring is therefore not made, since it would either do away with the rationale for share contracts, if worthwhile, or be irrelevant if uneconomical. However, the models I am aware of do not treat imperfect monitoring as the observation of an additional noisy signal, perhaps because of the lack of evidence that contracts are written this way. Instead, it is usually assumed that the worker or tenant supplies more effort the more he is monitored. For example, the Eswaran–Kotwal formulation was $E = E(S, L)$. Lucas (1979) has a similar formulation except that labour time and effort are not distinguished, so $L = L(S)$, and only fixed-wage workers are monitored. The problem with such a treatment is as follows. Suppose that supervision of amount S leads to a noisy signal $\tilde{L}$ of true labour input L. S determines the precision of $\tilde{L}$. Then in general the worker or tenant's payment should be $Y(Q, \tilde{L}; S)$, where S will affect the choice of the function Y since it affects the value of $\tilde{L}$ as a variable for determining payment. For example, a linear payment rule might be $\alpha Q + \beta \tilde{L} + C$, where α, β, and C depend on S, for a given S. Now given α, b, C, the tenant chooses his labour input L. This depends on S, but through the contract form rather than exogenously. In summary, how supervision or monitoring affects labour input depends on the rewards and penalties attached to the results of supervision: these are endogenous, so the relationship between monitoring and effort is endogenous. Hence there is a problem with the Eswaran–Kotwal and Lucas specifications. Note that the above model is completed by the landlord choosing α, β, C, and S, taking into account the tenant or worker's optimal response. The optimal S will depend on costs of supervision, which may be low if the landlord is supplying managerial input as well.[54]

Alston, Datta, and Nugent avoid some of the above problems. They allow for probabilistic detection of "shirking," that is, under-provision of contracted labour by the landlord, although this is well defined only for wage labour, since the sharecropper in their model does not contract the amount of labour.[55] The probability is essentially that of paying a fine or penalty. The less the labour input, the higher this probability. The penalties, however, are not optimally determined by the landlord, but are exogenously given functions. For wage contracts the penalty is assumed to increase with the extent of shirking. Similarly, for share contracts the penalty is assumed to decrease as effort increases. There is a logical problem here as well, since, even if penalties are exogenous, if the landlord knows what penalty to impose he must know how much labour input was supplied, but this contradicts the original notion of probabilistic detection.

The above model also has another difficulty, shared by that of Lucas. These analyses assume that monitoring cost functions differ for different types of contracts. However, they do not allow for any differences in production technology or inputs that might explain such differences. The example of a landlord supplying managerial inputs and therefore having lower monitoring costs was noted above. If the production technology is the same, then what differs from contract to contract are the benefits of monitoring, not the cost function. For example, a landlord who gives a tenant a fixed-rent contract could equally monitor him as well as a sharecropper. However, there is no benefit to supervising the former, while it pays to check on the share tenant. If the landlord supplies implements or bullocks to the sharecropper, he will also incur the cost of monitoring their use to prevent abuse. Again, however, this is not a difference in cost functions: the landlord could monitor the tenant's use of his own implements, but he gains nothing from doing so—it is the benefits that differ. As a modelling strategy, therefore, it seems to make better sense to specify a cost function for monitoring that does not exogenously depend on the form of contract. The equilibrium amount of monitoring, its cost, and the nature of the contract are all simultaneously determined.

This concludes the section on incentives. It seems that there are several avenues for fruitful theoretical research. First, there is the application of the dynamic model of Holmstrom and Milgrom. Second, further work should be done on the nature of equilibrium when the landlord contributes non-marketable inputs. Finally, monitoring, which is empirically important in share contracts, remains to be properly integrated into incentive models.

5   Sharecropping and Screening

The basic idea behind this explanation is that the landlord cannot directly observe some characteristic of potential tenants that affects productivity, such as entrepreneurial or other ability. Then, by offering a menu of contracts, including share contracts, the landlord can get individuals of different ability to select different contracts. Tenants are thus "screened" according to ability. In general, someone—landlord or tenant, depending on market structure—will be better off than if only wage and fixed-rent contracts were available. Note that the lowest-ability individuals might not receive a contract at all— they might be screened out of the market.

The screening model has several attractive features in terms of the stylized facts. First, it explains the coexistence of sharecropping with fixed-rent and wage contracts. Second, it fits with the observation that share tenancy is often associated with lower productivity than fixed-rent tenancy (see e.g. Bell 1977), since the model predicts that the more able (and more productive) tenants will choose fixed-rent contracts and the less able will choose sharecropping. Third, and related to the second point, the model seems to agree with the agricultural ladder hypothesis, which is based on the observation that, as agricultural workers gain physical and human capital, they progress from wage labour to sharecropping, then to renting, and finally to owner-operation (see e.g. Spillman 1919, and Cox 1944).

Hallagan (1978) and Newbery and Stiglitz (1979) independently introduced similar models of screening or self-selection by contractual choice.[56] Critiques were provided by Allen (1982) and Basu (1982). Based on his critique, Allen (1982) extended the basic model to allow for heterogenous landlords. Finally, Allen (1985a) provided a rather different screening model, which was distinguished by having default possibilities and more than one time-period. I shall begin by presenting a version of Hallagan's model and shall then discuss the critiques of Basu and Allen. Next, I shall do the same with Newbery and Stiglitz's analysis. Finally, I shall present and discuss Allen's work.

Hallagan (1978) does not construct a formal model, but what follows captures the essential features of his argument. We initially assume that there is a single landlord with two identical plots of land. He chooses not to, or is constrained not to, cultivate them himself. There are several potential tenants, of whom one has higher ability than the rest. However, one person can just manage a single plot by himself, so the landlord must give his plots to two different tenants. He would like one to be the high-ability person, who has a higher productivity. To abstract from risk-sharing effects, all individuals are assumed to be risk-neutral. Hence, while there is uncertainty in production, this need not be treated explicitly, since only expected values matter. Also, incentive considerations are mostly avoided, although we appeal to them to avoid indeterminacy of the contractual form in some instances. Hence input choices need not be treated explicitly. Finally, there are no binding wealth constraints, so, for example, a tenant can always make the payment specified by a fixed-rent contract. Reviewing the above assumptions, we may note that the other major explanations of sharecropping—risk-sharing, incentives and input provision, and wealth constraints—have been ruled out so that we may concentrate on the screening explanation.

We now begin with the formal model. Each potential tenant, including the high-ability person, has a reservation expected income of $\bar{Y}$. Thus, implicitly, the high-ability person's skills are specific to tenant farming. This is not essential, as I shall point out below. The high-ability individual's expected output from farming is Q_1, while that of any of the low-ability individuals is Q_2, $Q_2 < Q_1$. The actual outputs are $\tilde{Q}_1, \tilde{Q}_2$ because of uncertainty: this means that ability cannot be deduced from actual output. We assume that disutility of labour is the same in tenant farming and the best alternative occupation, and that there are no other inputs. Hence a tenancy contract will be acceptable if it provides expected income $Y(Q_i) \geq \bar{Y}$. We assume that if this holds with equality, the tenancy is chosen. Also, we assume that $Q_i > \bar{Y}$, so that farming is worthwhile.

Initially, suppose that the landlord knows everyone's ability. Acting as a monopolist, he will charge a rent R_i such that $Q_i - R_i = \bar{Y}$, and

his expected income will be $Q_1 + Q_2 - 2\bar{Y}$. Note that there is an indeterminacy, in that sharecropping contracts would also suffice. If α_i
is the tenant's share, the landlord can set α_i such that $\alpha_i Q_i = \bar{Y}$, and
achieve the same expected income. Hence we assume that there is
some incentive effect, enough to ensure that the fixed rent contracts
are better.

Now suppose that the landlord cannot observe anyone's ability.
Also, because of the uncertainty in production, he cannot infer ability
from actual output. Then he cannot discriminate as above, where he
charges $R_1 > R_2$ to the more able tenant, because the latter would
always claim to be of lower ability and ask for the lower rent. On
the other hand, charging R_1 will attract only the more able tenant
and the other plot will go unrented. Below it is demonstrated that
the landlord can do better than collecting $R_1 = Q_1 - \bar{Y}$, or $2R_2 =
2Q_2 - 2\bar{Y}$, by offering a choice of a fixed-rent and a share contract: the
more able individual will prefer the fixed-rent contract, and will
choose it, while the less able individuals will prefer the share contract, and one of them will become a sharecropper.

Let the contract menu be (R_s, α_s), where 's' stands for screening.
Then, for the above contract selection to occur, it must be true that

$$Q_1 - R_s \geq \alpha_s Q_1, \tag{29}$$

$$\alpha_s Q_2 \geq Q_2 - R_s. \tag{30}$$

These are known in the literature as the self-selection or incentive
compatibility constraints. The first inequality says that the more able
person prefers the fixed-rent contract, the second that the less able
person prefers the share contract. The inequalities may be rearranged
slightly to give

$$(1 - \alpha_s)Q_1 \geq R_s \tag{31}$$

and

$$(1 - \alpha_s)Q_2 \leq R_s. \tag{32}$$

Hence we see that the two inequalities are compatible, since $Q_1 > Q_2$.
This would not be the case if they were reversed: it cannot be that the
more able person prefers the share contract and the less able one the
fixed-rent contract.

Now, assuming that the landlord rents both plots, he chooses
(R_s, α_s) to maximize his expected income,

$R_s + (1 - \alpha_s)Q_2,$

subject to the self-selection constraints above, and the contract acceptance constraints

$$Q_1 - R_s \geq \bar{Y} \tag{33}$$

and

$$\alpha_s Q_2 \geq \bar{Y}. \tag{34}$$

Since both self-selection constraints cannot be simultaneously binding, we consider each possibility in turn. If that for the more able person is binding, $R_s = (1 - \alpha_s)Q_1$, and the landlord's expected income is $(1 - \alpha_s)(Q_1 + Q_2)$. This is maximized by setting α_s as small as possible, i.e. $\alpha_s = \bar{Y}/Q_2$, so that the less able person will just accept the share contract. Note that then $Q_1 - R_s = \alpha_s Q_1 > \bar{Y}$, so that the more able person is better off than with his alternative. The landlord's expected income is

$$(1 - \bar{Y}/Q_2)(Q_1 + Q_2) = Q_1 - \bar{Y}Q_1/Q_2 + Q_2 - \bar{Y}. \tag{35}$$

If, on the other hand, the less able person is indifferent between the two contracts, then $R_s = (1 - \alpha_s)Q_2$; but α_s must be the same, from the acceptance constraints, so that the landlord's expected income is $2Q_2 - 2\bar{Y}$, which is lower. Hence the first possibility is better. In fact, this is a special case of a more general result (see, e.g. Cooper 1984 for a good exposition) that the self-selection constraint will be binding on the person who has an incentive to pretend to be someone else: we noted above that the more able person would claim to be less able, faced with rental contracts (R_1, R_2). This is demonstrated here to elucidate the workings of the model.

It remains to check that the screening contract is better for the landlord than the alternatives. Clearly, it is better than charging R_2 to each tenant, since $2R_2 = 2Q_2 - 2\bar{Y}$. It is better than just collecting $R_1 = Q_1 - \bar{Y}$ from the more able tenant if

$$Q_2 - \bar{Y}Q_1/Q_2 > 0 \tag{36}$$

or

$$Q_2/\bar{Y} > Q_1/Q_2. \tag{37}$$

This condition is violated if the more able person is much more productive than the others. In that case, the equilibrium still involves screening, since individuals of different ability are distinguished *ex post*, but there is no role for sharecropping. Instead, there is adverse selection: the lower-ability individuals are shut out of the tenancy market. If the last inequality is satisfied, however, the equilibrium involves screening, with an essential role for share contracts in that process.

The above model involves one important simplification from Hallagan's argument: wage contracts are neglected. This was done for expositional convenience and does not alter the fundamental structure of the screening model, or sharecropping's role in it. I next describe what happens when wage contracts are allowed.

We may introduce wage contracts indirectly. In the above model, suppose that the share contract also has a fixed side-payment, C, so that the share tenant receives $\alpha_s \tilde{Q}_2 + C$. Then it turns out to be optimal for the landlord to set $\alpha_s = 0$ and $C = \bar{Y}$, that is, to offer a fixed-wage contract. Screening thus is achieved by offering a choice between a fixed-rent and a fixed-wage contract. However, sharecropping in general has a role if there are three or more types of potential tenants, for then wage and rent contracts together will not suffice for complete screening. If that is optimal for the landlord, he will use share contracts as well. The formal model for three or more types is similar to the above two-ability model. If there are n ability levels, there will be $n(n-1)$ self-selection constraints, but at most $n-1$ will be binding in equilibrium: each ability level will be indifferent between that individual's contract and the one chosen by those in the next lowest ability level. The most able and least able individuals will choose rent and wage contracts respectively, and those in between will choose different share contracts, distinguished by different share and side-payment combinations. I shall not present the general model here, since it adds no new insights. Instead, I turn to Basu's critique of Hallagan's screening model.

Basu allows for competition among landlords, and this destroys the screening result in Hallagan's model. Note that this is not perfect competition in the sense of price-taking behaviour: instead, it is monopolistic competition. In terms of the simplified two-ability model presented above, suppose there are two landlords. Then the equilibrium cannot be the screening equilibrium, since there the landlord renting to the high-ability persons earns more on that plot of land. With more than one landlord, they will bid up the "price" of the high-ability person so that the return on any plot of land is the same, namely, $Q_2 - \bar{Y}$, the return from renting to the less able person. Hence $R = Q_2 - \bar{Y}$ for the more able tenant. But this is exactly what the less able tenant pays in expected terms with a share contract $\alpha = \bar{Y}/Q_2$, so he might as well receive a fixed-rent contract. The same argument applies to a situation with many landlords, many potential tenants, and more than two ability levels: equilibrium will involve all tenants receiving fixed-rent contracts, and landlords getting a rent equal to the expected surplus of the tenant of marginal ability. There is no screening and no role for share contracts.

Allen (1982) makes a similar point to Basu. He introduces competition as price-taking behaviour. He allows plot size to vary, which is not strictly in Hallagan's model. He also assumes a competitive market for labour. He then argues, as a special case of the general result, that competitive equilibrium is Pareto-efficient; in the equilibrium individuals will hire land and labour in or out so that the standard marginal conditions are satisfied. Hence there is no role for share contracts since fixed-rent contracts achieve efficiency. The crux of the argument is that incomplete information about ability does not matter, since each person as producer knows his own ability and will make efficient input decisions based on that knowledge.[57] Hence there is no role for screening. While Allen's formulation is more general in allowing for variable amounts of land and labour, the assumption of price-taking behaviour by all market participants seems unrealistic. The usual justification in terms of the limit of monopolistic competition or other strategic behaviour may not hold when there is asymmetric information. In any case, it is clear that the screening explanation needs a stronger basis than is provided by Hallagan.

Newbery and Stiglitz (1979) independently suggested screening as a rationale for sharecropping. Their model is more general, in that they also allow for the landlord to vary the plot size. This turns out to be a crucial feature if sharecropping is to serve a screening function when there is some form of competition among landlords. Newbery and Stiglitz assume that ability multiplies labour effort in the production function, but this is inessential to their argument. I present a simplified version of their model, ignoring labour input, since it is fixed in their formulation, and concentrating on the case of two ability levels and a choice between fixed-rent and share contracts. Again, these simplifications are for expositional ease—the model is more general. I shall not present a full solution of the model, but instead shall focus on why the Newbery–Stiglitz formulation avoids some problems of Hallagan's model.

Let us assume that the production function form and amount of land are such that each landlord will want to have more than one tenant, and that there are more landlords than high-ability potential tenants. The typical higher-ability person's average production function is $Q_1(T)$, where T is the amount of land. The lower-ability person's average production function is $Q_2(T)$, with $Q_1(T) > Q_2(T)$ and $Q_1'(T) > Q_2'(T)$.[58] Furthermore, as usual $Q_i' > 0$ and $Q_i'' < 0, i = 1, 2$. Let r_i be the rental rate for a tenant of type i, and T_i be the amount of land he is given. Thus, the landlord with perfect information about potential tenants' abilities offers two different rental "packages," (r_1, T_1) and (r_2, T_2).[59] He seeks to maximize $r_1 T_1 + r_2 T_2$ subject to the availability of his land, $T_1 + T_2 = \bar{T}$,[60] and to the contract acceptance constraints of the tenants, which are

$$Q_1(T_1) - r_1 T_1 \geq \bar{Y} \tag{38}$$

and

$$Q_2(T_2) - r_2 T_2 \geq \bar{Y}. \tag{39}$$

It is easy to see that the solution will involve the landlord equating marginal products on the two plots, and setting rental rates so that each tenant gets just $\bar{Y}$.

Now suppose that there is competition among landlords.[61] Then this will force the return per acre, that is the rental rate, on all land to be the same.[62] Hence any landlord is restricted to offering contracts (r, T_1) and (r, T_2). In this case, both acceptance constraints may or may not be binding at the equilibrium,[63] depending on the precise form of the production functions.[64] Now if the landlord does not observe potential tenants' abilities, he still may offer contracts of the above form, and it is possible that each type will prefer a different contract. However, the landlord can do better by offering a fixed-rent and a share contract, as I now demonstrate.

Suppose that the typical landlord offers contracts (r, T_1) and (α, T_2). The self-selection constraints are

$$Q_1(T_1) - r T_1 \geq \alpha Q_1(T_2) \tag{40}$$

and

$$\alpha Q_2(T_2) \geq Q_2(T_1) - r T_1. \tag{41}$$

Competitive behaviour by landlords requires that

$$r = (1 - \alpha)Q_2(T_2)/T_2,^{65} \tag{42}$$

so that the return per acre from each contract is equalized. This is equivalent to

$$rT_2 = (1 - \alpha)Q_2(T_2). \tag{43}$$

Hence

$$rT_2 < (1 - \alpha)Q_1(T_2), \tag{44}$$

so that

$$\alpha Q_1(T_2) < Q_1(T_2) - rT_2. \tag{45}$$

If the self-selection constraint for the higher-ability tenant is binding in equilibrium, it follows that

$$Q_1(T_1) - rT_1 < Q_1(T_2) - rT_2. \tag{46}$$

In words, the self-selection constraint would be violated by the pair of rental contracts $(r, T_1), (r, T_2)$. What I have shown is that, while screening could be accomplished by offering a choice of two rental contracts, it can be done more effectively from the landlord's perspective by offering a choice between a fixed-rent and a share contract. And screening is possible even with competition, as long as the landlord has an additional dimension of control, namely the size of the plot to be rented.

The above formulation allows landlords to choose contract parameters subject to contract acceptance and the equalizing effect of competition among landlords for high-ability tenants. This is not competition in the sense of price-taking behaviour. Allen's (1982) critique of screening in Hallagan's model based on price-taking behaviour in all markets applies equally to the Newbery–Stiglitz model *if* price-taking behaviour is assumed in the latter as well. The equilibrium is then Pareto-efficient, and there is no role for share contracts or for screening. However, as argued in Section 2, this seems unrealistic.

Next we examine some flaws of the above models as explanations of sharecropping. One seemingly attractive feature of these screening models, as noted in the beginning of this section, is that they are consistent with the agricultural ladder hypothesis. However, as Basu points out, Spillman's version of this is quite different, being "a rather Shakespearean account of the stages of a farmer's life. It focuses more on the development of farmer's skills over time than on inter-farmer differences in one situation." On the other hand, there is cross-sectional evidence of a similar pattern (e.g. Cox 1944, and Brown and Atkinson 1981), which one might also call an agricultural ladder.

A more telling criticism does emerge from a consideration of what happens over time. In screening models, ability or land quality is generally revealed sooner or later, through self-selection of contract terms. In the real world, one would also expect such knowledge to be gained gradually by direct observation. Once this happens, screening is unnecessary and only wage and rent contracts are needed. Hence, the validity of such models in agricultural contexts where there is little in-migration and limited use of new techniques is questionable: one would expect abilities and land qualities to be well known. This seems to be the major problem with the above screening models.

Allen (1985a) presents an ingenious model that avoids the above strictures. His model predicts that share contracts will be used even after potential tenants are screened. Furthermore, only three types of contracts are used, although a continuum of ability levels is allowed for. While the possibility of default plays an essential role in this model, its interesting predictions depend on the initial lack of information about potential tenants' abilities, and the resulting screening. Hence we consider the model here, rather than in Section 3 or Section 6.

Allen's model assumes that there is a continuum of abilities, A, in the interval $[0, A_u]$. Everyone's labour supply is fixed. The production function for a person of ability A with land T is $AQ(T)$, where Q has the usual properties. Uncertainty is abstracted from, though we may think of AQ as expected output. Each person knows his own ability, but this cannot be known by anybody else until he has been seen to produce for one period. It will then be known to all the landlords in the locality. However, if the person moves, landlords elsewhere will again be initially unaware of his ability.

There is an infinite number of discrete production periods, and contracts are agreed on each period. However, at the end of each period, a tenant may choose to default on the agreed-upon payment to the landlord. He must then move to another place to avoid penalties. Initially, no moving costs are assumed, but this is not essential.

People are risk-neutral, and their utility of consumption is

$$U = \sum_{t=1}^{\infty} \delta^{t-1} c_t \tag{47}$$

where $\delta(<1)$ is the discount factor. There is no saving or wealth of tenants. Finally, it is necessary to assume that each period there is some exogenously determined turnover of population in any locality. This ensures that there are always people to be screened.

There are two stages of contracting. First, when ability is unobserved, the contract involves a payment R_s to the landlord for T_s units of land. Since landlords will offer a menu of such contracts for screening, we may think of R_s and T_s as functions of A. The landlord's opportunity cost of land is r per unit; hence it must be that

$$R_s(A) \geq rT_s(A). \tag{48}$$

With competition among landlords, this will hold with equality, and the tenant's (expected) utility,

$$AQ\{T_s(A)\} - R_s(A),$$

is maximized. Since ability is unknown, the menu of contracts must satisfy the self-selection constraints,

$$AQ\{T_s(A)\} - R_s(A) \geq AQ\{T_s(A')\} - R_s(A') \quad \text{for all } A, A'. \tag{49}$$

There are several other constraints. Potential tenants have opportunity cost W per period. If the contract when ability is known is $\{R(A), T(A)\}$, it must be true that

$$AQ\{T_s(A)\} - R_s(A) + \frac{\delta}{1-\delta}[AQ\{T(A)\} - R(A)] \geq \frac{W}{1-\delta}. \tag{50}$$

The left-hand side is the utility of tenancy, and the right-hand side is the utility of working elsewhere: these are calculated using equation (47). If this inequality is binding, it defines a marginal level of ability A_0: it turns out the tenancy contract will be accepted if and only if $A \geq A_0$. Next, suppose a person of ability A_0 receives just enough land to cover his opportunity cost if he undertakes the tenancy for one period, then defaults. Let this amount be $T_0(A_0)$, which is defined by

$$A_0 Q(T_0) = W. \tag{51}$$

To avoid this problem and consequent losses, the landlord is restricted to

$$T_s(A) \leq T_0(A_0). \tag{52}$$

Also, obviously,

$$T_s(A) \geq 0. \tag{53}$$

Finally, for a contract to be enforceable in this model, it must be worthwhile for tenants to make the agreed-upon payment. The benefit of default, the screening period payment, must be less than the cost, the present value of the loss from being rescreened in another area. Thus we have the following constraint, which is essential to the model:

$$R_s(A) \leq \delta \langle AQ\{T(A)\} - R(A) - [AQ\{T_s(A)\} - R_s(A)] \rangle. \tag{54}$$

Note that at the first stage $R(A)$, $T(A)$ are taken as given.

The second stage of contracting is when abilities are known. The contracts then solve the following problem, which is similar to the previous one with the constraints imposed by asymmetric information omitted:

$$\max_{R(A),T(A)} \quad AQ\{T(A)\} - R(A)$$

s.t. $\quad R(A) \geq rT(A)$,

$$R(A) \leq \delta \langle AQ\{T(A)\} - R(A) - [AQ\{T_s(A)\} - R_s(A)] \rangle,$$

$$T(A) \geq 0, \tag{55}$$

with $R_s(A)$ and $T_s(A)$ being given.

I shall now outline the implications of this model. The complete solution is quite complicated (see Allen 1985a for details), but I can highlight some insights. First, in the screening period, the incentives of the marginal tenant of ability A_0 provide the binding constraint. To prevent this default, the screening contract must have $T_s(A) = T_0(A_0)$. Also, competition among landlords ensures that $R_s(A) = rT_s(A)$. Hence the equilibrium contract is

$$\left.\begin{array}{l} R_s(A) = rT_0(A_0) \\ T_s(A) = T_0(A_0), \end{array}\right\} \tag{56}$$

so every tenant gets the same contract in the screening period. Note that ability subsequently becomes known not through self-selection of contracts, since there is only one, but through direct observation.

In the subsequent periods, if the default constraint in (55) does not bind for a tenant, it must be that $R(A)$, $T(A)$ maximizes $AQ(T) - rT$, since $R(A) = rT(A)$. But this implies that the marginal product of land is equated to its opportunity cost. Hence this is a standard fixed-rent contract: the landlord could equivalently allow the tenant to select T given the rental rate r. On the other hand, if the default constraint binds, it determines the amount of land offered, which will be such that the marginal product at that value exceeds the "rental rate" r: hence this cannot be interpreted as a fixed-rent contract. Let the equilibrium amount of land in this case be $T^*(A, A_0)$—it depends on A_0 through the influence of the screening contract on the default constraint. Then the corresponding equilibrium payment is

$$R(A) = \frac{\delta}{1+\delta} AQ\{T^*(A, A_0)\} - C \tag{57}$$

where

$$C = \frac{\delta}{1+\delta} [AQ\{T_0(A_0)\} - rT_0(A_0). \tag{58}$$

Hence the contract for such tenants is a share contract with an associated side-payment to the tenant.

The question remains as to when the default constraint is binding. Allen provides an example with a quadratic production function, where the lowest-ability persons do not become tenants, those of middle ability become sharecroppers, and those of high ability get fixed-rent contracts. However, as he demonstrates, in general this need not be true, in that, while the lowest two groups are always non-tenants and sharecroppers respectively, thereafter there may be alternating groups who get share and fixed-rent contracts: hence there is no obvious "ladder." Furthermore, for the production function $Q = \sqrt{T}$, no fixed-rent contracts will be used.

Finally, Allen argues convincingly that the introduction of uncertainty, risk aversion, variations in technology across regions, or moving costs[66] does not substantively change the predictions of the model.

I shall now evaluate this framework. As noted, the model predicts that sharecropping will be used even after tenants are screened.

This is because there is the possibility of default. On the other hand, default is constrained by the cost of being rescreened elsewhere. Hence, in Allen's model, sharecropping persists, unlike the previous self-selection models. Second, while there are potentially many ability levels, all share contracts are predicted to involve a share $\delta/(1+\delta)$. This deals with the problem in other models of "too many share contracts." There are additional attractive features. First, the predicted share is close to one-half for reasonable values of the discount factor; for example, $\delta = 0.9$ implies a share of 0.47. Second, since the model relies on the absence of direct enforcement mechanisms such as saving and the use of collateral, their introduction in the course of economic development would explain a concurrent decline in share tenancy.

There remain some shortcomings, of course. The model still predicts a continuum of different side-payments. Furthermore, as noted, for plausible production functions it predicts no use of fixed-rent contracts. Finally, it does not give clear-cut predictions about the variation of contract type with ability. However, overall, it does seem that Allen's work focuses on some important features of the institutional setup in less developed agriculture, and provides extremely useful insights into the role of sharecropping.

6   Sharecropping and Cost-sharing

Input cost-sharing is a common arrangement in share contracts.[67] If sharecropping exists for reasons such as risk-sharing, incentive provision, or screening, cost-sharing might be a convenient way of ensuring that such inputs are used at efficient levels by the tenant, even if the landlord could directly specify input levels. In a simple model, if the cost share is set equal to the output share, then the use of the input will satisfy the usual condition that marginal (value) product equals price.[68] Although the tenant receives only a fraction of the product, he pays only the same fraction of the cost. An argument that runs in the other direction, from cost-sharing to sharecropping, is less obvious. This is made by Jaynes (1982, 1984) and is based on imperfections in the market for the shared input, which is interpreted as capital. I shall now discuss this model as a rationale for share contracts.

The formal model has no uncertainty in it. The production function is thus $Q(L, T, I)$, where L and T are labour and land, as before, and I is some other input such as fertilizer or seeds. The price of I is p. The tenant's output share is α, and his cost share is β. There is a fixed payment of C, and his wealth is W. Hence his utility is

$$U(\alpha Q + W - \beta pI + C, L), \qquad (59)$$

which is increasing in the first argument, income, and decreasing in the second argument, labour input. The tenant is assumed to choose I independently. Hence his input choice satisfies

$$\alpha Q_I - \beta p = 0. \qquad (60)$$

Jaynes's justification for this is that the tenant cannot be forced to contribute more or less capital to the productive venture than he deems optimal. The landlord is assumed to maximize his utility, which is linear in income, subject to (60), and to providing the tenant with his reservation utility level, $K(W)$. The landlord's income is

$$(1 - \alpha)Q(L, T, I) - (1 - \beta)pI - C - rT.$$

Here r is the opportunity cost of land. The landlord's choice variables are $\alpha, \beta, C, L,$ and T (and, notionally, I as well).

Jaynes also allows for monitoring costs, but this is not essential. His main point is that the cost-sharing, captured by $\beta < 1$, potentially occurs because the landlord does not have enough capital himself, and hence seeks households with sufficient wealth. Jaynes shows that at the landlord's optimum $\alpha = \beta$, and hence there is output-sharing if there is cost-sharing. Cost-sharing emerges because the landlord is implicitly capital-considered and the tenant is explicitly so constrained as well.

Jaynes also addresses the question of why landlords do not offer fixed-rent contracts. He says that in that case the landlord would still have to provide some credit to the tenant. This would have to earn the landlord its opportunity cost, and the tenant would get only the return to his own labour, reducing him to a wage labourer. However, the last two clauses do *not* follow. If the tenant is still providing some capital of his own, he would get some return on that. In any case, if the landlord is capital-constrained and has to compete for wealthier tenants, such tenants should be able to earn the same with fixed-rent contracts as with Jaynes's sharecropping–cost-sharing solution. With fixed-rent contracts, the landlord would simply make a lump-sum loan, rather than subsidizing the input at the margin. Provided the tenant can borrow enough, B, from the landlord so that $pI \le W + B$

when $Q_I = p$, the optimum can be achieved. If B is not large enough, then the landlord will also not be able to provide enough of a subsidy through cost-sharing to ensure $Q_I = p$. To summarize, the efficient solution can be achieved in Jaynes's model with fixed-rent contracts and without cost-sharing, but with a production loan from the landlord.

Several other points are worth noting. First, if, unlike in Jaynes's model, labour input cannot be determined by the landlord, a fixed-rent contract has the advantage of providing efficient incentives for labour input. Second, fixed-rent contracts may no longer be optimal if there is uncertainty and the tenant is risk-averse, but then, it is sharecropping that leads to cost-sharing, rather than the other way around. Third, Jaynes's justification for the tenant independently choosing the level of input I seems weak. If the landlord can observe and enforce the level of input I, he might as well do so. (He has monopolistic power in choosing all other variables, subject to attracting the tenant.) On the other hand, if he cannot observe the level of input I, then he cannot sensibly agree to provide a fraction of the cost. In fact, Bardhan and Singh (1982, 1987)[69] have shown that in this case an attempt at cost-sharing at the margin will not necessarily have the desired effect. This seeming problem with justifying cost-sharing itself—either it is unnecessary or it does not have the desired effect—is carefully dealt with by Braverman and Stiglitz (1986a). They show that, if the tenant's input decision is made after he obtains additional private information about productivity, the landlord will prefer cost-sharing to specifying the input level. This is because cost-sharing delegates the input decision to the person with better information. Note that in general, $\alpha \neq \beta$ in this model. Furthermore, if there is no incentive problem and no uncertainty, the optimal contract involves a fixed rent and no cost-sharing at the margin—the landlord may simply make a lump-sum production loan. This is because the tenant will then make fully efficient decisions. Hence it is incentives and uncertainty that drive the result that share contracts will be used, and cost-sharing follows from that.

I conclude this section, therefore, by stating that it seems that, while capital constraints and cost-sharing are important and can both be usefully incorporated into models of sharecropping, they do not explain the institution itself. At best, we can say that both sharecropping and cost-sharing are the result of uncertainty and asymmetries in information.

7 Conclusion

I have already offered something of a conclusion in the introduction: sharecropping is a diverse phenomenon, and explanations of sharecropping are necessarily going to be diverse. The common theme, however, is, that sharecropping is a response to uncertainty and asymmetries in information. One may also view it as a response to different types of market failure, in labour, insurance, credit, and capital markets. Typically, however, these market failures can be traced back to imperfect or incomplete information as the cause. It does not follow, though, that institutions such as sharecropping will lead to outcomes that are efficient relative to the structure of information. While this may be the case, often there will be general equilibrium distortions that can be corrected by government tax and subsidy policies that are also constrained by available information, and hence are strictly feasible. Briefly, this is because, in a many-commodity, second-best world, taxes or subsidies on observable commodities can favourably affect choices of unobservables such as labour input—pecuniary externalities matter. This is an issue that has been treated by Arnott and Stiglitz in several papers (1984, 1985, 1986). This is aside from gains that might be made by improving the information structure (e.g. accreditation, licensing) and thereby mitigating market imperfections. Hence there are two general sorts of policies that might usefully be pursued in the context of agriculture with sharecropping. The detailed policy implications of the models considered above seem well worth pursuing—but in another place.

Notes

1. The classical and neoclassical literature starts with Smith (1776), and includes Young (1788), Sismondi (1818), Jones (1831), Mill (1848), and Marshall (1920). Historical studies include Alston (1981), Alston and Higgs (1982), H. Higgs (1894), R. Higgs (1974), Reid (1975), Winters (1974), and Wright (1978).

2. Descriptive and empirical studies include Ahmed (1974), Bardhan (1977, 1984), Bell (1977), Bliss and Stern (1982), Hendry (1960), Huang (1971, 1975), Issawi (1957), Johnson (1971), Jodha (1984), Pant (1983), Rao (1971), Roumasset (1984), Roumasset and James (1979), Ruttan (1966), and Shaban (1987). An interesting collection of studies is in Byres (1983), and an excellent recent work is that of Robertson (1987).

3. For example, I touch on some of the "neglected themes" mentioned by Binswanger and Rosenzweig.

4. Binswanger's and Rosenzweig's Figure 1–2 (1984) provides a schematic representation of the kind of classification I have provided, though it is not identical.

5. See, for example, Reid (1976), Lucas (1979), Bell and Braverman (1981), Quibria (1982), Alston, Datta, and Nugent (1984), and Quibria and Rashid (1984). A good basic survey is in Bliss and Stern (1982).

6. There are parallel problems or paradoxes as well in terms of the landlord's decisions. See Lucas (1979) and Bell and Braverman (1981). Also see the discussion of Jaynes below.

7. See Section 6 on sharecropping and cost-sharing.

8. They assume that only a single share contract, specifying α, is available. In their model, the tenant faces some exogenous expected penalty that is inversely related to the labour-land ratio. This places a constraint on his demand for land. The landlord, on the other hand, is constrained in a different manner. In the Jaynes model, if faced with a given share, the landlord would wish to always increase the labour-land ratio, unless the marginal product of labour falls to zero. Here, instead, the landlord assumes that however much land he chooses to provide on share terms, the labour-land ratio will be the same, i.e. rather than taking the tenant's labour input decision as given, he assumes the tenant will always adjust his labour input to maintain the labour-land ratio on sharecropped land. This is not a usual type of competitive assumption. There are other difficulties as well: the landlord does not benefit from penalties on the tenant, so it is not clear what these are; the landlord does not even realize that this monitoring affects the share tenant's behaviour; the exogeneity of penalties and differences in monitoring cost functions are not well motivated (see Section 4). Hence, while the model provided by Alston, Datta and Nugent is ingenious, it seems unsatisfactory in some respects.

9. An alternative is an explicit bargaining approach. See Bell's Chapter 4 below.

10. See, for example, the Symposium on the Limits of Non-co-operative Equilibrium in the *Journal of Economic Theory*, 1980. An early, non-rigorous attempt in the context of sharecropping is Koo (1973).

11. For example, Lucas (1979) does this in the last model in his paper.

12. See Arnott and Stiglitz (1984, 1985, 1986). By exclusivity, I mean that the landlord can require that his tenant does not contract with other landlords as well.

13. Stiglitz (1974a), Newbery (1975, 1977), and Newbery and Stiglitz (1979).

14. So the central planner is also unable to make state-contingent adjustments.

15. Thus, let (α, C) be the optimal contract for the landlord, with inputs (L, T), so that the sharecropper gets $\alpha \tilde{Q}(L, T, \theta) + C$. Suppose that the landlord can instead offer a rental contract at rental rate r for cultivation with inputs (kL, kT), and a wage contract at wage rate w for the remaining $\{(1 - k)L, (1 - k)T\}$. The tenant's return in state of the world θ is then

$$\tilde{Q}(kL, kT, \theta) - rkT + w(1 - k)L = k\tilde{Q}(L, T, \theta) - rkT + w(1 - k)L,$$

by the assumption of CRS. For this to duplicate the returns from the share contract, it must be that $k = \alpha$. Then, for the side payments to be equal,

$$w(1 - \alpha)L - r\alpha T = C.$$

Clearly, the landlord can always find a w and r so that this holds. In fact, even if he must offer a market-determined wage, w, he can select an appropriate rental rate. The key here is that the landlord has some monopoly power. If both w and r for this tenant are set by the market, then of course he cannot be necessarily driven to his reservation utility level, and instead the landlord must compete by adjusting the share and side-payment; we are back to the Newbery model, with the addition of side-payments.

16. The production decision is akin to investing in an asset with risky returns.

17. A linear sharing rule is optimal only if the utility functions have absolute risk aversions whose reciprocals are linear. See Wilson (1968).

18. These are thirteenth-century England, nineteenth-century Germany, Chile, and Peru.

19. Newbery (1977) and Newbery and Stiglitz (1979) also look at economies of scale and indivisibilities. They see these as limiting the scope of their result on the irrelevance of share contracts for risk-sharing. However, *if* the conditions Allen describes hold, their result is more general.

20. Alternatively or additionally, the rental rate could be random. Bell (1986) has suggested that the timing of the randomness may be such that the wage is known when cultivation decisions are made. Then the following argument does not hold. Newbery and Stiglitz also discuss this point.

21. A rigorous demonstration is in Newbery (1977), where it is also shown that the equilibrium share will be $\alpha^* = LQ_L/Q$, i.e. the imputed share of labour with no uncertainty.

22. Eswaran and Kotwal (1985c) look at these inputs, but the emphasis is on incentive problems, so their analysis is treated in the next section.

23. Such models are considered in Chapter 4 below.

24. This assumes that monitoring is prohibitively costly. This is relaxed in the next section.

25. One can treat other inputs similarly from an analytical point of view.

26. Mostly through Marshall's footnote.

27. If it can, there is no incentive problem, of course.

28. Empirically, monitoring is often important.

29. The literature is enormous. See the recent survey by Hart and Holmstrom (1987) for an excellent exposition and a partial bibliography.

30. Mazumdar (1975) and Sen (1981) make similar points, but not centrally to their analyses.

31. The Shetty and Eswaran–Kotwal models are actually also pure moral hazard models (or 'hidden action', in Arrow's terminology), but they do not rely on risk aversion. The Hurwicz–Shapiro model is a 'hidden information' model (see Arrow 1985).

32. Again we may refer to Hart and Holmstrom (1987) for details.

33. This is easily shown; see, for example, Harris and Raviv (1979).

34. For a discussion of such issues, see Hart and Holmstrom (1987).

35. Roughly, since $U'' < 0$, U' and θ are negatively correlated, so $E(U'\theta) - E(U')E(\theta) < 0$ and $E(\theta) = 1$.

36. With risk neutrality, $C_\alpha = Q$ and $\alpha = 1$, as we would expect: a fixed-rent contract is used. Otherwise, note that equation (9) does not give an explicit formula for the share, since the right-hand side also depends on α.

37. The analysis involves obtaining an expression for L_α, which turns out to be quite messy. Similar sorts of comparative statics with uncertainty are common in the literature; see e.g. Arrow (1971).

38. See Chapter 12 below, and Robertson (1987).

39. This point is made by Singh (1983) in a two-period model.

40. Alternative models, where agents get more than their opportunity cost and hence suffer if dismissed, are those of Stiglitz and Weiss (1983) and Shapiro and Stiglitz (1984).

41. The parameter ε is suppressed in what follows.

42. This is a situation where each person's choice is the best response to the other's equilibrium choice. It is easy to show that this equilibrium exists. It is assumed unique.

43. It is plausible that he can precommit these, but not his input M.

44. This applies to materials in their model as well.

45. This is hence a hidden information model in Arrow's terminology.

46. In the published proof, differentiability is imposed. In general, $Y(Q)$ may be kinked or discontinuous.

47. See Section 5 below on screening for more discussion of this hypothesis. Also see Wright (1978: 176).

48. In Shetty's model these are constant, and there is cost-sharing in the proportion of the output share.

49. The following derivation turns out to contain an error. The correct result is that α exceeds one, unless restricted to not do so. See Ray and Singh (1998) for a correct analysis, discussion and references.

50. Note that, while θ_1 is a function of L, C, and α, the derivatives with respect to θ_1 cancel out, from its definition.

51. This is easy to demonstrate mathematically. The intuition (for which I am grateful to Steve Stoft) is that the center of gravity of the distribution is shifted to the right by removing the left tail.

52. For general results, see Holmstrom (1979, 1982). For an application, see Singh (1985).

53. It is not clear if share contracts that specify labour inputs (e.g. as in Cheung's observations) are of this form, with penalties for non-fulfilment. Possibly, observed labour time is always supplied as contracted, and effort is still unobservable, so the incentive problem remains.

54. This is thus a different idea from Eswaran and Kotwal, where there are no such economies of scope. I am grateful to Lee Alston (private correspondence) for this idea on why supervision costs might be low.

55. Fixed-rent contracts are considered in their model, presumably because of asset or wealth limitations, since everyone is risk-neutral. However, these are not made explicit.

56. The idea can actually be traced to Reid (1976).

57. The details of the model are not presented, since it is a standard Walrasian one.

58. The assumption that marginal products are also ordered by ability is typically necessary in screening or self-selection models; see e.g. Cooper (1984). It is consistent with ability being multiplicative; i.e., $Q_i(T) = Q(A_iT)$.

59. In an analogy to conventional theory, the landlord is acting as a perfectly discriminating monopolist.

60. I assume that the endowment T is such that this constraint is always binding.

61. Again, this is a form of monopolistic competition since landlords still choose contract parameters.

62. Here I follow Newbery and Stiglitz. An alternative notion of competition could be that the total return from any contract is equalized. For fixed plot size, of course, the two are the same.

63. I omit a detailed analysis.

64. The self-selection constraints are then

$$Q_1(T_1) - rT_1 \geq Q_1(T_2) - rT_2$$
$$Q_2(T_2) - rT_2 \geq Q_2(T_1) - rT_1.$$

These can both be satisfied, e.g. if T_i maximizes $Q_i(T) - rT$.

65. Since plot size is variable, this equality does not completely determine the landlord's choice, unlike in the fixed-plot size case.

66. That is, provided these costs are not too high, they only change the side-payment, which may then be of either sign. If they are high enough, they may lead to irrelevance of the additional constraints in the screening period. Thus, Bell's (1986) criticism on this point is only partially valid.

67. See e.g. Ladejinsky (1977), Rao (1975), and Rudra (1975).

68. This argument was made by Heady (1947) and formalized by Adams and Rask (1968).

69. See also Bardhan (1984: Ch. 7).

Bibliography

Adams, D. W. and Rask, N. (1968). "Economics of Cost-sharing in Less Developed Countries." *American Journal of Agricultural Economics*, 50, 935–45.

Ahmed, M. (1974). "Farm Efficiency under Owner Cultivation and Share Tenancy." *Pakistan Economic and Social Review*, 12, 132–43.

Allen, F. (1982). "On Share Contracts and Screening." *Bell Journal of Economics*, 13, 541–7.

——— (1984). "Mixed Wage and Rent Contracts as Reinterpretations of Share Contracts." *Journal of Development Economics*, 16, 313–17.

——— (1985a). "On the Fixed Nature of Sharecropping Contracts." *Economic Journal*, 95, 30–48.

——— (1985b). "Repeated Principal–Agent Relationships with Lending and Borrowing." *Economic Letters*, 17, 27–31.

Alston, L. (1981). "Tenure Choice in Southern Agriculture, 1930–1960." *Explorations in Economic History*, 18, 211–32.

——— Datta, S. and Nugent, J. (1984). "Tenancy Choice in a Competitive Framework with Transaction Costs." *Journal of Political Economy*, 92, 1121–33.

——— and Higgs, R. (1982). "Contractual Mix in Southern Agriculture Since the Civil War: Facts, Hypotheses, and Tests." *Journal of Economic History*, 42, 327–53.

Arnott, R. J. and Stiglitz, J. E. (1984). "Equilibrium in Competitive Insurance Markets: The Welfare Economics of Moral Hazard." Mimeo, Princeton University.

——— (1985). "Labor Turnover, Wage Structures, and Moral Hazard: The Inefficiency of Competitive Markets." *Journal of Labour Economics*, 3, 434–62.

——— (1986). "Moral Hazard and Optimal Commodity Taxation." *Journal of Public Economics*, 29, 1–24.

Arrow, J. (1971). *Essays in the Theory of Risk-bearing*. Amsterdam: North-Holland (first published 1965).

——— (1985). "The Economics of Agency." In J. Pratt and R. Zeckhauser (eds.), *Principals and Agents: The Structure of Business*, pp. 37–51. Boston: Harvard Business School Press.

Bardhan, P. K. (1977). "Variations in Forms of Tenancy in a Peasant Economy." *Journal of Development Economics*, 4, 105–18.

——— (1984). *Land, Labor, and Rural Proverty: Essays in Development Economics*. Delhi: Oxford University Press/New York: Columbia University Press.

——— and Singh, N. (1982). "A Note on Cost Sharing and Incentives in Sharecropping." Mimeo, University of California at Berkeley.

——— and Singh, N. (1987). "A Note on Moral Hazard and Cost Sharing in Sharecropping." *American Journal of Agricultural Economics*, 69, 382–3.

——— and Srinivasan, T. N. (1971). "Cropsharing Tenancy in Agriculture: A Theoretical and Empirical Analysis." *American Economic Review*, 61, 48–64.

Basu, K. (1982). "On the Existence of Share Tenancy in a Screening Model." Mimeo, CORE, Louvain-la-Neuve.

Bell, C. (1977). "Alternative Theories of Sharecropping: Some Tests Using Evidence from North-East India." *Journal of Development Studies*, 13, 317–46.

——— (1986). "The Choice of Tenancy Contract." Mimeo, Vanderbilt University.

——— and Braverman, A. (1981). "On the Nonexistence of 'Marshallian' Sharecropping Contracts." *Indian Economic Review*, 15, 201–3.

Binswanger, H. and Rosenzweig, M. R. (eds.) (1984). *Contractual Arrangements, Employment, and Wages in Rural Labor Markets in Asia.* New Haven, Conn: Yale University Press.

Bliss, C. and Stern, N. H. (1982). *Palanpur: The Economy of an Indian Village.* Oxford: Clarendon Press.

Bonin, J. P. (1977), "Work Incentives and Uncertainty on a Collective Farm." *Journal of Comparative Economics*, 1, 77–97.

Braverman, A. and Stiglitz, J. E. (1982). "Sharecropping and the Interlinking of Agrarian Markets." *American Economic Review*, 72, 695–715.

────── (1986a). "Cost-sharing Arrangements under Sharecropping: Moral Hazard, Incentive Flexibility, and Risk." *American Journal of Agricultural Economics*, 68, 642–52.

Byres, T. J. (ed.) (1983). *Sharecropping and Sharecroppers.* London: Frank Cass.

Cheung, S. N. S. (1968). "Private Property Rights and Sharecropping." *Journal of Political Economy*, 76, 107–22.

────── (1969a). *The Theory of Share Tenancy.* Chicago: University Press.

────── (1969b). "Transaction Costs, Risk Aversion, and the Choice of Contractual Arrangements." *Journal of Law and Economics*, 12, 23–43.

Cooper, R. (1984). "On Allocative Distoritons in Problems of Self-selection." *Rand Journal of Economics*, 15, 568–77.

Cox, L. S. (1944). "Tenancy in the United States, 1865–1900: A Consideration of the Validity of the Agricultural Ladder Hypothesis." *Agricultural History*, 18, 97–105.

Eswaran, M. and Kotwal, A. (1985c). "A Theory of Contractual Structure in Agriculture." *American Economic Review*, 75, 352–67.

Hallagan, W. (1978). "Self-selection by Contractual Choice and the Theory of Sharecropping." *Bell Journal of Economics*, 9, 344–54.

Harris, M. and Raviv, A. (1979). "Optimal Incentive Contracts with Imperfect Information." *Journal of Economic Theory*, 20, 231–59.

Hart, O. and Holmstrom, B. (1987). "The Theory of Contracts." In T. Bewley (ed.), *Advances in Economic Theory.* Cambridge: University Press.

Heady, E. (1947). "Economics of Farm Leasing Systems." *Journal of Farm Economics*, 29, 659–78.

Hendry, J. B. (1960). "Land Tenure in South Vietnam." *Economic Development and Cultural Change*, 9, 27–44.

Higgs, H. (1894). "Metayage in Western France." *Economic Journal*, 4, 1–13.

Higgs, R. (1974). "Patterns of Farm Rental in the Georgia Cotton Belt, 1880–1900." *Journal of Economic History*, 34, 468–82.

Holmström, B. (1979). "Moral Hazard and Observability." *Bell Journal of Economics*, 10, 74–91.

────── (1982). "Moral Hazard in Teams." *Bell Journal of Economics*, 13, 324–40.

—— and Milgrom, P. (1987). "Aggregation and Linearity in the Provision of Intertemporal Incentives." *Econometrica*, 55, 303–28.

Huang, Y. (1971). "Allocative Efficiency in a Developing Agricultural Economy in Malaya." *American Journal of Agricultural Economics*, 53, 514–16.

—— (1975). "Tenancy Patterns, Productivity, and Rentals in Malaysia." *Economic Development and Cultural Change*, 23, 703–18.

Hurwicz, L. and Shapiro, L. (1978). "Incentive Structures Maximizing Residual Gain Under Incomplete Information." *Bell Journal of Economics*, 9, 180–192.

Issawi, C. (1957). "Farm Output under Fixed Rents and Share Tenancy." *Land Economics*, 38, 74–7.

Jaynes, D. G. (1982). "Production and Distribution in Agrarian Economies." *Oxford Economic Papers*, 34, 346–67.

—— (1984). "Economic Theory and Land Tenure." In Binswanger and Rosenzweig (1984).

Jodha, N. (1984). "Agricultural Tenancy in Semi-arid Tropical India." In Binswanger and Rosenzweig (1984).

Johnson, A. W. (1971). *Sharecroppers of the Sertao*. Stanford: University Press.

Johnson, D. G. (1950). "Resource Allocation under Share Contracts." *Journal of Political Economy*, 58, 111–23.

Jones, R. (1831). *An Essay on the Distribution of Wealth on the Sources of Taxation*. Part 1: *Rent*. London: John Murray.

Koo, A. Y. (1973). "Towards a More General Model of Land Tenancy and Reform." *Quarterly Journal of Economics*, 87, 567–80.

Ladejinsky, W. (1977). "Agrarian Reform in India." In L. Y. Walinsky (ed.), *The Selected Papers of Wolf Ladejinsky: Agrarian Reform as Unfinished Business*. New York: Oxford University Press.

Lucas, R. E. B. (1979). "Sharing, Monitoring, and Incentives: Marshallian Misallocation Reassessed." *Journal of Political Economy*, 87, 501–20.

Marshall, A. (1920). *Principles of Economics*. London: Macmillan.

Mazumder, D. (1975). "The Theory of Sharecropping and Labor Market Dualism." *Economica*, 32, 161–73.

Mill, J. S. (1848). *Principles of Political Economy*. London: W. Parker.

Mirrlees, J. A. (1974). "Notes on Welfare Economics, Information, and Uncertainty." In M. Balch, D. McFadden, and S. Wu (eds.), *Essays in Economic Behaviour under Uncertainty*, pp. 243–58. Amsterdam: North-Holland.

Newbery, D. M. G. (1974). "Cropsharing Tenancy in Agriculture: Comment." *American Economic Review*, 64, 1060–6.

—— (1975). "The Choice of Rental Contract in Peasant Agriculture." In L. Reynolds (ed.), *Agriculture in Development Theory*, Ch. 5. New Haven: Yale University Press.

—————— (1977). "Risk-sharing, Sharecropping, and Uncertain Labour Markets." *Review of Economic Studies*, 44, 585–94.

—————— and Stiglitz, J. E. (1979). "Sharecropping, Risk-sharing, and the Importance of Imperfect Information." In J. A. Roumasset, J. M. Boussard, and I. Singh (eds.), *Risk, Uncertainty, and Agricultural Development*, Ch. 17. New York: Agricultural Development Council.

Pant, C. (1983). "Tenancy and Family Resources: A Model and Some Empirical Analysis." *Journal of Development Economics*, 12, 27–39.

Quibria, M. G. (1982). "A 'Layman's' Geometric Proof why 'Marshallian' Sharecropping Contracts Should Not Exist." *Bangladesh Development Studies*, 9, 97–99.

—————— and Rashid, S. (1984). "The Puzzle of Sharecropping: A Survey of Theories." *World Development Report*, 12, 103–14.

Radner, R. (1981). "Monitoring Cooperative Agreements in a Repeated Principal–Agent Relationship." *Econometrica*, 49, 1127–48.

Rao, C. H. H. (1971). "Uncertainty, Entrepreneurship, and Sharecropping in India." *Journal of Political Economy*, 79, 578–95.

—————— (1975). *Technological Change and Distribution of Gains in Indian Agriculture*. New Delhi: Macmillan.

Rao, J. Mohan (1986). "Agriculture in Recent Development Theory." *Journal of Development Economics*, 22, 41–86.

Ray, Tridip and Nivrikar Singh, "A Note on 'Limited Liability, Wealth Differences and Tenancy Contracts in Agrarian Economies,'" UCSC Working Paper, http://econ.ucsc.edu/~boxjenk/limliab2.pdf.

Reid, J. D., Jr. (1975). "Sharecropping in History and Theory." *Agricultural History*, 49, 426–40.

—————— (1976). "Sharecropping and Agricultural Uncertainty." *Economic Development and Cultural Change*, 24, 549–76.

—————— (1977). "The Theory of Share Tenancy Revisited—Again." *Journal of Political Economy*, 85, 403–7.

Richards, A. (1986). *Development and Modes of Production in Marxian Economics: A Critical Evaluation*, Chur, Switzerland: Harwood Academic Publishers.

Robertson, A. F. (1987). *The Dynamics of Productive Relationships: African Share Contracts in Comparative Perspective*. Cambridge: University Press.

Ross, S. (1973). "The Economic Theory of Agency: The Principal's Problem." *American Economic Review, Proceedings*, 63, 134–9.

Roumasset, J. (1984). "Explaining Patterns in Landowner Shares: Rice, Corn, Coconut, and Abaca in the Philippines." In Binswanger and Rosenzweig (1984).

—————— and James, W. (1979). "Explaining Variations in Share Contracts: Land Quality, Population Pressures, and Technological Change." *Australian Journal of Agricultural Economics*, 23: 116–27.

Rubinstein, A. (1979). "Offenses that May Have Been Committed By Accident: An Optimal Policy of Retribution." In S. Brahms, A. Shotter, and G. Schrodianer (eds.), *Applied Game Theory*, pp. 406–13. Wurtzburg: Physica-Verlag.

Rudra, A. (1975). "Sharecropping Arrangements in West Bengal." *Economic and Political Weekly*, 10, A58–A63.

Ruttan, V. W. (1966). "Tenure and Productivity of Philippine Rice Producing Farms." *Philippine Economic Journal*, 5, 42–63.

Sen, Abhijit (1981). "Market Failure and Control of Labor Power: Towards an Explanation of 'Structure' and Change in Indian Agriculture." *Cambridge Journal of Economics*, 5, 201–28 and 327–50.

Shaban, R., (1987). "Testing between Competing Models of Sharecropping." *Journal of Political Economy*, 95, 893–920.

Shapiro, C. and Stiglitz, J. (1984). "Equilibrium Unemployment as a Worker Discipline Device." *American Economic Review*, 74, 433–44.

Shetty, S. (1988). "Limited Liability, Wealth Differences, and the Tenancy Ladder in Agrarian Economies." *Journal of Development Economics*, 29, 1–22.

Singh, N. (1983). "The Possibility of Nonrenewal of a Contract as an Incentive Device in Principal–Agent Models." University of California at Santa Cruz, Working Paper no. 117.

—— (1985). "Monitoring and Hierarchies: The Marginal Value of Information in a Principal–Agent Model." *Journal of Politcal Economy*, 93, 599–609.

Sismondi, J. L. S. de (1818). *Political Economy*. New York: Augustus Kelly, 1966.

Smith, A. (1776). *The Wealth of Nations*. New York: Modern Library, 1937.

Spillman, W. J. (1919). "The Agricultural Ladder." *American Economic Review*, Papers and Proceedings, 9, 170–9.

Stiglitz, J. E. (1974a). "Incentives and Risk-sharing in Sharecropping." *Review of Economic Studies*, 41, 219–55.

—— (1983). "Incentive Effects of Termination: Applications to the Credit and Labour Markets." *American Economic Review*, 73, 912–27.

Wilson, R. (1968). "The Theory of Syndicates." *Econometrica*, 36, 119–32.

Winters, D. L. (1974). "Tenant Farming in Iowa, 1860–1900: A Study of the Terms of Rental Leases." *Agricultural History*, 48, 130–50.

Wright, G. (1978). *The Political Economy of the Cotton South*. New York: W. W. Norton.

Young, A. (1788). *Travels in France during the Years 1787, 1788, 1778*, Vol 2. Dublin reprint, 1973.

3 Fragmented Duopoly: Theory and Applications to Backward Agriculture

Kaushik Basu and Clive Bell

1 Introduction

In certain trades trust is a precondition for exchange or transaction to occur. This would be true where information asymmetries are strong. In buying used cars most of us would prefer to make a purchase from friends and acquaintances (or at least from some of them!). It is well known that in informal credit markets, where formal legal institutions are weak, a person would lend money only to those whom he can trust or over whom he has some control. Thus a landlord may agree to lend money only to his laborers and a merchant may agree to lend only to his regular customers. This has led to a view that credit markets are "fragmented."[1] However, when it has come to actually modelling such a case the usual recourse has been to treat it as a case of several monopoly islands. Strictly speaking, however, the market just described is neither a monopoly nor a duopoly since the set of potential borrowers of the landlord would, typically, have some intersection with the set of potential borrowers of the merchant but the two sets would not be identical. What we have is a case in between a monopoly and oligopoly. It is this "in between" case that is formally characterized and explored in this chapter.

Let us assume that there are n sellers of a certain commodity. Let S_i be the set of potential customers of seller i. To consumers outside S_i, i will never sell goods, irrespective of the price. Consider now two special cases. First, if it is true that

$$S_1 = S_2 = \cdots = S_n,$$

then we have a case of standard oligopoly with n firms. All firms are competing over the same set of customers.

If, on the other hand, $(S_1, S_2, \ldots, S_n)$ happens to be a partition over the set of all potential customers in the economy, then we have a case of n standard monopolies. Each seller has his own exclusive pool of customers.[2]

There is no reason why we have to restrict attention to these two polar cases. We may well have cases where for some i, j, the sets S_i and S_j have some common members but it is not the case that S_i is the same set for all i. We shall describe a market structure where this happens (along with the two polar cases just described) as a *fragmented oligopoly*.

Though we motivated the idea of fragmented oligopoly by talking about the role of trust and control in certain transactions,[3] we believe that this market structure could be usefully applied in many different areas. It clearly has relevance to models of industrial location. Indeed, certain features of location contribute to the fragmentation of rural credit markets when the pattern of settlement is nucleated, as in the case of South Asia's villages, rather than continuous, as in Hotelling's (1929) classic work. It is known, for example, that not all villages have resident moneylenders [Reserve Bank of India (1954)] and that commission agents and traders often have "territories" made up of several contiguous villages from which most of their clients in money-lending and trade are drawn.[4] Drawing upon these examples, suppose that there are three villages, A, B and C, in a row. Moneylender 1 lives in village A; and moneylender 2 lives in C. If we suppose that the inhabitants of A would go only to their "resident" moneylender and likewise for C, and that those of B would go to whoever charges less, then we have a case of fragmented duopoly. If N_X is a set of people in village X, then this is a special case of the above formal definition with $n = 2$ and $S_1 = N_A \cup N_B$ and $S_2 = N_C \cup N_B$. Thus, though the model that we construct does not belong to the class of location models based on Hotelling's [see, for example, D'Aspremont, Gabszewicz and Thisse (1979) and Bonanno (1987)] and the properties that we investigate are distinct from the ones that a model of location would focus on, the abstract structure could be used as a basis for a model of locational duopoly.

Another view of our model is that of an oligopoly with switching costs [e.g., von Weizsäcker (1984); Klemperer (1987a,b); and Bulow, Geanakoplos and Klemperer (1985)]. Indeed our model may be viewed as an application of switching cost theory, with prohibitive switching costs once the "domains" or "territories" of firms have been established, to the study of backward markets and agrarian relations. Though our initial model, in abstraction, is a kind of switching-cost model, we develop it in some detail as our aim is to address issues in development and to persuade development economists of the relevance of such models of industrial organization to agrarian theory.

Models of fragmented oligopoly could also find application in activities where because of asymmetric information each seller has a predetermined clientele that trusts him. International trade with prior political fragmentation is another area of possible application of this theory. Though this paper is an abstract analysis of fragmented duopoly and little depends on what actual motivation is used, our interest in the subject arose from an attempt to give a rigorous characterization of the idea of "market fragmentation" which is so central to development economics and particularly the theory of agrarian structure. It is for this reason that much of the paper dwells on problems of backward agriculture.

When firms possess captive segments of the market, it is natural to ask whether they can practice price discrimination between segments. This is indeed an open question. It is arguable that in fragmented agrarian markets, which are our central concern in this paper, arbitrage is not easy and so price discrimination ought to be treated as feasible. One must, however, remember that in personalized rural markets of the kind described in Bardhan (1984), the possibility of price discrimination may be thwarted by social norms. In different societies, different kinds of discrimination are treated by the people as "unjust." The origins of these norms lie in distant history but are often powerful enough to make certain kinds of discriminatory pricing infeasible. That is, the cost in terms of political dissension is too high from the seller's point of view. It is for this reason that we have in this paper devoted somewhat more attention to the non-discrimination model. We do, however, deal with the case of segment-specific price discrimination in separate sections.

The Cournot–Nash equilibria of a fragmented duopoly in which sellers cannot practice price discrimination are analyzed in section 2. Section 3 briefly describes the case where a seller can price-discriminate between market segments. In section 4 a two-period model is constructed in which in the first period the players fight to establish their domains, that is, the S_1's and the S_2's. In the second period they treat S_1 and S_2 as given and play a quantity-setting game. The subgame perfect equilibria of such a two-period game, with and without price discrimination, are examined. The case with price discrimination is taken up in section 5, and the possibility of rent-dissipation in this setting in section 6.

2   The Nash Equilibrium of a Fragmented Duopoly without Price Discrimination

There are n identical consumers and each consumer's demand function for the commodity in question is given by

$$q = q(p),\tag{1}$$

where p is price and q is quantity demanded. We assume q is a continuous function and $q'(p) < 0$. The inverse demand function is written as follows:

$$p = p(q).\tag{2}$$

There are two sellers (or firms), 1 and 2. The n consumers are partitioned into three sets, N_1, N_2 and N_3, consisting of, respectively, n_1, n_2 and n_3 persons. Thus $n_1 + n_2 + n_3 = n$. The members of N_1 would buy goods from only firm 1. Members of N_2 would buy from only 2. The third group would buy from whoever offers better terms. These three groups will be referred to as the three *segments* of the market. N_i is firm i's *captive segment*, for $i = 1, 2$; and N_3 will be referred to as the *contested segment*.[5]

Both firms have the same cost function: A cost of c units has to be incurred to produce each unit of the good. An immediate consequence of this assumption is that were the firm able to charge the monopoly price, p^m, in its captive segment of the market, p^m would depend only on the shape of the individual's demand function and c. That is, p^m is then independent of the pattern of market segmentation. This is taken up further in sections 3 and 5.

Consider now firm i's problem. It has to decide how much to supply to its captive segment, x_i, and how much to apply to the contested segment, q_i. To begin with, it will be assumed that a firm cannot discriminate between consumers in terms of the price charged. The consequence of relaxing this assumption is discussed in section 3.

Suppose each firm has chosen a strategy. That is, we are given (x_1, q_1, x_2, q_2). Clearly the price of the good in the contested segment will be

$p = p(q_1 + q_2)/n_3.$

If $q_i > 0$, then the fact that a firm must charge the same price to all customers means that i must charge a price of $p((q_1 + q_2)/n_3)$ even in its captive segment. As price depends on the other firm's choice of q_j, the firm's choice of x_i may not be consistent with demand in the captive segment of its market. Thus i's total profit will be

$$\left[p\left(\frac{q_1 + q_2}{n_3} \right) - c \right] \left\{ q_i + \min\left[x_i, n_i q\left(p\left(\frac{q_1 + q_2}{n_3} \right) \right) \right] \right\}. \tag{3}$$

Note that $n_i q(p((q_1 + q_2)/n_3))$ is the demand for the good in the captive segment when price is $p((q_1 + q_2)/n_3)$; and the shorter side of the market determines the volume of sales when supply is not equal to demand.

It is easy to see, however, that, given q_1 and q_2 (>0), firm i's choice of x_i can be deduced therefrom. Hence, we may define the profit of each firm in terms of only q_1 and q_2. Using π_i to denote firm i's profit, we have:[6]

$$\pi_i(q_1, q_2) = \begin{cases} \max\limits_{x_i} \left[p\left(\dfrac{x_i}{n_i} \right) - c \right] x_i & \text{if } q_i = 0 \\[2ex] \left[p\left(\dfrac{q_1 + q_2}{n_3} \right) - c \right] \left[q_i + \dfrac{n_i}{n_3}(q_1 + q_2) \right] & \text{if } q_i > 0. \end{cases} \tag{4}$$

The interpretation of this profit function is as follows. Given (q_1, q_2), firm i supplies to its captive segment a profit-maximizing amount of goods. That is, given q_1 and q_2, price is determined by $p((q_1 + q_2)/n_3)$; so that if $q_i > 0$, then in its captive segment, firm i supplies exactly the amount that is demanded, which is equal to $(n_i/n_3)(q_1 + q_2)$. If $q_i = 0$, then the fact that a firm has to charge the same price to all its buyers places no restriction on the price it can charge in the captive segment. In such a case it can charge the monopoly price, p^m, and make monopoly profits. These features are captured in (4).

Let us define the *Nash equilibrium* of the *game* as a (q_1^*, q_2^*) such that $\pi_1(q_1^*, q_2^*) \geq \pi_1(q_1, q_2^*)$, for all q_1 and $\pi_2(q_1^*, q_2^*) \geq \pi_2(q_1^*, q_2)$, for all q_2.

It is useful to have a visual representation of the reaction functions. This would enable us to compare a fragmented duopoly with a traditional duopoly. In fig. 3.1, firm 1's reaction functions lie in the NE- and NW-quadrants. If q_2 is zero, firm 1 acts as a monopolist on both its captive segment and the contested segment. In that case, let OC be the amount it supplies on its captive segment and OA be the amount

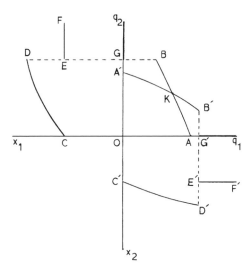

Figure 3.1
Reaction functions and equilibrium in a fragmented duopoly.

it supplies on the contested segment. As q_2 rises, firm 1's sales on the contested and captive segments are represented by the lines AB and CD. It will be shown later that AB will be steeper than the 45° line and CD will be a rising curve, as shown. As q_2 rises, supply in firm 1's captive segments deviates more and more from the monopoly output OC. This happens because a firm has to charge the same price to all customers. As q_2 keeps rising, a point will be reached where firm 1 would prefer to drop out of the contested market and sell the monopoly output to its captive segment. This happens when $q_2 = OG$. For all $q_2 > OG$, firm 1 sells $GE = OC$ units on its captive segment and zero in the contested market.

We have here drawn a case which gives a "stable" Nash equilibrium [in the sense of Friedman (1977)]. It is later shown that this must always be the case. In fig. 3.1 we also depict firm 2's reaction functions. These are denoted by the same letters with primes on them. The above discussion makes it clear that for analyzing the Nash equilibria of a fragmented duopoly we could concentrate exclusively on the NE-quadrant because the reactions in the captive segments (i.e., the NW- and SE-quadrants) could be derived mechanically from the happenings in the NE-quadrant.

In the case depicted in fig. 3.1 there is only one Nash equilibrium. But since the reaction functions have breaks it appears as if we can

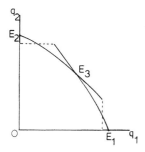

Figure 3.2
Multiple equilibria.

have corner equilibria as in models with fixed costs [e.g., Spence (1979), Dixit (1979, 1980), Basu and Singh (1990)]. as illustrated in fig. 3.2. If E_1 had occurred, then firm 1 would be selling OE_1 on the contested segment, whereas firm 2 would be selling only to its captive segment. It can, however, be shown that such equilibria can never arise in this model and in order to have such corner equilibria it may be necessary to introduce some fixed costs [Mishra (1991)]. It seems to us that in practice, markets do often get partitioned into zones within which each firm acts like a monopolist.[7] However, as things stand, equilibrium is always unique and occurs with both firms supplying to the contested segment.

Let us now take note of a property of the reaction functions which has important implications for our model. Let the function $R_i(q_j)$ denote firm i's optimal [in terms of (4)] choice of q_i given that the other firm has chosen q_j. In case there is more than one q_i which satisfies this condition, we shall assume that R_i specifies the smallest of these q_i's. Thus in fig. 3.1, if $q_2 = OG$, then $R_1(q_2) = 0$.

Suppose q_2 is such that $R_1(q_2) > 0$. Hence in maximizing π_1 we could [in eq. (4)] concentrate on the case where $q_1 > 0$. That is,

$$\pi_1(q_1, q_2) = \left[p\left(\frac{q_1 + q_2}{n_3} \right) - c \right] \left[q_1 + \frac{n_1}{n_3}(q_1 + q_2) \right].$$

Maximizing π_1 with respect to q_1 gives us the following first-order condition:

$$\frac{\partial \pi_1}{\partial q_1} = (p - c)\left(1 + \frac{n_1}{n_3} \right) + \frac{p'}{n_3} \cdot \left[\left(1 + \frac{n_1}{n_3} \right) q_1 + \frac{n_1}{n_3} q_2 \right] = 0. \tag{5}$$

This yields the following theorem.

THEOREM 1

If $R_1(q_2) > 0$, then $\partial R_1/\partial q_2 > -1$.

If $R_2(q_1) > 0$, then $\partial R_2/\partial q_1 > -1$.

Proof See appendix.

Theorem 1 asserts that as long as both firms are operating on the contested segment, a decrease in q_2 by one unit causes an increase in $R_1(q_2)$ by less than one unit; symmetrically, the same applies to firm 2's reaction function.

Using Theorem 1 we can quickly establish some corollaries. Observe that our Nash equilibrium must be stable in the sense that the reaction functions intersect in the "correct" direction. This is because Theorem 1 implies that in the NE-quadrant of fig. 3.1, firm 1's reaction function must be steeper (in magnitude) than firm 2's reaction function.

COROLLARY 1   As long as firm 1 operates on the contested market, a fall in q_2 would cause firm 1's supply on its own captive segment to fall.

Corollary 1 tells us that the slope of the *CD* curve will be in the direction shown. To see this, check that, by Theorem 1, as q_2 falls $q_2 + R_1(q_2)$ must fall. Hence price in the contested segment rises. Since the firm charges all its customers the same price, the price charged by firm 1 in the captive segment rises. Hence, the amount sold on the captive segment must fall.

It is easily shown that if the entire industry (i.e., all the captive and contested segments) was served by a monopolist, output would be less than or equal to that in a fragmented duopoly. It follows that price in a fragmented duopoly would be less than or equal to monopoly price.

First, observe that since all consumers are identical, the volume of output in the industry would be the same whether it was served by one monopolist or t monopolists. If firm 1 is a monopolist supplying $n_1 + n_3$ customers and firm 2 a monopolist supplying n_2 customers, firm 1 would supply *CA* units and 2 would supply *OC'* units (in fig. 3.1). Hence a single monopolist selling to all n consumers would supply $CA + OC'$ units. Let $(x_1^*, q_1^*, x_2^*, q_2^*)$ be the equilibrium of a fragmented duopoly. If $q_1^* = 0$ or $q_2^* = 0$, then clearly $x_1^* + q_1^* + x_2^* + q_2^* =$

$CA + OC'$. If $(q_1^*, q_2^*) > 0$, i.e., the industry is at a point like K, then Theorem 1 implies $q_1^* + q_2^* > OA$. Since OA is the monopoly output with n_3 buyers, price in the fragmented duopoly equilibrium is less than monopoly price; and output is greater than monopoly output. The above claim, along with Corollary 2 below, tells us that, in some sense, a fragmented duopoly lies where we expect it to lie— somewhere *between* a standard duopoly and a monopoly.

Let us now turn to the properties of the Nash equilibrium and do some comparative statics. If with n_2 and n remaining constant n_1 increases, what happens to firm 1's share in the contested market? In other words, how does the size of one's captive segment affect one's share in the contested segment? The next theorem asserts that this relationship is a negative one. There is here an interesting analogy with Fudenberg and Tirole's (1986, pp. 23–24) analysis in which an incumbent firm, planning to deter entry, prefers not to have a large captive segment.

THEOREM 2   If n_1 increases with n and n_2 constant, then a Nash equilibrium, (q_1, q_2), where $(q_1, q_2) > 0$, changes such that 1's relative market share in the contested segment falls (i.e., q_1/q_2 falls).

Since we are looking at a case where in the Nash equilibrium $(q_1, q_2) > 0$, (q_1, q_2) must satisfy (5) and, by symmetry, the following:

$$(p - c)\left(1 + \frac{n_2}{n_3}\right) + \frac{p'}{n_3} \cdot \left[\left(1 + \frac{n_2}{n_3}\right)q_2 + \frac{n_2}{n_3}q_1\right] = 0. \tag{6}$$

Eqs. (5) and (6) imply

$$\frac{n_1 + n_3}{n_2 + n_3} = \frac{(n_1 + n_3)q_1 + n_1 q_2}{(n_2 + n_3)q_2 + n_2 q_1}.$$

Cross-multiplying and substituting $n - n_1 - n_2$ for n_3, we get

$$\frac{q_1}{q_2} = \frac{n - n_1}{n - n_2}. \tag{7}$$

The theorem is immediate.

Just before stating the theorem we claimed that we were going to look into the effect of n_1 on the market share. Clearly, this can be interpreted in several ways. What Theorem 2 examined was the effect of n_1 on q_1/q_2 with n_2 and n held constant. What, it may be asked, will be the effect of raising n_1 on q_1/q_2 if n_2 and n_3 are held constant?

To answer this, note that (7) implies $q_1/q_2 = (n_2 + n_3)/(n_1 + n_3)$. Hence, firm 1's market share falls if n_1 increases and n is also increased by the same amount.

Eq. (7) tells us more than Theorem 2. Market shares in the contested segment in a Nash equilibrium are independent of c and approach equality as n increases with n_1 and n_2 constant.

THEOREM 3   The equilibrium price does not vary with changes in n_1 and n_2 as long as $n_1 + n_2$ and n remain unchanged, excepting in the special case where the change in n_1 and n_2 causes a firm to enter or withdraw from the contested market.

This is a somewhat surprising result. It asserts that in the determination of the industry's price and output, what matters is how much of the market is contested and how much captive. Excepting the special case mentioned in the theorem, the exact break-up of the total captive segment into firm 1's and 2's segments is inconsequential.

To prove this, consider first an "interior solution," i.e., $(q_1, q_2) > 0$. Rewriting (5) and (6) and using (7), we get

$$\frac{p'q_1}{p-c} = -(n - (n_1 + n_2))\frac{(n - n_1)}{n}, \tag{8}$$

$$\frac{p'q_2}{p-c} = -(n - (n_1 + n_2))\frac{(n - n_2)}{n}. \tag{9}$$

Writing z for $(q_1 + q_2)/(n - (n_1 + n_2))$, from (8) and (9) we get

$$z = \frac{p(z) - c}{-p'(z)} \cdot \frac{2n - (n_1 + n_2)}{n}. \tag{10}$$

Eq. (10) implies that z will be unchanged as long as $n, n_1 + n_2$ and c remain unchanged. Since price depends on z, price remains unchanged as long as n, $n_1 + n_2$ and c remain unchanged.

If we have a corner solution, the monopoly price will prevail no matter how the segmentation occurs.

It is interesting to observe that (10) implies that we cannot predict the direction of changes in price induced by changes in n or $n_1 + n_2$, unless we impose restrictions on p''. It is easily checked using (10) that a rise in $(n_1 + n_2)$ will cause z to fall, and hence price to rise, if $p'' \leq 0$. In other words, as the contested segment becomes smaller, $p'' \leq 0$ is a strongly sufficient condition for the equilibrium price to rise towards the monopoly price. As a standard duopoly is characterized by $n_1 = n_2 = 0$, we also have.

COROLLARY 2   If $p'' \leq 0$, industry output (price) in a fragmented duopoly will be less (greater) than that in a standard duopoly.

It is possible to use this model to do more comparative statics exercises and deduce other properties, but that is not the aim here. Instead we apply the theory of fragmented duopoly to a problem in backward agriculture and, in that context, explore how the captive segments of the market are established in a two-period setting. But before doing so, we make a brief digression to show how our model may be adapted to allow segment-specific price discrimination.

3   Fragmented Duopoly with Price Discrimination

Let us assume, as before, that seller i chooses q_i and x_i but that he is free to set the price in his captive market, wherever he wishes.

Given profit-maximizing behaviour and given q_1, q_2, x_i, firm i will set a price of $p(x_i/n_i)$ in its captive market, and in the contested market price will be given by $p((q_1 + q_2)/n_3)$. If we continue to assume a constant marginal cost, then all the segments get completely dismembered and equilibrium can be worked out separately for each. The monopoly price, p^m, will be charged in each of the captive segments, while the standard duopoly price will hold in the contested segment.

The problem is much more interesting if we suppose that firm i's total cost function, $c_i(\cdot)$, is increasing and convex. Firm i's profit, $\hat{\pi}_i$, is given as follows:

$$\hat{\pi}_i(q_1, q_2, x_i) = p\left(\frac{x_i}{n_i}\right) \cdot x_i + p\left(\frac{q_1 + q_2}{n_3}\right) q_i - c_i(q_i + x_i), \qquad i = 1, 2.$$

Firm i maximizes this by choosing q_i and x_i. Its first-order conditions are:

$$\frac{x_i}{n_i} p'\left(\frac{x_i}{n_i}\right) + \left(\frac{x_i}{n_i}\right) = c_i'(q_i + n_i) \tag{11}$$

and

$$\frac{q_i}{n_3} p'\left(\frac{q_1 + q_2}{n_3}\right) + \left(\frac{q_1 + q_2}{n_3}\right) = c_i'(q_i + n_i). \tag{12}$$

The *Nash equilibrium* of a *price-discriminating fragmented duopoly* is given by the (x_1, q_1, x_2, q_2) derived from solving the four equations described by (11) and (12) and by setting i equal to 1 and 2.

Comparative-statics results may be derived in much the same way as in the previous section. For example, assuming that the marginal revenue curve is downward sloping [i.e., the left-hand term in (11) falls as x_i rises and the left-hand term in (12) falls as q_i rises], Corollary 1 can be derived even for the price-discrimination model. Moreover, following Bulow, Geanakoplos and Klemperer (1985), this model can be used to illustrate some surprising results, like how a subsidy in the captive segment of a seller can actually result in the seller being worse off in equilibrium. With these remarks we turn to the analysis of agrarian relations and the determination of the size of the captive and contested segments. We return to the subject of price discrimination in section 5.

4   Subgame Perfection in a Two-Period Model of Agrarian Relations

Since n_1 and n_2 influence the outcome of the one-period fragmented duopoly described in sections 2 and 3, it is but natural that firms will try to influence n_1 and n_2 to the extent that they can. For the sake of illustration consider a rural economy with n laborers and two landlords. In period 1 each landlord i decides on the number, n_i, of laborers he will employ on his land.[8] In period 2 the landlords supply credit to them and to the contested segment of the market for loans. This periodization reflects more the priorities of decision than the actual sequence of time. Moreover, in reality period 2 will be further split up involving a first sub-period when the loan is received by the laborers and a second sub-period when the wage is received and the principal and interest is repaid. We, however, ignore this further temporal partitioning of period 2.

We shall assume—and this is not unrealistic—that each landlord has the power to forbid his employees from taking credit from the other landlord. Further, this is in a setting where everybody knows everybody and the landlords consider it safe to give credit to any laborer from this set of villages. Thus the n_1 and n_2 chosen in period 1 become parameters in the second period in the fragmented credit market. Moreover n_1 and n_2 have the same significance as the n_1 and

n_2 in sections 2 and 3 above since landlord i can lend to $n_i + n_3$ laborers where $n_3 = n - n_1 - n_2$.

It is immediately clear that in this model landlord i may hire employees not just to work as laborers but keeping in mind that a larger n_i alters the kind of leverage he has in the credit market. Hence this theory provides a rationale for interlinkage, albeit of a very different kind from the ones found in the literature [e.g., Braverman and Srinivasan (1981), Braverman and Stiglitz (1982), Basu (1983), Mitra (1983), Bell (1988)].

The natural solution criterion to use in such a two-period model is that of sub-game perfection. We shall first give an abstract characterization of this and then scrutinize a special case.

Let landlord i's production function be

$$X_i = X_i(n_i), \qquad X_i' \geq 0, \qquad X_i'' \leq 0.$$

To keep the model simple, we assume that laborers have access to other employment opportunities at an exogenous wage, w. In period 2 each landlord earns profits from production and interest from the credit market depending on what Nash equilibrium emerges from a fragmented duopoly characterized by n_1 and n_2.

In order to state this more formally note that if in a fragmented duopoly n and c are fixed, the fragmented duopoly is entirely defined by (n_1, n_2).

Let us now define a *Nash equilibrium correspondence*, N, as follows. For every pair of non-negative integers n_1 and n_2 such that $n_1 + n_2 \leq n$,

$$N(n_1, n_2) \equiv \{(q_1, q_2) | (q_1, q_2) \text{ is a Nash equilibrium in a fragmented} \\ \text{duopoly defined by } (n_1, n_2)\}.$$

A specification of which Nash equilibrium will occur in period 2 for each game (n_1, n_2) is a *selection*, f, from the Nash equilibrium correspondence N. That is, $f(n_1, n_2)$ is an element of $N(n_1, n_2)$, for all (n_1, n_2).

Given that c represents the opportunity cost of giving credit and p is the price of credit, we could use π_i as defined in section 2 to be i's profit function in period 2.

For every selection, f, from the correspondence N, we can define each player's profit in the two-period game (assuming zero discounting) as

$$\Omega_i(n_1, n_2, f) = X_i(n_i) - wn_i + \pi_i(f(n_1, n_2)), \qquad i = 1, 2, \tag{13}$$

where the absence of price discrimination in the credit market implies that all laborers will pay the same price and hence that both landlords will pay their laborers the exogenous wage w.

The triple (n_1^*, n_2^*, f^*) is a (subgame-) perfect equilibrium if and only if

$$\Omega_1(n_1^*, n_2^*, f^*) \geq \Omega_1(n_1, n_2^*, f^*) \qquad \text{for all } n_1, \text{ and}$$

$$\Omega_2(n_1^*, n_2^*, f^*) \geq \Omega_2(n_1^*, n_2, f^*) \qquad \text{for all } n_2.$$

Distorting terminology slightly, we may refer to (n_1^*, n_2^*) as a "perfect equilibrium" if there exists an f^* such that (n_1^*, n_2^*, f^*) is a perfect equilibrium.

In this setting, laborers are fully rational and make their choices after evaluating the consequences of joining one or other of the captive segments of the market, as opposed to dealing in the contested segment. However, we assume that n is large and laborers do not collude, so that each takes the pattern of segmentation (n_1, n_2) as exogenously given. As noted above, the assumption of a constant marginal cost of funds, c, for both landlords implies that the monopoly price, p^m, is independent of the size of each captive market. Hence, if the laborer conjectures that the market will contain no contested segmented (i.e., $n_1 + n_2 = n$), he will face a price p^m from both landlords; and since the wage is exogenously given, he will therefore be indifferent between them. If, on the other hand, there is a contested segment, then in the absence of price discrimination, the same price will rule everywhere; and again he will be indifferent as to which segment he joins. That is to say, an interlinked wage and credit contract with either landlord will yield a laborer the same utility as an unbundled deal. Thus, although laborers are not strategic in the sense that the actual choice of n_i is effectively in the hands of the landlords alone, they are fully rational. In brief we model laborers in the same way as consumers are modeled in oligopoly theory.

We analyze the perfect equilibria of the two-period game in the special case where the demand schedule of an individual consumer is linear over the relevant range of outcomes:

$$p = a - bq. \tag{14}$$

We assume that n is so large and the marginal product of labor, i.e., $X_i'(n_i)$, falls so fast that landlords 1 and 2 will never choose n_1 and

n_2 for which there is a Nash equilibrium where one firm abandons the contested segment totally. Hence, we could focus on the unique "interior" Nash equilibrium that occurs for each relevant (n_1, n_2). Let $f(n_1, n_2)$ refer to such a Nash equilibrium.

Using (5), (6) and (14), we get

$$\pi_i(f(n_1, n_2)) = \frac{(a-c)^2}{b} \cdot \frac{(n-n_j)n^2}{(3n-n_1-n_2)^2}, \qquad i = 1, 2. \tag{15}$$

Hence, using $\bar{\Omega}_i(n_1, n_2)$ to denote $\Omega_i(n_1, n_2, f)$, we have

$$\bar{\Omega}_i(n_1, n_2) = [X_i(n_i) - wn_i] + \left[\frac{(a-c)^2}{b} \cdot \frac{(n-n_j)n^2}{(3n-n_1-n_2)^2}\right], \qquad i = 1, 2. \tag{16}$$

Clearly, if n_1^* and n_2^* are such that n_1^* maximizes $\bar{\Omega}_1(n_1, n_2^*)$ and n_2^* maximizes $\bar{\Omega}_2(n_1^*, n_2)$, then (n_1^*, n_2^*) is a perfect equilibrium.

The first interesting feature of the perfect equilibrium to note is that in equilibrium each landlord will be employing labor up to a point where the wage rate exceeds the marginal product of labor. Let $\hat{n}_i$ be such that

$$X_i'(\hat{n}_i) = w.$$

It is easy to see that for all n_2, and all $n_1 < \hat{n}_1$, $\bar{\Omega}_1(\hat{n}_1, n_2) > \bar{\Omega}(n_1, n_2)$. At $n_1 = \hat{n}_1$ a further increase in n_1 causes $\bar{\Omega}_1$ to rise since, at this point, the first expression within brackets in (16) is stationary and the second expression is rising. Hence, landlords always employ in excess of what pure marginal productivity and wage considerations would lead them to do. This result is quite in keeping with Klemperer's (1987b) finding of heightened competition in the 'first' period. It could also be thought of as providing a rationale for the idea that landlords have a penchant for maintaining an excessive number of dependent laborers [see, e.g., Bhaduri (1983)]. In addition, this model gives some new insight into the phenomenon of disguised unemployment and surplus labor, since it is possible for marginal product to be not only less than w, but even zero (if X_i' vanishes for finite n_i).

From the first-order conditions of maximizing $\bar{\Omega}_1(n_1, n_2)$ with respect to n_1 and $\bar{\Omega}_2(n_1, n_2)$ with respect to n_2 and denoting the equilibrium values with a star, we have

$$X_1'(n_1^*) + \frac{2(a-c)^2 n^2 (n - n_2^*)}{b(3n - n_1^* - n_2^*)^3} = w$$

and

$$X_2'(n_2^*) + \frac{2(a-c)^2 n^2 (n-n_1^*)}{b(3n - n_1^* - n_2^*)^3} = w.$$

These, in turn, imply

$$\frac{X_1'(n_1^*) - w}{X_2'(n_2^*) - w} = \frac{n - n_2^*}{n - n_1^*}. \tag{17}$$

Hence, if $n_2^* > n_1^*$, then $X_1'(n_1^*) > X_2'(n_2^*)$, since from the reasoning above we know that $X_i'(n_1^*) - w < 0$, $i = 1, 2$. It is important to appreciate that this is true though the production functions of the two landlords need not be the same. If we use the extent of divergence of $X_i'(n_1^*)$ from w as an index of production inefficiency, then what we have established is that larger farms (in terms of numbers of workers employed) are the ones exhibiting greater production inefficiency. Also, larger farms have larger shares of the contested segment of the credit market,[9] and hence are larger overall.

5 Equilibrium in Agrarian Markets with Price Discrimination

If landlords can practice price discrimination, the laborer who accepts an interlinked contract by going into a captive segment of the credit market knows that he will be charged the monopoly price, p^m, which exceeds that in the contested segment, p^o, should one exist.[10] Thus, in order to make an interlinked contract attractive to laborers, landlords will have to offer a wage premium, δ say, in compensation for the higher rate of interest. Landlords are therefore constrained by the utility equivalence condition

$$v(p^m, w + \delta) = v(p^o, w), \tag{18}$$

where $v(\cdot)$ is the indirect utility of a laborer.

In this case, (13) becomes

$$\Omega_i(n_1, n_2, f) = [X_i(n_i) - (w + \delta)n_i] + \pi_i(f(n_1, n_2)) \tag{13'}$$

with the reminder that f now pertains to the Nash equilibrium as in section 3 (i.e. with price discrimination allowed).

$$\pi_i(f(n_1, n_2)) = n_i p^m \cdot q(p^m) + p\left(\frac{q_1 + q_2}{n_3}\right) \cdot q_i - c(n_i q(p^m) + q_i), \tag{19}$$

where $(q_1, q_2) = f(n_1, n_2)$.

With a linear demand function,

$$p^m = (a+c)/2 \quad \text{and} \quad q^m = (a-c)/2b.$$

In a standard duopoly, with $n_3 = n - n_1 - n_2$ given exogenously,

$$p^o = (a+2c)/3 \quad \text{and} \quad q^o = (q_1^o + q_2^o)/n_3 = 2(a-c)/3b,$$

and by symmetry,

$$q_1^o = q_2^o = n_3 q^o/2.$$

Substituting for $(p^m, q^m, p^o, q_1^o, q_2^o)$ in (19), some manipulation yields

$$\pi_i(f(n_1, n_2)) = \frac{(a-c)^2}{b} \cdot \left(\frac{5n_i - 4n_j}{36} + \frac{n}{9} \right) \qquad i = 1, 2, \ i \neq j, \tag{20}$$

which, unlike (15), is linear in (n_1, n_2).

The next step is to obtain the wage premium δ from (18). While the value of δ depends on $v(\cdot)$, it follows at once from the fact that (p^m, p^o, w) are all independent of (n_1, n_2) that δ must be likewise. Hence, substituting for $\pi_i(\cdot)$ from (20) in (13'), we have

$$\bar{\Omega}_i(n_1, n_2) = [X_i(n_i) - (w+\delta)n_i] + \frac{(a-c)^2}{b} \cdot \left(\frac{5n_i - 4n_j}{36} + \frac{n}{9} \right), \qquad i = 1, 2. \tag{21}$$

As in section 4, in equilibrium each landlord will be employing labor up to a point where the wage rate (including the premium δ in this case) exceeds the marginal product of labor. For when $[X_i(n_i) - (w+\delta)n_i]$ is stationary, π_i is increasing in n_i. Denoting the values of (n_1, n_2) in equilibrium with a star, we have, from (21),

$$X_1'(n_1^*) = (w+\delta) - \frac{5}{36} \frac{(a-c)^2}{b}, \qquad i = 1, 2. \tag{22}$$

Hence, unlike the case without price discrimination, the marginal product of labor is identical on the farms of both landlords.

This result is not very surprising in the light of the fact that the assumption of constant marginal costs makes all the parameters of an individual's wage and credit contracts independent of the pattern of market segmentation, if landlords can practice price discrimination. As we saw in section 3, the cost functions (in this case, for lending) must be increasing and convex for interesting situations to arise from the one-period game with (n_1, n_2) fixed. It is certainly plausible that the cost of lending, for example, is increasing and convex with the size of the captive market, since the landlord must prevent each of his captive clients from borrowing from the other landlord in period 2 and recover monopoly interest charges from them subsequently.

6 Rent Dissipation

There remains the question of whether competition for captive segments of the market in period 1 will more than dissipate the rents from lock-in in period 2 [Klemperer (1987a)]. Suppose, therefore, that interlinking was banned. In a standard duopoly with $n_1 = n_2 = 0$ and $n_3 = n$, the profit of each landlord from moneylending is, under the above assumptions about costs and demand,

$$\pi_i^o = n(a - c)^2/9b. \tag{23}$$

In this case, the total profit of landlord i in equilibrium is

$$\Omega_i^o = [X_i(\hat{n}_i) - w\hat{n}_i] + n(a - c)^2/9b, \tag{24}$$

where $X_i'(\hat{n}_i) = w$. Subtracting (24) from (21), we obtain

$$\bar{\Omega}_i(n_1^*, n_2^*) - \Omega_i^o = [X_i(n_i^*) - wn_i^*] - [X_i(\hat{n}_i) - w\hat{n}_i] - \delta n_i^*$$

$$+ \frac{(a - c)^2}{b} \left(\frac{5n_i^* - 4n_j^*}{36} \right), \qquad i = 1, 2. \tag{25}$$

Since $\hat{n}_i$ maximizes $[X_i(n_i) - wn_i]$,

$$\xi_i \equiv [X_i(n_i^*) - wn_i^*] - [X_i(\hat{n}_i) - w\hat{n}_i] < 0$$

and the (algebraic) sum of the first three terms on the right-hand side of (25) is negative.

Now suppose that one landlord (1, say) has more land than the other; so that, by virtue of (22) and an assumption that land and labor are complementary, $n_1^* > n_2^*$. Now, if the difference in holdings is such that $n_2^* \leqq 4n_1^*/5$, it follows at once that the landlord who has the smaller holding would be better off if interlinking were banned.

In order to examine whether the combined rents from lock in of both landlords are more than fully dissipated by heightened competition for captive segments in period 1, we sum over i in (25) and obtain

$$\sum_i [\bar{\Omega}_i(n_1^*, n_2^*) - \Omega_i^o(n_1, n_2)] = (\xi_1 + \xi_2) - (n_1^* + n_2^*)[\delta - (a - c)^2/36b].$$

$$\tag{26}$$

Since $\xi_i < 0$, a strongly sufficient condition for the said rents to be more than dissipated is

$$\delta > (a - c)^2/36b. \tag{27}$$

Now the loss in an individual's net consumer surplus that results from being charged the monopoly price as opposed to the duopoly price is

$$(p^m - p^o)(q^m + q^o)/2 = 7(a - c)^2/72b > (a - c)^2/36b.$$

Hence, as δ is the compensating variation with respect to the increase in price from p^o to p^m, (27) will indeed hold if consumption in each period is a non-inferior good for a laborer. We have therefore shown that rents from second period lock-in can be more than dissipated in our model, a possibility which appears in other models in the related literature.

By way of comparison, we now examine whether this result will hold if landlords cannot practice price discrimination. Summing (18) over i and subtracting $(\Omega_1^o + \Omega_2^o)$, we obtain, in this case,

$$\sum[\bar{\Omega}_i(n_1^*, n_2^*) - \Omega_i^o(n_1, n_2)] = (\xi_1 + \xi_2) + \frac{(a - c)^2 n}{b}\left[\frac{n(n + n_3^*)}{(2n + n_3^*)^2} - \frac{1}{9}\right]. \tag{28}$$

Since $9n(n + n_3^*) > (2n + n_3^*)^2$, strong claims about whether rents are more than fully dissipated cannot be made without knowledge of the shape of $X_i(n_i)$ over the domain $(\hat{n}_i, n_i^*)$, all of which determine the magnitude of ξ_i. We leave this as an open question.

7 Conclusion

This paper started by analyzing a market structure in which each firm has a *predetermined* set of potential customers. These sets may overlap but they need not coincide totally with one another. Such a structure could emerge in a location-model of oligopoly, but it emerges more naturally in trades where the problem of asymmetric information and moral hazard is high. Such markets were referred to as fragmented oligopolies, and the basic properties of a fragmented duopoly were analyzed formally. The next step was to make each firm's set of potential customers endogenous by embedding a fragmented duopoly in a two-period model and then examine its perfect equilibrium. This was done in the context of labor and credit markets in backward agrarian economies. There emerged a rationale for interlinking, albeit of a sort quite different from that advanced in the extant literature on that subject.

Fragmented oligopolies, it was argued, are relevant in a wide variety of situations. The particular model constructed in this paper was meant to be illustrative. By considering alternative strategy sets for firms and different solution concepts, a range of different models of fragmented oligopoly can be constructed. There is, in brief, room for much further exploration.

Appendix: Proof of Theorem 1

Given the symmetric nature of the two parts of Theorem 1, it is clearly sufficient to prove either.

From the second-order condition we have

$$\frac{\partial^2 \pi_1}{\partial q_1^2} = 2\frac{p'}{n_3} \cdot \left(1 + \frac{n_1}{n_3}\right) + \frac{p''}{n_3^2} \cdot \left[\left(1 + \frac{n_1}{n_3}\right)q_1 + \frac{n_1}{n_3}q_2\right] < 0. \tag{A.1}$$

Taking total differentials in (5), we get

$$p' \cdot \left(\frac{dq_1}{n_3} + \frac{dq_2}{n_3}\right)\left(1 + \frac{n_1}{n_3}\right) + \frac{p''}{n_3} \cdot \left(\frac{dq_1}{n_3} + \frac{dq_2}{n_3}\right)\left[\left(1 + \frac{n_1}{n_3}\right)q_1 + \frac{n_1}{n_3}q_2\right]$$

$$+ \frac{p'}{n_3} \cdot \left[\left(1 + \frac{n_1}{n_3}\right)dq_1 + \frac{n_1}{n_3}dq_2\right] = 0.$$

Rearranging terms this may be rewritten as

$$\frac{dq_1}{dq_2} = -\frac{2\frac{p'}{n_3} \cdot \left(1 + \frac{n_1}{n_3}\right) + \frac{p''}{n_3^2} \cdot \left[\left(1 + \frac{n_1}{n_3}\right)q_1 + \frac{n_1}{n_3}q_2\right] - \frac{p'}{n_3}}{2\frac{p'}{n_3} \cdot \left(1 + \frac{n_1}{n_3}\right) + \frac{p''}{n_3^2} \cdot \left[\left(1 + \frac{n_1}{n_3}\right)q_1 + \frac{n_1}{n_3}q_2\right]} \tag{A.2}$$

Given (A.1) and $p' < 0$, it follows that $(dq_1/dq_2) > -1$. Since (5) implicitly defines the reaction function $R_1(\cdot)$, we have proved Theorem 1.

Notes

1. See Bhaduri (1983), Basu (1983), Bardhan (1984), Platteau and Abraham (1987).

2. Such a model is developed in Basu (1987) where the rural credit market is modelled as a collection of independent credit islands.

3. Trust plays an important role not only in backward markets but in a whole range of interactions in any economy: see Dasgupta (1986).

4. This was revealed in conversations between commission agents and Bell in the course of fieldwork in Andhra Pradesh and Punjab, India.

5. This ought not to be confused with the concept of "contestable" markets in the literature.

6. We assume throughout that $\max_{x_i}[p(x_i/n_i) - c]x_i > 0$, for $i = 1$ or 2. This ensures that production is profitable.

7. Recall that in this model both monopolists will charge the same price, since customers are identical. If, however, we allow for heterogeneity among customers, then the prices may be different.

8. We shall assume that the parameters of the model are such that firm 1's chosen n_1 and firm 2's chosen n_2 never sum to greater than n.

9. From (5) and (6), we get $(q_1/q_2) = (n - n_1^*)/(n - n_2^*)$. Substituting into (15) yields the required result.

10. This argument uses subgame perfection with rules out the possibility of landlords committing themselves to some price different from p^m.

References

Bardhan, P. K., 1984, *Land, labor and rural poverty* (Columbia University Press, New York).

Basu, K., 1983, The emergence of isolation and interlinkage in rural markets, *Oxford Economic Papers* 35, 262–280.

Basu, K., 1987, Disneyland monopoly, interlinkage and usurious interest rates, *Journal of Public Economics* 34, 1–18.

Basu, K. and N. Singh, 1990, Entry-deterrence in Stackelberg perfect equilibria, *International Economic Review* 31, 61–71.

Bell, C., 1988, Credit markets and interlinked transactions, in: H. B. Chenery and T. N. Srinivasan, eds., *Handbook of Development Economics* (North-Holland, Amsterdam).

Bhaduri, A., 1983, *The economic structure of backward agriculture* (Academic Press, London).

Bonanno, G., 1987, Location choice, product proliferation and entry deterrence, *Review of Economic Studies* 54, 37–45.

Braverman, A. and T. N. Srinivasan, 1981, Credit and sharecropping in agrarian societies, *Journal of Development Economics* 9, 289–312.

Braverman, A. and J. E. Stiglitz, 1982, Sharecropping and the interlinking of agrarian markets, *American Economic Review* 72, 695–715.

Bulow, J. I., J. D. Geanakoplos and P. D. Klemperer, 1985, Multimarket oligopoly: Strategic substitutes and complements, *Journal of Political Economy* 93, 488–511.

Dasgupta, P., 1986, Trust as a commodity, Economic theory discussion paper no. 101 (Cambridge University, Cambridge).

D'Aspremont, C., J. J. Gabszewicz and J.-F. Thisse, 1979, On Hotelling's "stability in competition," *Econometrica* 47, 1145–1150.

Dixit, A., 1979, A model of duopoly suggesting a theory of entry barriers, *Bell Journal of Economics* 10, 20–32.

Dixit, A., 1980, The role of investment in entry-deterrence, *Economic Journal* 90, 95–106.

Friedman, J., 1977, *Oligopoly and the theory of games* (North-Holland, Amsterdam).

Fudenberg, D. and J. Tirole, 1986, *Dynamic models of oligopoly* (Harwood Academic Publishers, London).

Geertz, C., 1978, The bazaar economy: Information and search in peasant marketing, *American Economic Review* 68, 28–32.

Hotelling, H., 1929, Stability in competition, *Economic Journal* 39, 41–57.

Klemperer, P. D., 1987a, The competitiveness of markets with switching costs, *Rand Journal of Economics* 18, 138–150.

Klemperer, P. D., 1987b, Markets with consumer switching costs, *Quarterly Journal of Economics* 102, 375–394.

Mishra, A., 1991, Clientelization and fragmentation in backward agriculture: A model based on forward induction, Mimeo. (Delhi School of Economics, New Delhi).

Mitra, P., 1983, A theory of interlined rural transactions, *Journal of Public Economics* 20, 169–191.

Platteau, J. P. and A. Abraham, 1987, An inquiry into quasi-credit systems in traditional fisherman communities: The role of reciprocal credit and mixed contracts, *Journal of Development Studies* 23, 461–490.

Reserve Bank of India, 1954, *All India rural credit survey*, Vol. 1, Part 2 (Credit Agencies) (R. B. I., Bombay).

Spence, A. M., 1977, Entry, capacity, investment and oligopolistic pricing, *Bell Journal of Economics* 8, 534–544.

von Weizsäcker, C. C., 1984, The costs of substitution, *Econometrica* 52, 1085–1116.

4 Occupational Choice and the Process of Development

Abhijit V. Banerjee and
Andrew F. Newman

I Introduction

Why does one country remain populated by small proprietors, artisans, and peasants while another becomes a nation of entrepreneurs employing industrial workers in large factories? Why should two seemingly identical countries follow radically different development paths, one leading to prosperity, the other to stagnation? Questions like these are of central concern to both development economists and economic historians, who have been interested in the study of the evolution of institutional forms, particularly those under which production and exchange are organized. Yet most of these institutional questions have resisted formal treatment except in a static context (see Stiglitz [1988] for a review), whereas the dynamic issues that are peculiarly developmental have for the most part been restricted to the narrower questions of output growth or technical change. This chapter takes a first step in the direction of providing a dynamic account of institutional change by focusing on the evolution of occupational patterns, the contractual forms through which people exchange labor services.[1]

There are several ways in which the dynamics of occupational choice influence the process of development. Most obvious among them is the effect on the distribution of income and wealth. Insofar as distribution can affect saving, investment, risk bearing, fertility, and the composition of demand and production, there is a clear link with the economy's rate of growth and hence with development in its narrowest sense.

Just as important is the connection that arises when one considers development to mean institutional transformation as well as economic growth (Stiglitz 1988; Townsend 1988; Khan 1989). One of the most significant elements of the institutional structure of any economy is the dominant form of organization of production: it has "external" consequences considerably beyond the efficiency of current production. Some of these effects may be politico-economic, but there are also some that are purely economic. It has been argued, for example, that the introduction of the factory system in the early years of the Industrial Revolution left the technology unaffected and generated little efficiency gain initially. But it seems very likely that in the long run this new form of production organization helped to make possible the major innovations of the Industrial Revolution (see, e.g., Cohen 1981; Millward 1981; North 1981).

Conversely, the process of development also affects the structure of occupations. It alters the demand for and supply of different types of labor and, hence, the returns to and allocations of occupations. It transforms the nature of risks and the possibilities for innovations. And, of course, it changes the distribution of wealth. Since one's wealth typically affects one's incentives to enter different occupations, the effect on the wealth distribution generates a parallel effect on the occupational structure.

Our aim here is to build a model that focuses directly on this interplay between the pattern of occupational choice and the process of development. The basic structure of interaction is very simple. Because of capital market imperfections, people can borrow only limited amounts. As a result, occupations that require high levels of investment are beyond the reach of poor people, who choose instead to work for other, wealthier, employers; thus wage contracts are viewed primarily as substitutes for financial contracts. The wage rate and the pattern of occupational choice are then determined by the condition that the labor market must clear.[2] Depending on labor market conditions and on their wealth, other agents become self-employed in low-scale production or remain idle.

The pattern of occupational choice is therefore determined by the initial distribution of wealth, but the structure of occupational choice in turn determines how much people save and what risks they bear. These factors then give rise to the new distribution of wealth. We shall be concerned with the long-run behavior of this dynamic process.

Despite its simplicity, our model's structure is somewhat nonstandard. As a rule, the dynamics are nonlinear and the state space—the set of all wealth distributions—is very large, so that reasonably complicated behavior may be expected. While a complete mathematical analysis of the model is beyond the scope of this chapter, we confine our attention to two special cases that admit considerable dimensional reduction. These examples afford complete study: they are simple enough to allow diagrammatic exposition in which we trace out entire paths of development, including institutional evolution, and with them we generate robust and natural instances of hysteresis or long-run dependence on initial conditions.

In one of our examples (Sec. IVD), the ultimate fate of the economy —prosperity or stagnation—depends in a crucial way on the initial distribution of wealth. If the economy initially has a high ratio of very poor people to very rich people, then the process of development runs out of steam and ends up in a situation of low employment and low wages (this may happen even when the initial per capita income is quite high, as long as the distribution is sufficiently skewed). By contrast, if the economy initially has few very poor people (the per capita income can still be quite low), it will "take off" and converge to a high-wage, high-employment steady state.

That an economy's long-term prosperity may depend on initial conditions is a familiar idea in the development literature, and some recent papers capture different aspects of this phenomenon in a formal model (e.g., Romer 1986; Lucas 1988; Murphy, Shleifer, and Vishny 1989a, 1989b; Matsuyama 1991; Galor and Zeira, in press). This chapter differs from these in several respects. First, most of the papers study technological increasing returns, originating either in the production technology itself or in various kinds of productivity spillovers. We consider instead a kind of "pecuniary" increasing returns stemming from an imperfect capital market (Galor and Zeira also follow this tack). Second, distribution tends not to play a causal role in this literature. A notable exception is Murphy et al. (1989a), but there the mechanism is the structure of demand for produced commodities rather than the occupational choice mediated by the capital market: moreover, their model is static and therefore does not endogenize the distribution.

Third, and most important, none of these papers emphasizes the endogeneity of economic institutions as part of the process of development. This distinction is highlighted by the example we examine in Section IVC, in which there appears a different kind of dependence on initial conditions. We show that the economy might converge to a steady state in which there is (almost) only self-employment in small-scale production; alternatively, it may end up in a situation in which an active labor market and both large- and small-scale production prevail. Which of the two types of production organization eventually predominates once again depends on the initial distribution of wealth. Specifically, an economy that starts with a large number of relatively poor people is more likely to develop wage employment and large-scale production than an economy with few very poor people. This result provides a formalization of the classical view that despite the fact that capitalism is the more dynamic economic system, its initial emergence does depend on the existence of a population of dispossessed whose best choice is to work for a wage.

In Section II we set up the basic model. Section III examines single-period equilibrium. The main results on the dynamics of occupational choice and the process of development are in Section IV. We conclude in Section V with a brief discussion of some qualitative properties of this class of models.

II   The Model

A   *Environment*

There is a large population (a continuum) of agents with identical preferences; the population at time t is described by a distribution function $G_t(w)$, which gives the measure of the population with wealth less than w.

At the beginning of life, agents receive their initial wealth in the form of a bequest from their parents. They also have an endowment of one unit of labor; the effort they actually exert, however, is not observable except under costly monitoring by another agent.

When agents become economically active, they may apply for a loan. Enforcement of loan contracts is imperfect, and agents immediately have an opportunity to renege; lenders will limit borrowing and require collateral in order to ensure that agents do not. The agents choose an occupation, which determines how they invest their labor and capital. They then learn investment outcomes and settle outside claims. Finally, they bequeath to their children, consume what remains, and pass from the scene.

Although the model is naturally recursive, we prefer to study dynamics in continuous time and to impose an overlapping demographic structure. These modifications permit us to avoid unrealistic jumps and overshooting, which can arise as artifacts of discrete time and simultaneous demographics. We therefore shall assume that all the economic activity other than inheritance—borrowing, investment, work, and bequests—takes place at the instant the agents reach maturity. The age of maturity in turn is distributed exponentially with parameter λ across the population and independently from wealth.[3] The total population is stationary and is normalized to unity; that is, a cohort of size λ is active at each instant.

These assumptions, though artificial, greatly simplify the analysis. For instance, they imply that in an interval of time dt, a measure $\lambda G_t(w)\,dt$ of agents with wealth below w are active: the measure of active agents in a wealth interval is always proportional to the measure of the entire (immature) population in that interval. Thus differential changes in the wealth distribution at each instant will depend only on the current distribution. Moreover, the differential dynamics will be related to the recursive dynamics in a transparent manner so that it will be easy to switch attention from the (recursive) dynamics of a lineage to the (continuous) dynamics of the economy.

Agents are risk-neutral: preferences over commodities are represented by $c^\gamma b^{1-\gamma} - z$, where c is an agent's consumption of the sole physical good in the economy, b is the amount of this good left as a bequest to his offspring (the "warm glow" [Andreoni 1989] is much more tractable than other bequest motives), and z is the amount of labor he supplies. Denote the income realization by y; utility then takes the form $\delta y - z$, where $\delta \equiv \gamma^\gamma (1 - \gamma)^{1-\gamma}$.

B Production Technology and Occupations

The economy's single good may be used for consumption or as capital. There are three ways to invest. First, there is a divisible, safe asset that requires no labor and yields a fixed gross return $\hat{r} < 1/(1 - \gamma)$.[4] One may think of it as financial claims mediated by foreign banks that borrow and lend at the fixed international interest rate $\hat{r} - 1$.[5] Agents may invest in this asset regardless of how they use their labor. Anyone who invests only in the safe asset is said to be idle or to be subsisting.

Second, there is a risky, indivisible investment project such as a farm or machine that requires no special skill to operate. To succeed, it must have an initial investment of I units of capital and one unit of labor; with any lower level of either input, it will not generate any returns. If the project succeeds, it generates a random return rI, where

r is r_0 or r_1 with probabilities $1 - q$ and q, respectively ($0 < r_0 < r_1$), and has mean $\bar{r}$. Such a project may be operated efficiently by a self-employed agent insofar as it produces enough output to cover its labor cost: $I(\bar{r} - \hat{r}) - (1/\delta) \geq \max\{0, I(r_0 - \hat{r})\}$.

Finally, there is a monitoring technology that permits aggregated production. By putting in an effort of one, one entrepreneur can perfectly monitor the actions of $\mu > 1$ individuals; less effort yields no information. This activity is indivisible, and it is impossible to monitor another monitor.

Using this technology, an entrepreneur can hire μ workers, each at a competitive wage v. Workers undertake projects that require I' units of capital and one unit of labor and generate random returns $r'I'$; r' takes on the values r_0' and r_1' (also with $0 < r_0' < r_1'$) with probabilities $1 - q'$ and q'. It is natural to imagine that the projects individual workers are running are similar to the projects being run by the self-employed. To facilitate this interpretation, we assume that $I' = I$ and that r' and r have the same mean (note that $q' \neq q$, however). The returns on each of the projects belonging to a single entrepreneur are perfectly correlated. Entrepreneurial production is feasible in the sense that at the lowest possible wage rate (which is $1/\delta$, since at a lower wage the worker is better off idle) it is more profitable than self-employment: $\mu[I(\bar{r} - \hat{r}) - (1/\delta)] - (1/\delta) \geq \max\{I(\bar{r} - \hat{r}) - (1/\delta), \mu[I(r_0' - \hat{r}) - (1/\delta)]\}$.

The main difference between the two types of production lies not so much in the technology but rather in the contracts under which output is distributed. In one, the worker runs a project for himself: he is the claimant on output and therefore needs no monitoring. In the other, the worker runs it for someone else, which entails the monitoring function of the entrepreneur.

To summarize, there are four occupational options: (1) subsistence, (2) working, (3) self-employment, and (4) entrepreneurship. There may be a question of how we rule out other possibilities. Entrepreneurs cannot control more than μ projects because one cannot monitor a monitor. Being a part-time entrepreneur (sharing with someone else) is ruled out by the indivisible monitoring technology and in any case would not be attractive because of risk neutrality. Raising capital through partnership is precluded by the same contract enforcement problems that exists between the bank and borrowers: one partner could as easily default on another partner as default on the bank (thus without loss of generality we need consider only debt and can ignore equity). The same arguments rule out combining self-employment with any other activity.

C Markets

In the market for labor, demand comes from entrepreneurial production and supply from individuals' occupational choices. This market is competitive, with the wage moving to equate supply and demand. The goods market is competitive as well, but it is otherwise pretty trivial.

It remains to discuss the market for loans. We assume that lenders can enter freely; what distinguishes this market is the possibility that a borrower might renege on a debt. The story we have in mind is similar to that proposed by Kehoe and Levine (in press). To abstract from bankruptcy issues, assume that project returns are always high enough to ensure that borrowers can afford repayment. Suppose that an agent puts up all his wealth w (the maximum he can provide) as collateral and borrows an amount L. He may now attempt to avoid his obligations by fleeing from his village, albeit at the cost of lost collateral $w\hat{r}$; flight makes any income accruing to the borrower inaccessible to lenders. Fleeing does not diminish investment opportunities, however, and having L in hand permits the agent to achieve $V(L)$ in expected gross income net of effort (under our assumptions, his ensuing decisions and therefore $V(L)$ are independent of his choice whether to renege). At the end of the production period, he will have succeeded in escaping the lender's attempts to find him with a large probability $1 - \pi$, in which case he avoids paying $L\hat{r}$. Should he be caught, though, he will have had ample time to dispose of his income, and therefore he can be subjected to only a non-monetary punishment F (such as flogging or imprisonment), which enters additively into his utility. Reneging therefore yields a payoff of $V(L) - \pi F$, and repaying yields $V(L) + w\hat{r} - L\hat{r}$; the borrower will renege whenever $w\hat{r} + \pi F < L\hat{r}$. Knowing this, lenders will make only loans that satisfy $L \leq w + (\pi F/\hat{r})$. All loans made in equilibrium will satisfy this constraint, and the borrower will never renege.[6]

The only reason to borrow in this model is to finance self-employment or entrepreneurship. The target levels of capital are therefore I and μI (we assume that wages are paid at the end of the period so there is no need to finance them). Someone with a wealth level $w < I$ who wants to become self-employed therefore uses w

as collateral and needs to borrow I.[7] He will be able to borrow this amount if and only if $I \leq w + (\pi F/\hat{r})$. Thus the minimum wealth level w^* necessary to qualify for a loan large enough to finance self-employment is equal to $I - (\pi F/\hat{r})$ (the escape probability $1 - \pi$ is large enough that $w^* > 0$). The smallest wealth needed to borrow enough to be an entrepreneur, denoted w^{**}, is derived by a parallel argument and is equal to $\mu I - (\pi F/\hat{r})$. Since μ exceeds unity, w^{**} is greater than w^*; moreover, neither of these values depends on the wage.

The model of the capital market we have chosen here yields a rather extreme version of increasing returns to wealth. In effect, it is not terribly different from the models of Sappington (1983) and Bernanke and Gertler (1989, 1990) or the numerous discussions of credit markets in the development literature (see Bell [1988] for a survey). Using such models would not alter the dependence of borrowing costs on wealth or of occupational structure on distribution. But as we shall see, the present model is simple enough in some cases to allow reduction to a dynamical system on the two-dimensional simplex, a procedure that would be impossible with a more elaborate specification.

III Static Equilibrium

Recall that the distribution of wealth at time t is denoted by $G_t(w)$ and that because the age to maturity is exponentially distributed and independent of wealth, $\lambda G_t(w)$ represents the distribution of wealth for the cohort active at t. The (expected) returns to self-employment and subsistence are given exogenously by the model's parameters; the wage v determines the returns to the other two occupations. The returns and the borrowing constraints determine the occupational choice made at each level of wealth. Integrating these choices with respect to $\lambda G_t(w)$ gives us the demand for and the supply of labor. To find the instantaneous equilibrium, we need only find the wage that clears the labor market (we can assume that the goods market clears; as for the capital market, the interest rate has already been fixed at $\hat{r}$).

All agents who do not choose subsistence will have the incentive to expend full effort. Therefore, the payoffs to each occupation (for someone who can choose any of them) are subsistence, $\delta w \hat{r}$; worker, $\delta(w \hat{r} + v) - 1$; self-employed, $\delta[w \hat{r} + I(\bar{r} - \hat{r})] - 1$; and entrepreneur, $\delta[w \hat{r} + \mu I(\bar{r} - \hat{r}) - \mu v] - 1$. Since only entrepreneurs demand labor, these expressions imply that demand will be positive only if the wage does not exceed $\bar{v} \equiv [(\mu - 1)/\mu]I(\bar{r} - \hat{r})$. Moreover, since only agents with $w \geq w^{**}$ will be entrepreneurs, the labor demand correspondence is

0 if $v > \bar{v}$,

$[0, \mu\lambda[1 - G_t(w^{**})]]$ if $v = \bar{v}$,

$\mu\lambda[1 - G_t(w^{**})]$ if $v < \bar{v}$.

Similar reasoning tells us that the supply of labor is (denote the minimum wage $1/\delta$ by $\underline{v}$)

0 if $v < \underline{v}$,

$[0, \lambda G_t(w^*)]$ if $v = \underline{v}$,

$\lambda G_t(w^*)$ if $\underline{v} < v < I(\bar{r} - \hat{r})$,

$[\lambda G_t(w^*), \lambda]$ if $v = I(\bar{r} - \hat{r})$,

λ if $v > I(\bar{r} - \hat{r})$.

The equilibrium wage will be $\underline{v}$ if $G_t(w^*) > \mu[1 - G_t(w^{**})]$ and $\bar{v}$ if $G_t(w^*) < \mu[1 - G_t(w^{**})]$. The singular case in which $G_t(w^*) = \mu[1 - G_t(w^{**})]$ gives rise to an indeterminate wage in $[\underline{v}, \bar{v}]$. The facts that the wage generically assumes one of only two values, that it depends on no more information about the distribution $G_t(\cdot)$ than its value at w^* and w^{**}, and that w^* and w^{**} do not depend on any endogenous variables of the model are the keys to the dimensional reduction that so simplifies our analysis below.

To summarize, the pattern of occupational choice that is generated in equilibrium is as follows: (1) Anyone with initial wealth less than w^* will be a worker unless wages are exactly $\underline{v}$, in which case the labor market clears by having some of the potential workers remain idle. (2) Agents with initial wealth between w^* and w^{**} will become self-employed; although they could choose working, they would do so only if $v \geq I(\bar{r} - \hat{r})$, which cannot occur in equilibrium. (3) Anybody who starts with wealth at or above w^{**} will be an entrepreneur as long as $v < \bar{v}$. If $v = \bar{v}$, all the potential entrepreneurs are equally happy with self-employment, so $1 - [G_t(w^*)/\mu] - G_t(w^{**})$ of them opt for the latter, and the labor market clears.

Thus despite the fact that everybody has the same abilities and the same preferences, different people choose different occupations.

What is more, the occupational choices made by individuals depend on the distribution of wealth. For example, if everyone is above w^*, everyone will be self-employed. Employment contracts emerge only if some people are below w^* and others are above w^{**}. With everyone below w^*, subsistence becomes the only option. Thus, as in Newman (1991), the institutional structure of the economy, represented by the pattern of occupations, depends on the distribution of wealth.[8] The question, of course, is whether this dependence of institutional structure on distribution that obtains in the short run also obtains in the long run, when the distribution itself is endogenous.

IV Dynamics

We have described how the equilibrium wage and occupational choices at time t are determined, given an initial wealth distribution. Knowledge of the realization of project returns then gives us each person's income and bequests, from which we can calculate the rate of change of this distribution.

A Individual Dynamics

A person active at t leaves $1 - \gamma$ of his realized income as a bequest b_t. The intergenerational evolution of wealth is then represented as follows: (1) subsistence: $b_t = (1 - \gamma)w_t \hat{r}$; (2) working: $b_t = (1 - \gamma)(w_t \hat{r} + v)$; (3) self-employment: $b_t = (1 - \gamma)[w_t \hat{r} + I(r - \hat{r})]$, which is random; and (4) entrepreneurship: $b_t = (1 - \gamma)\{w_t \hat{r} + \mu[I(r' - \hat{r}) - v]\}$, also random.

The transition diagram in figure 4.1 represents the dynamics of lineage wealth for the case $v = \bar{v}$. Everybody with wealth between zero and w^* will choose working, and their offspring's wealth as a function of their own wealth is given by the line segment AB. Agents between w^* and w^{**} will be self-employed, and their wealth dynamics are given by the two parallel lines CD and $C'D'$, each indicating one realization of the random variable r. Since the wage is $\bar{v}$, everyone above w^{**} will either be an entrepreneur or be self-employed; the two parallel lines DE and $D'E'$ represent the dynamics for a self-employed person and FG and $F'G'$ represent those for an entrepreneur.

A similar diagram can be constructed for the case in which $v = \underline{v}$. The specific positions of the different lines in these diagrams depend, of course, on the parameters of the model.

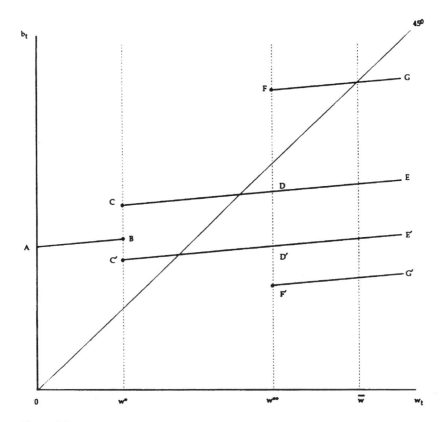

Figure 4.1
Individual recursion diagram for $v = \bar{v}$.

B The Dynamics of Distribution and Occupational Choice

From the point of view of an individual lineage, wealth follows a Markov process. If this process were stationary, we could go ahead and use the standard techniques (see, e.g., Stokey and Lucas 1989) to establish existence and global stability of an ergodic measure on the wealth space and, since we are assuming a continuum of agents, reinterpret this to be the limiting wealth distribution for the economy. Under the stationarity assumption, one can study Markov processes by considering (deterministic) maps from the space of distributions to itself; such maps are well known to be linear.

In our model, however, the stationarity assumption is not justified. At the time a lineage is active, its transition rule depends on the prevailing wage. The wage in turn depends on the current distribution of wealth across all active agents in the economy (which, as we have said, is the same as that for the entire population); as the distribution changes over time, so does the wage, thereby destroying the stationarity of the process.

In short, the state space for our model is not simply the wealth interval, but the set of distributions on that interval: this is the smallest set that provides us with all the information we need to fully describe the economy and predict its path through time. We have already shown that given the current distribution of wealth, we can determine the equilibrium level of wages and the pattern of occupational choices. Then, using the transition equations, the current distribution of wealth $G_t(\cdot)$, and the fact that we have a large number of agents receiving independent project returns, we can in principle derive the (deterministic) change in the distribution of wealth at time t. We therefore have a well-defined, deterministic, dynamical system on the space of wealth distributions.

Ordinarily, the dynamical system so derived may be quite complex, and unlike a system induced by the familiar stationary Markov process, which is defined on the same space, it is nonlinear. The nonlinearity already tells us that uniqueness, global stability, and other nice, easy-to-verify properties of linear systems are unlikely to obtain. But we want to say more about our economy than to simply state abstractly that it might display hysteresis, nonuniqueness, cycles, or other nonlinear behavior.[9]

Fortunately, if we restrict attention to certain sets of parameter values, we can achieve a rather precise characterization of the economy's behavior using methods that are elementary. In the rest of this section we shall look at two examples that obtain when the individual transition diagrams like figure 4.1 have certain configurations; these cases are illustrative of interesting historical patterns of development and occupational structure.

C   The Cottage versus the Factory

Consider the case in which the transition diagrams for $v = \underline{v}$ and $v = \bar{v}$ are given by figure 4.2a and b. The configuration represented in these diagrams will obtain when $\bar{v}$ is relatively high, $1 - \gamma$ is relatively low, and the riskiness of production (given by $r_1 - r_0$ and $r_1' - r_0'$) is quite large.

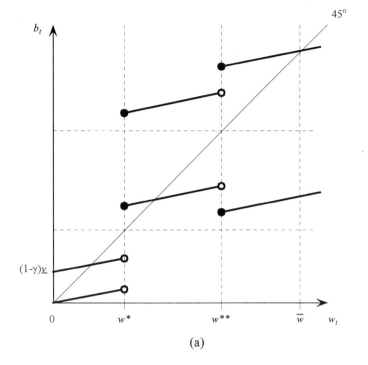

(a)

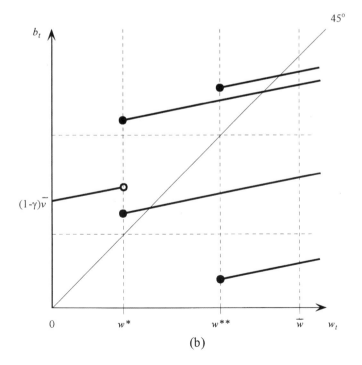

(b)

Figure 4.2
$a, \underline{v} = v$. $b, v = \bar{v}$.

Look now at figure 4.2a. Define $\bar{w}$ to be the fixed point of the inter-generational wealth transition map $b(w_t) = (1-\gamma)\{w_t\hat{r} + \mu[I(r_1' - \hat{r}) - \underline{v}]\}$, and observe that this is the highest possible wealth level that can be sustained in the long run (any lineage with wealth greater than this value is sure to fall below it eventually). Without loss of generality then, we restrict all our attention to wealth distributions on the interval $[0, \bar{w}]$.

Observe now that in figure 4.2a, a lineage currently with wealth in $[0, w^*)$ remains in that range in the next period. Any lineage initially in $[w^*, w^{**})$ either goes to $[w^{**}, \bar{w}]$ (if the project return is high) or remains in $[w^*, w^{**})$ (if the project return is low). Finally, the offspring of an agent who is in $[w^{**}, \bar{w}]$ either remains there (if lucky) or goes to $[w^*, w^{**})$ (if unlucky). The important point is that these transitions depend only on what interval one is in and not on the precise wealth level within that interval. Similarly, inspection of figure 4.2b shows that when the prevailing wage is $\bar{v}$, the transitions between the same three intervals also depend only on those intervals and not on the wealth levels within them.

As we showed in Section III, the equilibrium wage and the occupational structure depend only on the ratio of the number of people in $[0, w^*)$ and the number of people in $[w^{**}, \bar{w}]$, and not on any other properties of the distribution. Identify the three intervals $[0, w^*)$, $[w^*, w^{**})$, and $[w^{**}, \bar{w}]$ with three "classes" L, M, and U (for lower, middle, and upper); wealth distributions (fractions of the population in the three classes) are then given by probability vectors $\mathbf{p} = (p_L, p_M, p_U)$, that is, points in Δ^2, the two-dimensional unit simplex. The state space for our economy is then just this simplex: for our purposes, it contains all the information we need.[10]

Now suppose that at some instant $t, \lambda p_L > \mu \lambda p_U$ so that there is excess supply in the labor market and $v = \underline{v}$. In an interval of time dt a measure $\lambda p_U \, dt$ of the current upper class is active. The people in this class are replaced by their children, of whom a fraction q' will have parents who are lucky with their investment and therefore remain in the upper class. Among the children in the currently active middle class, q have lucky parents and ascend into the upper class. The change in the upper-class population in this interval is therefore

$$dp_U = \lambda(qp_M \, dt + q'p_U \, dt - p_U \, dt).$$

The evolution of the entire wealth distribution can be represented by a dynamical system on Δ^2, which may be written

$$\frac{d\mathbf{p}}{dt} = \mathbf{A}(\mathbf{p}(t))\mathbf{p}(t), \tag{1}$$

where $\mathbf{A}(\mathbf{p}(t))$ is a 3×3 matrix that depends on the current distribution $\mathbf{p}(t)$ in the sense that it takes two different forms depending on whether p_L is greater or less than μp_U. If $\lambda p_L > \mu \lambda p_U$, so that $v = \underline{v}$, then we have (for brevity, we set $\lambda = 1$ for the remainder of the paper)

$$\mathbf{A}(\mathbf{p}) = \begin{bmatrix} 0 & 0 & 0 \\ 0 & -q & 1-q' \\ 0 & q & q'-1 \end{bmatrix}, \qquad p_L > \mu p_U. \tag{2}$$

For the case $v = \bar{v}$, the situation is slightly more complicated since the individual transition probabilities for members of the class U depend on their occupation:

$$\mathbf{A}(\mathbf{p}) = \begin{bmatrix} -1 & 0 & (1-q')p_L/\mu p_U \\ 1 & -q & (1-q)[1-(p_L/\mu p_U)] \\ 0 & q & q+(q'-q)(p_L/\mu p_U)-1 \end{bmatrix}, \qquad p_L < \mu p_U. \tag{3}$$

The third column of this matrix is derived by noting that $p_L/\mu p_U$ of the agents with wealth greater than w^{**} become entrepreneurs; of these, q' get the high return and remain above w^{**}, and $1-q'$ fall below w^*; the remaining agents in U become self-employed and enter L and U in the proportions $1-q$ and q.

Now it will be convenient to study the dynamics of our economy by using a phase diagram; to do so we restrict our attention to the two variables p_L and p_U, since knowledge of them gives us p_M. This procedure gives us a piecewise-linear system of differential equations:

$$\dot{p}_L = \begin{cases} 0, & p_L > \mu p_U \\ \left(\dfrac{1-q'}{\mu} - 1\right)p_L, & p_L < \mu p_U \end{cases} \tag{4}$$

and

$$\dot{p}_U = \begin{cases} q - qp_L + (q'-q-1)p_U, & p_L > \mu p_U \\ q - \left(q + \dfrac{q}{\mu} - \dfrac{q'}{\mu}\right)p_L - p_U, & p_L < \mu p_U. \end{cases} \tag{5}$$

The phase diagram for this set of differential equations is given in figure 4.3a. The upper triangle represents distributions for which $v = \bar{v}$, and the lower triangle represents those for which $v = \underline{v}$. The

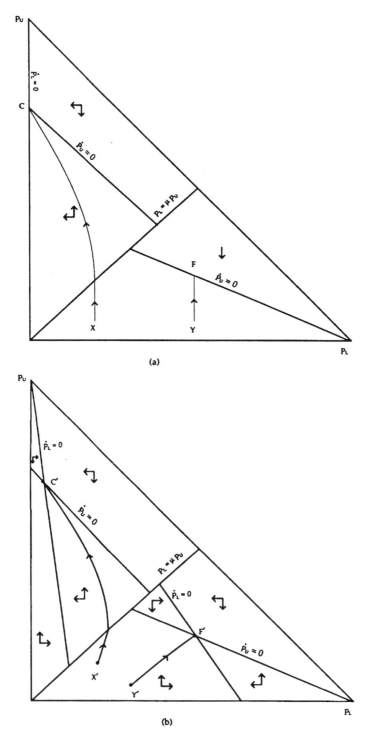

Figure 4.3
The cottage and the factory: *a*, original dynamics; *b*, perturbed dynamics.

heavy line is the "boundary" $p_L = \mu p_U$ between the two linear systems.[11]

In the upper triangle the point C represents a stationary distribution that is locally stable. In the lower triangle there is a continuum of stationary distributions since the $\dot{p}_L = 0$ locus includes the whole lower triangle. This is a consequence of the fact that there is no way in or out of state L. Hysteresis of a degenerate sort is therefore built into this model.

Since our interest lies in hysteresis generated by the workings of the labor market, we feel that it is best to eliminate the degeneracy. This is legitimate since all we need to do to get rid of it is to perturb the dynamics slightly by allowing individuals very small probabilities of moving from state L to the other two states and from the other two states to L.[12] The phase diagram for one such perturbation is given in figure 4.3b. As expected, the $\dot{p}_U = 0$ loci in both triangles have moved only very slightly, as has the $\dot{p}_L = 0$ locus in the upper triangle. The most significant change is that now we have a $\dot{p}_L = 0$ locus in the lower triangle that intersects the $\dot{p}_U = 0$ locus in that triangle at the point F'.

Both F' and C' represent stationary distributions, and both are locally stable. But they represent very different social situations. Point F' is an economy in which there are three distinct classes with very little social mobility between the top two and the bottom one (all mobility in and out of L is due to the small random perturbations we used to eliminate the degeneracy). The principal reason behind the limited mobility is that the ratio of workers to entrepreneurs is high; the consequent low wage rate makes it virtually impossible, given the propensity to bequest, for workers to accumulate enough wealth to enter state M. At the same time, the wage rate is low enough and the project returns (in particular the low ones) are high enough to ensure the self-employed and entrepreneurs against going to L.

By contrast, C' is a situation in which there is really only one occupation in the economy: the overwhelming majority of the population (in the unperturbed version of the model, *everyone*) is self-employed. While there are a substantial number of people in class U who therefore are wealthy enough to be entrepreneurs, most of them are self-employed because they cannot find any workers. Since the low outcome for the self-employed is still high enough to keep the next generation in state M, the supply of people in state L remains small and the original configuration is able to reproduce itself.

The economy always converges to one of these stationary states. Which of the two will result depends on the initial conditions. With the aid of the phase diagram we see what types of economies converge to C' rather than to F'. Roughly speaking, economies with a small fraction of poor relative to middle- and upper-class people tend to converge to C'.

By looking at some trajectories, we can be more precise and better understand the dynamics. The points X' and Y' are two points close to each other in the lower triangle that both have a small upper class but have slightly different mixes of the classes. Consider the trajectory starting at X', which has the relatively smaller lower class. Since the middle class is large and the upper class small, those moving up from M to U outnumber those who are moving the other way. The upper class grows. Because the size of the lower class changes very slowly, the ratio of the upper class to the lower class increases over time until μp_U becomes greater than p_L. At this point the wage increases to $\bar{v}$ and the dynamics change. The workers start rising into the middle class, reducing the fraction of potential entrepreneurs who can find workers. The rest of the upper class now adopts self-employment and the transitions into the lower class decline (the self-employed remain in the middle class even when they are unlucky). The fraction of the lower class in the population thus continues to decline, and the economy converges to a distribution like C'.

The trajectory that starts at Y' also moves in the same direction at first, but since the initial fraction of the middle class was smaller, the rate of increase in the upper class will be smaller. For this reason, and also because the initial fraction of the lower class was larger, p_L remains larger than μp_U, wages do not rise, and employing people remains profitable. Instead of converging to C', the economy ends up at F', which is a situation with both self-employment and entrepreneurial production.

If we identify self-employment with self-sufficient peasants and cottage industries and entrepreneurial production with large-scale capitalist agriculture and factory production, the dynamic patterns we describe above have historical parallels. The most famous of these might be the instance of England and France, which in terms of the level of development and technology were roughly comparable at the middle of the eighteenth century (O'Brien and Keyder 1978; Crafts 1985; Crouzet 1990) and yet went through radically different paths of development. England went on to develop and benefit hugely from the factory system and large-scale production, whereas France remained a nation of small farms and cottage industries for the next hundred years. In terms of our model, one possible explanation would be that England started at a point like Y' and France started at a point like X'.[13]

D   Prosperity and Stagnation

A somewhat different set of development paths can be generated with an alternative configuration of parameter values. Consider the case in which the transition map is as in figure 4.4a and b (corresponding once again to the cases $v = \underline{v}$ and $v = \bar{v}$). As before, the aggregate dynamic behavior can be reduced to a two-dimensional dynamical system in the simplex. Using the same definitions for the states as above, we follow a similar procedure to derive the dynamics of the wealth distribution. This process is described by the following system of piecewise-linear differential equations:

$$\dot{p}_L = \begin{cases} 1 - q - (1-q)p_L + (q-q')p_U, & p_L > \mu p_U \\ 1 - q - \left(2 - q + \dfrac{q'}{\mu} - \dfrac{q}{\mu}\right)p_L, & p_L < \mu p_U \end{cases} \tag{6}$$

and

$$\dot{p}_U = \begin{cases} q - qp_L + (q' - q - 1)p_U, & p_L > \mu p_U \\ q - \left(q + \dfrac{q}{\mu} - \dfrac{q'}{\mu}\right)p_L - p_U, & p_L < \mu p_U. \end{cases} \tag{7}$$

The corresponding phase diagram appears in figure 4.5. There are two stationary distributions, labeled S and P, and both are locally stable, with large basins of attraction.[14] Again, these stationary distributions are very different from each other. The distribution S is a state of economic collapse or stagnation: $p_L = 1$, so all agents have low wealth, which entails that they all remain in the subsistence sector. By contrast, P is a prosperous economy with both self-employment and an active labor market in which workers receive high wages; since the transition probabilities between the states are relatively high, there is also considerable social mobility. This contrasts with the case of factory production discussed above (point F' in fig. 4.3b) in which there is little mobility between L and the other two states.

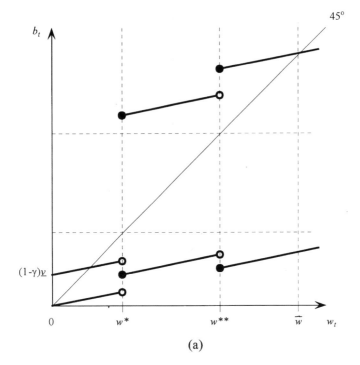

(a)

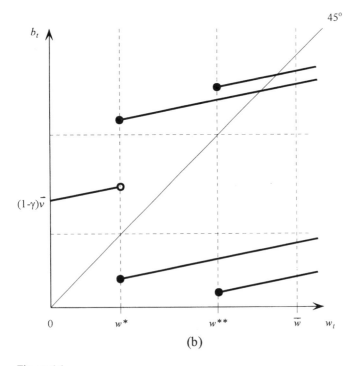

(b)

Figure 4.4
a, $\underline{v} = v$. b, $v = \bar{v}$.

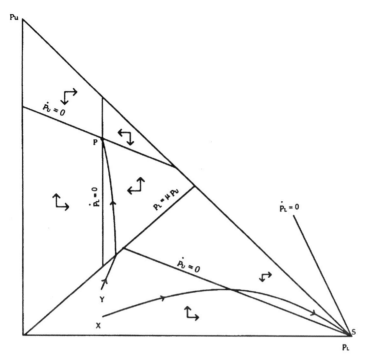

Figure 4.5
Prosperity and stagnation.

As before, the long-run behavior of this economy depends on the initial conditions: economies in which the initial ratio of workers to entrepreneurs is low are more likely to be above the boundary line, where they will be subject to the high-wage dynamics, and are therefore more likely to converge to P. Where the initial ratio of poor to wealthy is high, the economy will be subject instead to the low-wage dynamics.

Of course, by examining figure 4.5, we can see that even if an economy initially has a high ratio of poor to wealthy, it is not necessarily doomed to stagnate, particularly if the middle class is sufficiently large (distributions with a large middle class are located near the origin). Consider the path starting at the point Y. Here most agents in the economy are self-employed, and the few workers that there are receive low wages because there are so few entrepreneurs demanding their labor (recall that some agents in state L must be idle). Over time, some of the self-employed become entrepreneurs and the rest fall into the lower wealth class. Along this particular path, the number of agents in U grows sufficiently fast that all agents in L are eventually hired as workers, and the economy is brought to the boundary. Now there is excess demand for labor and the high-wage dynamics take over, with the number of wealthy agents growing rapidly (the number of workers declines slightly along this part of the development path, from which we infer that the ranks of the self-employed must be growing). Thus even though this economy begins with a high ratio of poor to wealthy, it eventually achieves prosperity.

Notice, however, that if we start at the nearby point X instead of Y, the upper class grows slightly faster than the lower class, with both growing at the expense of the middle class of self-employed. The wage remains low, however, and eventually the lower class begins to dominate until the economy collapses to the stationary point S.

We can also check whether an economy might adhere to standard accounts of development such as the Kuznets hypothesis. The present example shows that the path to prosperity need not follow this pattern. Along the path emanating from Y, equality, measured by the relative size of the middle class, declines all the way to the prosperous steady state P. We can, however, easily generate versions of figure 4.5 in which some paths to prosperity are indeed of the Kuznets type. An example is shown in figure 4.6, which is obtained when the probability q' of high returns for entrepreneurs is fairly large. Beginning at Y, the middle class declines until point Z, after which it grows as the economy converges to P. Thus, as Kuznets suggested, while mean wealth rises along the entire development path, inequality first increases and then decreases.

V Conclusion

In dynamic studies of income and wealth distribution, economists have tended to rely on what we have referred to as linear models, in which individual transitions are independent of aggregate variables (see Banerjee and Newman [1991] and the references therein). Our model of a developing economy, by contrast, is nonlinear because it violates this property of individual dynamics (see also Aghion and Bolton 1991). While it seems unlikely that other nonlinear models will admit the kind of dimensional reduction we have exploited, our examples do illustrate some of the fundamental differences between the two types of model.

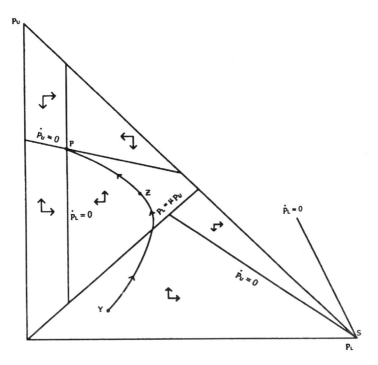

Figure 4.6
A development path that follows a Kuznets curve.

For one thing, they may have distinct policy implications. Under the guidance of the linear model, which usually displays global stability, one is led to conclude that continual redistributive taxation, with the distortion it often entails, is required for achieving equity. The nonlinear model, by contrast, raises the possibility that one-time redistributions may have permanent effects, thereby alleviating the need for distortionary policy.

The nonlinear model also provides a way to capture the empirically appealing notion that the same individual characteristics (e.g., wealth levels) can be observed under different stationary distributions. For all practical purposes, the very richest people in India are as wealthy as the very richest in the United States, and the very poorest Americans are no wealthier than their Indian counterparts. Yet standard Markov process models (including deterministic representative agent models) that give rise to multiple steady states or hysteresis preclude this possibility: any state observed under one stationary distribution cannot be observed under another, so that if

India and the United States correspond to different equilibria of the same standard model, then no Indian can enjoy the same wealth as any American.

Our examples (particularly C' and F' in fig. 4.3b) underscore a related point. Individual lineages can travel all over the wealth space under two very different stationary distributions.[15] Moreover, random perturbations to the individual-level dynamics will not significantly affect these distributions and cannot destroy the dependence of aggregate behavior on initial conditions. Contrary to the lessons of linear models, there need be no contradiction between individual mobility and aggregate hysteresis.

Notes

1. We use the term "occupation" to mean a contractual arrangement rather than a productive activity. A bricklayer and an accountant are in the same occupation if each is an independent contractor or if each works for a wage.

2. This static model of occupational choice is a simplified version of the one in Newman (1991), which also discusses the advantages of the capital market imperfections approach over preference-based approaches such as that of Kihlstrom and Laffont (1979). See also the related work of Eswaran and Kotwal (1989).

3. That is, an agent born at s is "immature" with probability $e^{\lambda(s-t)}$ at time $t > s$ ($1/\lambda$ is the average age of maturity of the population). These demographics resemble those in Blanchard (1985), although he does not assume instantaneous economic activity.

4. The restriction on the safe return ensures that the long-run dynamics are reasonable in the sense that people's wealth levels do not grow without bound.

5. Of course, $\hat{r}$ might instead represent the return to some physical subsistence activity that requires wealth but no effort; arbitrage considerations then dictate that this also be the return on loans.

6. An alternative interpretation is that πF is equal to a moving cost incurred by the borrower when he flees, with no chance for the lender to catch him.

7. By using all his wealth as collateral, the borrower maximizes the size of the loan he can obtain.

8. So does static efficiency. In this model, a first-best Pareto optimum is achieved only when everyone is self-employed. Even though the employment contract is optimal from the point of view of the parties involved, an equilibrium with employment contracts cannot be first-best efficient (some resources are being spent on monitoring instead of direct production).

9. As this article was going to press, we became aware of the work of Conlisk (1976) on interactive Markov chains, to which our model is closely related. His results do not apply to our case, however.

10. Thus if $G(\cdot)$ is the current wealth distribution, then $p_L = G(w^*)$, $p_M = G(w^{**}) - G(w^*)$, and $p_U = 1 - G(w^{**})$. Of course, some information is lost by our dimensional reduction: if $H(\cdot)$ is another distribution with $H(w^*) = G(w^*)$ and $H(w^{**}) = G(w^{**})$, then it will be indistinguishable from $G(\cdot)$, even if the two distributions have different means. The limits to which they converge will generally differ as well but will be equal at w^* and w^{**}.

11. We have assumed that on the boundary the high-wage dynamics apply. The behavior at the boundary is, of course, affected by which wage prevails there. Making alternative assumptions will not significantly change our results.

12. Think of these small probabilities as corresponding to winning the lottery and having a thunderbolt hit your house and factory.

13. A full study of the relevant data would be the subject of another paper, but there seems to be abundant evidence both for the poor performance of credit markets, at least in England (Deane 1965; Shapiro 1967; Ashton 1968), and for a more equal land distribution in France (especially after the Revolution) than in England (where the enclosure movement had generated a large population of landless poor). See Clapham (1936), Grantham (1975), and Soltow (1980).

14. Figure 4.5 is not the only possible phase diagram that can correspond to the configurations in fig. 4.4a and b. If q, q', and μ satisfy $\mu q(1 - q) < 1 + q' + q(q - q')$, the stationary point of the high-wage dynamics will actually lie *below* the $p_L = \mu p_U$ boundary. Then there is a unique steady state since in converging to the high-wage stationary point, the economy crosses the boundary and the low-wage dynamics take over: the economy inevitably stagnates.

15. The idea that a stationary economy is one in which aggregate characteristics are fixed, but in which individuals may occupy different states over time, is already common in economics (examples are Loury [1981], Banerjee and Newman [1991], and Hopenhayn [1992]); it is one motivation for seeking ergodic distributions. What is new here is the presence of multiple ergodic distributions with common support.

References

Aghion, Philippe, and Bolton, Patrick. "A Trickle-down Theory of Growth and Development with Debt Overhang." Manuscript. Paris: DELTA, 1991.

Andreoni, James. "Giving with Impure Altruism: Applications to Charity and Ricardian Equivalence." *J.P.E.* 97 (December 1989): 1447–58.

Ashton, Thomas S. *The Industrial Revolution, 1760–1830.* London: Oxford Univ. Press, 1968.

Banerjee, Abhijit V., and Newman, Andrew F. "Risk-bearing and the Theory of Income Distribution." *Rev. Econ. Studies* 58 (April 1991): 211–35.

Bell, Clive. "Credit Markets, Contracts and Interlinked Transactions." In *Handbook of Development Economics,* edited by Hollis Chenery and T. N. Srinivasan. New York: North-Holland, 1988.

Bernanke, Ben, and Gertler, Mark. "Agency Costs, Net Worth, and Business Fluctuations." *A.E.R.* 79 (March 1989): 14–31.

———. "Financial Fragility and Economic Performance." *Q.J.E.* 105 (February 1990): 87–114.

Blanchard, Olivier J. "Debt, Deficits, and Finite Horizons." *J.P.E.* 93 (April 1985): 223–47.

Clapham, John H. *Economic Development of France and Germany, 1815–1914.* 4th ed. Cambridge: Cambridge Univ. Press, 1936.

Cohen, Jon S. "Managers and Machinery: An Analysis of the Rise of Factory Production." *Australian Econ. Papers* 20 (June 1981): 24–41.

Conlisk, John. "Interactive Markov Chains." *J. Math. Sociology* 4 (July 1976): 157–85.

Crafts, N. F. R. "Industrial Revolution in England and France: Some Thoughts on the Question, 'Why Was England First?'" In *The Economics of the Industrial Revolution*, edited by Joel Mokyr. Totowa, N.J.: Rowman & Allanheld, 1985.

Crouzet, François. *Britain Ascendant: Comparative Studies in Franco-British Economic History.* Cambridge: Cambridge Univ. Press, 1990.

Deane, Phyllis. *The First Industrial Revolution.* Cambridge: Cambridge Univ. Press, 1965.

Eswaran, Mukesh, and Kotwal, Ashok, "Why Are Capitalists the Bosses?" *Econ. J.* 99 (March 1989): 162–76.

Galor, Oded, and Zeira, Joseph. "Income Distribution and Macroeconomics." *Rev. Econ. Studies* (in press).

Grantham, George W. "Scale and Organization in French Farming, 1840–1880." In *European Peasants and Their Markets: Essays in Agrarian Economic History*, edited by William N. Parker and Eric L. Jones. Princeton, N.J.: Princeton Univ. Press, 1975.

Hopenhayn, Hugo Andreas. "Entry, Exit, and Firm Dynamics in Long Run Equilibrium." *Econometrica* 60 (September 1992): 1127–50.

Kehoe, Timothy J., and Levine, David K. "Debt-constrained Asset Markets." *Rev. Econ. Studies* (in press).

Khan, M. Ali. "In Praise of Development Economics." Manuscript. Baltimore: Johns Hopkins Univ., 1989.

Kihlstrom, Richard E., and Laffont, Jean-Jacques. "A General Equilibrium Entrepreneurial Theory of Firm Formation Based on Risk Aversion." *J.P.E.* 87 (August 1979): 719–48.

Loury, Glenn C. "Intergenerational Transfers and the Distribution of Earnings." *Econometrica* 49 (July 1981): 843–67.

Lucas, Robert E., Jr. "On the Mechanics of Economic Development." *J. Monetary Econ.* 22 (July 1988): 3–42.

Matsuyama, Kiminori. "Increasing Returns, Industrialization, and Indeterminacy of Equilibrium." *Q.J.E.* 106 (May 1991): 617–50.

Millward, R. "The Emergence of Wage Labor in Early Modern England." *Explorations Econ. Hist.* 18 (January 1981): 21–39.

Murphy, Kevin M.; Shleifer, Andrei; and Vishny, Robert W. "Income Distribution, Market Size, and Industrialization." *Q.J.E.* 104 (August 1989): 537–64. (*a*)

———. "Industrialization and the Big Push." *J.P.E.* 97 (October 1989): 1003–26. (*b*)

Newman, Andrew F. "The Capital Market, Inequality, and the Employment Relation." Manuscript. Evanston, Ill.: Northwestern Univ., 1991.

North, Douglass C. *Structure and Change in Economic History.* New York: Norton, 1981.

O'Brien, Patrick K., and Keyder, Caglar. *Economic Growth in Britain and France, 1780–1914: Two Paths to the Twentieth Century.* London: Allen & Unwin, 1978.

Romer, Paul M. "Increasing Returns and Long-Run Growth." *J.P.E.* 94 (October 1986): 1002–37.

Sappington, David. "Limited Liability Contracts between Principal and Agent." *J. Econ. Theory* 29 (February 1983): 1–21.

Shapiro, Seymour. *Capital and the Cotton Industry in the Industrial Revolution.* Ithaca, N.Y.: Cornell Univ. Press, 1967.

Soltow, Lee. "Long-Run Changes in British Income Inequality." In *Wealth, Income, and Inequality,* 2d ed., edited by Anthony B. Atkinson. Oxford: Oxford Univ. Press, 1980.

Stiglitz, Joseph E. "Economic Organization, Information, and Development." In *Handbook of Development Economics,* edited by Hollis Chenery and T. N. Srinivasan. New York: North-Holland, 1988.

Stokey, Nancy L., and Lucas, Robert E., Jr. *Recursive Methods in Economic Dynamics.* Cambridge, Mass.: Harvard Univ. Press, 1989.

Townsend, Robert M. "Models as Economies." *Econ. J.* 98 (suppl., 1988): 1–24.

5   Economic Underdevelopment: The Case of a Missing Market for Human Capital

Lars Ljungqvist

1 Introduction

Dualism is a term often used in the characterization of underdeveloped countries. It refers to asymmetries in these societies which cannot be found in the developed world. A commonly asserted dualism is the coexistence of a modern industrial sector and a backward agricultural sector. Another economic asymmetry has to do with earnings differentials between various types of labor. Such an example is provided by Psacharopoulos (1973), who, in the 1960s, compared the relative average earnings of individuals by educational level for a group of developed and less developed countries. In the latter countries he found that workers with a university education on the average earned 6.4 times as much as the typical worker who had completed primary school, while the corresponding figure for the developed countries was 2.4.[1] A related empirical observation is the significantly higher private and social rates of return on education in the less developed countries compared to the developed ones as documented in a comprehensive survey article by Psacharopoulos (1985). It seems therefore puzzling that substantially higher relative wage differences in the underdeveloped world do not trigger a reallocation of labor which would reduce those differentials. Or stated as a more general question, is the existence of a dual economy consistent with individual rationality?

In the classic Lewis (1954) model of a dual economy, the level of wages in the urban industrial sector is assumed to be constant and determined as a fixed premium over a constant subsistence level of wages in the traditional agricultural sector. The earnings differential is such that a rural worker is indifferent between keeping his current employment or starting to work in the industrial sector. The model's inadequacy to deal with "excessive" relative wage differences is addressed by Harris and Todaro (1970), who assume a politically determined minimum urban wage at levels substantially higher than agricultural earnings. The resulting urban unemployment acts as an equilibrating force by reducing the expected earnings in the urban industry. Calvo (1978) shows how the urban wage can be determined endogenously after introducing a trade union into the Harris–Todaro model. However, it remains to be explored whether or not substantial relative wage differences can exist under pure competition. In doing so, we will combine Lewis' idea of economic dualism with Schultz's emphasis on the importance of human capital for understanding the situation in low-income countries. When these two economists shared the Nobel Prize in 1979, Schultz (1980) stressed also that poverty does not impair rationality and "poor people are no less concerned about improving their lot and that of their children than rich people are."

In the human capital literature, whose early contributors included Becker (1962) and Mincer (1958), educational decisions are based on maximizing behavior. A common assumption has also been that a perfect market for educational loans exists. This seems questionable, since the embodiment of human capital in people ought to affect its value as security for a loan. As Friedman (1962) pointed out, the productivity of human capital depends on the cooperativeness of the original borrower, and the prohibition of slavery makes it impossible to seize the capital from a borrower who does not honor his debt. It follows that credit constraints may be an important source of educational differences, which is also the conclusion in empirical work by Behrman et al. (1989) using U.S. data. This chapter adopts therefore the assumption of Loury (1981), which is that future labor earnings cannot serve as collateral on a loan.

The world economy in our model is assumed to be inhabited by agents who are identical with respect to preferences and innate abilities. An agent maximizes utility over an infinite horizon and can be thought of as representing a dynastic family. All countries have access to the same technologies concerning the production of a single good and education. The good can be used for consumption or investment. It is produced with physical capital, skilled workers and unskilled workers as inputs in a constant-returns-to-scale production function. Any unskilled agent can become skilled when being educated by an already skilled worker. The international economy exhibits free trade in consumption goods and physical capital, while labor is assumed to be completely immobile between countries.

Within this framework we ask the question, can developed and underdeveloped countries coexist indefinitely in a competitive world equilibrium? That is, can we find an allocation and price system supporting such a dynamic general equilibrium? It should be noted that the model itself makes it feasible for a country to reach the development level of any other country. The countries are assumed to be identical with respect to technology and the innate abilities of their labor forces. Moreover, all countries have access to the international capital market to finance their stocks of physical capital or as an outlet for net national savings. It is therefore not a foregone conclusion how there can exist underdeveloped countries in a stationary world equilibrium. Finally, the focus on stationary outcomes is meant to further our understanding of economic development by first exploring under what circumstances economic underdevelopment can persist over time.

Given indivisibilities in education, this paper establishes a continuum of steady states depending on the distribution of human and nonhuman wealth. An underdeveloped country is characterized by a high ratio of unskilled workers in the labor force, a small stock of physical capital, a low gross national product, a high rate of return on human capital and a corresponding large wage differential between skilled and unskilled workers. The perpetuation of such a situation can be explained as follows. In a country with a high ratio of unskilled labor, the wage of an uneducated worker is very low relative to the wage of a skilled worker. This means that the cost of education is high in comparison to the labor earnings of an unskilled agent. It turns out that an unskilled worker with no or few assets chooses not to obtain an education. The loss of utility from foregone consumption while saving for educational expenditures outweighs the welfare from higher future earnings.[2]

The precise structure of the model is set out in the following section. Equilibrium prices and quantities in a country are characterized in section 3. Section 4 studies individuals' optimization behavior. Section 5 proves the existence of multiple steady states for a country, while a stationary world equilibrium is described in section 6. Section 7 discusses economic growth in the context of our model, and section 8 contains the conclusions.

2   The Model

Consider a world economy inhabited by a continuum of infinitely lived agents. All agents are identical with respect to preferences and innate abilities. An agent's preferences at time t_0 over consumption streams take the usual additively separable, discounted form,

$$\int_{t0}^{\infty} e^{-\rho t} U(c_t)\, dt, \qquad \rho > 0. \tag{1}$$

The instantaneous utility function $U(c)$ is strictly increasing, concave and differentiable over the positive real numbers. The utility function is also assumed to satisfy the Inada condition

$$\lim_{c \to 0} U'(c) = \infty. \tag{2}$$

Each agent is endowed with a constant flow of time that can be devoted to work. As can be seen from the agent's preferences, there is no disutility associated with working.

The world economy produces a single good which can be used for either consumption or investment. A country's output at time t depends on its capital stock K_t and the employment levels in two different job categories. Let L_{st} denote the employment level for the skill-intensive type of work, which can only be performed by skilled workers. On the other hand, the employment in the labor-intensive job category, L_{ut}, can be made up of both unskilled and skilled workers. The good is then produced according to the aggregate production function

$$F(L_{st}, L_{ut}, K_t) = G(L_{st}, L_{ut})^{\alpha} K_t^{1-\alpha}, \qquad 0 < \alpha < 1. \tag{3}$$

The production function exhibits constant returns to scale with positive marginal products, i.e., the function $G(L_{st}, L_{ut})$ is linearly homogeneous with positive first derivatives. It is also assumed that the marginal rate of substitution between different labor is diminishing everywhere:

$$\frac{F_1(L_s, L_u, K)}{F_2(L_s, L_u, K)} = \frac{G_1(L_s, L_u)}{G_2(L_s, L_u)} \quad \text{is strictly decreasing in} \quad \frac{L_s}{L_u}. \tag{4}$$

(An integer i as a subscript on a function denotes the partial derivative with respect to the ith argument.) Moreover the marginal product of unskilled labor approaches zero when the fraction of skilled labor to unskilled labor goes to zero, while the marginal product of skilled labor remains strictly positive in that limit (for any positive stock of physical capital). The corresponding restrictions on the function G are

$$\lim_{L_s/L_u \to 0} G_1(L_s, L_u) > 0, \tag{5a}$$

$$\lim_{L_s/L_u \to 0} G_2(L_s, L_u) = 0. \tag{5b}$$

For simplicity, physical capital is assumed to not depreciate over time unless it is being consumed. Concerning the skilled labor force, there is an education technology which is also common across countries. A number γ of skilled workers can instantaneously transform an unskilled worker into a skilled worker. This education allows the worker to remain skilled for τ units of time.

The consumption good and physical capital are internationally traded without any transportation costs. However, labor is completely immobile between countries. Another critical assumption on feasible trades is that an agent's future labor earnings cannot serve as collateral on a loan. Physical capital can still be used as collateral security, but that is equivalent to selling and repurchasing capital in this world without uncertainty.[3]

We will focus on stationary equilibria for the described world economy. It turns out that a steady state, or, for that matter, a Pareto-optimal stationary allocation, will only exist if the education technology is sufficiently productive. In particular, the parameters must satisfy

$$1 - \rho\gamma > e^{-\rho\tau}, \tag{6}$$

which implies that $\tau > \gamma$.[4] If condition (6) is not satisfied, any constant stock of human capital would be unprofitable in an equilibrium. The rate of return would fall short of the subjective discount factor ρ as will be shown in (17) below. Even feasibility is violated if $\tau < \gamma$ as will be seen in (11) below. Such economies where human capital must necessarily vanish over time are left out from our analysis, i.e., condition (6) is assumed to hold throughout the paper.

3   Equilibrium Prices and Quantities in a Country

Let w_{st} and w_{ut} denote the real wages at time t for the country's workers employed in the skill-intensive and labor-intensive jobs,

respectively. In a competitive equilibrium, these two production factors are paid their marginal products:

$$w_{st} = F_1(L_{st}, L_{ut}, K_t) = \alpha G_1(L_{st}, L_{ut}) G(L_{st}, L_{ut})^{\alpha-1} K_t^{1-\alpha}, \tag{7a}$$

$$w_{ut} = F_2(L_{st}, L_{ut}, K_t) = \alpha G_2(L_{st}, L_{ut}) G(L_{st}, L_{ut})^{\alpha-1} K_t^{1-\alpha}. \tag{7b}$$

Since skilled workers can perform both types of work, it must also be
true that w_{st} is at least as high as w_{ut}. A similar argument implies that
the wage of educators is equal to w_{st}.

In a stationary world equilibrium, the internationally determined
real interest rate will be equal to the rate of time preference ρ. Given
this interest rate and the employment levels in the two job categories,
we can find an expression for the equilibrium stock of capital,

$$\rho = F_3(L_{st}, L_{ut}, K_t),$$

i.e.,

$$K_t = [\rho^{-1}(1-\alpha)]^{1/\alpha} G(L_{st}, L_{ut}). \tag{8}$$

Since the production technologies for goods and education exhibit
constant returns to scale, another implication of perfect competition
is that "pure" profits are zero and, therefore, the ownership of these
industries is immaterial.

Normalize the country's total labor endowment to unity and let L_{et}
denote the number of skilled workers employed as educators. Since
agents supply all labor inelastically, market clearing in the country's
labor market is obtained when

$$L_{st} + L_{ut} + L_{et} = 1. \tag{9}$$

If we let H_t denote the number of skilled workers at time t, feasibility
requires also that

$$L_{st} + L_{et} \leq H_t. \tag{10}$$

Due to international trade, there are no 'domestic' market clearing
conditions for goods and physical capital. However, any flows of
resources between countries must be consistent with individual
agents satisfying their budget constraints as shown in section 4.

Since we will only analyze stationary equilibria, it is convenient to
drop the time subscript from all variables. A country's steady state
will then turn out to be fully characterized by its ratio of skilled
workers H. This quantity is obviously related to the number of edu-

cators L_e. After noting that rational agents will not incur the cost of education as long as their skills are intact, it follows that

$$H = \int_0^\tau \gamma^{-1} L_e \, dt = \frac{\tau L_e}{\gamma},$$

i.e.,

$$L_e(H) = \frac{\gamma H}{\tau} \in (0, H). \tag{11}$$

$L_e(H)$ is strictly less than H by assumption (6), which ensures that any stationary ratio of skilled workers is feasible. Due to the resource cost associated with education, it must also be true in a steady state that no skilled workers are employed in the labor-intensive job category. After substituting (11) into (10) at equality, it can be seen that

$$L_s(H) = \frac{\tau - \gamma}{\tau} H \in (0, H), \tag{12a}$$

and by also using (9),

$$L_u(H) = 1 - H. \tag{12b}$$

It is then straightforward to express the capital stock in terms of H by substituting (12) into (8),

$$K(H) = [\rho^{-1}(1 - \alpha)]^{1/\alpha} G\left(\frac{\tau - \gamma}{\tau} H, 1 - H\right). \tag{13}$$

Similarly, the steady-state output level can be written as a function of H by substituting (12) and (13) into (3):

$$F(L_s(H), L_u(H), K(H)) = [\rho^{-1}(1 - \alpha)]^{(1-\alpha)/\alpha} G\left(\frac{\tau - \gamma}{\tau} H, 1 - H\right). \tag{14}$$

The steady-state wages can also be expressed in terms of H by substituting (12) and (13) into (7):

$$w_s(H) = \alpha[\rho^{-1}(1 - \alpha)]^{(1-\alpha)/\alpha} G_1\left(\frac{\tau - \gamma}{\tau} H, 1 - H\right), \tag{15a}$$

$$w_u(H) = \alpha[\rho^{-1}(1 - \alpha)]^{(1-\alpha)/\alpha} G_2\left(\frac{\tau - \gamma}{\tau} H, 1 - H\right). \tag{15b}$$

Finally, let $r(H)$ denote the rate of return on human capital in a steady state, which can be computed from

$$\gamma w_s(H) = \int_0^\tau e^{-r(H)t} [w_s(H) - w_u(H)]\, dt. \tag{16}$$

The left-hand side of this expression is the cost of education, while the right-hand side represents the present value of the increase in future labor income due to education.

4 Individuals' Optimization Behavior

This section examines what stationary prices are consistent with individuals' optimization behavior. In a steady state, it must be true that both skilled and unskilled workers *choose* to retain their respective educational status. We also know that an individual would prefer a constant consumption stream, since the rate of time preference is equal to the real interest rate.

Let us first examine for what stationary wages a skilled worker is willing to continue to bear the cost of education. The answer is simply; whenever the rate of return on human capital is at least as high as the rate of return on the alternative of investing in physical capital, i.e., $r(H) \geq \rho$. After using (16), this weak inequality can be rearranged to a restriction on the relative wage:

$$\frac{w_s}{w_u} \geq \frac{1 - e^{-\rho\tau}}{1 - e^{-\rho\tau} - \rho\gamma} \equiv \left(\frac{w_s}{w_u}\right)^* > 1. \tag{17}$$

Condition (17) ensures that the wage differential between skilled and unskilled labor is high enough to compensate skilled workers for their investment in human capital. Given that (17) is satisfied, it is straightforward to derive the optimal consumption and savings of a skilled worker. The mentioned desire to smooth consumption over time leads the individual to choose a constant flow of savings q out of labor income, which together with compound interest is exactly sufficient to finance the educational expenditure γw_s every τ units of time, i.e.,

$$\int_0^\tau e^{\rho t} q\, dt = \gamma w_s.$$

The necessary flow of savings is therefore equal to

$$q = \frac{\rho\gamma w_s}{e^{\rho\tau} - 1}. \tag{18}$$

In addition, let $\bar{a}$ denote the individual's assets in excess of those used for financing education. It follows that the optimal consumption flow of such a skilled worker can be written as

$$c_s(\bar{a}) = w_s - q + \rho\bar{a}. \tag{19}$$

We now turn to the optimization behavior of an unskilled worker. Let a_0 denote his assets. Given that the agent remains uneducated forever, the optimal consumption flow is

$$c_u(a_0) = w_u + \rho a_0 \tag{20}$$

with a corresponding life-time utility of

$$\int_0^\infty e^{-\rho t} U(c_u(a_0)) \, dt = \rho^{-1} U(c_u(a_0)). \tag{21}$$

Any unskilled worker is able to become skilled by acquiring education. However, if his assets are less than the educational expenses of γw_s, the agent must first accumulate sufficient funds. During this accumulation phase it will once again be optimal for the individual to choose a constant consumption stream, let say $\hat{c} < w_u + \rho a_0$.[5] This consumption level will then determine the length of the accumulation period, denoted $T(\hat{c})$. The pair $\hat{c}$ and $T(\hat{c})$ represents a tradeoff between the reduction in consumption while assets are being accumulated and the rapidity at which the higher income of a skilled worker is realized. In particular, a shorter accumulation period enables an individual to acquire an education faster but reduces also his consumption level as an unskilled worker. The formal relationship is

$$\int_0^{T(\hat{c})} e^{\rho t}(w_u - \hat{c}) \, dt + e^{\rho T(\hat{c})} a_0 = \gamma w_s,$$

i.e.,

$$T(\hat{c}) = \rho^{-1} \ln\left(\frac{w_u - \hat{c} + \rho\gamma w_s}{w_u - \hat{c} + \rho a_0}\right). \tag{22}$$

When the unskilled worker has obtained an education, the optimal consumption level is $c_s(0)$ as defined in (19). The equality between the discount rate and the real interest rate makes it unattractive to acquire any assets in excess of those used for financing education.

The optimal $\hat{c}$ is therefore found by solving the following optimization problem:

$$\max_{\hat{c}} \int_0^{T(\hat{c})} e^{-\rho t} U(\hat{c}) \, dt + \int_{T(\hat{c})}^{\infty} e^{-\rho t} U(c_s(0)) \, dt, \tag{23}$$

subject to

$$\hat{c} < w_u + \rho a_0,$$

$c_s(0)$ and $T(\hat{c})$ as defined in (19) and (22),

given

$a_0.$

The limiting value of the objective function when $\hat{c}$ approaches $w_u + \rho a_0$ is clearly the life-time utility of an agent who remains uneducated forever, given by (21). If this latter utility level cannot be improved upon by obtaining a future education, an unskilled worker with insufficient assets, $a_0 < \gamma w_s$, *chooses* to remain uneducated forever. After substituting (22) into (23), the condition for this can be seen to be

$$U(c_u(a_0)) \geq \rho \frac{\gamma w_s - a_0}{w_u - \hat{c} + \rho \gamma w_s} U(\hat{c}) + \frac{w_u - \hat{c} + \rho a_0}{w_u - \hat{c} + \rho \gamma w_s} U(c_s(0)) \tag{24}$$

for all $\hat{c} < w_u + \rho a_0$.

5   Steady States and Welfare in a Country

As demonstrated in section 3, a country's steady state is fully characterized by its ratio of skilled workers H. We will now prove that there exist equilibrium wages as defined in (15), which are consistent with individuals' optimization behavior. Proposition 1 establishes what is the highest possible H in a steady state, while a continuum of steady states is proven to exist in Proposition 2. Proposition 3 compares prices and quantities across such stationary equilibria. Proposition 4 concludes that a Pareto-optimal stationary allocation is only obtained for the steady state with the highest ratio of skilled workers.

PROPOSITION 1   The highest ratio of skilled workers consistent with a steady state in a country is H^* implied by

$$\frac{G_1((\tau - \gamma)\backslash\tau^{-1}H^*, 1 - H^*)}{G_2((\tau - \gamma)\backslash\tau^{-1}H^*, 1 - H^*)} = \left(\frac{w_s}{w_u}\right)^*, \tag{25}$$

where $(w_s/w_u)^*$ is defined in (17). If (25) is not satisfied for any ratio of skilled workers in the unit interval, H^* is equal to one.

Proof After substituting (15) into (17), the resulting expression (25) determines the highest H for which skilled workers would choose to remain educated. At this composition of the labor force, the equilibrium wages are such that the return on education net of "depreciation" is equal to the real interest rate ρ. People are therefore indifferent between acquiring an education or investing in physical capital. This means also that unskilled workers have no incentive to change their educational status. An unskilled worker's life-time utility is even reduced if education would have to be preceded by a period of asset accumulation.

The existence of a unique $H^* \in (0, 1]$ is guaranteed by assumptions (4) and (5). The latter assumption implies that the limit of the left-hand side of (25) is infinity when H approaches zero, and the expression is decreasing in H by the former assumption. However, the model does not preclude the possibility that the rate of return on education does not fall below ρ even if all workers are educated. H^* would then be equal to one. □

In addition to the highest possible steady state H^* in Proposition 1, the following proposition guarantees the existence of a continuum of steady states.

PROPOSITION 2   There exists $\bar{H} \in (0, 1]$ such that any ratio of skilled workers $H \in (0, \bar{H}]$ can be a steady state in a country whenever the unskilled workers have no assets.[6]

Proof See appendix.

The continuum of steady states may seem surprising in light of assumption (4) that the relative wage of unskilled labor is lower the smaller H is. One might therefore think that unskilled workers would like to educate themselves and start earning the higher wage. But at very low ratios of skilled workers in the economy, the educational cost is also high compared to the labor income of an unskilled worker. It turns out that the loss of utility from foregone consumption while saving for educational expenditures outweighs the welfare gain from higher future earnings. Moreover, the proof of Proposition 2 is "continuous" with respect to the unskilled workers' asset holdings. It can therefore be shown that a ratio of skilled workers strictly less than $\bar{H}$ is consistent with a steady state as long as the unskilled workers have sufficiently few assets.

PROPOSITION 3   The steady-state output level and stock of physical capital are increasing in the ratio of skilled workers in the labor force, while the wage of skilled labor in terms of unskilled labor and the rate of return on education are decreasing.

Proof   See appendix.

PROPOSITION 4   Given lump-sum transfers being available, a Pareto-optimal stationary allocation is only obtained when the ratio of skilled workers is equal to H^* as defined in Proposition 1.

Proof   Since all agents have the same discount factor ρ, a Pareto-optimal stationary allocation must implement all investment opportunities with a rate of return greater than or equal to ρ. The international market for physical capital can be said to accomplish this objective for nonhuman capital. But according to the proofs of Propositions 1 and 3, there are investment opportunities in human capital earning a rate of return greater (less) than ρ whenever H is less (greater) than H^*. It is straightforward to construct a Pareto-superior allocation for any stationary ratio of skilled workers other than H^* by gradually adjusting that ratio towards H^*.   □

6   World Equilibrium

The existence proofs of a country's steady states were partial equilibrium arguments, since they only imposed market clearing in the domestic labor market. A world equilibrium requires also that the international good market and physical capital market clear. We will now examine under what circumstances, supply is equal to demand in the world capital market. It then follows that market clearing for international trade in goods is ensured by Walras' Law.

Consider any number of countries and suppose that each country has a stationary ratio of skilled workers consistent with a steady state as discussed in section 5. The steady-state capital stock in a country is then given by expression (8), which depends on the composition of the country's labor force. A condition for a stationary world equilibrium is that the implied world capital stock is willingly held by the agents. First of all, assets are demanded by skilled workers who are saving for future educational expenditures. These agents have been shown to optimally accumulate assets until it is time for them to obtain a new education. Despite this sawtooth time pattern of each skilled agent's asset holdings, it is straightforward to verify that a country's total assets used for financing education stay constant over time in a steady state. After summing up all such assets across countries, this demand for assets cannot be allowed to exceed the supply, i.e., the world capital stock. It follows that a stationary world equilibrium with interest rate ρ will only exist if the implied stock of physical capital is at least as large as agents' savings for future educational expenditures.

Any physical capital not used for financing education can be owned by anyone in the world, as long as the ownership is consistent with all agents choosing to retain their educational status. In particular, it has been shown that unskilled workers in an underdeveloped country must be relatively poor, since they would otherwise like to obtain an education. On the other hand, unskilled workers in a country with the highest possible ratio of skilled workers can own any amount of assets. At this composition of the labor force, the rates of return on human and nonhuman capital are equalized. As a result, agents are indifferent between obtaining an education or investing in physical capital.

In a steady state, countries' aggregate asset holdings and individuals' consumption levels stay constant over time. Any net flows of goods between countries will only arise from factor payments for foreign-owned physical capital. The international capital market equalizes the rates of return on physical capital across countries. Agents are therefore indifferent to the location of their savings, and the allocation of the world's physical capital depends solely on countries' stocks of human capital. It follows that economic underdevelopment is caused by underinvestment in human capital. A reflection of this is the higher rates of return on education in less developed countries, which also correspond to larger relative wage differences between skilled and unskilled labor in these countries.

7 Economic Growth

We have studied the implications of a missing credit market for human capital in a stationary environment. It is clearly desirable to extend the analysis to an economy exhibiting economic growth. The following proposition is suggestive with respect to the effects of neutral technological change.

PROPOSITION 5   Suppose the production function in (3) is multiplied by a "technology level" A, and assume that the marginal utility of consumption remains strictly positive in the limit when consumption approaches infinity. It is then possible to eliminate any steady state other than H^* by choosing A sufficiently large.

Proof   See appendix.

The proof uses the fact that neutral technological change raises the marginal products of all inputs by the same factor. This implies that the rate of return on education is unchanged for any given ratio of skilled workers in the labor force. However, the higher wage of unskilled workers makes economic underdevelopment less likely. At a sufficiently high income level, everyone would like to save for an education as long as the rate of return on human capital exceeds the interest rate in the market for physical capital.

Even though economic growth may eventually loosen the impact of a missing market for human capital, it leaves open the question how the process of growth itself is affected by such a market imperfection. The answer will depend on which "growth mechanism" is chosen. The exogenous technological change in Solow's (1956) original neoclassical model has been superseded by the endogenous growth literature. Uzawa (1965) assumes that both intangible human capital and physical capital can be accumulated without limits making unbounded growth possible, while Arrow (1962) examines the effects of learning by doing. A more recent exploration of these concepts can be found in Romer (1986) and Lucas (1988). Another example of an endogenous growth model is the attempt by Becker and Barro (1988) to analyze fertility and capital accumulation decisions simultaneously within a general equilibrium framework. In future work, we intend to reexamine the implications of these models when markets for human capital are incomplete.

8   Conclusions

This paper has examined the effects of indivisibilities in education and a missing market for human capital, in a world economy with free trade in consumption goods and physical capital. Although technology and individuals' preferences are identical across countries, it is shown that both developed and underdeveloped countries can coexist in a stationary equilibrium. In fact, there is a continuum of steady states for the world economy corresponding to different distributions of human and nonhuman wealth. The perpetuation of economic underdevelopment is due to the inability to use future labor earnings as collateral on a loan and the nonconvexity in education. As a result, unskilled workers with little assets living in underdeveloped countries choose to remain uneducated despite the higher rates of return on education in these countries. The reason being that the loss of utility from foregone consumption while saving for educational expenditures, outweighs the welfare from higher future earnings.

Another model of an international economy with both skilled and unskilled labor is presented by Findlay and Kierzkowski (1983). Given a perfect student loan market, they show that skilled and unskilled workers attain the same utility level. This case corresponds to our unique Pareto–optimal production structure in Proposition 4, where an individual's welfare depends on the sum of his human and nonhuman assets but not on his educational status per se. The reason that the composition of the labor force can differ across countries in the model of Findlay and Kierzkowski, is the assumption of exogenously given levels of a specific educational input. Under our assumption that skilled labor is used to transform unskilled workers into skilled workers, it is shown with identical preferences that all countries are clones of each other. The market imperfection for human capital is therefore crucial for explaining economic underdevelopment in this framework when educational inputs are reproducible.

The constraint that future labor earnings cannot serve as collateral on a loan is also analyzed by Loury (1981), who writes down a model with human capital as the only intertemporal good. In the face of stochastic shocks to individuals' abilities, the economy is seen to converge to a unique income distribution. An important reason for multiple distributions being ruled out is the assumption that the recurrent education decision is a continuous choice variable. We have instead shown that indivisibilities in education can explain the persistence of economic underdevelopment, even when all agents can earn the market interest rate on any amount of savings chosen. We believe that the assumption of a lumpy education technology parallels more closely to actual circumstances. The common practice, for whatever reason, is to provide education in "packages" like high school and college degrees.

Our multiplicity of steady states resembles the idea of an underdevelopment trap by Azariadis and Drazen (1990). They assume that the technological rate at which individuals can accumulate human capital depends positively on the existing economy-wide stock of human resources. It is shown that a country can converge to a steady state with or without investments in human capital depending on whether or not the initial stock of human capital exceeds a critical threshold value. The positive externality of human capital, as in the earlier development paper by Lucas (1988), implies that rates of return on education are lower in less developed countries than in developed ones. Our model has the opposite implication, which is also supported by empirical work as mentioned in the introduction. To appreciate the differences in mechanism between the two types of models, we consider why an uneducated worker in an underdeveloped country would like to migrate to a developed country. In a model with technological externalities, the agent would enhance his own productivity by working in close proximity to highly educated individuals. In our model, his ability would not change, but he would earn a higher wage in the developed country because of the relative scarcity of unskilled labor compared to the stock of human and nonhuman capital.

Another implication of our analysis is a positive correlation between economic underdevelopment and income inequality within a country. The relationship is even exact when income derived from nonhuman assets is excluded. The income inequality can be said to reflect the severity of the credit constraint on human capital investments. This result is at variance with Kuznets' (1955) idea that inequality tends to increase in the early stages of economic development and to decrease in the later stages, the so-called "Kuznets curve." However, Fields and Jakubson (1990) argue that the existing empirical support of the Kuznets curve is entirely an artifact of the econometric method used. The inference is reversed as soon as country-specific effects are introduced in the estimation. Their conclusion that inequality tends to decrease with economic development is shown to be robust to alternative samples and functional form specifications.

The income distribution matters also in the model of industrialization by Murphy et al. (1989). They interpret industrialization as the introduction of increasing returns technologies. The assumption that international trade is costly attaches then importance to the size and composition of domestic demand. Industrialization is seen to take place if incomes are distributed broadly enough to materialize as demand for mass-produced domestic manufactures. A higher concentration of incomes to the very rich is not conducive to industrialization, since it means a shift of aggregate demand away from high volumes to more variety of goods. As a consequence, fewer industries may find it profitable to incur the fixed costs of introducing increasing returns technologies. These demand considerations are clearly absent in our model with unhampered international trade in goods, and the focus is instead on a relationship between the income distribution and the supply of human capital. At any rate, both models can be said to highlight economic interdependencies which are not present in a representative agent framework.

The fact that the steady state with the highest ratio of skilled workers is the only Pareto-optimal allocation implies that benevolent governments can do away with economic underdevelopment in our model. However, this may only be true if lump-sum transfers are available. Suppose, instead, that the economic reform must take the form of a student loan program. This would not only benefit the additional agents being educated but also the wage of workers remaining unskilled would increase due to the change in the labor force. On the other hand, the originally skilled workers would face a lower wage in terms of unskilled labor, and if there is an absolute decline in their income they would oppose the reform. Such an argument brings us back to the two economists referred to in the motivation of our paper. Both Lewis (1954, p. 409) and Schultz (1964, p. 196) spoke about underinvestment in human capital because of some agents' vested interests in maintaining the status quo. Romer (1990) resorts to similar reasoning when explaining import restrictions on producer durables, which slow down a country's economic growth but benefit domestic capital owners.

Lucas (1990) mentions that capital market imperfections can be a reason for countries remaining underdeveloped. Capital flows between countries are too small when there is no effective mechanism for enforcing international borrowing agreements. Our paper has shown that a similar constraint on households' financing of human capital can explain the same macroeconomic situation of under-development. The analysis suggests that the observed migration pressure between countries due to restrictions on immigration has its counterpart in a lack of "occupational migration" within under-developed economies because of imperfections in the process of human capital accumulation. The model is therefore consistent with Adelman's (1977) observation that newly industrialized countries, such as South Korea and Taiwan, implemented educational policies prior to their growth takeoffs in the early 1960s.

Appendix

Proof of Proposition 2

As shown in the proof of Proposition 1, skilled workers choose to remain educated for any $H \in (0, H^*]$. We will now have to prove the existence of H^u such that an unskilled worker without assets would not like to acquire an education for any $H \in (0, H^u]$. The proposition is then obviously true for $\bar{H} = \min\{H^*, H^u\}$.

According to (24), an unskilled worker without assets would not like to change his educational status if

$$U(c_u(0)) \geq \frac{p\gamma w_s}{w_u - \hat{c} + p\gamma w_s} U(\hat{c}) + \frac{w_u - \hat{c}}{w_u - \hat{c} + p\gamma w_s} U(c_s(0)) \qquad \text{for all } \hat{c} < w_u.$$

A sufficient condition is therefore that

$$U(c_u(0)) \geq U(\hat{c}) + \frac{w_u - \hat{c}}{p\gamma w_s} U(c_s(0)) \qquad \text{for all } \hat{c} < w_u.$$

After imposing (18)–(20), this weak inequality can be written as

$$\frac{U(w_u) - U(\hat{c})}{w_u - \hat{c}} \geq \frac{U(\phi w_s)}{p\gamma w_s} \qquad \text{for all } \hat{c} < w_u, \tag{A.1}$$

where

$$\phi = 1 - \frac{p\gamma}{e^{p\tau} - 1} > 0.$$

Assumption (6) ensures that the constant ϕ is positive. By using (2), (5) and (15), the limits of the two sides can be found for H approaching zero:

$$\lim_{w_u \to 0} \frac{U(w_u) - U(\hat{c})}{w_u - \hat{c}} \bigg|_{\hat{c} < w_u} = \lim_{c \to 0} U'(c) = \infty; \tag{A.2a}$$

$$\lim_{w_s \to \underline{w}_s} \frac{U(\phi w_s)}{p\gamma w_s}, \tag{A.2b}$$

where

$$\underline{w}_s = \alpha[\rho^{-1}(1-\alpha)]^{(1-\alpha)/\alpha} \lim_{L_s/L_u \to 0} G_1(L_s, L_u) > 0.$$

The limit in (A.2b) is always finite. This is obvious when $\underline{w}_s$ is finite or the utility function is bounded from above. If $\underline{w}_s$ is infinite and the utility function is unbounded, L'Hôpital's rule can be applied to obtain the limit $(\rho\gamma)^{-1}\phi U'(\infty)$ which is still finite. We can then conclude that condition (A.1) is satisfied for some interval $(0, H^u]$, i.e., an unskilled worker without assets chooses to remain uneducated if the ratio of skilled workers in the labor force is less than or equal to H^u.

Proof of Proposition 3

Given the equilibrium expressions for the allocation of labor in (12) and the wages in (15), assumption (4) implies that the wage of skilled labor in terms of unskilled labor is decreasing in the ratio of skilled workers in the labor force. After dividing both sides of (16) by $w_s(H)$, it then also follows that the rate of return on education is decreasing in H. To establish that the steady-state output level and stock of physical capital are increasing in H, it must be shown according to (13) and (14) that the function G is increasing in H for the relevant domain, i.e., for all values of H which can constitute steady states. When totally differentiating G with respect to H, it can be seen that G is an increasing function as long as

$$G_1\left(\frac{\tau-\gamma}{\tau}H, 1-H\right) \Big/ G_2\left(\frac{\tau-\gamma}{\tau}H, 1-H\right) > \frac{\tau}{\tau-\gamma}. \tag{A.3}$$

In a steady state, the left-hand side is equal to relative wage of skilled labor in terms of unskilled labor. The proof can therefore be completed by demonstrating that the lower bound on the steady-state wage in (17) is greater than the right-hand side of (A.3), i.e.,

$$\left(\frac{w_s}{w_u}\right)^* \equiv \frac{1-e^{-\rho\tau}}{1-e^{-\rho\tau}-\rho\gamma} > \frac{\tau}{\tau-\gamma} \Leftrightarrow e^{-\rho\tau} > 1-\rho\tau.$$

The inequality holds trivially for $\rho\tau \geq 1$. If $\rho\tau \in (0,1)$, take the natural logarithm of both sides and calculate the Taylor series expansion of the right-hand side around $\rho\tau = 0$. The result is the obviously true statement that

$$0 > -\sum_{i=2}^{\infty} i^{-1}(\rho\tau)^i.$$

Proof of Proposition 5

Let H be a steady state for some given technology level A, i.e. conditions (17) and (24) are satisfied for the corresponding equilibrium wages w_s and w_u. It can then be shown that condition (24) will eventually be violated when A goes to infinity unless H is equal to H^*. In particular, we will show that even unskilled workers without assets would like to start saving for an education at a sufficiently high A. First, choose an arbitrary savings plan implied by some consumption level $\hat{c} < w_u$. Second, multiply the resulting consumption allocation by the same factor as the contemplated increase in A, let say λ. This is clearly feasible since all wages are raised by λ in the case of neutral technological change. Our new version of (24) becomes

$$U(\lambda c_u(0)) \geqq \frac{\rho\gamma\lambda w_s}{\lambda w_u - \lambda\hat{c} + \rho\gamma\lambda w_s} U(\lambda\hat{c}) + \frac{\lambda w_u - \lambda\hat{c}}{\lambda w_u - \lambda\hat{c} + \rho\gamma\lambda w_s} U(\lambda c_s(0)).$$

After imposing (18)–(20), this can be rearranged to read

$$\frac{U(\lambda w_u) - U(\lambda\hat{c})}{U(\lambda\phi w_s) - U(\lambda w_u)} \geqq \frac{w_u - \hat{c}}{\rho\gamma w_s}, \tag{A.4}$$

where ϕ is defined in (A.1). The limit of the left-hand side when A, and therefore λ, goes to infinity

$$\lim_{\lambda\to\infty} \frac{U(\lambda w_u) - U(\lambda\hat{c})}{U(\lambda\phi w_s) - U(\lambda w_u)} = \lim_{\lambda\to\infty} \frac{w_u U'(\lambda w_u) - \hat{c} U'(\lambda\hat{c})}{\phi w_s U'(\lambda\phi w_s) - w_u U'(\lambda w_u)} = \frac{w_u - \hat{c}}{\phi w_s - w_u}. \tag{A.5}$$

Besides applying L'Hôpital's rule, we have used the assumption in Proposition 5 that the marginal utility of consumption remains positive when consumption approaches infinity. The marginal utilities in the numerator and denominator of (A.5) must therefore converge to the same number and cancel out. Finally, substitute this limit back into (A.4),

$$\frac{w_u - \hat{c}}{\phi w_s - w_u} \geqq \frac{w_u - \hat{c}}{\rho\gamma w_s} \Leftrightarrow \frac{w_s}{w_u} \leqq \frac{1 - e^{-\rho\tau}}{1 - e^{-\rho\tau} - \rho\gamma} \equiv \left(\frac{w_s}{w_u}\right)^*. \tag{A.6}$$

A limiting stationary equilibria with skilled and unskilled labor must satisfy both conditions (17) and (A.6), i.e. the only permissible relative wage is $(w_s/w_u)^*$ and H^* is the unique steady state according to Proposition 1. [If H^* is equal to one, there are no unskilled workers and condition (A.6) becomes irrelevant.]

Notes

1. United States, Canada, Great Britain, Netherlands, France and Norway constitute the group of developed countries, while the less developed countries include Malaysia, Philippines, Ghana, South Korea, Kenya, Uganda, Nigeria and India. See table 8.4 in Psacharopoulos (1973).

2. An economist from Ghana questioned the relevance of this model for his country where education is publicly subsidized. However, he later acknowledged that the low participation of the rural population in higher schooling was due to various costs related to education. These costs included tutoring necessary for passing entrance exams, lost labor income while studying, and higher living expenses in urban areas where institutes of higher learning are located.

3. Ljungqvist (1989) derives results similar to this paper in an overlapping generations framework. Following the approach of Becker (1974) and Barro (1974), the two-period lived agents in that model maximize an infinite-horizon objective function due to concern about their offspring. The critical assumption on feasible trades is that parents can only pass on nonnegative inheritance to their children.

4. The parameters ρ and γ are both strictly positive, so assumption (6) implies that $\rho\gamma \in (0,1)$. After taking the natural logarithm of (6) and calculating the Taylor series expansion of the left-hand side around $\rho\gamma = 0$, we arrive at

$$-\sum_{i=1}^{\infty} \frac{1}{i}(\rho\gamma)^i > -\rho\tau \Rightarrow \gamma + \sum_{i=2}^{\infty} \frac{1}{i}\rho^{i-1}\gamma^i < \tau \Rightarrow \gamma < \tau.$$

5. Any uneven consumption flow while saving for educational expenditures can be improved upon by cutting off the peaks and filling in the troughs at the interest rate ρ. It is clearly feasible for the individual to delay consumption by investing in physical capital. The ongoing accumulation of educational funds implies also that consumption smoothing is possible in the opposite direction through a reduction of early savings.

6. Please note that the highest possible steady state H^* in Proposition 1 may or may not be included in the set $(0,\bar{H}]$ since $H^* \geq \bar{H}$.

References

Adelman, Irma, 1977, *Redistribution before growth—A strategy for developing countries*, Inaugural lecture (Leyden University, Leyden, The Netherlands).

Arrow, Kenneth J., 1962, The economic implications of learning by doing, *Review of Economic Studies* 29, 155–173.

Azariadis, Costas and Allan Drazen, 1990, Threshold externalities in economic development, *Quarterly Journal of Economics* 105, no. 2, 501–526.

Barro, Robert J., 1974, Are government bonds net wealth?, *Journal of Political Economy* 82, no. 6, 1095–1117.

Becker, Gary S., 1962, Investment in human capital: A theoretical analysis, *Journal of Political Economy* 70, no. 5, 9–49.

Becker, Gary S., 1974, A theory of social interactions, *Journal of Political Economy* 82, no. 6, 1063–1093.

Becker, Gary S. and Robert J. Barro, 1988, A reformulation of the economic theory of fertility, *Quarterly Journal of Economics* 103, no. 1, 1–25.

Behrman, Jere R., Robert A. Pollak and Paul Taubman, 1989, Family resources, family size, and access to financing for college education, *Journal of Political Economy* 97, no. 2, 398–419.

Calvo, Guillermo A., 1978, Urban unemployment and wage determination in LDC's: Trade unions in the Harris–Todaro model, *International Economic Review* 19, no. 1, 65–81.

Fields, Gary S. and George H. Jakubson, 1990, The inequality–development relationship in developing countries, Manuscript (Cornell University, Ithaca, NY).

Findlay, Ronald and Henryk Kierzkowski, 1983, International trade and human capital: A simple general equilibrium model, *Journal of Political Economy* 91, no. 6, 957–978.

Friedman, Milton, 1962, *Capitalism and freedom* (University of Chicago Press, Chicago, IL).

Harris, John R. and Michael P. Todaro, 1970, Migration, unemployment and development: A two sector analysis, *American Economic Review* 60, no. 1, 126–142.

Kuznets, Simon, 1955, Economic growth and income inequality, *American Economic Review* 45, no. 1, 1–28.

Lewis, W. Arthur, 1954, Economic development with unlimited supplies of labour, *Manchester School of Economic and Social Studies* 22, no. 2, 139–191. Reprinted in: A. N. Agarwala and S. P. Singh, eds., *The economics of underdevelopment* (Oxford University Press, London, 1958).

Ljungqvist, Lars, 1989, Insufficient human capital accumulation resulting in a dual economy caught in a poverty trap, SSRI workshop series no. 8902 (University of Wisconsin-Madison, Madison, WI).

Loury, Glenn C., 1981, Intergenerational transfers and the distribution of earnings, *Econometrica* 49, no. 4, 843–867.

Lucas, Robert E., Jr., 1988, On the mechanics of economic development, *Journal of Monetary Economics* 22, no. 1, 3–42.

Lucas, Robert E., Jr., 1990, Why doesn't capital flow from rich to poor countries?, *American Economic Review Papers and Proceedings* 80, no. 2, 92–96.

Mincer, Jacob, 1958, Investment in human capital and personal income distribution, *Journal of Political Economy* 66, no. 4, 281–302.

Murphy, Kevin M., Andrei Shleifer and Robert Vishny, 1989, Income distribution, market size, and industrialization, *Quarterly Journal of Economics* 104, no. 3, 537–564.

Psacharopoulos, George, 1973, *Returns to education: An international comparison* (Elsevier–Jossey Bass, San Francisco, CA).

Psacharopoulos, George, 1985, Returns to education: A further international update and implications, *Journal of Human Resources* 20, no. 4, 583–604.

Romer, Paul M., 1986, Increasing returns and long-run growth, *Journal of Political Economy* 94, no. 5, 1002–1037.

Romer, Paul M., 1990, Trade, politics, and growth in a small, less developed economy, Paper presented at a CEPR/IIES Conference in Stockholm, June.

Schultz, Theodore W., 1964, *Transforming traditional agriculture* (Yale University Press, New Haven, CT).

Schultz, Theodore W., 1980, Nobel lecture: The economics of being poor, *Journal of Political Economy* 88, no. 4, 639–651.

Solow, Robert M., 1956, A contribution to the theory of economic growth, *Quarterly Journal of Economics* 70, no. 1, 65–94.

Uzawa, Hirofumi, 1965, Optimum technical change in an aggregative model of economic growth, *International Economic Review* 6, no. 1, 18–31.

6

Thy Neighbor's Keeper: The Design of a Credit Cooperative with Theory and a Test

Abhijit V. Banerjee,
Timothy Besley, and
Timothy W. Guinnane

I Introduction

Economists now appreciate that resource allocation in less developed economies is influenced by nonfirm economic institutions such as credit cooperatives, sharecropping [Stiglitz 1974], market inter-linkages [Braverman and Stiglitz 1982], rotating savings and credit associations [Besley, Coate, and Loury 1993], gift exchange arrangements, and the extended family. However, while an extensive body of literature has gone into understanding the way in which firms are organized (see, for example, Williamson [1975]), our understanding of nonfirm institutions is limited to a number of alternative theories about the possible function served by a particular institution. (An exception is Eswaran and Kotwal [1985].) These theories are all plausible but imply different answers to policy and other questions. In this chapter we illustrate a method for discriminating between them, using the example of Germany's nineteenth century credit cooperatives.

There are three main reasons why cooperatives might function better than conventional banking arrangements in less developed economies. The first, essentially sociological, view stresses the role of the community in sustaining nonopportunistic behavior among participants. Social sanctions are typically not available to a conventional bank, but are available in a co-op [Besley and Coate 1992]. The second view sees the cooperative as sustained by repeated interactions among the participants. Both of these views are similar in giving reasons why privately optimal, shortsighted behavior may be curtailed in a credit cooperative. The policy implications of these two views are also similar: cooperatives should be designed to ensure that members have durable long-term relations among themselves or else identify sufficiently with the collective. Thus, we treat these two as a single hypothesis, which we call the *long-term interaction* view of credit cooperatives.

We compare this with the hypothesis that a cooperative provides an efficient way to induce monitoring of borrowers which, following Stiglitz [1990], we call the *peer monitoring* view.[1] Although the community lacks capital, necessitating outside funding from a bank, neighbors are assumed to have better information about borrowers than banks. The efficient outcome is then to have community-based monitoring, an idea first analyzed in Varian [1989] and Stiglitz [1990]. For such monitoring to be effective, the cooperative's structure must create incentives for its members to monitor one another.

This view thus predicts that a cooperative will adopt a constitution that provides monitoring incentives. Here, we suggest three ways in which this can be done.

1. The other members of the cooperative may be made liable, in whole or in part, for any loan on which the cooperative defaults.

2. Part of each loan may be financed by another cooperative member, so that if the borrower defaults, then the other co-op members also lose something.

3. The interest on the part of the loan financed by other members may be increased, enhancing the members' stake in ensuring that the loan is repaid.

Our model is of a Principal (the bank), Supervisor (the nonborrowing co-op member), and an Agent (the borrower). While such models have been studied in general (see Tirole [1988]), we use the German cooperatives as a template for restricting the model, giving us a basis for characterizing the optimal organizational form. The model is also of interest in the context of the burgeoning literature on nonmarket credit institutions reviewed in Besley [1993]. Liability, borrowing from inside, and the interest paid to members are the three instruments that are optimally chosen by each cooperative.

Although the data from nineteenth century Germany are not extensive enough to permit formal statistical testing of hypotheses, they are invaluable for the current exercise. The choice of instruments in Germany was made at the cooperative level, making it possible for the constitution to reflect optimally its idiosyncratic environment. The long time-horizon for the data also makes it likely that each cooperative adopted its best constitutional form. In Ireland the life of the cooperatives was short, reflecting poor institutional design (see Guinnane [1994]).

Our *test* of the peer monitoring view has two main limitations. First, we have no direct evidence on the optimality of the chosen instruments. Instead, we derive the comparative-static properties and compare these with cross-sectional data on cooperatives. Second, the long-term interaction and peer monitoring views are *not* inconsistent. Hence, finding that the predictions of the peer monitoring model agree with the data does not necessarily prove that this is the correct model. We can only find evidence *against* this view by finding that its comparative statics do not fit the data.

The remainder of the chapter is organized as follows. In Sections II–IV we construct a model of the optimal credit cooperative and derive some predictions from it. Section V tests these predictions against the data on the nineteenth century cooperatives. Section VI contains concluding remarks.

II   The Model

The model is based on the structure of the German cooperatives. Although our representation is inevitably stylized, the structure of the model captures the salient features of the institutions. We discuss the correspondence between the model and historical cooperatives briefly at the end of Section III and in detail in Section V.

The cooperative has two members each of whom owns two assets; a plot of land and monetary wealth of k. At the beginning of time, nature endows (only) one co-op member with an opportunity to make his land more productive. This requires an investment of $K + k$ units of capital, thus necessitating a loan if it is to be undertaken. The other member is assumed to have no opportunity to invest and receives a deterministic return of θ on his land. We assume that $k < K$, implying that total monetary wealth within the co-op is insufficient to finance the investment. Thus, some part of the loan must be obtained from outside sources. The cooperative borrows b from outside, and the monitor lends $K - b$ to the borrower. We denote the interest rate to be paid on outside funds by R and on inside funds by r.[2]

The nonborrowing member serves three potential functions. First, he is a lender. Second, he is a guarantor and hence may stand liable if the borrower fails to repay some of what is owed to the outside borrower. We denote the amount of this liability by $l(\leq bR)$. Finally, he may monitor the borrower.

Once funds for the project are in place, the nonborrower chooses his monitoring level to affect the borrower's project choice. The borrower selects a project, whose return is subsequently realized. If he has sufficient funds, then the borrower repays the monitor and the outside lender. Otherwise, he defaults and the monitor has to pay out l.

The monitor can also earn a return on his monetary wealth outside the co-op. He has access to an outside opportunity on which he receives a gross return of ρ. However, the net return is $\rho - \delta$, where δ can be positive or negative in general. A positive δ might represent the fact that the cooperative is a more convenient repository for funds, while a negative value of δ represents a case in which the outside bank yields other services (e.g., advice) unavailable in the co-op. Since the borrower may default, the return to lending inside the co-op must compensate the nonborrowing member for the risk that he bears. Thus, r must be at least as high as the nonborrower's opportunity cost of funds allowing for the possibility of default. The cooperative's constitution is defined in terms of (b, l, r): the amount of internal borrowing, the liability of the nonborrowing member, and the interest rate paid on internal borrowing.

III   Project Selection

Projects are selected by the borrower but can be influenced by the nonborrowing member. This section characterizes this project choice as a function of (b, l, r). Projects are indexed by a success probability: $\pi \in [\underline{\pi}, 1]$. A project yields some return with probability π and nothing otherwise. The expected return from a project is denoted by $E(\pi) \equiv \pi\phi(\pi)$. We assume that $E'(\pi) > 0$ and $\phi'(\pi) < 0$. This first of these says that *projects with higher expected returns are also safer*.

Let ρ denote the lender's opportunity cost of funds. The interest rate paid on outside funds in a competitive credit market is found using the lender's zero profit condition:

$$\pi Rb + (1 - \pi)l = \rho b. \tag{1}$$

With probability π the loan is repaid, and with probability $(1 - \pi)$ the lender receives an amount l from the nonborrowing member. The cost of funds is ρb. Solving for R in (1), the total interest payment owed on any project is

$$\bar{r} \equiv bR + (K - b)r = (\rho b - (1 - \pi)l + (K - b)r\pi)/\pi, \qquad (2)$$

which is just the sum of repayments on borrowing from outside and inside sources. To capture the idea that the borrower will choose projects that are too risky from a social point of view, we assume that

$$\pi(\phi(\pi) - \rho K) \qquad (3)$$

is *decreasing* in π. Thus, if he could borrow at the outside lender's opportunity cost of funds, ρ, the borrower would find it worthwhile to choose the riskiest project $\underline{\pi}$. This would be inconsistent with the lender breaking even, necessitating a higher interest rate. The lender prefers a high π while the borrower prefers a low one.

The nonborrowing member can affect the project choice. We model this as a penalty imposed on the borrower if he chooses $\underline{\pi}$. Thus, for a project π to be selected, it must be preferred to choosing $\underline{\pi}$ and paying the penalty c. The borrower will select the project π, therefore, if it satisfies the following incentive compatibility constraint:

$$\pi(\phi(\pi) - \bar{r}) \geq \underline{\pi}(\phi(\underline{\pi}) - \bar{r}) - c. \qquad (4)$$

The monitor chooses c and, we assume, is committed to punishing the borrower if he deviates to $\underline{\pi}$. This abstracts from two problems. First, the borrower is not allowed to bribe the monitor to change his behavior. Second, we ignore the fact that the punishment may not be credible because it is costly for the monitor to inflict. The cost of imposing a penalty c, is given by an increasing and convex function, $M(c)$.[3]

The monitor is assumed to set c before the borrower chooses π. The project chosen in equilibrium will be that for which (4) is an equality (assuming an interior solution). But since *in equilibrium* $\bar{r}$ depends upon π and the vector (b, l, r) via (2), the equilibrium project can be written as the fixed point relationship:

$$\pi = h(\bar{r}(\underline{\pi}, b, l, r), c), \qquad (5)$$

derived from (4). The value of π that satisfies (4) is unique if $\partial h(\cdot)/\partial \bar{r} \cdot \partial \bar{r}/\partial \pi < |1|$ which holds if $\underline{\pi}$ is large enough,[4] so that we can write $\pi = g(b, l, r, c)$ to represent the project chosen as a function of the three parameters representing the co-op's design and the penalty level chosen by the monitor.

We now investigate how the choice of π depends upon the co-operative's design, holding c fixed (see Appendix A for details). Such effects are mediated through the interest payment $\bar{r}$. Since an increase in the liability on the nonborrower, l, reduces the interest rate required by the outside lender, it raises π. An increase in r has the opposite effect since it raises $\bar{r}$. The effect of changing b depends upon the sign of $(R - r)$; whether a change in the balance of financing between inside and outside sources raises or lowers the interest rate depends upon whether inside or outside capital is cheaper.

The monitor chooses c to maximize $\pi(K - b) - (1 - \pi)l - M(c)$, recognizing that π is determined by the function $h(\cdot)$. This yields the first-order condition:

$$((K - b)r + l)\frac{\partial h}{\partial c} = M'(c). \tag{6}$$

The term multiplying $\partial h/\partial c$ represents the gain to the nonborrower of the project being successful over its failure, and thus measures the incentive for the monitor to increase π. Solving (6) yields $c = f(b, l, r, \pi)$, i.e., the penalty choice as a function of the co-op's design and the project chosen.

To investigate the comparative static properties of (6), there are two effects to consider (see Appendix A). The first, or *direct* effect, operates via changes in $((K - b)r + l)$ and the second, or *indirect* effect, via the impact of (b, l, r) on $\partial h/\partial c$ operating through the interest payment $\bar{r}$. The latter represents how the co-op's design affects the *marginal* impact of c on project selection. An increase in l raises the incentive to monitor directly and also raises $\partial h/\partial c$ when it reduces $\bar{r}$. Thus, more liability increases c other things being equal. The effect of an increase in r is ambiguous. Its direct effect encourages monitoring, but it also raises $\bar{r}$ yielding an unfavorable indirect effect. Finally, an increase in b reduces incentives for the nonborrower to engage in costly monitoring if $R > r$. The direct effect always discourages monitoring and the indirect effect is also negative if $\bar{r}$ is increased, which it will be if $R > r$.

Equilibrium values of c and π are obtained as fixed points of the mappings $\pi = g(b, r, l, c)$ and $c = f(b, r, l, \pi)$ (see Appendix A for details). These are denoted by $c^*(b, r, l)$ and $\pi^*(b, l, r)$. Thus, project selection and the monitor's choice can be written as functions of the co-op's design. This will prove useful in the next section which investigates how these parameters should optimally be set within a cooperative.

The model makes several specific assumptions that are based on the nineteenth century German institutions. We discuss a defense of a number of these here. First, we have ruled out collateral. In doing so, we appeal to the fact that land collateralization worked imperfectly and that the cooperative's members were mainly those with few assets to pledge. In any case, introducing *partial* collateralization would not change anything of substance. Second, our assumption that the return on internal funds must exceed their opportunity cost reflects the reality that cooperative members could use other financial intermediaries as repositories for their savings if they wished. In reality, as we discuss further below, the interest rate in cooperatives was most often higher than that available outside. In any case, it would have been difficult to force individuals to deposit their savings in a cooperative. Third, we assumed away partial default. As far as we know, this was treated just the same as full default, leading to ejection from the cooperative. This is plausible given that there were probably natural indivisibilities in punishments such as social ostracism or being ejected from the co-op, making the punishment for partial default much the same as that for full default. While the model could be extended to handle partial default, it is not clear that there are significant gains from pursuing this. Fourth, we assume away problems of collusion. We have no direct evidence that collusion was not a problem, although reference to it never seems to show up in the documents of the time. If anything, the problem of free-riding when members failed to attend management meetings seemed to be more of a concern.

IV   Optimal Credit Cooperatives

This section studies optimally designed credit cooperatives, i.e., how the parameters (b, l, r) should be set to foster incentives for monitoring and project selection. We assume that the objective of the co-op is to maximize its ex ante[5] surplus, given by

$$V \equiv E(\pi) - M(c) - \rho K + (K - b)\delta. \tag{7}$$

This equals the expected project return less monitoring costs and the opportunity cost of capital. The final term is the gain/loss if the opportunity cost of funds is different inside the co-op.

There are two agency problems faced by the co-op. The first is standard: borrowers may not choose surplus maximizing projects. This may be offset by having a monitor who can punish the borrower. However, there is a second agency in having the monitor choose the punishment optimally. The cooperative can specify rules about borrowing outside, liability, and internal interest rates. It cannot, however, directly specify the choice of project or level of monitoring. Thus, it must respect the incentive constraints (4) and (6). An *optimal constitution* for the credit cooperative involves choosing (b, l, r) to maximize ex ante surplus, with π and c determined by (4) and (6).

We begin by considering what happens if first π and c, and then only c, can be chosen directly as features of co-op design. In the first case, $\pi = 1$ and $c = 0$ would be chosen, since safer projects have the highest expected returns and monitoring is costly. Whether internal funds are used depends upon whether $\delta \gtreqqless 0$. Other aspects of the co-op's constitution then serve no purpose in affecting its performance.

In the case where c but not π can be chosen, the parameters (b, l, r) can be set to affect project choice. However, since c can be stipulated, it will be chosen to maximize (7) yielding

$$R'(\pi)\frac{\partial g}{\partial c} - M'(c) = 0. \tag{8}$$

Thus, the marginal value of monitoring, which is the increase in the expected profit project return when c is increased, is set equal to its marginal cost. Some monitoring is now worthwhile to counteract the incentives of borrowers. The level of monitoring implied by (8) is not necessarily optimal in the presence of an agency problem in monitoring since it ignores the effect of (b, l, r) on project choice via $\bar{r}$. However, (8) is a useful benchmark case to which we return below.

Our exploration of the optimal credit cooperative begins by deriving the first-order conditions for (b, l, r). The first-order condition for b is

$$R'(\pi)\frac{\partial \pi^*}{\partial b} - M'(c)\frac{\partial c^*}{\partial b} - \delta = 0, \tag{9}$$

with equality if $0 < b < K$. There are three terms. The first is the effect on project choice. This has a direct component (operating through $\bar{r}$) and an indirect one operating through the change in c. The second term represents the effect on costs of changing c. The third is an effect whose sign depends upon whether internal or external funds have a higher opportunity cost. The first-order condition for liability choice is

$$R'(\pi)\frac{\partial \pi^*}{\partial l} - M'(c)\frac{\partial c^*}{\partial l} \geq 0, \qquad (10)$$

with equality if $0 \leq l < bR$. This basically parallels the case of b, except for the absence of the final term. The first-order condition for the choice of r is likewise

$$R'(\pi)\frac{\partial \pi^*}{\partial r} - M'(c)\frac{\partial c^*}{\partial r} \leq 0 \qquad (11)$$

with equality if $r > (\rho - \delta)/\pi$, since the cooperative must pay at least the opportunity cost of funds if nonborrowing members are willing to lend. Equation (11) again displays the same two basic terms. We refer to setting $r = (\rho - \delta)/\pi$ and $l = 0$ as the *default options* for these parameters, i.e., to denote situations in which neither of these is set to foster monitoring incentives.

We begin by looking at how the level of c induced by an optimal constitution compares with that given by (8). This is answered in

PROPOSITION 1   The optimally designed co-op generates more monitoring than in the case where c can be directly stipulated. If (b, l, r) are determined optimally, then the monitor chooses a level of c so that the marginal product of monitoring $(R'(\pi)\partial g/\partial c)$ is less than its marginal cost $(M'(c))$.

Proof of Proposition 1   See Appendix B.

Suppose that monitoring were valuable on the margin. Then, since increasing l increases both c and π while reducing $\bar{r}$, it will be set at its maximum possible value. The monitor will then owe the bank the interest independently of whether the project succeeds. At the same time he will keep the whole of $\bar{r}$ which (ex hypothesi) is greater than $E'(\pi)$ which measures the social benefit from monitoring. Thus, the private return to monitoring exceeds the social return.

Proposition 1 is a general result concerning the optimum when a vector (b, l, r) is being optimally set. We would like, however, to understand each separate aspect of co-op design. Our next set of results illustrates how the three features of the co-op design should be optimally chosen.

The first result is on the choice of r and l. Should the cooperative ever set the interest rate on internal funds above their opportunity cost? Proposition 1 suggests an immediate answer. Since c is "too high," and increasing r always reduces π and may sometimes increase c, there is no need to raise r above $(\rho - \delta)/\pi$ unless it will reduce c. Thus, we have

PROPOSITION 2 If internal funds receive more than their opportunity cost, then the marginal effect of an increase in r must be to *reduce* the penalty imposed by the nonborrower.

Proof of Proposition 2 See Appendix B.

The next result concerns the choice between l and r as ways of affecting the choice of c. Since from Proposition 1 we know that reducing c at the margin raises ex ante surplus, we would like to choose parameter values to accomplish this task. We now compare liability and the interest on internal funds as devices to achieve this. From the previous result the effect at the margin of increasing r is to reduce c and π. Reducing l also reduces both c and π (by raising $\bar{r}$). However, increasing r only reduces c through its effect on $\bar{r}$. Its direct effect is to *increase* c, whereas *both* the direct effect and the indirect effect of reducing l go in the direction of reducing c. Hence, for a given reduction in π, reducing l generates a bigger reduction in c than an increase in $\bar{r}$. As long as the reduction in l is feasible, it is, therefore, a preferred instrument.

PROPOSITION 3 If the co-op pays the nonborrowing member more than his opportunity cost of funds, then liability will be set to zero.

Proof of Proposition 3 See Appendix B.

Our final result concerns the effect of having $\delta < 0$, i.e., a lower opportunity cost of funds inside the co-op. In this case the funds borrowed by the co-op will be entirely from outside.

PROPOSITION 4 If the opportunity cost of funds is greater outside the co-op ($\delta < 0$), then the co-op will not borrow at all from its members, but will use the nonborrowing member as a guarantor (with $l > 0$), thus generating incentives for him to monitor.

Proof of Proposition 4 See Appendix B.

The result says that, if there is a better lending deal outside the co-op, it will pay the monitor to place his funds there. In this case the co-op will generate incentives for the nonborrowing member to commit to punishing the borrower by offering an interest rate above the opportunity cost of funds. (Note that the Proposition does not say anything about the case where $\delta \geq 0$.)

This concludes the formal part of the paper. Our next task is to compare the theoretical predictions of our model with data on the German credit cooperatives in the nineteenth and early twentieth centuries.

V   A Test

1   Background

German credit cooperatives were founded in the second half of the nineteenth century under the leadership of Hermann Schulze-Delitzsch and Friederich Raiffeisen [1951 (1887)], both of whom viewed credit market problems as significant contributors to poverty.[6] While these two and other leaders differed on many features of cooperative organization, they agreed that the cooperative's purpose was to make loans to those excluded from banks and other formal institutions: the poor and those lacking collateral. In this they succeeded. The Raiffeisen organization reported that, in 1910, 72 percent of all new loans were backed by personal security while 43 percent of all loans outstanding were for 300 marks or less [Cahill 1913, pp. 108–09]. More generally, the credit cooperatives thrived; by 1909 there were over 14,500 rural credit cooperatives with some 1.4 million members, or about 5.6 cooperatives per 1000 rural Germans. By one estimate nearly one-third of all rural German households at the turn of the twentieth century belonged to a credit cooperative [Grabein 1908, p. 9].[7]

2   The German Debate

German cooperators conducted a lively debate over the best structure for a credit cooperative. This *Systemstreit* focused especially on liability and the payment of dividends. Unlimited liability meant that if a cooperative failed, any unsatisfied creditor could sue any cooperative member for up to the full amount owed to that creditor. Many Schulze-Delitzsch cooperatives adopted limited liability when it became legal in 1889. Dividend policy also divided the cooperative organizations. Raiffeisen-style cooperatives had only nominal shares and paid no dividends to members; any profits in a business year were placed in a permanent reserve fund. Schulze-Delitzsch credit cooperatives, on the other hand, had larger shares and paid dividends to members.

Cooperative advocates used both economic and noneconomic arguments to support their views of the best cooperative structure. Raiffeisen himself stressed a noneconomic interpretation; to him, limited liability and dividends were undesirable because they undermined the cooperative spirit. Others, however, took the economic view and argued that the basic organizational issues boiled down to practical matters of adapting the cooperative's constitution to local conditions. The Haas federation of cooperatives, which by 1914 had admitted the majority of German credit cooperatives, recognized these practical issues by permitting individual cooperatives to choose their own form of liability. Because of these differences across German cooperatives, we can test our model against cross-sectional variations in cooperative structure. Rigorous econometric tests of these propositions are beyond the scope of this paper. Given the limitations of the published statistical sources, that effort requires work with manuscript sources as outlined in Guinnane [1992a, 1992b]. Here we limit ourselves to a discussion of the relationship between our model's predictions and aggregate information drawn from published studies of cooperatives. The data we discuss below are accurate, and pertain to most if not all credit cooperatives in Germany. Their main defect is that the definitions of the published data do not always correspond precisely to the variables in our model.

3   Comparing the Results with the Data

The model shows that monitoring will be pushed to a point where its marginal value is negative. This result casts different light on one of the proud boasts of the German credit cooperative movement: their extremely low rate of failure. In 1909–1910, years in which there were approximately 15,000 rural credit cooperatives in Germany, none of those with unlimited liability failed, and only three with limited liability failed. Viewed comparatively, private credit institutions were 55 times more likely to fail than were rural credit cooperatives in the period 1895–1905 [Great Britain 1914, p. 315].

For some of the relationships implied by the theory, it will prove helpful to supplement the analytical results from the last section with simulations. We study an example where $R(\pi) = \theta + \beta\pi$ and $M(c) = \alpha c^2/2$. (Appendix C shows that this satisfies necessary regularity conditions for large enough α.) We varied three exogenous variable: the relative costs of inside and outside capital δ, the cost of monitoring α,

Table 6.1
Summary of simulation results

Exogenous parameters[a]	Function value[b]	Interest premium[c]	Scaled cost of monitoring[d]	π at opt	Optimal values for policy variables		
					l	r^a	b^e
$\beta = 0.01$							
$\alpha = 5, \delta = 0.03$	33.91	−0.001	0.92	0.927	0	0.10	1.38
$\alpha = 5$	33.59	0.010	0.96	0.900	0.01	—	2
$\alpha = 5, \underline{\pi} = 0.5$	33.77	0.004	0.95	0.515	0	0.98	1.37
$\beta = 0.2$							
$\alpha = 20$	39.86	0.006	0.02	0.902	0.2	—	2
$\beta = 0.5$							
Baseline	52.31	0.129	0.20	0.910	0.6	—	2
$\delta = 0.03$	54.20	−0.021	2.49	0.936	0	0.09	0.13
$\alpha = 50$	52.25	0.55	0.005	0.903	0.52	—	2
$\beta = 0.8$							
$\alpha = 100$	68.49	0.007	0.10	0.904	0.85	—	2
$\alpha = 100, \delta = 0.03$	72.35	−0.008	6.93	0.911	0	0.12	0.01
$\delta = 0.03$	71.55	−0.037	2.93	0.953	0	0.07	0.19
$\alpha = 100, \delta = 0$	68.49	0.010	0.10	0.904	0.85	—	2

Source: Authors' calculations.
a. Unless otherwise indicated, $\alpha = 20$, $\theta = 1$, $\underline{\pi} = 0.9$, $\rho = 0.05$, $K = 2$, and $\delta = -0.03$.
b. The function maximized is equation (7) with the example provided in subsection V.3. Function value reported as $100 \times \exp{(U)}$.
c. Scaled monitoring cost $- 100\alpha m^2 / 2(\theta + \beta\pi)$.
d. Interest premium $= (\rho - \delta)/\pi$.
e. When $b = 2$, r is meaningless.

and a parameter representing the sensitivity of expected return to the borrower's action, β. Note that a higher β represents a higher social return for any given π, thus parameterizing the extent of divergence between the private and the social incentives of the borrower.

Table 6.1 reports the main simulation results. Note that worsening the agency problem, either by increasing α or β, leads the cooperative to use its incentive instruments more intensively. For example, as β increases from 0.2 to 0.5, liability increases threefold from 0.2 to 0.6. Increasing π reduces the interest rate paid on internal borrowing significantly. We find that setting the worst available project $\underline{\pi}$ equal to 0.8 or higher is needed to get plausible-looking interest rate premiums. In light of the relatively rare failure rate of the cooperatives, this does not seem unreasonable. We return to other simulation results in the course of discussing specific findings.

The model (Proposition 2) predicts that l and r would never be set above their default values together, implying that unlimited-liability cooperatives would charge lower interest rates to lenders. Published data make it quite difficult to compare l and r on a cooperative-by-cooperative basis. The basic organizational difference does, however, support this prediction. Schulze-Delitzsch cooperatives paid dividends to members while Raiffeisen cooperatives did not. In fact, Schulze-Delitzsch cooperatives were sometimes accused of caring as much about dividends for members as low-cost loans for members. In the polemics of the day this difference was attributed by the Raiffeisen adherents to their desire to keep costs low for borrowers. The model implies something different: given the Raiffeisen commitment to unlimited liability, higher interest rates were redundant as an incentive device. In any case, this finding appears consistent with our theoretical model.

The model, especially Proposition 4, suggests that the sign of δ is an important determinant of whether a liability incentive is used to provide incentives for the monitor, with unlimited liability being more likely when δ is negative.[8] Rural cooperatives were predominantly of the unlimited liability variety. In 1908, 93 percent of all rural credit cooperatives had unlimited liability, compared with 54 percent of urban credit cooperatives [Wygodzinski 1911, p. 60]. Can the sign of δ explain this?

At first sight, the relative isolation of rural cooperatives would seem to imply that δ was positive. Germany's system of *Sparkassen* (state-supported savings institutions) rarely extended beyond cities and towns. Prior to the introduction of a local credit cooperative, one authority claimed, savers would keep their money at home, in cash, rather than undertake a long journey to a savings institution [Grabein 1908, pp. 54–55]. Yet, rural credit cooperatives paid an interest rate *premium* over the *Sparkassen*. One group, for example, paid depositors 3.65 percent on average in 1901, compared with 3.42 percent for the relevant *Sparkassen* [Grabein 1908, p. 59]. While this could be explained by the greater risk associated with cooperative deposits, it suggests that δ is *negative*. Since both rural cooperatives and *Sparkassen* almost never failed to honor their depositors, little of the interest rate premium could plausibly be attributed to failure risk. The

Table 6.2
Simulation results: The effect of δ[a]

Exogenous parameters[b]	Optimal values for policy variables		
	l	r^c	b
$\beta = 0.8$			
$\delta = 0.001$	0.98	—	2
$\delta = 0.002$	0.17	1.28	1.21
$\delta = 0.003$	0	1.27	1.05
$\beta = 0.9$			
$\delta = 0.005$	0	1.24	1.2
$\delta = 0.01$	0	1.24	1
$\delta = 0.002$	1	—	2

Source: Authors' calculations.
a. The function maximized is equation (7) with the example provided in subsection V.3. Function value reported as $100 \times \exp(U)$.
b. Unless otherwise indicated, $\alpha = 20$, $\theta = 1$, $\underline{\pi} = 0.9$, $\rho = 0.05$, and $K = 2$.
c. When $b = 2$, r is meaningless.

possibility that δ was in fact negative is reinforced by the observation that most cooperatives offered a less complete range of services to depositors than would be available in a *Sparkasse* or a commercial bank. Overall, while the limited information available suggests that δ is negative, reaching any firm conclusion on the sign of δ is problematic.

The effect of changing δ on liability choice is investigated in greater detail using the simulation results reported in Table 6.2. As Proposition 4 predicts, a negative value of δ implies positive liability. As we allow the value of δ to climb, the liability level falls. There exists a (typically small) positive value of δ at which the optimal design of the credit cooperative changes quite dramatically. The cooperative switches from using a liability incentive to using internal borrowing with an interest rate incentive, as in the case described in Proposition 2. We pointed out above that reaching a firm conclusion about the sign of δ is quite difficult. These simulations show that the prediction about the design of a credit cooperative in the face of varying δ can be quite dramatic. In favor of our model, this shows how relatively small differences in δ could account for the significant difference between the urban and rural cooperatives. It could also help to explain why approximately half of the Schulze-Delitzsch were unlimited liability, and a few rural cooperatives had limited liability.

The simulations also reveal that raising α reduces reliance on liability and increases the amount borrowed from within the cooperative. The historical experience is consistent with this prediction about α. Some observers argued that differences between urban and rural environments fully explained the differences between the design of Schulze-Delitzsch and Raiffeisen cooperatives. The Raiffeisen organization reported in 1913 that 80 percent of their credit cooperatives were located in towns of 3000 or fewer persons [Winkler 1933, p. 65]. Urban credit cooperatives tended to be much larger than their rural counterparts. In 1908 the average urban German credit cooperative had 469 members; the average rural cooperative, 94 members. Several urban credit cooperatives were enormous: Munich had one with 2600 members [Wygodzinski 1911, pp. 80–81]. One would expect monitoring costs to be higher in urban environments and in larger cooperatives; cooperative members were dispersed throughout a town or city and less likely to come into day-to-day contact. In addition, the projects for which they borrowed were not so publicly visible as agricultural investments. The Raiffeisen organization insisted on restricting membership to a small region to maximize the availability of information on members. Lower monitoring costs, as the simulations demonstrate, encourage the use of high liabilities.[9] The size of this effect, however, is rather weak. This is consistent with our intuitive understanding of the model. A change in α changes both the private and the social incentives to monitor, but not necessarily the wedge between the private and the social incentives. It is the latter that determines the choice of instruments.

The simulations show that a low β also implies little use of liability while a large β encourages the cooperative to use liability to increase monitoring. For high enough β, we would expect high liability even with a positive δ. If we were to assume that the agency problem is greater in urban areas, then this could also explain the importance of liability incentives there. In fact, the predominantly urban Schulze-Delitzsch co-ops deliberately discouraged the very poor from joining. Only a relatively small number of borrowers from these limited-liability cooperatives would have so few assets that disappearing with loan capital would be attractive. Moreover, they emphasized short-term loans, making it more difficult to acquire a large loan intended for a long-term project and then either misusing it or absconding with the money. The rural cooperatives, on the other hand, often made small and long-term loans to very poor individuals, people who might well (in the absence of the cooperative's monitoring) have been tempted to disappear with a loan, or to choose an extremely risky project. On the other hand, the same reasons that made the cost of monitoring higher in urban areas might also make β higher there.

The model further predicts that r and b are used to provide incentives only if δ is positive. This proposition is the most difficult to test from available data. We have already referred to the difficulties of signing δ empirically, and published information does not tell us how much of deposits comes from co-op members. The cooperatives had three basic sources of loan capital: loans from outsiders, loans from insiders (that is, member deposits), and the cooperative's own funds. Published accounts lump together all deposits (member and nonmember alike) and distinguish them only from *eigene Mittel*, the cooperative's own funds formed from entrance fees, share capital, and retained earnings. The more urban Schulze-Delitzsch cooperatives relied relatively more on their own funds for loan capital. In 1908, of the liabilities of the 12,000 credit cooperatives in the Haas organization (primarily rural and unlimited-liability), only about 4 percent was *eigene Mittel*. The comparable figure for the 1000 Schulze-Delitzsch cooperatives was 28 percent [Wygodzinski 1911, pp. 139, 164]. Since the *eigene Mittel* belonged to the members, and loans made from this source were in a sense loans from insiders, the information available tends to suggest that more borrowing from inside went with a lower value of δ, contrary to our prediction.[10]

Of the three main propositions suggested by the theory, we conclude that only one, that liability and interest rate incentives would not be used together, is clearly supported by the data. The other two propositions are not rejected by the data, but they are not unreservedly confirmed.

4   Extensions

Here, we consider some further features of credit cooperatives that may be important in explaining their design. Unlimited liability can also be used as a signaling device; it may serve to convince lenders that the cooperative was well run [Buchrucher 1905, p. 15]. There is some plausibility to this argument given that the unlimited liability co-ops in Germany tended to have poorer members who might find it important to signal that they were responsible. However the very fact that these people are poor, and have few assets, also tends to lower the credibility of such a signal.

Another explanation of the importance of unlimited liability is based on some cooperatives being poorer than others. We have assumed so far that every co-op has the same ability to borrow from its members, yet poorer co-ops would find this more difficult, necessitating greater use of liability. This is consonant with the poorer co-ops borrowing more from outside and explains why the poorer Raiffeisen co-ops relied on liability, despite being rural. But for poor members the use of liability is strictly limited by lack of assets. Thus, it would seem that poorer co-ops would have no effective way of providing monitoring incentives, implying a higher failure rate. But rural cooperatives had *lower* failure rates than urban cooperatives. Another potential weakness of our model is the absence of risk aversion. However, if people were highly risk averse, this would deter the poor most of all from participating in unlimited liability co-ops, which appears contrary to the evidence.

One assumption that it would be desirable to relax is that the cooperative maximizes total surplus. This assumption permits us to derive tight implications in this first analysis of credit cooperatives, but should be relaxed in further research. It is most natural where co-op members are identical, since then maximizing the total surplus also maximizes the return to each participant. However, member heterogeneity in both wealth and need for funds was a real feature of cooperatives [Guinnane 1992b]. Differences in borrowing probabilities or in wealth would require substantial alterations in our stylized model to maintain to participation by members.

Raiffeisen-type cooperatives, which emphasized high liability, were problematic for sufficiently heterogeneous populations. One observer noted that in some of the limited liability cooperatives in Pomerania, one member might have shares worth 100 marks, while another had many shares totaling 20,000 marks. If the latter bore all responsibility, as they effectively would in an unlimited-liability structure, then the wealthy would be unlikely to join (quoted in Grabein [1908, p. 13, note 1]). Rural, unlimited-liability cooperatives were in fact relatively uncommon in the Prussian provinces of Saxony and Pomerania, two areas with considerable numbers of very large farms. When the Irish Agricultural Organization Society introduced credit cooperatives into Ireland in 1894, it unfortunately chose to adhere strictly to the Raiffeisen model. Irish credit cooperatives never succeeded, with some observers pointing to the unwillingness of the more prosperous to join an institution in which they would shoulder most of the liability.[11]

VI Concluding Remarks

This chapter constructs a simple model of an optimal credit cooperative. Using the historical German experience, we have examined some implications of the peer monitoring view of credit cooperatives. We find qualified support for this model in the data. However, there are some features of credit cooperatives that we have not addressed in our work and require some further investigation. Of the extensions that we discussed above, introducing heterogeneity in the cooperative's membership is perhaps the most important, along with building detailed models of the long-term interaction view to compare their predictions with the data.

Apart from the specific task of understanding the design of credit cooperatives, our paper also emphasizes the use of comparative static predictions to explore the organization of nonstandard institutions. We argued that it is not enough for our model to be *consistent* with the existence of credit cooperatives. The way in which the organization adapts to different economic environments must also be as theory would predict. This is a stiffer test of both the theory and the data than is most often used. However, it is a challenge that is worth facing in trying to make sense of the reasons behind different organizational forms.

Appendix A

Here we justify some assertions made in the text. First recall that

$$\pi = h(\bar{r}(\pi, \xi), c) \tag{12}$$

from equality in (4) where $\xi \equiv (b, l, r)$. We then write $\pi = g(\xi, c)$. The choice of c satisfies

$$((K - b)r + l)\frac{\partial h}{\partial c}(\xi, c) = M'(c), \tag{13}$$

from which $c = f(\xi, \pi)$. A pair (π, c) constitutes an *equilibrium* if $c = f(\xi, \pi)$ and $\pi = g(\xi, c)$. They will be differentiable functions of ξ in the relevant domain if $\partial f/\partial \pi \times \partial g/\partial c < 1$. To calculate the derivatives of these functions, define

$$\Omega \equiv M'(c)\{E'(\pi) - \bar{r}\}^2 > 0. \tag{14}$$

Then, using (13), we have

$$\frac{\partial f}{\partial b} = \frac{\{(E'(\pi) - \bar{r})r - (l + (K - b)r)(R - r)\}}{\Omega}, \tag{15}$$

$$\frac{\partial f}{\partial l} = \frac{-\{(E'(\pi) - \bar{r}) - (l + (K - b)r)(1 - \pi)/\pi\}}{\Omega} > 0, \tag{16}$$

and

$$\frac{\partial f}{\partial r} = \frac{-(K - b)\{(E'(\pi) - \bar{r}) - (l + (K - b)r)\}}{\Omega}. \tag{17}$$

For the function $g(\cdot)$ we use equality in (4) to derive

$$\frac{\partial g}{\partial c} = \frac{-1}{\{E'(\pi) - \bar{r}\}\{1 - \partial h/\partial \pi\}} > 0, \tag{18}$$

$$\frac{\partial g}{\partial l} = \frac{-(\pi - \underline{\pi})(1 - \pi)}{\pi\{E'(\pi) - \bar{r}\}\{1 - \partial h/\partial \pi\}} > 0, \tag{19}$$

$$\frac{\partial g}{\partial b} = \frac{(\pi - \underline{\pi})(R - r)}{\{E'(\pi) - \bar{r}\}\{1 - \partial h/\partial \pi\}}, \tag{20}$$

and

$$\frac{\partial g}{\partial r} = \frac{(\pi - \underline{\pi})(K - b)}{\{E'(\pi) - \bar{r}\}\{1 - \partial h/\partial \pi\}} < 0. \tag{21}$$

Appendix B

Proof of Proposition 1 Suppose not. Then $E'(\pi)\partial g/\partial c - M'(c) \geq 0$. It is easy to check that this implies that (10) is strictly positive for all l and hence that $l = Rb$. In that case $\partial \bar{r}/\partial \pi = 0$, and $\partial g/\partial c = \partial h/\partial c$. From (6) we thus have $M'(c) = (r(K - b) + \rho b)\partial h/\partial c = \bar{r}\partial h/\partial c > E'(\pi)\partial h/\partial c = E'(\pi)\partial g/\partial c$, which is a contradiction.

Proof of Proposition 2 Observe that (11) can be written as

$$\frac{1}{1 - g_c f_\pi}(E'(\pi)(g_r + g_c f_r) - M'(c)(f_r + g_r f_\pi))$$

$$= \frac{1}{1 - g_c f_\pi}(E'(\pi)g_c - M'(c))\frac{\partial c^*}{\partial r} + E'(\pi)g_r. \tag{22}$$

If this is positive, then since $g_r < 0$ (see 21), we must have $\partial c^*/\partial r < 0$.

Proof of Proposition 3 The key to the proof is showing that $\partial V/\partial r \geq 0$ implies that $\partial V/\partial l < 0$. First note that

$$\frac{\partial V}{\partial l} \bigg/ \frac{\partial g}{\partial l} = \left\{E'(\pi)\frac{\partial g}{\partial c} - M'(c)\right\}\left(\frac{\partial f}{\partial l} \bigg/ \frac{\partial g}{\partial l}\right) + \left\{E'(\pi) - M'(c)\frac{\partial f}{\partial c}\right\} \tag{23}$$

and

$$\frac{\partial V}{\partial r} \bigg/ \frac{\partial g}{\partial r} = \left\{E'(\pi)\frac{\partial g}{\partial c} - M'(c)\right\}\left(\frac{\partial f}{\partial r} \bigg/ \frac{\partial g}{\partial r}\right) + \left\{E'(\pi) - M'(c)\frac{\partial f}{\partial c}\right\}. \tag{24}$$

Now from (17) and (21),

$$\frac{\partial f}{\partial r} \Big/ \frac{\partial g}{\partial r} = \frac{\{(E'(\pi) - \bar{r}) + ((K - b)r + l)\}}{\Omega(\pi - \underline{\pi})(E'(\pi) - \bar{r})(1 - \partial h/\partial \pi)}, \tag{25}$$

and from (15) and (19),

$$\frac{\partial f}{\partial l} \Big/ \frac{\partial g}{\partial l} = \frac{\{(E'(\pi) - \bar{r})[\pi/(1 - \pi)] - ((K - b)r + l)\}}{\Omega(\pi - \underline{\pi})(E'(\pi) - \bar{r})(1 - \partial h/\partial \pi)}. \tag{26}$$

Thus,

$$\frac{\partial f}{\partial l} \Big/ \frac{\partial g}{\partial l} - \frac{\partial f}{\partial r} \Big/ \frac{\partial g}{\partial r} = \frac{1/(1 - \pi)}{\Omega(\pi - \underline{\pi})(E'(\pi) - \bar{r})(1 - \partial h/\partial \pi)} > 0, \tag{27}$$

which, since $E'(\pi)\partial g/\partial c - M'(c) < 0$, implies that

$$\frac{\partial V}{\partial r} \Big/ \frac{\partial g}{\partial r} > \frac{\partial V}{\partial l} \Big/ \frac{\partial g}{\partial l}.$$

But since $\partial g/\partial r < 0$ and $\partial g/\partial l > 0$, then $\partial V/\partial r \geq 0$ implies that $\partial V/\partial l < 0$, as claimed. But r exceeds the opportunity cost of funds only if $\partial V/\partial r \geq 0$. Hence in that case we must have $\partial V/\partial l < 0$, which implies that $l = 0$.

Proof of Proposition 4 Since $R \leq \rho/\pi$ (using (1)), then $\delta < 0$ implies that $r > R$, which implies (from (20)) that $\partial g/\partial b > 0$. Next, observe that

$$\frac{\partial V}{\partial b} \Big/ \frac{\partial g}{\partial b} = \left\{ E'(\pi)\frac{\partial g}{\partial c} - M'(c) \right\} \left(\frac{\partial f}{\partial b} \Big/ \frac{\partial g}{\partial b} \right) + \left\{ E'(\pi) - M'(c)\frac{\partial f}{\partial c} \right\} \left(-\delta \Big/ \frac{\partial g}{\partial b} \right). \tag{28}$$

Now suppose that $l > 0$ and $(K - b) > 0$. Then we must have

$$\frac{\partial V}{\partial b} \Big/ \frac{\partial g}{\partial b} \leq 0 \quad \text{and} \quad \frac{\partial V}{\partial l} \Big/ \frac{\partial g}{\partial l} \geq 0.$$

Note that

$$\frac{\partial f}{\partial b} \Big/ \frac{\partial g}{\partial b} = \frac{\{(E'(\pi) - \bar{r})[r/(R - r)] - ((K - b)r + l)\}}{\Omega(\pi - \underline{\pi})(E'(\pi) - \bar{r})(1 - \partial h/\partial \pi)}. \tag{29}$$

Thus,

$$\frac{\partial f}{\partial b} \Big/ \frac{\partial g}{\partial b} - \frac{\partial f}{\partial l} \Big/ \frac{\partial g}{\partial l} = \frac{\{[\pi/(1 - \pi)] + [r/(r - R)]\}}{\Omega(\pi - \underline{\pi})(1 - \partial h/\partial \pi)} < 0. \tag{30}$$

But then since $E'(\pi)\partial g/\partial c - M'(c) < 0$,

$$\frac{\partial V}{\partial l} \Big/ \frac{\partial g}{\partial l} \leq \frac{\partial V}{\partial b} \Big/ \frac{\partial g}{\partial b},$$

implying that $l = 0$. Recall that an alternative way to write the expression for $\partial V/\partial b$ is

$$\frac{\partial V}{\partial b} = \frac{1}{1 - g_c f_\pi}(E'(\pi)g_c - M'(c))\frac{\partial c^*}{\partial b} + E'(\pi)g_b. \tag{31}$$

Since the last two terms here are positive, if $\partial V/\partial b \leq 0$ (required for an optimum with $b < K$), then $\partial c^*/\partial b > 0$ at the optimum. Let (b^*, r^*) be the values of b and r at the optimum (we have already shown that $l^* = 0$). Note that the configuration $b' = K$, $r = r^*$, and $l = 0$ results in $c = 0$ (there is no incentive to monitor). Yet, at the optimum with $b = b^* < K$, $c > 0$ and $\partial c^*/\partial b > 0$. So keeping l fixed at 0 and r at r^*, if there is an increase in b from b^* to K, then c

must first rise and then fall. Therefore, there must exist a value of b, call it $\hat{b}$, with $\hat{b} > b^*$, such that the configuration $b = \hat{b}$, $l = 0$, $r = r^*$ generates the same value of c as the social optimum. Since $\hat{b} > b^*$, and $g_b > 0$, the resulting value of π will be higher than that at the suggested optimum. Also since $\delta < 0$, this will also reduce the cost of capital to the cooperative. Thus, the original choice of parameters at $(b^*, r^*, l^* = 0)$ could not have been optimal. This proves that $b = K$ at the optimum and r is also, therefore, effectively redundant. But then we must have $l > 0$ at the optimum as claimed.

Appendix C

Here we show that the example yields well-behaved $c(\cdot)$ and $\pi(\cdot)$ functions. For any given value of π, we can determine c from

$$\alpha c = \frac{l + (K - b)r}{(\rho b - l)/\pi + (K - b)r - \beta}. \tag{32}$$

The choice of π is determined from

$$c = (\pi - \underline{\pi})\{(\rho b - l)/\pi + (K - b)r - \beta\}. \tag{33}$$

Thus, we are looking for a fixed point of the map:

$$\pi = \underline{\pi} + \frac{l + (K - b)r}{\alpha\{l + (K - b)r - \beta + (\rho b - l)/\pi\}^2}. \tag{34}$$

Now at $\pi = \underline{\pi}$, the right-hand side of (34) exceeds the left-hand side. Moreover, the right-hand side of (34) is increasing in π. Thus, we have a fixed point provided that

$$1 - \underline{\pi} > \frac{l + (K - b)r}{\alpha\{l + (K - b)r - \beta + (\rho b - l)/\pi\}^2}, \tag{35}$$

which holds if α is large enough. It will be unique if

$$\frac{2[l + (K - b)r](\rho b - l)/\pi}{\alpha\{[l + (K - b)r] - \beta + (\rho b - l)/\pi\}^3} < 1,$$

which also holds for large enough α. Hence, for large enough α, we have a unique fixed point between $\underline{\pi}$ and 1. Thus, π will be a differentiable function of (b, r, l), as required.

Notes

1. That monitoring is an important aspect of cooperatives is succinctly captured in Fagneux [1908]. He refers to the small villages as places "where one's eyes are so attentive to what occurs among the neighbors" [p. 39] (authors' translation).

2. We assume that $\theta > R$ to ensure that the nonborrower's wealth is greater than the maximum amount that he could be required to pay to the outside lender.

3. The penalty is never actually imposed in equilibrium. We assume, however, that it is costly for the nonborrowing member of the co-op to put himself in a position to

penalize if necessary. Costs of imposing penalities may thus partly reflect information gathering, but also the fact that a monitor may have to rearrange his affairs to watch over the borrower at crucial stages of the project. Because there is only one monitor, there is no free-rider problem in monitoring here, which may arise for large co-ops.

4. *Proof.* Note that $\partial h/\partial \pi = \{(\pi-\underline{\pi})\partial \bar{r}/\partial \pi\}/(E'(\pi)-\bar{r}) = \{(\pi-\underline{\pi})/\underline{\pi}\}(Rb-l)/\pi(\bar{r}-R'(\pi))\}$. Since the first term in $\{\cdot\}$ goes to zero as $\underline{\pi} \to 1$ and the second term in $\{\cdot\}$ is bounded, the claim follows.

5. The idea is that either member of the co-op has an equal probability of being the borrowing or nonborrowing member at the time at which the co-op's constitution is being designed.

6. Verein fur Socialpolitik [1887] is a survey of rural credit conditions in most of Germany. Bonus and Schmidt [1990] is one of the few papers discussing the German cooperatives.

7. 20 marks = 1 pound sterling = $4.86 under the gold-standard exchange rates. An unskilled German laborer would earn in the neighborhood of 10–20 marks per week in the first decade of the twentieth century. Cooperatives data are from the Deutsche Bundesbank [1976, DI, Tables 1.07 and 1.08]. Rural population of Germany for 1910 is defined as persons in places with fewer than 2000 people [Marschalk 1984, Tables 1.3 and 5.5]. We do not discuss two related features of German credit cooperatives. Most cooperatives had accounts at regional cooperative banks that aided in smoothing correlated shocks across cooperatives. In addition, some credit cooperatives were closely allied to purchasing and marketing cooperatives. The latter alliances were the subject of controversy.

8. The parameter δ is positive (negative) if the cooperative is a better (worse) place for local savers to keep their funds.

9. Some agriculturalists belonged to Schulze-Delitzsch cooperatives, and some town-dwellers belonged to Raiffeisen-style cooperatives, but Schulze-Delitzsch cooperatives were much more likely to be located in large population centers. The membership of the Schulze-Delitzsch cooperatives in 1912 included 28 percent farmers or farm laborers [Great Britain 1914, p. 311]. The greater occupational heterogeneity in a Schulze-Delitzsch cooperative would also imply a larger α, since it would be more difficult for urban workers to screen and monitor agricultural projects and vice versa.

10. A long article in *Blätter für Genossenschaftswesen* 1904 (50), the organ of the Schulze-Delitzsch group, criticizes reliance on deposits in the Raiffeisen organization.

11. One of the few successful Irish credit cooperatives in the early twentieth century had limited liability. See Guinnane [1994].

References

Besley, Timothy, "Savings, Credit and Insurance," Jere Behrman and T. N. Srinivasan, eds. *Handbook of Development Economics Volume III* (Amsterdam: North-Holland, 1993).

Besley, Timothy, and Stephen Coate, "Group Lending, Repayment Incentives and Social Collateral," Working paper, 1992, *Journal of Development Economics*, forthcoming, 1994.

168   Abhijit V. Banerjee, Timothy Besley, and Timothy W. Guinnane

Besley, Timothy, Stephen Coate, and Glenn Loury, "The Economics of Rotating Savings and Credit Associations," *American Economic Review*, LXXXIII (1993), 792–810.

Bonus, Holger, and Georg Schmidt, 1990, "The Cooperative Banking Group in the Federal Republic of Germany: Aspects of Institutional Change," *Journal of Institutional and Theoretical Economics*, CXLVI (1990), 180–207.

Braverman, Avi, and Joseph E. Stiglitz, "Sharecropping and the Interlinking of Agrarian Markets," *American Economic Review*, LXXII (1982), 695–715.

Buchrucher, Albert, *Unbeschränkte oder beschränkte Haftpflicht: Welche Art der Rechts form ist für ländliche Kreditgenossenchaften die geeignetste?* (Neuwied: Raiffeisen-Druckerei, 1905).

Deutsche Bundesbank, *Deutsches Geld- und Bankwesen in Zahlen 1876–1975*, (Frankfurt: Fritz Knapp, 1976).

Eswaran, Mushek, and Ashok Kotwal, "A Theory of Contractual Structure in Agriculture," *American Economic Review*, LXXV (1985), 352–67.

Fagneux, Louis, *La Caisse de Crédit Raiffeisen: Le Raiffeisenism en France et à l'Etranger...*, Paris, 1908.

Grabein, Max, *Wirtschaftliche und soziale Bedeutung der ländlichen Genossenschaften in Deutschland.* (Tübingen: H. Laupp, 1913).

Great Britain, "Report of the Departmental Committee on Agricultural Credit in Ireland," *House of Commons Sessional Papers*, Vol. 13 (1914).

Guinnane, Timothy W., "Financial Intermediation for Poor People: The Case of German Credit Cooperatives, 1850–1914," Working paper, Department of Economics, Princeton University, 1992a.

———, "What Do Cooperatives Really Do? Evidence from Micro-Studies of Nineteenth Century German Credit Cooperatives," Working paper, Department of Economics, Princeton University, 1992b.

———, "A Failed Institutional Transplant: Raiffeisen's Credit Cooperatives in Ireland, 1894–1914." *Explorations in Economic History* (1994), 38–61.

Marschalk, Peter, *Bevölkerungsgeschichte Deutschlands im 19. und 20. Jahrhundert* (Frankfurt; Suhrkanp, 1984).

Raiffeisen, Friedrich W., *Die Darlehnskassen-Vereine als Mittel zur Abhilfe der Noth der ländlichen Bevölkerung*, 7th edition, unaltered reprint of the 5th edition of 1887; (Neuwied: Raiffeisen-Druckerei, 1951 [1887]).

Stiglitz, Joseph E., "Risk Sharing and Incentives in Sharecropping," *Review of Economic Studies*, XLI (1974), 219–56.

———, "Peer Monitoring in Credit Markets," *World Bank Economic Review*, IV (1990), 351–66.

Tirole, Jean, *The Theory of Industrial Organization* (Cambridge, MA: MIT Press, 1988).

United States Senate, *Agricultural Credit and Cooperation in Germany*, U.S. Senate Document Number 17, 63rd Congress, 1st Session, 1913.

Varian, Hal R., "Monitoring Agents with Other Agents," *Journal of Institutional and Theoretical Economics*, CXLVI (1990), 153–74.

Verein für Socialpolitik, *Der Wucher auf dem Land., Schriften des Vereins für Socialpolitik XXXV* (Leipzig: Duncker & Humblot, 1887).

Williamson, Oliver E., *Markets and Hierarchies: Analysis and Antitrust Implications* (New York, NY: The Free Press, 1975).

Winkler, Horst, "Die Landwirtschaftlichen Kreditgenossenschaften und die Grundsätze Raiffeisens," *Jahrbuch für Nationalökonomie und Statistik* (138, Band III; Band 83 Erst Hefte, pp. 59–76, 1933).

Wygodzinski, Willi, *Das Genossenschaftswesen in Deutschland* (Leipzig und Berlin: Teubner, 1911).

7 Industrialization and the Big Push

Kevin M. Murphy,
Andrei Shleifer, and
Robert W. Vishny

I Introduction

Virtually every country that experienced rapid growth of productivity and living standards over the last 200 years has done so by industrializing. Countries that have successfully industrialized—turned to production of manufactures taking advantage of scale economies—are the ones that grew rich, be they eighteenth-century Britain or twentieth-century Korea and Japan. Yet despite the evident gains from industrialization and the success of many countries in achieving it, numerous other countries remain unindustrialized and poor. What is it that allows some but not other countries to industrialize? And can government intervention accelerate the process?

Of the many causes of lack of growth of underdeveloped countries, a particularly important and frequently discussed constraint on industrialization is the small size of the domestic market. When domestic markets are small and world trade is not free and costless, firms may not be able to generate enough sales to make adoption of increasing returns technologies profitable, and hence industrialization is stalled. In this chapter, we present some models of economies with small domestic markets and discuss how these markets can expand so that a country can get out of the no-industrialization trap. In particular, we focus on the contribution of industrialization of one sector to enlarging the size of the market in other sectors. Such spillovers give rise to the possibility that coordination of investments across sectors—which the government can promote—is essential for industrialization. This idea of coordinated investment is the basis of the concept of the "big push," introduced by Rosenstein-Rodan (1943) and discussed by many others.

According to Rosenstein-Rodan, if various sectors of the economy adopted increasing returns technologies simultaneously, they could each create income that becomes a source of demand for goods in other sectors, and so enlarge their markets and make industrialization profitable. In fact, simultaneous industrialization of many sectors can be self-sustaining even if *no* sector could break even industrializing alone. This insight has been developed by Nurkse (1953), Scitovsky (1954), and Fleming (1955) into a doctrine of balanced growth or the big push, with two important elements. First, the same economy must be capable of both the backward preindustrial and the modern industrialized state. No exogenous improvement in endowments or technological opportunities is needed to move to industrialization, only the simultaneous investment by all the sectors using the available technology. Second, industrialization is associated with a better state of affairs. The population of a country benefits from its leap into the industrial state.

In this chapter, we attempt to understand the importance of demand spillovers between sectors by looking at simple stylized models of a less developed economy in which these spillovers are strong enough to generate a big push. In doing so, we chiefly associate the big push with multiple equilibria of the economy and interpret it as a switch from the cottage production equilibrium to industrial equilibrium. The main question we address is, What does it take for such multiple equilibria to exist? In addition, we ask when the equilibrium in which various sectors of the economy "industrialize" is Pareto-preferred to the equilibrium in which they do not. We thus make precise the sense in which industrialization benefits an economy with fixed preferences, endowments, and technological opportunities.

In all the models described in this chapter, the source of multiplicity of equilibria is pecuniary externalities generated by imperfect competition with large fixed costs.[1] Yet such multiplicity is not automatic: in Section III we show that even where pecuniary externalities are important, equilibrium can be unique. The idea behind the uniqueness result is that if a firm contributes to the demand for other firms' goods *only* by distributing its profits and raising aggregate income, then unprofitable investments must *reduce* income and therefore the size of other firms' markets. Starting from the equilibrium in which no firm wants to adopt increasing returns, each investing firm would then lose money and therefore make it even less attractive for other firms to invest. As a result, the second equilibrium with a higher level of industrialization cannot exist. When profits are the only channel of spillovers, the industrialized equilibrium cannot coexist with the unindustrialized one.

In contrast, multiple equilibria arise naturally if an industrializing firm *raises* the size of other firms' markets even when it itself loses money. This occurs when firms raise the profit of other industrial firms through channels other than their own profits. In the models we present, industrialization in one sector can increase spending in other manufacturing sectors by altering the composition of demand. In the model of Section IV, industrialization raises the demand for manufactures because workers are paid higher wages to entice them to work in industrial plants. Hence, even a firm losing money can benefit firms in other sectors because it raises labor income and hence demand for their products.

The model of Section V focuses on the intertemporal aspect of industrialization. In that model, industrialization has the effect of giving up current income for future income because the benefits of current investment in cost reduction are realized over a long period of time. The more sectors industrialize, the higher is the level of future spending. But this means that the profitability of investment depends on there being enough other sectors to industrialize so that high future spending justifies putting down a large-scale plant today. Since an investing firm generates a positive cash flow in the future, it raises the demand for the output in other sectors even if its own investment has a negative net present value. In the models of both Sections IV and V, coordinated investment across sectors leads to the expansion of markets for all industrial goods and can thus be self-sustaining even when no firm can break even investing alone.

The effect of a firm's investment on the size of the markets for output in other sectors is not the only relevant pecuniary externality. An important component of industrialization for which pecuniary externalities can be crucial is investment in jointly used intermediate goods, for example, infrastructure such as railroads and training facilities. To the extent that the cost of an infrastructure is largely fixed, each industrializing firm that uses it helps defray this fixed cost and so brings the building of the infrastructure closer to profitability. In this way, each user indirectly helps other users and hence makes their industrialization more likely. As a result, infrastructure develops only when many sectors industrialize and become its users. In Section VI we associate the big push with the economy making large investments in a shared infrastructure. This approach has the advantage of being important even in a completely open economy.

The emphasis of this chapter on the efficiency of industrialization warrants some explanation. All the deviations from the first-best are ultimately driven by imperfect competition and the resulting divergence of the price of output from marginal cost. But inefficiency manifests itself in two distinct ways. First, at any positive level of industrialization, there is a static monopoly pricing inefficiency in that industrial goods are overpriced relative to cottage-produced goods. Second, given monopoly pricing in industrial sectors, the level of industrialization can be too low from a second-best welfare point of view. In particular, welfare is lower in the nonindustrialized equilibrium than in the fully industrialized equilibrium. In our discussion of government policy, we take monopoly pricing in industrial sectors as given and always focus on second-best policies that bring about a Pareto-preferred, higher level of industrialization. We stress, however, that because all our models are highly stylized and capture what we can only hope to be one aspect of reality, policies suggested by these models should be interpreted with caution.[2]

II   The Importance of Domestic Markets

Except for the example of infrastructure (Sec. VI), our analysis relies crucially on the importance of domestic markets for industrialization. Such analysis runs into an obvious objection. If world trade is free and costless, then an industry faces a world market, the size of which cannot plausibly constrain adoption of increasing returns technologies. Yet despite this theoretical objection, there is now considerable empirical evidence pointing to the importance of the domestic market as an outlet for sales of domestic industry.

The best evidence comes from the work of Chenery and Syrquin (1975) and Chenery, Robinson, and Syrquin (1986). Using a sample of rapidly growing economies over the period from the early 1950s to the early 1970s, Chenery et al. look at a change in domestic industrial output over that period in each country and divide it between a change in domestic demand and a change in exports. Because some outputs are also used as intermediate goods and the structure of production as measured by the input-output matrix is changing, Chenery et al. correct their results for changes in technology. By far the most important sources of growth in output, however, are growth in domestic demand and growth in exports.

The findings of Chenery et al. point to a dominant share of domestic demand in growth of domestic industrial output. In countries with populations over 20 million, expansion of domestic demand accounts for 72–74 percent of the increase in domestic industrial output (1986, p. 156).[3] In such countries, when per capita income is between 200 and 800 1964 U.S. dollars, the share of industry in gross national product is five to six percentage points higher than in countries with populations under 20 million, with the difference concentrated in industries with important economies of scale, such as basic metals, paper, chemicals, and rubber products (Chenery and Syrquin 1975, p. 78). In small primary goods-oriented countries with populations under 20 million, a rise in domestic sales accounts for 70–72 percent of the increase in the domestic industrial output (Chenery et al. 1986, p. 156). Even in small manufacturing-oriented countries with populations under 20 million, expansion of domestic demand accounts for about 50–60 percent of industrial output expansion (p. 156). In Korea—the paragon of an open, export-oriented economy—domestic demand expansion accounted for 53 percent of growth of industrial output between 1955 and 1973 (p. 158) and a much larger fraction if one abstracts from export-intensive sectors such as textiles. Moreover, the intensive export of manufactures began only after the industry became established in the domestic market (Chenery and Syrquin 1975, p. 101). Whether the causes of limited trade are natural, such as transport costs or taste differences across countries, or man-made, such as tariffs, the bottom line is the overwhelming importance of domestic demand for most of domestic industry.

III   A Simple Aggregate Demand Spillovers Model with a Unique Equilibrium

The existence of multiple, Pareto-ranked equilibria of the type envisioned in the big push literature requires that the economy be capable of sustaining two alternative levels of industrialization. This means that industrialization must be individually unprofitable at a low aggregate level of industrialization but individually profitable as long as a sufficient number of other sectors industrialize. Put another way, even individually unprofitable industrialization must have spillover effects on other sectors that make industrialization in other sectors more profitable.

In this section, we discuss a simple model in which profit spillovers across sectors are present, but they are still not sufficient to generate the conditions for the big push. The firm in this model has a positive spillover on the demands (profits) of other sectors if and only if it makes a positive profit itself. Hence, even though the firm does not internalize the effect of its dividends on the profits in other sectors, it still makes a (second-best) efficient investment decision and has a positive spillover on other firms only to the extent that its own industrialization decision is individually profitable. We start with this model in order to illustrate the fact that the conditions for individually unprofitable investments to raise the profitability of investment in other sectors are more stringent than those loosely expressed in much of the big push literature of the 1940s and 1950s (see, e.g., Rosenstein-Rodan 1943).

Consider a one-period economy with a representative consumer, with Cobb-Douglas utility function $\int_0^1 \ln x(q)\, dq$ defined over a unit interval of goods indexed by q.[4] All goods have the same expenditure shares. Thus when his income is y, the consumer can be thought of as spending y on every good $x(q)$. The consumer is endowed with L units of labor, which he supplies inelastically, and he owns all the profits of this economy. If his wage is taken as numeraire, his budget constraint is given by

$$y = \Pi + L, \tag{1}$$

where Π is aggregate profits.

Each good is produced in its own sector, and each sector consists of two types of firms. First, each sector has a competitive fringe of firms that convert one unit of labor input into one unit of output with a constant returns to scale (cottage production) technology. Second, each sector has a unique firm with access to an increasing returns (mass production) technology. This firm is alone in having access to that technology in its sector and hence will be referred to as a monopolist (even though, as we specify below, it does not always operate). Industrialization requires the input of F units of labor and allows each additional unit of labor to produce $\alpha > 1$ units of output.

The monopolist in each sector decides whether to industrialize or to abstain from production altogether. We assume that the monopolist maximizes his profit taking the demand curve as given.[5] He industrializes ("invests") only if he can earn a profit at the price he charges. That price equals one since the monopolist loses all his sales to the fringe if he charges more, and he would not want to charge less when facing a unit elastic demand curve. When income is y, the profit of a monopolist who spends F to industrialize is

$$\pi = \frac{\alpha - 1}{\alpha} y - F \equiv ay - F, \tag{2}$$

where a is the difference between price and marginal cost, or markup.

When a fraction n of the sectors in the economy industrialize, aggregate profits are

$$\Pi(n) = n(ay - F). \tag{3}$$

Substituting (3) into (1) yields aggregate income as a function of the fraction of sectors industrializing:

$$y(n) = \frac{L - nF}{1 - na}. \tag{4}$$

The numerator of (4) is the amount of labor used in the economy for actual production of output, after investment outlays. One over the denominator is the multiplier showing that an increase in effective labor raises income by more than one for one since expansion of low-cost sectors also raises profits. To see this more explicitly, note that

$$\frac{dy(n)}{dn} = \frac{\pi(n)}{1 - an}, \tag{5}$$

where $\pi(n)$ is the profit of the last firm to invest. When the last firm earns this profit, it distributes it to shareholders, who in turn spend it on all goods and thus raise profits in all industrial firms in the economy. The effect of this firm's profit is therefore enhanced by the increases in profits of all industrial firms resulting from increased spending. Since there are a fraction n of such firms, the multiplier is increasing in the number of firms that benefit from the spillover of the marginal firm. The more firms invest, the greater is the cumulative increase in profits and therefore income resulting from a positive net present value investment by the last firm.

For an alternative interpretation of (5), notice that since the price of labor is unity, the profit of the last firm, $\pi(n)$, is exactly equal to the net labor saved from its investment in cost reduction. The numerator of (5) is therefore the increase in labor available to the economy as a result of the investment by the last firm. In equilibrium, this freed-up labor moves into all sectors. However, its marginal product is higher in industrialized sectors than in nonindustrialized sectors. The more sectors industrialize (i.e., the higher is n), the greater is the increase in total output resulting from the inflow of freed-up labor into these sectors. In fact, the denominator of (5) is just the average of marginal labor costs across sectors, which is clearly a decreasing function of n. This interpretation connects (5) to (4), which explicitly states that income is a multiple of productive labor and that the multiplier is increasing in n.

Despite the fact that the firm ignores the profit spillover from its investment, it is easy to see that there is a unique Nash equilibrium in which either all firms industrialize or none of them do (i.e., there is no big push). In order for there to be a no-industrialization equilibrium, it must be the case that when aggregate income is equal to L, a single firm loses money from industrializing. But if no firm can break even from investing when income is L, then there cannot be an equilibrium in which any firms invest. For suppose that a single firm decides to invest. Since it loses money, it only reduces aggregate income, making the profit from industrialization in any other sectors even lower. Hence if it is unprofitable for a single firm to invest, it is even less profitable for more firms to do so, making the existence of the second equilibrium impossible. As is clear from (5), a firm's spillover is positive if and only if its own profits are positive. The multiplier changes only the magnitude of the effect of a firm's investment on income, and not the sign.

The remainder of the paper presents three modifications of this model in which a firm engaging in unprofitable investment can still benefit other sectors and make it more likely that they will find it profitable to invest. By doing so, we get away from the uniqueness result of this section and generate a big push.

IV   A Model with a Factory Wage Premium

The first model of the big push we present comes closest in its spirit to Rosenstein-Rodan's (1943) paper. According to this theory, to bring farm laborers to work in a factory, a firm has to pay them a wage premium. But unless the firm can generate enough sales to people other than its own workers, it will not be able to afford to pay higher wages. If this firm is the only one to start production, its sales might be too low for it to break even. In contrast, if firms producing different products all invest and expand production together, they can all sell their output to each other's workers and so can afford to pay a wage premium and still break even. In this section, we construct a model along these lines.[6]

We assume that higher wages are paid in the factory to compensate workers for disutility of such work. Accordingly, we take utility to be $\exp[\int_0^1 \ln x(q)\,dq]$ if a person is employed in cottage production and $\exp[\int_0^1 \ln x(q)\,dq] - v$ if he or she is employed in a factory using increasing returns. Although factory workers earn higher wages, they have the same unit elastic demand curves for manufactures as cottage production workers, and so we can calculate demands based on the aggregate income, y.[7] Specifically, when the total profit and labor income is y, we can think of it as expenditure y on each good. Workers engage in either constant returns to scale (CRS) cottage production of manufactures or in factory work in which increasing returns to scale (IRS) technologies are used.[8] Cottage production wage is set to one as numeraire, and total labor supply is fixed at L.

As before, the cottage technology for each good yields one unit of output for each unit of labor input. Cottage producers who use this technology are competitive. In contrast, the IRS technology requires a fixed cost of F units of labor to set up a factory but then yields $\alpha > 1$ units of output for one unit of labor input. We assume that access to the IRS technology is restricted to a separate monopolist in each sector.

The monopolist will choose to operate his technology only if he expects to make a profit taking the demand curve as given. If he does operate, he could not raise his price above one without losing the business to the fringe. But he also would not want to cut the price since demand is unit elastic.

Since all prices are always kept at unity, it is easy to calculate the competitive factory wage, w. Each monopolist must pay a wage that makes a worker indifferent between factory and cottage production employment:

$$w = 1 + v > 1. \tag{6}$$

In this pure compensating differentials model, factory employees get the minimum wage necessary to get them out of cottage production and hence get no surplus from industrialization except as profit owners.

When aggregate income is y, the monopolist's profit is given by

$$\pi = y\left(1 - \frac{1+v}{\alpha}\right) - F(1+v), \tag{7}$$

where 1 is the price he gets and $(1+v)/\alpha$ is his unit variable cost. The monopolist will incur $F(1+v)$ only if he expects income to be high enough for this investment to make money.

As is clear from (7), for this model to be at all interesting, the productivity gain from using the IRS technology must exceed the compensating differential that must be paid to a worker, that is,

$$\alpha - 1 > v. \tag{8}$$

If this condition does not hold, the factory will not be able to afford any labor even if it surrenders to it all the efficiency gain over the cottage technology. As a result, the factory could not possibly break even, whatever the level of income.

Under the conditions discussed below, this model can have two equilibria, one with and one without industrialization. In the first equilibrium, no firm incurs the fixed cost for fear of not being able to break even, and the population stays in cottage production. Income is equal to L, the wage bill of the cottage labor, since no profits are earned. For this to be an equilibrium, it must be the cast that in no sector would a monopolist want to set up a factory if he has to pay the required factory wage. That is, for no industrialization to take place, we must have

$$L\left(1 - \frac{1+v}{\alpha}\right) - F(1+v) < 0. \tag{9}$$

In a second equilibrium, all sectors industrialize. By symmetry, the quantity of output produced in each sector is $\alpha(L-F)$, which at unit prices is also the value of output. Since the only input is labor, total factor payments are wages, which are equal to $L(1+v)$. For this to be an equilibrium, profits must be positive:

$$\pi = \alpha(L-F) - L(1+v) > 0. \tag{10}$$

When (10) holds, all firms expect a high level of income and sales resulting from simultaneous labor-saving industrialization of many sectors and are consequently happy to incur the fixed cost $F(1+v)$ to set up a factory. This of course makes the expectation of industrialization self-fulfilling.

An examination of (9) and (10) suggests that there always exist some values of F for which both equilibria exist, provided (8) holds. For these values of F, the economy is capable of a big push, whereby it moves from the unindustrialized equilibrium to one with industrialization when all its sectors coordinate investments. The reason for the multiplicity of equilibria is that a link between a firm's profit and its contribution to demand for products of other sectors is now broken. Because a firm that sets up a factory pays a wage premium, it increases the size of the market for producers of other manufactures, even if its investment loses money. Consequently, the firm's profit in this model is not an adequate measure of its contribution to the aggregate demand for manufactures since a second component of this contribution—the extra wages it pays—is not captured by the profits.

In this model, the Pareto superiority of the equilibrium with industrialization is apparent. Since prices do not change, workers are equally well off as wage earners in the second equilibrium, but they also get some profits. They have higher income at the same prices and hence must be better off. Firms making investment decisions in the no-industrialization equilibrium ignore the fact that, even when they lose money, the higher factory wages they pay generate profits in other industrializing sectors by increasing the demand for manufactures. As a result, these firms underinvest in the no-industrialization equilibrium, and an inefficiency results. As is commonly supposed in the discussion of industrialization, it indeed creates wealth and represents a better outcome.

The big push resulting from higher factory wages could also be obtained using a different but related model of industrialization. Instead of focusing on a compensating differential, we could assume that cottage production is located on the farm and factories are located in the cities, and that city dwellers' demand is more concentrated on manufactures. For example, living in a city might require consumption of processed food if fresh food is expensive to transport from the farm. Urbanization also leads to increased consumption of other manufactures, such as textiles, leather goods, and furniture (Reynolds 1983). If these changes in demand are important, then urbanization in the process of industrialization leads to an increase in the demand for manufactures. In this way industrialization can be self-sustaining even if there is no compensating wage differential for factory work, but only a shift in the consumption bundle toward manufactures.

V A Dynamic Model of Investment

This section presents a second example in which an investment that loses money nonetheless raises aggregate income. A firm that uses resources to invest at one point in time, but generates the labor savings from this investment at a later point, decreases aggregate demand today and raises it tomorrow. This shift in the composition of demand away from today's goods and toward tomorrow's goods can also give rise to multiple equilibria and inefficient underinvestment, unless the government coordinates investment or entrepreneurs are spontaneously "bullish."

One historical account (Sawyer [1954]; quoted in Cole [1959]) motivates this model in the context of nineteenth-century American economic growth. According to Sawyer, even when a cold economic calculation dictated otherwise, irrationally bullish and overoptimistic American entrepreneurs insisted on investing. But with enough people making this mistake, optimistic projections became self-fulfilling (cf. Keynes's [1936] account of entrepreneurial optimism):

To the extent that it worked in an economic sense—that an over-anticipation of prospects in fact paid off in either a private or social balance sheet, we find ourselves on the perilous edge of an "economics of euphoria"—a dizzy world in which if enough people make parallel errors of over-estimation, and their resulting investment decisions fall in reasonable approximation to the course of growth, they may collectively generate the conditions of realizing their original vision. It suggests, historically, a sort of self-fulfilling prophecy, in which the generalized belief in growth operated to shift the marginal efficiency of capital schedule to the right, and in which the multiple centers of initiative, acting in terms of exaggerated prospects of growth, pulled capital and labor from home and from the available reservoirs abroad, and so acted as to create the conditions on which their initial decisions were predicated. [Sawyer 1954, pt. C, p. 3]

Our model shows that Sawyer's ideas about self-fulfilling expectations of growth do not really rely on assuming entrepreneurial irrationality.

A two-period model suffices to illustrate the big push in a dynamic context. Consider a representative consumer with preferences defined over the same unit interval of goods in both the first and the second periods. If we denote by $x_1(q)$ and $x_2(q)$, with q between zero and one, his consumption of good q in periods 1 and 2, respectively, the consumer's utility is given by

$$U = \left[\int_0^1 x_1^\gamma(q)\,dq\right]^{\theta/\gamma} + \beta\left[\int_0^1 x_2^\gamma(q)\,dq\right]^{\theta/\gamma} \tag{11}$$

In this expression, $1/(1 - \theta)$ is the intertemporal elasticity of substitution, and $1/(1 - \gamma)$ is the elasticity of substitution between different goods within a period. For example, in the special case in which $\gamma = 0$ and $\theta = 1$, to which we return below, the consumer has unit elastic demand for each good q and is indifferent about when to consume his income. The representative consumer is endowed with L units of labor each period that he supplies inelastically, and he owns all the profits. Without loss of generality, each period's wage is set equal to one.

Each good q in the first period must be produced using a CRS technology converting one unit of labor into one unit of output. The same technology is also available in the second period. The CRS technology is used by a competitive fringe of firms. In addition to this CRS technology, each sector q has a potential monopolist who can invest F units of labor in the *first* period and then produce $\alpha > 1$ units of output per unit of labor in the *second* period. Each monopolist in this model thus has an intertemporal investment decision since the benefits of the IRS technology obtain only with a lag. His decision whether or not to invest depends both on the equilibrium interest rate and on income in period 2.

To analyze the decision of a monopolist in a representative sector, denote his profits by π, equilibrium discount factor by β^*,[9] and periods 1 and 2 aggregate incomes by y_1 and y_2, respectively. As before, the price the monopolist can charge in the second period if he invests is bounded above by one, the price of the competitive fringe. We assume that

$$\alpha < \frac{1}{\gamma}. \tag{12}$$

The demand curve in each sector is sufficiently inelastic that the monopolist does not want to cut the price below one. If we denote by $a = 1 - (1/\alpha)$ the marginal profit rate of the monopolist per dollar of sales, his profits can now be written as

$$\pi = \beta^* a y_2 - F. \tag{13}$$

The monopolist will incur the fixed cost F in the first period whenever the net present value of his profits given by (13) is positive.

For some parameter values, this model has two equilibria. In the first equilibrium, no sector incurs the fixed cost F in period 1, and no industrialization takes place. Income each period is equal to wage income:

$$y_1 = y_2 = L. \tag{14}$$

Furthermore, the equilibrium discount factor at which the consumers are willing to accept the constant expenditure L on consumption in both periods is equal to β. For this to be an equilibrium, it must not pay a monopolist in a representative sector to incur F in the first period if he expects income in the second period to be L and if the discount factor is β. By (13), the monopolist will not invest if

$$\pi = \beta aL - F < 0. \tag{15}$$

When this condition holds, the demand that firms expect to obtain in the second period is too low for them to break even on their investments. Since they do not invest, the realized level of income is indeed low, and the no-industrialization equilibrium is sustained.

An important feature of this model is that, whereas what matters for a firm is the present value of its profits, what matters for its contribution to aggregate demand in the second period is its second-period cash flow. Thus even if an investing firm loses money, it still raises second-period income. Put differently, even an unprofitable investment transfers income from the first to the second period and thereby makes investment for other firms, which sell only in the second period, more attractive, ceteris paribus. Of course, this shift of income across periods resulting from investment is in part offset by an increase in the interest rate. Nonetheless, the income effect is in many cases more important than the interest rate effect, and, as a result, simultaneous investment by many firms can become profitable even when each loses money investing in isolation. This gives rise to a second equilibrium, in which the economy makes the "big push."

In this equilibrium with industrialization, each sector incurs the fixed cost F in the first period, and as a result the first-period income is

$$y_1 = L - F. \tag{16}$$

The second-period income is higher because of higher profits:

$$y_2 = L + \pi = L + ay_2 = \alpha L. \tag{17}$$

One way to think about these equations for income is that, in the first period, there are no markups charged, and hence the multiplier is one, while in the second period the multiplier is α because each sector marks up the price over cost.

For the consumer to accept a higher level of consumption in period 2 than in period 1, the discount factor in this equilibrium must be

$$\beta^* = \beta\left(\frac{\alpha L}{L - F}\right)^{\theta-1} \tag{18}$$

The interest rate rises in equilibrium to prevent the consumer from wanting to smooth his consumption. The higher θ is, the less averse the consumer is to intertemporal substitution, and hence the lower is the interest rate needed to equilibrate the loan market at zero. In the limiting case in which $\theta = 1$ and the consumer is perfectly happy to substitute consumption across time, the equilibrium discount rate is simply his rate of time preference β.

For the proposed allocation to be an equilibrium, it must pay the firm expecting income y_2 from (17) and faced with a discount rate from (18) to invest in the first period. This will be the case provided

$$(a\alpha L)\beta\left(\frac{\alpha L}{L - F}\right)^{\theta-1} - F > 0. \tag{19}$$

When condition (19) holds, the interest rate does not rise too much when consumption is growing. As a result, there exists an equilibrium in which firms expect other firms to invest and income to rise, and all firms in fact invest in anticipation of profiting from the higher income. Our interpretation of the possibility of the big push is the coexistence of both equilibria for the same parameter values. In that case, firms invest if they expect other firms to do the same and income to grow, and they do not invest if they expect the economy to remain stationary.

The key to the coexistence of the two equilibria is the fact that a firm's profits are not an adequate measure of its contribution to demand for manufactures. An investing firm, even if it loses money, reduces period 1 income and raises period 2 income. Aside from the effect of this investment on the rate of interest, the main consequence of this action by the firm is to reduce the demand for manufactures in the first period—which is irrelevant for investment—and to raise the demand for manufactures of other firms in the second period— which is key to their investment decisions. As a result, the investment by a firm makes investment by other firms more attractive. All that is needed for this to be the case is that the second-period cash flow of the firm be positive. Then the whole cash flow contributes to the second-period demand for manufactures and raises the profitability of investment of all other firms in the economy (as long as the interest rate does not rise too much). The result of the investment, then, is to shift the composition of demand across periods in a way that makes the investment by other firms more attractive. This shift of income makes the big push possible, even if the net present value of a firm investing alone in the economy is negative. As before, the possibility of the big push turns on the divergence between the firm's profits and its contribution to the demand for manufactures of other investing firms.

In this model, the equilibrium with industrialization is Pareto-preferred to that without industrialization. This can be most easily seen from the fact that spot prices of manufacturing goods are the same in the two equilibria in both periods, but that the present value of income is higher in the second equilibrium even though the interest rate has risen. The reason for the Pareto ranking has to do with the difference in multipliers across the two periods. An investing firm uses up labor in the first period, when the contribution of labor to income is exactly equal to its wage. The same firm saves labor in the second period, which goes on to generate *both* wages and profits in other sectors. Hence the firm undervalues the labor it saves in the second period when making its investment decision. This is equivalent to saying that a dollar of a firm's positive cash flow in the second period generates more than a dollar in income since the dividends the firm pays become a source of demand and hence of profits in other sectors. In contrast, a dollar of negative cash flow in the first period reduces income by only a dollar. Both the labor market version of the story and the demand generation version explain why a dollar of the firm's profit in the second period raises income by $\$\alpha$, that is, has a multiplier associated with it. Because the firm ignores this multiplier in making its investment decision, it will in general underinvest in the no-industrialization equilibrium. The variation of multipliers across periods thus explains the Pareto ranking of the two equilibria.

We stress that the reasons for multiplicity of equilibria and for their Pareto ranking are not the same. To see this, suppose that the first-period technologies are also used by monopolists in the various sectors, who mark up the price over cost but get imitated by the competitive fringe in the second period. As before, monopolists can also further reduce costs and stay ahead of competition in the second period if they invest F in the first period. If the markup in the first period is larger, the multiplier in the first period will be larger than the multiplier in the second period, even if monopolists invest to cut second-period costs below the competitive price. In this case, we might still have two equilibria. In the first, firms do not invest because they expect too few others to invest and raise second-period income. In the second equilibrium, firms invest and shift income from period 1 to period 2 and thus create high enough period 2 cash flows for other firms to justify their investments. In this case, however, the high investment equilibrium might be less efficient since firms are using up labor to build plants in the first period, when markups elsewhere in the economy are high, and saving labor in the second period, when the wage is closer to its contribution to income.[10] The point is that multiplicity is affected by gross cash flows in the two periods, whereas the relative efficiency of equilibria is determined by the difference in the multipliers.

At least at the initial stages of industrialization, it is plausible to think of the economy as moving from the use of competitive CRS backstop technologies to the use of less competitive IRS technologies. In this case, our model yields both a positive and a normative result concerning the big push. First, the big push indeed might take the form of simultaneous industrialization of many sectors, each generating future income that helps the profitability of other sectors. The mutual reinforcement of sectors is thus a key property of this big push. Second, the big push, or simultaneous industrialization, is good in this economy because it uses up labor when it is least productive (i.e., when it is stuck in backstop) and frees up labor when it is most productive (i.e., when industrialization has occurred).

The inefficiency of unindustrialized equilibrium raises the possibility of a government role either in encouraging agents to invest or, alternatively, in discouraging current consumption. In our model, persuasion and encouragement of investment alone might be an effective enough tool since these steps might coordinate agents' plans on a better equilibrium. Alternatively, the government can use investment subsidies as long as they are widely enough spread to bring about a critical mass of investment needed to sustain a big push.[11]

VI A Model of Investment in Infrastructure

For a large infrastructure project, such as a railroad, the size of the market can be particularly important since most of the costs are fixed.

As a result, the building of a railroad often depends on the demand from potential users. These users, in turn, can access much larger markets if they can cheaply transport their goods using a railroad. It is not surprising in this context that infrastructure in general and railroads in particular have been commonly credited with being an important component of the big push (Rostow 1960; Rosenstein-Rodan 1961), although there is some debate on whether they have been absolutely pivotal (Fogel 1964; Fishlow 1965).

In our context, building a railroad is especially important because it interacts so closely with industrialization. In particular, since many sectors share in paying for the railroad and the railroad brings down effective production costs, an industrializing sector essentially has the effect of reducing the total production costs of the other sectors. These external effects of an investment are not captured by the firm making it, and hence we again have room for multiple equilibria. The railroad might not get built and industrialization might not take place unless there are enough potential industrial customers.

There are two separate reasons why a railroad might not get built even when it is socially efficient to build it. First, if a railroad is unable to price-discriminate between its users, it can extract only part of the social surplus that it generates. This reflects just the usual reason why a monopolist underinvests in a new technology. If the railroad could extract from each firm all the profits obtained through the use of its services, this inefficiency would not result. In addition, a railroad might not get built if, once it is built, there still remains extrinsic uncertainty about whether the economy industrializes. As in the model of the previous section, if it pays a sector to build a factory only when other sectors do the same even after the railroad is built, then there is always a chance of the bad equilibrium with no industrialization. If the railroad builder is sufficiently averse to this outcome, in which he gets no customers, the railroad will not be built.

We illustrate these results using a modified version of the intertemporal investment model from the previous section. First, we use the same utility function (11) as before, but since we do not care about the interest rate effects, we assume that $\theta = 1$ and $\gamma = 0$. The representative consumer is indifferent about when he consumes his income and spends equal shares of his income in each period on all goods. We also assume that the consumers' time discount factor β is equal to one, so that the equilibrium interest rate is always zero.

It is natural to suppose that the CRS cottage technologies can be set up in all locations and hence do not require the use of a railroad. In contrast, IRS technologies are operated in only one location, and hence each unit of output produced with these technologies must be transported to get sold. We assume that industrialization cannot take place in the absence of the railroad. We also assume for simplicity that the transportation input is the same for all units manufactured using IRS.

In addition, we assume that there are now two types of IRS technologies. A fraction n of sectors (1-firms) requires the fixed cost F_1 to be incurred in the first period to build a factory, whereas the fraction $1 - n$ (2-firms) requires the fixed cost $F_2 > F_1$. In the second period, all fixed-cost firms have labor productivity α. We introduce the two types of sectors in order to address the case in which the railroad fails to extract all the surplus it generates. We also assume that it takes a fixed cost of R units of labor in the first period to build the railroad and that the marginal cost of using it is zero. The latter assumption is used only for simplicity.

To address the question of surplus extraction by the railroad, we note that if the railroad does not observe the fixed cost of each firm, all firms look the same in the first period. As a result, the railroad cannot price-discriminate between them. A further issue is that to the extent that costs F_i are sunk in the first period, a railroad that extracts all the period 2 cash flows from the investing firms will make all their investments money-losing. Accordingly, we assume that the railroad can commit itself to a price it will charge in the second period before the potential industrial firms make their investments.

Throughout this section we also assume that there is no way that low-fixed-cost firms, even if they could profitably industrialize alone, would generate enough surplus to pay for the railroad; both types must industrialize to pay for it. This assumption amounts to

$$n\left(\frac{aL}{1 - an} - F_1\right) < R, \tag{20}$$

which is essentially an upper bound on the profits 1-firms can generate. Note that (20) is also an efficiency condition for 1-firms industrializing alone since we are assuming that the railroad extracts all the surplus.

Under our assumptions, the price the railroad charges enables it to extract all the profits from high- but not low-fixed-cost firms. This seems to us to be the easiest way to model the realistic notion that the railroad owners do not capture all the social benefits of the investment.

A necessary and sufficient condition for there to exist an equilibrium in which a railroad is built and all sectors industrialize is

$$a\alpha L - F_2 > R. \tag{21}$$

Condition (21) implies that the railroad can cover its costs when it charges each firm the amount equal to the profit of a 2-firm. Since the railroad cannot price-discriminate, each high-fixed-cost firm will then earn a zero profit, and each low-fixed-cost firm will earn a profit of $F_2 - F_1$. Condition (21) also implies that the high-fixed-cost firms can break even since period 2 income is αL. It is easy to see, then, that (21) guarantees both that all firms are prepared to invest when the railroad is built and other firms invest, and that the railroad can be paid for by tariffs charged to investing firms.

In some circumstances, building of the railroad and industrialization of all sectors will not take place even if this outcome is efficient. Building the railroad is efficient whenever the surplus from industrialization is positive, which happens if

$$a\alpha L - nF_1 - (1 - n)F_2 > R. \tag{22}$$

Since (22) is less stringent than (21), the railroad sometimes is not built even when it is efficient. This happens precisely because the railroad can charge each firm only the amount equal to the profits of 2-firms, which are smaller than the profits of 1-firms. At the same time, it would be efficient to build the railroad if it can break even extracting both the surplus of 1-firms and that of 2-firms. The impossibility of price discrimination gives rise to the outcome in which the railroad is not built and industrialization does not take place even when efficiency dictates otherwise.

This is a very simple reason for a failure of an efficient industrialization. When (22) holds but (21) fails, the market for railroad services is too small in the sense that some users do not end up paying as much as the services are worth to them, even if all firms would industrialize with a railroad. If the railroad could price-discriminate better, the efficient outcome would be achieved and there would be a large increase in income due to the large amount of producer and consumer surplus created by the railroad. As it is, there is a unique equilibrium in which the railroad is not built because it is privately unprofitable, even though it is socially very desirable.

The discussion thus far leaves open the question whether (21) suffices for the railroad to be built. In other words, will the railroad be built for sure if once it is built industrialization is a feasible equilibrium? The answer of course is no since industrialization need not be the only equilibrium that can occur once the railroad is built. What would keep the railroad from being built is the extrinsic uncertainty over whether or not the potential users of the railroad do in fact make their fixed-cost investments and thus become actual users. This uncertainty thus concerns the selection of equilibrium between sectors. If the railroad must be built without a prior knowledge of the actions of manufacturing sectors, its organizers might refuse to accept the uncertainty about the future demand, in which case the railroad is not built and industrialization does not occur.

For both equilibria to exist after the railroad is built, it suffices to look at parameter values for which (21) holds, and it also does not pay a 1-firm to invest when expected income is L, that is,

$$aL - F_1 < 0. \tag{23}$$

For these parameter values, the railroad will make money on its first-period investment if the economy industrializes but will incur a large loss if no industrialization takes place and there are no consumers of its services. The investment R might then not be made because the proprietors of the railroad are averse to the possibility that the bad equilibrium obtains. We then have a standoff in which the railroad is not built for fear that an insufficient number of sectors will industrialize, and this in turn ensures that firms do not make the large-scale investments needed to industrialize.

This discussion reveals two ways in which investment by a sector benefits other sectors in a way that is not captured by profits. First, just as in the previous section, an investing firm raises the demand in the second period and hence helps other firms make money. Second, by using railroad services, an investing firm helps pay for the fixed cost of the railroad. The railroad, in turn, reduces the production costs of other sectors. Indirectly, then, an investing firm contributes to the reduction of total costs of the other industrializing sectors. These effects give rise to the possibility that a firm actually benefits other firms even if it loses money, and so to big push type results.

Furthermore, for reasons identical to those in the previous section, the equilibrium with industrialization is Pareto-preferred.

The failures of an efficient railroad to be built suggest some clear functions for the government in this model. Subsidizing the railroad might be helpful but not sufficient. What is also needed is a coordination of investments by enough private users of the railroad to get to the equilibrium with industrialization. Without industrialization by such users, the railroad can become a classic "white elephant" project that is not needed when it is built. This problem can of course be ameliorated if railroad users are sufficiently optimistic that they are eager to invest: this might be the description of America's nineteenth-century experience. The problem can also be solved if one large sector of the economy demands enough railroad services to cover the fixed cost: Colombia's coffee boom in the 1880s is a case in point. In the absence of such favorable circumstances, however, government intervention in support of the railroad might be essential.

The railroad is one of a number of examples of infrastructure projects that require substantial demand by industry (or by other customers) to break even and that might need public subsidies if built ahead of demand. Other examples include power stations, roads, airports, and perhaps, most important, training facilities (Rosenstein-Rodan 1961). One reason for underinvestment in such facilities is the inability of firms to prevent workers they train from moving to other firms and so appropriating the returns from training. A second important reason why a country with little industry will have too few training facilities concerns the ignorance of untrained workers about what they are good at. Some education is necessary to discover one's comparative advantage. A worker will invest in such education only if a broad range of different industries offer employment, so that he can take advantage of his skills. But a broad range of industries is less likely to develop in the first place if the labor force is uneducated.

In the context of market size models, infrastructure can be a particularly appealing area for state intervention. First, coordination issues are especially important since the infrastructure serves many sectors simultaneously. Second, the projects tend to be large and time-consuming, so that capital market constraints and substantial uncertainty can deter private participation. Third, projects are fairly standard, and hence "local knowledge" (Hayek 1945), which is perhaps the main advantage of private entrepreneurs over government, is not as essential as in other activities. It is not surprising then that most governments support infrastructure, and the most successful ones—such as Korea—coordinate that support with general industrial development.

VII Conclusion

The analysis of this chapter has established some, though by no means all, conditions under which a backward economy can make a big push into industrialization by coordinating investments across sectors. The principal idea is that the big push is possible in economies in which industrialized firms capture in their profits only a fraction of the total contribution of their investment to the profits of other industrializing firms. In our examples, a firm adopting increasing returns must be shifting demand toward manufactured goods, redistributing demand toward the periods in which other firms sell, or paying part of the cost of the essential infrastructure, such as a railroad. In these cases, the firm can help foster a mutually profitable big push even when it would lose money industrializing alone. All our models have the common feature that complementarities between industrializing sectors work through market size effects. In the first two models, industrialization of one sector raises the demand for other manufactures directly and so makes large-scale production in other sectors more attractive. In the railroad model, industrialization in one sector increases the size of the market for railroad services used by other sectors and so renders the provision of these services more viable.

The analysis may also have some implications for the role of government in the development process. First, a program that encourages industrialization in many sectors simultaneously can substantially boost income and welfare even when investment in any one sector appears unprofitable. This is especially true for a country whose access to foreign markets is limited by high transportation costs or trade restrictions. The net payoff from a program of simultaneous industrialization can also be high when all markets are open, but a shared infrastructure—such as a railroad or a stock of managers—is necessary to operate profitably in any given sector. In the latter case, simultaneous development of many export sectors may be necessary to sustain any one of them.

Our analysis also suggests that countries such as South Korea that have implemented a coordinated investment program can achieve industrialization of each sector at a lower explicit cost in terms of temporary tariffs and subsidies than a country that industrializes piecemeal. The reason is that potentially large implicit subsidies flow across sectors under a program of simultaneous industrialization. Any cost-benefit analysis of subsidies or of temporary protection should reflect both the lower direct costs and the higher net benefit of a program that is coordinated across sectors.

Notes

1. The pecuniary externalities analyzed in this paper should be contrasted with technological externalities that can also give rise to interesting growth paths (Romer 1986a; Lucas 1988). Romer and Lucas also look at increasing returns, except in their models increasing returns are external to the firm. Earlier attempts outside the development literature to model pecuniary externalities in the growth context include important work of Young (1928) and Kaldor (1966) and recent work of Romer (1986b) and Shleifer (1986). Also related is some work in macroeconomics, e.g., Hart (1982), Weitzman (1982), and Kiyotaki (1988).

2. Farrell and Saloner (1985) suggest that multiplicity of equilibria is not a problem if one redefines the game to be sequential. We believe that for the problem we address the multiple equilibrium model we present captures the essential aspects of reality.

3. Our own calculations are based on table 6.3 in Chenery et al. (1986).

4. The discussion that follows partly draws on Shleifer and Vishny (1988).

5. The assumption that each monopolist maximizes profits rather than the welfare of his shareholders is what allows pecuniary externalities to matter. Shleifer (1986) justifies this assumption in some detail.

6. Factory employment is usually associated with working in a city. Lewis (1967) and many others confirm the empirical validity of the assumption that higher real wages are paid in cities.

7. All the models we study assume unit elastic demand. Historically, however, price-elastic demand for manufactures has played an important role in growth of industry (Deane 1979). Price-elastic demand leads to price cuts by a monopolist and the increase in consumer surplus, which is an additional reason for a big push.

8. For simplicity, there is no agricultural sector, although one could be added (see Murphy, Shleifer, and Vishny 1989).

9. If r is the equilibrium interest rate, then $\beta^* = 1/(1 + r)$.

10. An example demonstrating this possibility is available from the authors.

11. Policies coordinating private investment across sectors appear in Rosenstein-Rodan's (1943) proposal for the East European Investment Trust. According to that proposal, foreign lenders and donors should insist that the money they lend to the economy be spent on investment and not on consumption. This is entirely consistent with their concern for the welfare of aid recipients as well as with a concern for getting their money back.

References

Chenery, Hollis B.; Robinson, Sherman; and Syrquin, Moshe. *Industrialization and Growth: A Comparative Study*. New York: Oxford Univ. Press (for World Bank), 1986.

Chenery, Hollis B., and Syrquin, Moshe. *Patterns of Development, 1950–1970*. London: Oxford Univ. Press (for World Bank), 1975.

Cole, Arthur H. *Business Enterprise in Its Social Setting*. Cambridge, Mass.: Harvard Univ. Press, 1959.

Deane, Phyllis. *The First Industrial Revolution*. 2d ed. Cambridge: Cambridge Univ. Press, 1979.

Farrell, Joseph, and Saloner, Garth. "Standardization, Compatibility, and Innovation." *Rand J. Econ.* 16 (Spring 1985): 70–83.

Fishlow, Albert. *American Railroads and the Transformation of the Ante-Bellum Economy*. Cambridge, Mass.: Harvard Univ. Press, 1965.

Fleming, J. Marcus. "External Economies and the Doctrine of Balanced Growth." *Econ. J.* 65 (June 1955): 241–56.

Fogel, Robert W. *Railroads and American Economic Growth: Essays in Econometric History*. Baltimore: Johns Hopkins Press, 1964.

Hart, Oliver D. "A Model of Imperfect Competition with Keynesian Features." *Q.J.E.* 97 (February 1982): 109–38.

Hayek, Friedrich A. von. "The Use of Knowledge in Society." *A.E.R.* 35 (September 1945): 519–30.

Kaldor, Nicholas. *Causes of the Slow Rate of Economic Growth of the United Kingdom: An Inaugural Lecture*. Cambridge: Cambridge Univ. Press, 1966.

Keynes, John Maynard. *The General Theory of Employment, Interest and Money*. London: Macmillan, 1936.

Kiyotaki, Nobuhiro. "Multiple Expectations Equilibria under Monopolistic Competition." *Q.J.E.* 103 (November 1988): 695–714.

Lewis, W. Arthur. "Unemployment in Developing Countries." *World Today* 23 (January 1967): 13–22.

Lucas, Robert E., Jr. "On the Mechanics of Economic Development." *J. Monetary Econ.* 22 (July 1988): 3–42.

Murphy, Kevin M.; Shleifer, Andrei; and Vishny, Robert W. "Income Distribution, Market Size, and Industrialization." *Q.J.E.* 104 (August 1989).

Nurkse, Ragnar. *Problems of Capital Formation in Underdeveloped Countries*. New York: Oxford Univ. Press, 1953.

Reynolds, Lloyd G. "The Spread of Economic Growth to the Third World: 1850–1980." *J. Econ. Literature* 21 (September 1983): 941–80.

Romer, Paul M. "Increasing Returns and Long-Run Growth." *J.P.E.* 94 (October 1986): 1002–37. (a)

———. "Increasing Returns, Specialization, and External Economies: Growth as Described by Allyn Young." Manuscript. Rochester, N.Y.: Univ. Rochester, 1986. (b)

Rosenstein-Rodan, Paul N. "Problems of Industrialisation of Eastern and South-eastern Europe." *Econ. J.* 53 (June–September 1943): 202–11.

———. "Notes on the Theory of the 'Big Push.'" In *Economic Development for Latin America*, edited by Howard S. Ellis and Henry C. Wallich. New York: St. Martin's, 1961.

Rostow, Walt W. *The Stages of Economic Growth: A Non-Communist Manifesto.* Cambridge: Cambridge Univ. Press, 1960.

Sawyer, John E. "Entrepreneurship in Periods of Rapid Growth: The United States in the 19th Century." Paper presented at a conference on Entrepreneurship and Economic Growth, Cambridge, Mass., November 12–13, 1954.

Scitovsky, Tibor. "Two Concepts of External Economies." *J.P.E.* 62 (April 1954): 143–51.

Shleifer, Andrei. "Implementation Cycles." *J.P.E.* 94 (December 1986): 1163–90.

Shleifer, Andrei, and Vishny, Robert W. "The Efficiency of Investment in the Presence of Aggregate Demand Spillovers." *J.P.E.* 96 (December 1988): 1221–31.

Weitzman, Martin L. "Increasing Returns and the Foundations of Unemployment Theory." *Econ. J.* 92 (December 1982): 787–804.

Young, Allyn A. "Increasing Returns and Economic Progress." *Econ. J.* 38 (December 1928): 527–42.

8 Complementarities and Cumulative Processes in Models of Monopolistic Competition

Kiminori Matsuyama

1 Introduction

In recent years, the paradigm of monopolistic competition has been applied to model a variety of aggregate phenomena in macroeconomics, international and interregional economics, and economic growth and development. Monopolistic competition typically is defined as a situation of imperfect competition with the following features:

a) The products are differentiated. Each firm, as the sole producer of its own brand, is aware of its monopoly power and sets the price of its product.

b) The number of firms (and products) is so large that each firm ignores its strategic interactions with other firms; its action is negligible in the aggregate economy.

c) Entry is unrestricted and takes place until the profits of incumbent firms are driven down to zero.

These features make the paradigm of monopolistic competition very useful for modeling aggregate phenomena. First, as a form of imperfect competition, it allows us to describe decentralized allocations in the presence of increasing returns. Second, unlike oligopoly models, it helps us to focus on the aggregate implications of increasing returns without worrying about strategic interactions among firms and the validity of profit maximization as the objective of firms. Third, the explicit analysis of entry-exit processes makes it suitable for capturing the role of net business formations across business cycles. Furthermore, in models of monopolistic competition, the range of products supplied in the market can be endogenized through entry and exit. This feature also makes monopolistic competition a useful

apparatus within which to formalize growth and development processes, as economies grow and our standards of living rise not so
much by producing or consuming more of the same products, but by
adding new products to the list of those we already produce and
consume.

In this chapter, I present a highly selective review of recent developments in this area. Central to the discussion is the notion of complementarity. Broadly speaking, complementarities are said to exist
when two phenomena (or two actions, or two activities) reinforce
each other. For example, if expansion of industry A leads to expansion of industry B, which in turn leads to further expansion of A,
then the two industries are complementary to each other. Or, if the
arrival of a new store makes the neighborhood a desirable location
for other stores, then there are complementarities in the locational
decisions. Such complementarity introduces some circularity in the
economic system, which has profound implications for the stability
of the system. If a change in a certain activity is initiated by an exogenous shock, this leads to a similar change in complementary activities and starts a cumulative process of mutual interaction in which
the change in one activity is continuously supported by the reaction
of the others in a circular manner. Many writers of the past, such as
John Hicks (1950), Nicholas Kaldor (1985), Michal Kalecki (1939),
Gunnar Myrdal (1957), and Ragnar Nurkse (1953), among others,
have stressed that cumulative processes of this kind should be an
essential element in explaining business cycles, underdevelopment,
economic growth, and regional inequalities.

On the other hand, the standard neoclassical paradigm, exemplified by Kenneth Arrow and Frank Hahn (1971), emphasizes the self-
adjusting mechanisms of market forces with its efficient resource
allocation. As different activities compete for scarce resources, expansion of one activity comes only at the expense of others, which
tends to dampen any perturbation to the system. Imperfect competition and incomplete markets (through an endogenous change in the
range of products offered in the market), as departures from the standard paradigm, leave more room for complementarities, and make
the system more conducive to circular and cumulative causation, as
complementarities help the system break away from the stabilizing
forces of resource constraints.

Ever since the publication of Edward Chamberlin (1933) and Joan
Robinson (1933), a large number of studies has applied the paradigm

of monopolistic competition in a variety of contexts. Indeed, there are already many excellent surveys, such as John Beath and Yannis Katsoulacos (1991), Curtis Eaton and Richard Lipsey (1989), Joseph Stiglitz (1986), and Jean Tirole (1988). These studies, however, are written from a different perspective. They address questions like: "How do models of monopolistic competition differ from oligopoly models?" or "What is the most appropriate way of modeling product differentiation?" or "Does market equilibrium provide optimal product diversity and selection?" i.e., they are written from predominantly partial equilibrium or industrial organization perspectives. Some studies, such as Jean-Pascal Benassy (1991) and Oliver Hart (1985), discuss general equilibrium models of monopolistic competition, but their concerns remain largely theoretical, such as the existence of equilibrium, its uniqueness, and limit theorems. In contrast, this chapter discusses how general equilibrium models of monopolistic competition can be applied to explain complementarities and cumulative phenomena and their implications in the context of macroeconomics, international and regional economics, as well as growth and development.[1] To put it differently, the main goal is to point out the commonality of ideas across a wide range of fields, using the notion of complementarity as an organizing principle.

The rest of this chapter is hence organized according to different mechanisms behind complementarity, In each section, my strategy is first to develop a basic model to illustrate the underlying logic, and then to use variations of it for discussing the literature. Section 2 focuses on the role of price distortions in generating multiplier processes, by developing a class of models in which the range of products offered is fixed. Section 3 focuses on endogenous product variety and increasing returns, by developing a class of models in which all products are marked up at the same rate. Section 4 combines the two elements by developing models with both endogenous product variety and differential markups. Section 5 discusses some methodological issues concerning the logic of coordination failures. Section 6 offers some concluding remarks.

2 Monopoly Pricing Distortions and Multiplier Processes

The departure from perfect competition means that the firm, faced with downward sloping demand, sets price above marginal cost. In the presence of such a distortion, aggregate demand management could be effective in stimulating aggregate economic activity, as well as in raising the welfare of the economy. To grasp the intuition behind the mechanism, suppose the government increases its demand for monopolistically competitive goods, financed by a lump-sum tax. Because prices exceed marginal costs, such a shift in demand would increase the level of monopoly profits in the economy and thus national income. This increased income would generate additional demand for monopolistically competitive goods, which further raises profits and income and so on. With monopoly price distortion, the equilibrium behavior of the economy resembles the multiplier process described in a simple textbook Keynesian model.

2.A   The Basic Model

The idea can be modeled as follows. To focus on monopoly pricing distortions, I will ignore the entry process and endogenous changes in product variety, i.e., it is assumed that the economy produces a fixed set of products, each of which is supplied by a sole monopolist. Let $z \in [0, 1]$ be an index of a product, as well as of the monopolist producing it. The assumption of restricted entry may be defended simply by arguing that the model describes the short-run equilibrium.[2]

The representative consumer is endowed with L units of labor, holds ownership shares of all profit-making firms, and maximizes the following preferences,

$$\alpha \int_0^1 \ln c(z)\, dz + (1 - \alpha) \ln(N),$$

where $c(z)$ denotes consumption of variety z, and N leisure, respectively; α represents the budget share of the product group, $z \in [0, 1]$, and is assumed to be between zero and one. Taking leisure as a numeraire, the budget constraint is given by

$$\int_0^1 p(z) c(z)\, dz + N \leq Y - T,$$

where $Y = L + \Pi$, represents aggregate income, which is equal to the sum of labor income, L, and profit, Π, while T is the lump sum tax. As a solution to this consumption decision problem, one can obtain demand for each variety of good as,

$$c(z) = \frac{\alpha(Y - T)}{p(z)}.$$

Let us assume that the government spends G equally for all goods regardless of their prices. Then, the total demand for each good is given by $q(z) = \{\alpha(Y - T) + G\}/p(z)$. The government also hires N' units of labor; the budget constraint requires $T = G + N'$.

Each variety can be produced by two types of firms. First, there is a competitive fringe of firms that can convert one unit of labor input into one unit of output with constant returns to scale technology. (Alternatively, one may interpret it as the technology of home production.) Second, there is a unique monopolist firm with access to an increasing returns to scale technology. This firm alone knows how to produce q units of output by using $aq + F$ units of labor input, where $0 \le a < 1$, and F represents the fixed cost. This firm chooses $p(z)$ to maximize its profit, $\pi(z) = p(z)q(z) - [aq(z) + F]$. In doing so, it treats Y as a fixed parameter; although this firm has some monopoly power over its own variety, it is negligible relative to the aggregate economy. Because of the unit elasticity of demand and the competitive fringe, the monopolist adopts the limit pricing rule, $p(z) = 1$, and thus $\mu \equiv 1 - a = \{p(z) - a\}/p(z)$ can be interpreted as the profit margin. Because all monopolists face the same incentive, $c(z) = \alpha(Y - T)$ and $q(z) = \alpha(Y - T) + G$ for all $z \in [0, 1]$. Aggregate profit is therefore equal to $\Pi = \pi(z) = \mu[\alpha(Y - T) + G] - F$. Note that higher aggregate demand increases aggregate profit because of the positive profit margin, μ.

The income identity implies $Y = L + \Pi = L + \mu[\alpha(Y - T) + G] - F$, or

$$Y = A + \mu\alpha Y, \tag{1}$$

where

$$A \equiv L - F + \mu(G - \alpha T)$$

is the "autonomous" component of aggregate income. Solving the income identity equation (1) for equilibrium income yields

$$Y = \frac{A}{1 - \mu\alpha} = \frac{L - F + \mu(G - \alpha T)}{1 - \mu\alpha}. \tag{2}$$

Note that a unit increase in government spending on the monopolistically competitive products raises A by μ when unaccompanied by a tax increase, and by $\mu(1 - \alpha)$ when financed by a lump-sum tax. This autonomous increase in income generates an induced demand increase by α, hence further increasing income by $\mu\alpha$. Through such a cumulative process, aggregate income increases by an amount equal to the original increase in the "autonomous" component of aggregate income, "multiplied" by $1 + \mu\alpha + (\mu\alpha)^2 + \cdots = 1/(1 - \mu\alpha)$.

It is easy to show that an increase in G, when financed by a reduction in N', improves the welfare of the representative consumer. This is because in equilibrium noncompetitive goods are consumed too little, due to the pricing distortions. Alternatively, this inefficiency can be understood in terms of aggregate demand spillovers. To see this, suppose that all consumers simultaneously increase their demand for noncompetitive goods; this leads to a more efficient allocation of resources, as the marginal benefit of consumption exceeds the social cost of production. Nevertheless, no individual consumer has any incentive to demand more in equilibrium. The discrepancy between the effects of coordinated versus unilateral demand increases arises, as the potential gains generated by a unilateral shift in demand, materialized as an increase in monopoly profit, will be widely dispersed in the economy. This spillover effect creates a kind of free-rider problem in consumption decisions. An increase in government spending improves welfare as it solves the free-rider problem.

Benassy (1978) and Takashi Negishi (1978, 1979) demonstrated underemployment and insufficient aggregate demand in monopolistically competitive economies, under the so-called "subjective demand" approach. For the "objective demand" approach, see Olivier Blanchard and Nobuhiro Kiyotaki (1987), Hart (1982), Richard Startz (1989), Martin Weitzman (1982), as well as the survey by Joaquim Silvestre (1993). Some of these studies emphasized aggregate demand management policies, both fiscal and monetary, as a way of solving the free-rider problems that arise from aggregate demand spillovers. To discuss the effectiveness of monetary policies, it would be necessary to introduce nominal price stickiness into the model, for which I refer to the surveys by Robert Gordon (1990) and Julio Rotemberg (1987) on the "New Keynesian Macroeconomics" literature.[3]

2.B Vertical Complementarity

The magnitude of the multiplier can be large even when the profit margin enjoyed by a typical firm is small, if a shift in demand ignites a chain reaction across a large number of firms. To see this, let us extend the basic model to multi-stage production. Suppose that there are S stages in production and, in each stage, there is a continuum of varieties, $z_j \in [0, 1]$, $(j = 1, 2, \ldots, S)$. Here, $j = 1$ represents consumption goods, $j = 2$ represents inputs to the consumption goods, etc. As before, each product can be produced either by a competitive fringe of firms, or a single monopolist, which has unique access to the superior technology. For all $1 \le j \le S - 1$, the competitive fringe uses the constant returns to scale technology given by

$$q(z_j) = \exp\left[\int_0^1 \ln q(z_{j+1})\, dz_{j+1}\right],$$

and the technology of the monopolist is given by

$$(1 - \mu_j)q(z_j) + F_j = \exp\left[\int_0^1 \ln q(z_{j+1})\, dz_{j+1}\right].$$

For $j = S$, the competitive fringe converts one unit of labor to one unit of output, while the labor input function of the monopolist is $(1 - \mu_S)q(z_S) + F_S$. Under this specification, each firm is negligibly small as a purchaser of its inputs, and hence takes input prices given. Then, each monopolist firm, as a producer, faces unit elastic demand, and hence sets its output price equal to the unit cost of the competitive fringe. This implies that $p(z_j) = 1$ for all products, and hence, the output level and profit in each stage can be solved as a function of Y, recursively from $q_1 = \alpha(Y - T) + G$, $q_{j+1} = (1 - \mu_j)q_j + F_j$, $\Pi_j = \mu_j q_j - F_j$, for $1 \le j \le S$. Combining them with the income identity,

$$Y = L + \sum_{j=1}^{S} \Pi_j,$$

one can show that equilibrium income can be written in the following form:

$$Y = \frac{A_0 + \mu(G - \alpha T)}{1 - \mu\alpha},$$

where

$$A_0 = L - \sum_{j=1}^{S}\left[F_j \prod_{k=j+1}^{S} (1 - \mu_k)\right],$$

$$\mu \equiv 1 - \prod_{j=1}^{S} (1 - \mu_j).$$

According to this formula, μ can be close to one for a long chain of production, as long as there are some price distortions at each stage of production. For illustration, let us take a couple of numbers from the range estimated by Ian Domowitz, Glenn Hubbard, and Bruce Petersen (1988) and Robert Hall (1988). If $\mu_j = 0.3$, $\mu = 0.76$ for $S = 4$ and $\mu = 0.94$ for $S = 8$. If $\mu_j = 0.4$, $\mu = 0.87$ for $S = 4$ and $\mu = 0.98$ for $S = 8$.

In this model, an exogenous rise in the final goods demand causes a chain reaction of output and profit increases through vertical complementarity, running from downstream to upstream industries. The multiplier can be large even with a small profit margin, because the double (multiple) marginalization generates a large inefficiency at the aggregate level. See Hart (1982) for another model of two-stage (producers and unions) monopolistic competition, although his main reason for introducing monopolistic labor unions was to generate unemployment.

2.C Horizontal Complementarity

In a perfectly competitive world, a sectoral shock helps to expand some sectors only at the expense of other sectors. In a monopolistically competitive world, on the other hand, a favorable sectoral shock can lead to an economy-wide boom, in which all producers benefit simultaneously. Aggregate demand spillovers create a horizontal complementarity across all sectors of the economy. To see this, let us now extend the basic model to have two product groups, $i = 1$ and 2, with n_i being the size of group i. Let α_i, μ_i and Π_i be the budget share, the profit margin, and the profit level of product group i. Then, $Y = L + \Pi_1 + \Pi_2$, and, if the government spends G_i on product group i, $\Pi_i = \mu_i[\alpha_i(Y - T) + G_i] - n_i F$. The profits of the two groups thus satisfy

$$\Pi_1 = A_1 + \mu_1\alpha_1(\Pi_1 + \Pi_2), \tag{3}$$

$$\Pi_2 = A_2 + \mu_2\alpha_2(\Pi_1 + \Pi_2), \tag{4}$$

where

$$A_1 \equiv \mu_1[G_1 + \alpha_1(L - T)] - n_1 F$$

$$A_2 \equiv \mu_2[G_2 + \alpha_2(L - T)] - n_2 F$$

summarize the autonomous components of the profits in the two groups. The second terms in (3) and (4) represent the induced components; a unit increase in total income generates additional demand for sector i by α_i, which increases its profit by $\alpha_i \mu_i$. Solving these equations simultaneously yields

$$\begin{bmatrix} \Pi_1 \\ \Pi_2 \end{bmatrix} = \frac{1}{1 - \mu_1 \alpha_1 - \mu_2 \alpha_2} \begin{bmatrix} 1 - \mu_2 \alpha_2 & \mu_1 \alpha_1 \\ \mu_2 \alpha_2 & 1 - \mu_1 \alpha_1 \end{bmatrix} \begin{bmatrix} A_1 \\ A_2 \end{bmatrix}.$$

Note that an increase in government spending on one group increases not only the profit (and the output) of that group, but also the profit and the output of the other group. Thus, an expansion of one sector benefits the other sector; the two sectors now become complementary to each other through demand spillover effects.

This implication can be carried over into international contexts. An increase in the autonomous demand for domestic products leads to a higher level of monopoly profits in the economy and thus of national income. This increased income will generate additional demand for domestic products, leading to a multiplier process. To the extent that increased income in demand falls on foreign goods and raises aggregate profits abroad, it also creates similar chain reactions and lead to an increase in income abroad. Thus, under imperfect competition, there are positive transmissions of country specific demand shocks: see Matsuyama (1992a) for a formal demonstration.

2.D   Economic Development

The profit multiplier process and aggregate spillover effects are also important in understanding some problems in economic development. To see this, let us modify the basic model in two ways. First, the monopolist in each industry, instead of being equipped with the increasing returns to scale technology, decides whether to adopt the technology or to stay with the competitive fringe. Second, the fixed cost involves the use of products, instead of labor, as follows:

$$F = \exp \left[\int_0^1 \ln f(z) \, dz \right],$$

where $f(z)$ represents the investment demand for variety z by a monopolist, who decides to use the increasing returns to scale technology. This specification implies that the investment demand, and hence the total demand curve, of each product are also unit elastic. Again, facing the unit elastic demand and the competitive fringe, the monopolist using the increasing returns to scale technology sets the price equal to one. Hence, the output is equal to $q = \alpha(Y-T) + G + sF$, where s is a fraction of the monopolists that invest. The monopoly profit is $\pi = \mu q - F = \mu[\alpha(Y - T) + G + sF] - F$. The income identity is now $Y = L + s\pi$, so that the aggregate income and the monopolist profit can be derived as functions of s,

$$Y(s) = \frac{L + s\mu(G - \alpha T) - (1 - \mu s)sF}{1 - \mu\alpha s},$$

$$\pi(s) = \frac{\mu\{G + \alpha(L - T)\} - (1 - \mu s)F}{1 - \mu\alpha s}.$$

Note that the multiplier is now equal to $1/(1 - \mu\alpha s)$, because an induced demand increase, α, caused by a unit increase in autonomous income, generates the profit, μ, only in a fraction s of the industries, in which the monopoly adopts the increasing returns to scale technology.

The incentive to adopt the increasing returns to scale technology, of course, depends on the profit, which in turn depends positively on s, i.e., on how widely the technology is used in the economy. Furthermore, if

$$\frac{1}{\mu}F > G + \alpha(L - T) > \frac{1 - \mu}{\mu}F,$$

then $\pi(0) < 0$ and $\pi(1) > 0$, as depicted in Figure 8.1. Under this condition, the complementarity of investment decisions across industries leads to a coexistence of a good equilibrium $(s = 1)$ and a bad equilibrium $(s = 0)$. In the former, all industries invest and use the increasing returns to scale technologies; in the latter, no investment takes place and all industries stay with constant returns to scale technologies, which can be interpreted as an underdevelopment trap. It is also straightforward to show that $\pi(1) > 0$ ensures that the welfare level is higher at the good equilibrium than at the bad equilibrium. In this model, because of the fixed cost, the incentive to invest depends on the market size. But the market size depends on the investment demand. This circularity generates the complementarity and multiple equilibria.

With multiple equilibria, government spending may have a large impact on the economy. Suppose that the above condition is met and

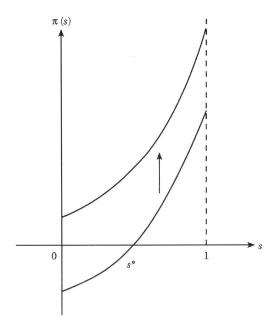

Figure 8.1

the economy is trapped in the bad equilibrium. A sufficiently large increase in G can shift the profit curve upward to eliminate the bad equilibrium, as depicted in Figure 8.1. In fact, even a small and "temporary" increase may be enough to lift the economy out of the state toward which it would otherwise gravitate.

Kevin Murphy, Andrei Shleifer, and Robert Vishny (1989a) argued, using models similar to one discussed above, that aggregate demand spillovers are crucial in understanding the problem of underdevelopment. In one of their models, it is assumed that workers suffer disutility from working in the factory (increasing returns to scale). In order to attract labor from villages, where cottage production is used (competitive fringe), monopolists have to pay a factory wage premium. In this model, the market size depends on the purchasing power of workers, which in turn depends on the extent of industrialization in the economy (through the factory wage premium), which generates the complementarity of investment across industries and multiple equilibria.

Arguably, these models capture the old idea, which dates back to Paul Rosenstein-Rodan (1943), Nurkse (1953), and Albert Hirschman

(1958), that the complementarity of modernization efforts across industries is the main obstacle to economic development. Rosenstein-Rodan, in particular, uses this idea to advocate for a large-scale development planning as a way of breaking away from underdevelopment traps. It should be stressed, however, that the complementarity of investment across industries does not necessarily provide the rationale for comprehensive central planning, as coordinated investment could be achieved through "the infectious influence of business psychology" (Nurkse 1961, p. 249), which may be orchestrated by no more than some form of indicative planning: see Matsuyama (1992b) for more on this issue.[4]

In the models discussed above, the range of products in the economy is fixed, and hence rents are not dissipated away by the process of entry. If unrestricted entry is possible, rents would disappear and so would the complementarity through the multiplier process. Startz (1989), for example, argues that the multiplier should be much smaller in the long run than in the short run. However, free entry brings another source of complementarity if the entry of new firms expands the variety of products supplied in the market. For the remainder of the paper, I will turn to this mechanism of complementarities, based on the endogeneity of the product space.

3 Expanding Product Variety and Aggregate Increasing Returns

To understand how the entry process could lead to a complementarity, it is important to note that entry of new firms, by introducing new products and services to the market, gives rise to increasing returns at the aggregate level. The idea itself is not new. Allyn Young (1928), for example, stressed that progressive division and specialization of industries, rather than subdivision of labor within a firm, as an essential part of the process by which increasing returns are realized. The formal modeling of this idea is, however, fairly recent.

3.A The Basic Model

To demonstrate the idea, I will use the following stripped down version of the Avinash Dixit and Stiglitz (1977) model. Suppose that a single consumption good is produced by assembling a variety of differentiated intermediate inputs. The technology satisfies the property of constant returns to scale for a given set of inputs. More specifically, the production function takes a form of symmetric CES;

$$X = \left[\int_0^n [x(z)]^{1-(1/\sigma)} \, dz \right]^{\sigma/(\sigma-1)}, \qquad (\sigma > 1)$$

with $x(z)$ being the amount of input z employed in production, and $[0, n]$ represents the range of intermediate inputs available in the marketplace. It assumes that the direct partial elasticity of substitution between every pair is equal to σ. The restriction, $\sigma > 1$, implies that no input is essential; X is well defined even if some differentiated inputs are not used at all. Such a restriction is necessary as we consider the situation in which the range of products offered may vary.

One implication of this specification of product differentiation deserves special emphasis. That is, the productivity of intermediate inputs increases the greater the range of inputs available. To see this, let us suppose that all varieties are produced by the same amount, which, in fact, would be the case in optimal and equilibrium allocations. By letting $x(z) = x$, we have

$$X = n^{\sigma/(\sigma-1)}x. \qquad (5)$$

Let $M = nx$ be the total inputs used. Then, the average productivity of inputs, $X/M = n^{1/(\sigma-1)}$, increases with n. This arguably captures the notion that the introduction of new capital goods and producer services of a highly specialized character would enhance the efficiency of the economy. Wilfred Ethier (1982a) and Paul Romer (1987) earlier interpreted this property of the CES specification as increasing returns due to specialization, or to the division of labor, in production. This interpretation has recently been given a formal treatment by Weitzman (1994).

The costs of expanding product variety and of increasing specialization come from economies of scale in the production of differentiated intermediate inputs. If there were no scale economies, then productivity could rise indefinitely by adding more and more varieties to the list of differentiated products, and producing less and less of each variety. As before, let us suppose that production of x units of each variety requires $ax + F$ units of labor; F is the fixed cost and a is the marginal labor requirement. For notational convenience, let us choose the unit for measurement so that $a = 1 - 1/\sigma$. Finally, the labor resource constraint is

$$L = n(ax + F), \tag{6}$$

where L is the total labor supply in the economy. Combining (5) and (6) yields

$$X = \frac{n^{1/(\sigma-1)}}{a}(L - nF).$$

Hence, the optimal product variety, one that maximizes the above expression, and per capita consumption are

$$n^* = \frac{L}{\sigma F}, \qquad \frac{X^*}{L} = \left[\frac{L}{\sigma F}\right]^{1/(\sigma-1)}.$$

They are larger a) when the fixed cost is small, b) when the products are less substitutable, and c) when the size of the economy is large.

A market equilibrium for this economy consists of the competitive final goods sector with the constant returns to scale production function X and the monopolistically competitive intermediate inputs sector with the labor input function, $ax + F$. Taking the range of intermediate inputs available in the market n, the prices of intermediate inputs, $p(z)$ for $z \in [0, n]$, and the price of the final good P, as fixed, the final goods producers seek to maximize their profit by choosing the cost-minimizing input combination. It is straightforward to derive the demand function for each input

$$\frac{x(z)}{X} = \left[\frac{p(z)}{P}\right]^{-\sigma}.$$

Furthermore, the zero profit condition implies that the output price must be equal to the unit cost:

$$P = \left[\int_0^n [p(z)]^{1-\sigma} dz\right]^{1/(1-\sigma)}.$$

Given the demand function derived above, each intermediate producer sets the price to maximize its profit. In doing so, it takes P and X as fixed. This means that the elasticity of demand with respect to its own price is σ, so that the profit-maximizing price satisfies $p(z)(1 - 1/\sigma) = a$, or $p(z) = 1$. The equilibrium price of the final good is hence

$$P = n^{1/(1-\sigma)}. \tag{7}$$

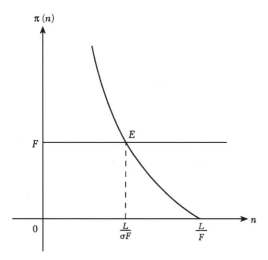

Figure 8.2

Note that an increasing availability of specialized inputs leads to a lower output price, although each input price remains constant. This is nothing but the mirror image of the efficiency effect of increasing specialization pointed out earlier.

The gross profit of each intermediate input firm (i.e., gross of the fixed costs) can be shown to be proportional to output produced:

$$\pi = (p - a)x = \frac{x}{\sigma}. \tag{8}$$

The labor market clearing condition is given by (6). Inserting this expression into (8), gross profit can now be expressed as a function of the number of firms;

$$\pi(n) = \frac{1}{\sigma - 1}\left[\frac{L}{n} - F\right]. \tag{9}$$

Note that this is a decreasing function of n, as shown in Figure 8.2. Entry of firms hence reduces the profit of incumbent firms, The entry process continues as long as gross profit exceeds the fixed cost, F. Thus, there is a unique equilibrium, depicted as point E in Figure 8.2. Some algebra shows that equilibrium product variety and per capita consumption are

$$n^e = \frac{L}{\sigma F}, \qquad \frac{X^e}{L} = \left[\frac{L}{\sigma F}\right]^{1/(\sigma-1)}.$$

In market equilibrium, the variety of intermediate inputs, or the division of labor, is limited by the extent of the market; as the economy size increases, more firms stay and a wider range of products are offered in the market; this division of labor enhances the efficiency of production, and therefore consumers living in a larger economy will be better off. (As equilibrium profit is zero, the aggregate income consists only of wage income, so per capita output is equal to the equilibrium real wage in this model.) The equilibrium output of each firm is

$$x^e = \sigma F,$$

which is to say that, with a large fixed cost and in the presence of close substitutes, firms need to sell more to break even.

One may be surprised to see that the equilibrium allocation is efficient in this model. This is certainly not a robust feature of the model: a slight change in functional forms can destroy the equivalence of equilibrium and efficient allocations. Yet, it is worth asking why the equilibrium can be efficient in spite of monopoly pricing. The answer can be found in terms of the theory of second best: the price distortion happens to offset the other distortion present in this model. But, what is the other distortion? I will come back to this problem in Section 3.E.

3.B   Economic Integration: The Effects of Trade

The basic model can easily be applied to international and interregional economics. Imagine that there exist two economies of the kind analyzed above, say East and West, and that they are originally isolated from each other. Furthermore, assume that the two economies have identical tastes and technologies. They differ only in labor supply. L^E denotes the labor supply of East and L^W that of West. Now let us ask; "What would happen if the two economies are integrated?" The answer to this question crucially depends on the mobility of goods and labor.

First, suppose that the products can be transported at zero cost, but labor is immobile. Free trade in goods ensures that the same set of intermediate inputs is available everywhere, so that the final goods sector in both economies achieves the same level of efficiency, while the varieties produced in each region are determined by the labor resource constraint. Symmetry implies that the number of intermediate inputs produced in each region is proportional to the labor supply; East produces $n^E = L^E/\sigma F$ varieties, and West produces $n^W = L^W/\sigma F$ varieties. Both regions enjoy the same level of productivity, and per capita income in both regions is equal to

$$\left[\frac{L^E + L^W}{\sigma F}\right]^{1/(\sigma-1)}.$$

As productivity depends on the availability of differentiated inputs in this model, economic integration through trade improves efficiency in both regions, and hence it is mutually beneficial. True, the larger economy may boast a much wider array of inputs produced than the smaller economy. However, as long as all the inputs are available at the same prices, this would not handicap the smaller economy. In fact, by comparing the situations before and after economic integration, it is easily seen that productivity gains are larger for the smaller economy.

With the notable exceptions of Negishi (1972) and others, imperfect competition and economies of scale received little attention in the theoretical trade literature for many years. The systematic study of trade in differentiated products has grown enormously during the last decade, following the path-breaking studies by Dixit and Victor Norman (1980, ch. 9), Paul Krugman (1979), and Kevin Lancaster (1979, ch. 10). I have touched on only one of many important lessons that come out of this literature: see Elhanan Helpman and Krugman (1985, chs. 6–9) and Helpman (1990) for more.

3.C   Economic Integration: The Effects of Factor Mobility

Let us now suppose that there are impediments to trade, but economic integration makes it possible for some workers to migrate across the economies. Footloose workers migrate from the smaller economy to the larger economy, where the equilibrium wage is higher. As a result, the population distribution becomes more lopsided. New firms are created in the larger economy, while firms are forced to close down in the smaller economy, which makes those who stay in the smaller economy worse off. With limited mobility of goods, increasing returns are now region-specific. This induces footloose workers to concentrate into one region. Economies of scale are realized only through agglomeration. It should be noted that economic integration benefits the immobile workers in the larger economy, while hurting those left behind in the smaller economy. This provides a striking contrast with the case of trade in differentiated goods, where all (immobile) workers gain and those in the smaller economy gain most. Riccardo Faini (1984), Masahisa Fujita (1989, ch. 8.4), Helpman and Krugman (1985, chs. 10–11), Francisco Rivera-Batiz (1988), and Matsuyama and Takaaki Takahashi (1994) among others, discuss the effects of impediments to trade in differentiated goods on the regional distribution of economic activity.

In the policy debates concerning Europe 1992, North American Free Trade Area (NAFTA), and other regional trading blocs, much has been discussed about the possible impact on smaller economies. Many argue that, incorporated into a larger market area, small economies can enjoy all the benefits of economies of scale, and become main beneficiaries of economic integration. Others believe, however, that economic integration and the free movement of labor and capital lead to a concentration of economic activities into the center, leaving the peripheries underdeveloped. The above analysis suggests that both arguments have some theoretical merit and we need more detailed information about the process of economic integration in order to determine the impacts. See Krugman and Anthony Venables (1990) and Krugman (1991) for further exploration of this issue.

3.D Clustering Phenomena

The regional disparities caused by the migration of workers represent just one example of clustering phenomena, more general patterns that we observe everywhere in the real world. For instance, many industries tend to concentrate into a few areas within a country (Glen Ellison and Edward Glaeser 1994). On a much smaller scale, retail stores and restaurants tend to cluster together in certain sections within a city. Some sort of complementarity is obviously important for explaining retail store clustering, but we cannot entirely attribute it to the physical characteristics of products sold by these stores. True, restaurants and theaters tend to cluster together, as they offer complementary services. In more extreme cases, such as nuts and bolts or left and right shoes, complementarities are so strong that they are sold together in the same store. What is less obvious is why stores selling very similar products and hence competing directly for customers also cluster together. Examples abound, such as automobile dealers, bookstores, camera shops, electronics shops, furniture stores, hair dressers, etc. Why are these stores not spread out geographically? The need to share common infrastructure may be one reason, but the universality suggests that there is something more that makes them cluster together.

A slight modification of the basic model, taken from Matsuyama (1992c), helps to explain why stores that sell similar products cluster together. The differentiated products, now interpreted as consumer goods, are divided into two groups, 1 and 2. Preferences are now given by $V(X_1, X_2)$, where

$$X_i = \left[\int_0^{n_i} [x(z_i)]^{1-(1/\sigma)} dz_i \right]^{\sigma/(\sigma-1)}, \qquad (\sigma > 1)$$

and n_i denotes the product variety offered in group i for $i = 1$ and 2. The upper-tier utility function, V, which aggregates the two composites of differentiated goods, is assumed to be homothetic. There are two types of labor, managers and workers, whose total supplies are K and L, respectively. Producing x units of each good requires $ax = (1 - 1/\sigma)x$ workers, as well as F managers. The services of managers are required independent of x and hence constitute the fixed cost. From the market clearing condition for managers, the total number of firms is constant and equal to $K/F = n_1 + n_2$. This feature of the model helps us focus on the distribution of firms across the two groups.

Normalize the wage paid to a worker to one. As before, demand for each product has the constant price elasticity equal to σ, for any given distribution of firms across the two groups. With the marginal cost equal to $a = 1 - 1/\sigma$, each firm sets the price to be equal to one, $p(z_i) = 1$ for all $z_i \in [0, n_i]$. Hence, all firms in the same group operate at the same scale, $x(z_i) = x_i$ for all $z_i \in [0, n_i]$, and thus $X_i = n_i^{\sigma/(\sigma-1)} x_i$ and the gross profit per firm is $\pi_i = x_i/\sigma$. (This means that each manager employed in group i is paid $x_i/\sigma F$ for her services.) The price index of each group is $P_i = n_i^{1/(1-\sigma)}$. The relative demand of the two composites can be written, due to the homotheticity of V, as $X_1/X_2 = \Psi(P_1/P_2)$, $\Psi' < 0$, so that the ratio of the gross profit in the two groups depends solely on the ratio of product variety:

$$\frac{\pi_1}{\pi_2} = \frac{x_1}{x_2} = \frac{X_1}{X_2} \left[\frac{n_1}{n_2} \right]^{\sigma/(1-\sigma)} = \Psi\left(\frac{P_1}{P_2} \right) \left[\frac{n_1}{n_2} \right]^{\sigma/(1-\sigma)} = \Psi\left(\left[\frac{n_1}{n_2} \right]^{1/(1-\sigma)} \right) \left[\frac{n_1}{n_2} \right]^{\sigma/(1-\sigma)}.$$

To see what is involved in this expression, suppose that V is a CES: $\Psi(P_1/P_2) = \beta[P_1/P_2]^{-\varepsilon}$, where ε represents the intergroup elasticity of substitution, while σ may now be referred to as the intragroup elasticity of substitution. Then,

$$\frac{\pi_1}{\pi_2} = \beta\left[\frac{P_1}{P_2}\right]^{-\varepsilon}\left[\frac{n_1}{n_2}\right]^{\sigma/(1-\sigma)} = \beta\left[\frac{n_1}{n_2}\right]^{(\varepsilon-\sigma)/(\sigma-1)}.$$

The relation between profit level and product variety depends on the relative magnitude of ε and σ.

For example, suppose that group 1 consists of restaurants and group 2 retail stores. A pair of restaurants or a pair of stores are much closer substitutes than dining and shopping ($\varepsilon < \sigma$). Then, the profit level is negatively related to variety. If there are too many restaurants and a few stores in the city, restaurants will close down and new stores will open in the long run. Entry and exit processes balance the numbers of the two types of establishments so as to equalize the profit rate across the two groups.

On the other hand, suppose that there are two streets in the city and products are grouped according to their location. It is costly to move back and forth between the two streets, but ex ante consumers are almost indifferent between the two locations. Then, ε is close to infinity, so that $\varepsilon > \sigma$ and hence the profit level is positively related to the number of shops. Entry of a new firm, by attracting more customers, would benefit existing firms in the same street. This introduces complementarity in the locational decision, and entry and exit processes lead to all stores clustering into a single location. Of course, with the right distribution, firms may be indifferent between the two locations. Yet, such an equilibrium is unstable. The two stable equilibria in this example both correspond to complete concentration in the same location. It should be pointed out that, when clustering happens, there is no guarantee that the market mechanism picks the right place to cluster. For example, if $\beta > 1$ in the above example, it is better to cluster in location 1 than in 2. Yet, clustering in location 2 is a stable equilibrium allocation.

Note also that clustering of two products (and stores) can occur even when the direct partial elasticity of substitution between them, σ, is high, i.e., even when they are very similar products. What makes a pair of products complementary to each other is the presence of a third alternative, rather than the physical characteristics of the two products. In other words, what matters is the Hicks-Allen notion of complementarity. In criticizing the notion of complementarity defined by earlier writers, Hicks and R. C. D. Allen (1934) argued that the notion of complementary goods should be based on the property of market demand and proposed that two goods should be regarded as complements if what is now known as the Allen partial elasticity of substitution is positive. In fact, an explicit calculation shows that in our model the compensated demand function satisfies

$$\frac{P_i}{x_i(z)} \frac{dx_i(z)}{dP_i} \bigg|_{V=const.} = \varepsilon - \sigma$$

so that products in the same group are Hicks-Allen complements, whenever $\varepsilon > \sigma$. Intuitively, when other shops in your area reduce their prices, you lose some of your customers; σ captures this business-stealing effect. Yet, your sale may still go up if the lower prices attract customers to your area, the effect captured by ε, more than enough to offset the business-stealing effect. If this is the case, then your shop and other shops in your area are complementary to each other in the sense of Hicks and Allen.

The discussion above assumed that V is a CES, but the main implications do not depend on this assumption. With a more general upper-tier utility function, this model can have any odd number of equilibria, with stable and unstable equilibria alternating. When evaluated at a stable (an unstable) equilibrium, products in the same group are Hicks-Allen substitutes (complements) with each other.

The traditional explanation of retail store clustering was based on Harold Hotelling's (1929) "principle of minimum differentiation," which is not robust to small specification changes. Recent literature, such as Asher Wolinsky (1983), emphasizes the role of consumer search in the presence of incomplete information. Much of modeling efforts is devoted to make products offered in the same location imperfect substitutes (i.e., finite σ). The analysis here suggests that the consumer's ex ante indifference between the locations is the reason why even a small amount of incomplete information often causes clustering in this literature.

The above model, with some modifications, can easily be applied to other contexts, as well. For example, the two groups can be interpreted as the two alternative transportation systems, say automobiles and railroads. Products are classified by whether they cater to the need of drivers or of train riders. To the extent that the two modes of transportation are close substitutes, there are two stable equilibria, which can explain diversity across societies. In some societies, people use trains frequently and there are more shops around stations than along highways, and there are many pocket-sized products. In others, people tend to drive more and there are more shops along highways than around railroad stations.[5]

Alternatively, groups can be classified according to dates. By interpreting ε as the intertemporal rate of substitution, the model can be extended to explain regular temporal variations, within a day, or a week, or a year. In such a model, there is no guarantee that the market mechanism chooses the right time to cluster activities. If this is the case, the government may be able to play a critical role in coordination, such as by introducing the daylight savings time or mandatory store closing hours.

3.E Anatomy of Market Failure

In demonstrating clustering phenomena, it was also argued that the model of Section 3.D yields the possibility of inefficiency. Market equilibrium does not necessarily pick the right place or the right time in which to concentrate economic activities. Or, society may be stuck with a relatively inefficient industrial standard, despite there being a technologically feasible alternative, which would enhance efficiency if adopted widely.

The natural question is then: "What is the source of inefficiency?" Because the model does not have any technological externalities, one might be tempted to attribute the inefficiency to the pricing distortion. However, in the model discussed above, all goods produced are marked up at the same rate (due to the symmetry of the products and the absence of an outside good), so that there is no distortion in relative price. Free entry ensures that managers work in the firms offering the highest returns. Then, without any discrepancy between social and private costs/benefits of any individual action, why is there inefficiency?

The source of inefficiency is the coordination failure across firms. Starting with an inefficient clustering equilibrium, no individual firm has an incentive to move to the other group, given that other firms continue to stay. But, why does the price mechanism fail to coordinate the actions of firms?

It might be instructive to interpret this inefficiency result in light of the First Fundamental Theorem of Welfare Economics. This theorem says that in economies with complete markets, competitive equilibria are Pareto optimal. This theorem is remarkable in that few restrictions on the properties of technologies are required. In particular, neither nonconvex technologies nor nonconvex consumption sets would cause any problem for Pareto optimality. The reason why this theorem does not apply to our model even in the absence of price distortions is the lack of complete markets. In order to be able to apply the theorem to the environment of our model, there must be competitive markets for all commodities (i.e., all potential products), as well as the markets for the two factors, in which prices are publicly quoted so that firms and consumers can signal their demand and supply for each commodity simultaneously for any vector of prices. This is indeed a very strong hypothesis. In the model above and in any monopolistic competition models, it is assumed more realistically that consumers demand only products that are available in the marketplace. What is critical here is that, before a new product is introduced, its price is not publicly quoted, so that there is no way for consumers to signal their demand for the product. When the firm enters, it not only creates a new product but also creates the market for that product.

The incompleteness of markets would not cause any coordination failure if all products are Hicks-Allen substitutes. When there are Hicks-Allen complements, however, a whole set of complementary products may fail to be introduced even when it is more efficient to introduce them. To understand this, it is useful to think that, from the consumer's point of view, products not yet offered can be regarded as products offered at prices equal to infinity. When a single firm contemplates offering one of the products, quoting a finite price does not generate any demand for the product if complementary products remain prohibitively expensive. Only when a large set of complementary products are offered simultaneously and become available at reasonable prices, consumers are induced to signal sufficiently high demand for each good. This is the reason why the costs-benefit calculation of individual entry differs from that of simultaneous entry, regardless of whether one takes social or private points of view. In the standard general equilibrium model with complete markets, this coordination problem is artificially resolved by the Walrasian auctioneer, who quotes the prices for all potential commodities to which both consumers and producers respond.[6]

That the lack of complete markets is responsible for the inefficiency in the model should also become clear by showing that any equilibrium allocation is the solution to the optimal allocation problem, conditional on the set of goods produced, which will be left to the reader as an exercise.[7] The important message is that the market mechanism may be an efficient algorithm for solving *how much* to consume and produce, once a more fundamental problem of *which* commodities to consume and produce has been solved. In reality, of course, there are so many potential commodities that it is impossible to open markets for all: we must decide which market to open. The paradox is that we need to open all markets in order to collect the necessary information to know which market to open.

Above, I have developed a monopolistic competition model with no price distortion in order to isolate the lack of complete markets as a sole source of inefficiency. It should be pointed out that the distortion due to the incompleteness of the market would not disappear in models with price distortions. Sometimes, the two forms of distortions can interact to produce a rather surprising result. For example, in the basic model of Section 3.A, the market equilibrium allocation is efficient. This is because the two forms of distortion exactly offset each other.

In many ways, the market failure in clustering phenomena discussed in this section resembles the "counterexamples" analyzed by Hart (1980) and Louis Makowski (1980), who interpret them as a formalization of the pecuniary externalities discussed by Tibor Scitovsky (1954). In their examples, the inefficiency occurs when a set of complementary products fails to be produced, while in the model above the inefficiency occurs when a wrong set of complementary products are produced. Their examples also assume directly complementarity between the two goods, the nut and the bolt, produced by two independent firms, for which the coordination failure is difficult to justify. On the other hand, the possibility of inefficiency here arises as the lack of coordination among a large number of firms, possibly selling very similar products.

The possibility of inefficient clusters discussed above arises because the market mechanism may fail to pick the right place in which to cluster economic activities. In the model, there is another clustering equilibrium, which is efficient. Hence, there is nothing wrong with clustering per se. This is an important point to keep in mind, particularly in the context of regional policies, as policy debates in this area often take it for granted that unbalanced regional growth is undesirable. However, this is not to say that an inefficient clustering equilibrium always coexists with an efficient clustering equilibrium. Indeed, one can construct a variation of the above model, in which all clustering equilibria are inefficient, relative to the (unstable) equilibrium in which all types of products are offered. For such a model, see Matsuyama and Takahashi (1994), which discusses the possibility of inefficient unbalanced regional growth.

4 Circular and Cumulative Causation in Growth and Development

Complementarity in the entry process and associated expanding product variety is also useful for understanding some fundamental problems of economic growth and development. Satisfactory treatments of these issues, of course, require a dynamic model, and the literature has evolved primarily by extending the dynamic monopolistic competition model of Kenneth Judd (1985). Nonetheless, I will refrain from developing dynamic models, as the static framework can illustrate many ideas in the literature.

4.A Underdevelopment Traps

One critical aspect of the development process is that productivity growth is realized through an ever greater indirectness in production. One of the main obstacles to economic development is that complicated technologies often require a variety of local inputs and producer services. In underdeveloped regions, the lack of local support industries force the use of relatively simple production methods in downstream industries. This in turn implies a small market size for specialized inputs; the lack of local demand prevents a network of support industries from springing up in the economy. Thus, the two factors, the lack of demand and the lack of support industries, are mutually interrelated. Not only is the division of labor limited by the extent of the market, but also the extent of the market is limited by the division of labor. Such circular causation creates underdevelopment traps. Of course, the circularity does not always imply a vicious circle. If the economy acquires more than a critical mass of support industries, the very fact that the relation is circular generates a virtuous circle. Over time, the division of labor becomes far more elaborate, the production process more indirect, involving an increasing degree of specialized inputs. Through such a cumulative process, the economy experiences productivity growth and a rising standard of living. In the presence of complementarity, nothing succeeds like success, and poverty becomes its own cause.

Again, a slight extension of the model of Section 3, taken from Matsuyama (1992c, sec. 3), helps to capture this idea. Let us now suppose that a single consumption good is produced with the following constant returns to scale production function,

$$C = F(X, N),$$

where N is labor input. This specification allows the final goods industry to substitute between labor intensive and intermediate inputs intensive technologies. The relative demand for N and X is given by an increasing function of P,

$$\frac{N}{X} = \Phi(P), \tag{10}$$

with the elasticity of substitution between X and N being equal to $\varepsilon(P) \equiv d \log \Phi(P)/d \log P$. The pricing behavior of monopolistically competitive firms is the same as before, so that $p(z) = 1$ for all $z \in [0, n]$ and all varieties are produced by the same amount; hence (5) and (7) remain valid. The labor market clearing condition now becomes, instead of (6),

$$n(ax + F) + N = L. \tag{6'}$$

For any n, equations (5), (6'), (7), and (10) can be solved for x. From (8), the gross profit per firm satisfies

$$\pi(n) = \frac{L - nF}{(\sigma - 1)n + \sigma\Phi(n^{1/(1-\sigma)})n^{\sigma/(\sigma-1)}}. \tag{9'}$$

With a large $\varepsilon(P)$, the profit function can be increasing in n. For example, suppose that $F(X, N)$ is CES, with $\varepsilon(P) \equiv \varepsilon$. Then, $\Phi(P) = \beta P^{\varepsilon}$ and the profit function has a single peak when $\varepsilon > \sigma$. In this case, there are three equilibria, as shown in Figure 8.3. The middle equilibrium, S_M, represents the threshold level below which the firms make losses. If the economy is slightly above the middle equilibrium, there is an inducement to start new firms. Profit per firm rises with the

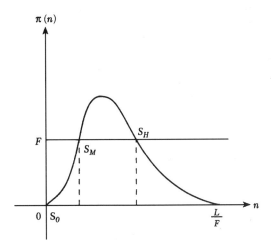

Figure 8.3

number of firms around the middle equilibrium, which makes it unstable. The other two equilibria, S_0 and S_H, are both stable. In the lower range, the limited availability of specialized inputs induces the final goods sector to use relatively labor intensive technologies, which implies a small market size for inputs producers. No firm is able to stay in the market, and $n = 0$, or S_0, represents a state of underdevelopment toward which the economy gravitates. The higher level equilibrium, S_H, on the other hand, is characterized by a wider range of intermediate inputs, a higher share of the intermediate inputs sector in GNP, and a higher total factor productivity.

More generally, this model could have an arbitrary number of stable equilibria, as constant returns to scale imposes very few restrictions on the relative factor demand function $\Phi(P)$. An example can easily be constructed by allowing the final goods sector to have access to a finite number of Leontief (i.e., fixed coefficient) technologies. Furthermore, it can be shown that per capita consumption (and labor productivity) is positively related to product variety across equilibria. The model is thus consistent with the idea of the stages of economic development.

The multiplicity of stable equilibria arises in this model because the benefits of a new input are not completely appropriated by the firm that introduces it. With an increasing variety of inputs, entry induces the final goods sector to switch to more intermediate inputs intensive technologies, thereby generating demand for other inputs. No individual firm, however, takes into account such pecuniary externalities. Of course, coordinated, simultaneous entry of firms would solve the demand spillover effects, making it possible for the economy to jump from S_0 to S_H. However, this is partly due to the static nature of the model. In an explicit dynamic setting, where starting up new firms require reallocation of current resources from production and the benefits of productivity growth are realized only in the future, Antonio Ciccone and Matsuyama (1992) show that the resource constraint makes coordinated entry unprofitable, and the economy cannot escape from the state of underdevelopment; thus $n = 0$ becomes a poverty "trap."

It is worth pointing out that, at a more formal level, the mechanisms generating multiple equilibria in this model are similar to those discussed in Section 3.D. The possibility of substitution between labor intensive and intermediate inputs intensive technologies makes intermediate inputs complementary to each other (in the sense of Hicks and Allen), even when the rate of substitution between two intermediate inputs, σ, is high. It should also be noted that, although monopoly price distortions play a significant role, the underdevelopment trap cannot be eliminated merely by correcting price distortions. For the same reason discussed in Section 3.E, multiple equilibria and inefficient traps could still exist without any price distortion: see Matsuyama (1992c, sec. 3).

4.B International Economics

The above model also suggests that international trade could be responsible for uneven development. To see this, consider the following model of a small open economy, adopted from Rodríguez-Clare (1993). There are two tradeable consumer goods, A and B, and preferences are given by $C_A^\alpha C_B^{1-\alpha}$. Both consumer goods sectors are competitive, and the production functions are $F_A(X_A, N_A) = X_A^\gamma N_A^{1-\gamma}$ and $F_B(X_B, N_B) = X_B^\delta N_B^{1-\delta}$, where $0 < \delta < \gamma < 1$. In the absence of international trade, this is analytically equivalent to an economy of a single final goods industry with the production function $F(X, N) = KX^{\alpha^*}N^{1-\alpha^*}$, where K is a positive constant and $\alpha^* \equiv \alpha\gamma + (1-\alpha)\delta$ (hence $\gamma > \alpha^* > \delta$). Relative demand is then $\Phi(P) = (1/\alpha^* - 1)P$ and the profit function is, from (9'),

$$\pi(n) = \frac{\alpha^*}{\sigma - \alpha^*}\left[\frac{L}{n} - F\right],$$

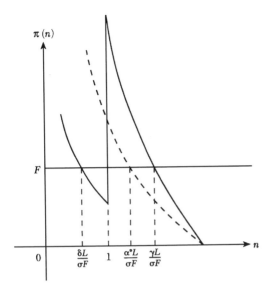

Figure 8.4

which is decreasing in n, as depicted by the dotted curve in Figure 8.4. There is a unique stable equilibrium, in which the economy produces both consumer goods. Equilibrium product variety is given by

$$n = \frac{\alpha^* L}{\sigma F}.$$

Suppose now that the economy trades in the world market, where the relative price of the two tradeable goods is exogenously given and equal to one. This open economy effectively becomes equivalent to a closed economy of a single final goods industry with the production function, $F(X, N) = \text{MAX}\{X_A^\gamma N_A^{1-\gamma} + X_B^\delta N_B^{1-\delta}, \text{s.t. } X_A + X_B \leq X$ and $N_A + N_B \leq N\}$, whose elasticity of substitution between X and N is infinite at $P = 1$. This is because the possiblity of trade makes the two consumer goods perfect substitutes for the competitive firms. With $\sigma < \varepsilon(1) = \infty$, the economy may now have underdevelopment traps.

More specifically, the unit cost is equal to P^γ in sector A and P^δ in sector B, so that the economy specializes in A when $P^{\gamma - \delta} = n^{(\gamma - \delta)/(1 - \sigma)} < 1$ or $n > 1$; it specializes in B when $n < 1$. The relative demand function is thus $\Phi(P) = (1/\gamma - 1)P$ and $\Phi(P) = (1/\delta - 1)P$, respectively. The gross profit is hence equal to

$$\pi(n) = \frac{\gamma}{\sigma - \gamma} \left[\frac{L}{n} - F \right],$$

if $n > 1$, and

$$\pi(n) = \frac{\delta}{\sigma - \delta} \left[\frac{L}{n} - F \right],$$

if $n < 1$. Note that the profit function jumps at $n = 1$, at which the economy switches between the two sectors. If $\gamma > \sigma F/L > \delta$, there are two stable equilibria, $n_A = \gamma L/\sigma F$ and $n_B = \delta L/\sigma F$, with $n = 1$ being the threshold level, as shown in Figure 8.4. In this example, international trade creates an underdevelopment trap. An economy with a small industrial base specializes in B, which make little use of local specialized inputs, hindering the development of an industrial base.

When an economy finds itself in such a trap, government intervention could be effective. For example, imposing sufficiently heavy taxes on the production of B can reduce the threshold level below n_B. This eliminates the low equilibrium trap, leaving n_A the only equilibrium (Dani Rodrik forthcoming). If $\alpha^* L > \delta F$, autarky would also help to generate a critical mass of support industries, so that temporary isolation would help the economy to escape the underdevelopment trap.

Let us now briefly consider some implications of this model from the global point of view. Suppose that the world economy consists of many identical national economies of the kind analyzed above. Because the world as a whole is a closed economy, some economies have to specialize in B, while others specialize in A. Without any innate differences, national economies need to be separated into the rich and the poor. Furthermore, as a larger fraction of the national economies succeeds in development, the world supply of A goes up relative to B, which reduces the relative price of A. This change in the relative price raises the threshold level of n, making the problem of development even harder for those remaining underdeveloped. See James Markusen (1991) for the dynamic analysis along this line, demonstrating first-mover advantages in economic development in the presence of international trade.

The above model thus captures an element of the radical or structuralist views, expressed by Paul Baran (1957), Myrdal (1957), and most notably by Raul Prebisch (1950). Nevertheless, its policy implications should be interpreted with caution. First, the economy may be better off in the low equilibrium trap than in autarky. Specializing in B under free trade is worse than specializing in A under free trade, but this does not necessarily imply that specializing in B under free trade is worse than autarky. Second, the analysis treats nontradeability (or, more generally, transport costs) of specialized inputs as given. As Markusen (1989) and others have pointed out, reducing trade barriers on specialized inputs is generally desirable. This is the case even when some inputs are truly nontradeable. For example, in the above example, suppose that some specialized inputs are tradeable, while others are nontradeable. Initially, all tradeable inputs are banned, and the economy is in the low equilibrium trap. Removing trade barriers on some tradeable inputs can help the economy to cross the threshold, which increases demand for inputs, including nontradeable ones. Hence, there is complementarity between tradeable and nontradeable inputs.[8]

4.C   Sustainable Growth

Note that in the previous model, the cumulative process of growth and development ultimately peters out. This is because the resource constraint eventually becomes strong enough to counteract demand complementarities. In industrialized countries, however, all indices seem to point steadily upwards. On average and in the long run there are no signs of a slacking of economic development in these countries (Angus Maddison 1982, ch. 2; Romer 1986). The recent literature on endogenous growth shows that complementarity in the technologies of entry processes itself may be important for sustainable growth.

Again, the basic model of Section 3.A can be used to illustrate the basic idea. As shown in Figure 8.2, the benefit of entry, gross profit, declines with new entries. In order to offset smaller profits, the cost of entry must also decline. One way of doing this, taken from Luis Rivera-Batiz and Romer (1991) and Robert Barro and Xavier Sala-i-Martin (1992), is to assume that starting new firms requires F units of the final good, instead of labor. The idea is that new generations of computers would help scientists design new products, hence this model is called "the lab equipment model" by L. Rivera-Batiz and Romer. Under this specification, entry also benefits from increasing returns due to specialization, which introduces a complementarity in the entry process and makes growth sustainable.

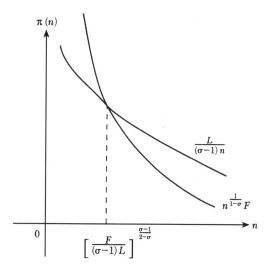

Figure 8.5

As labor is used only in manufacturing of inputs, the labor market condition becomes simply $nax = L$. Gross profit is thus $\pi = x/\sigma = L/(\sigma - 1)n$, which is declining in n. The cost of entry, on the other hand, becomes PF, so that entry of new firms would continue as long as

$$\pi(n) = \frac{L}{(\sigma - 1)n} \geq n^{1/(1-\sigma)}F, \tag{9''}$$

or

$$\frac{L}{(\sigma - 1)F} \geq n^{(2-\sigma)/(1-\sigma)}.$$

If $\sigma = 2$, then both the benefits and costs of entry fall at the same rate, and the inducement to start up new firms always exists as long as $L > (\sigma - 1)F$. If $\sigma < 2$, the case shown in Figure 8.5, the cost of entry falls faster than the benefit. This creates a threshold for development, but the cumulative process of growth, once started, will never stop.

An alternative way of generating sustainable growth, taken from Romer (1990) and Gene Grossman and Helpman (1991, ch. 3) and others, is to introduce learning-by-doing in the process of entry, while maintaining the assumption of the fixed cost being paid by labor. More specifically, let us suppose that the amount of labor required in start-up operations declines with the number of firms, say, F/n^λ. Then the stock of knowledge useful for setting up new firms is increasing in n. The idea is that entrepreneurs starting new businesses or scientists designing new products can learn from past experience, hence named "the knowledge-driven model" by L. Rivera-Batiz and Romer. The labor market clearing condition is now

$$L = n\left[ax + \frac{F}{n^\lambda}\right].$$

By substituting this expression in (8), one can show that the entry of new firms would continue as long as

$$\pi(n) = \frac{1}{\sigma - 1}\left[\frac{L}{n} - \frac{F}{n^\lambda}\right] \geq \frac{F}{n^\lambda}$$

or

$$\frac{L}{\sigma F} \geq n^{1-\lambda}.$$

If labor productivity in start-up operations is proportional to the number of firms ($\lambda = 1$), as assumed in Romer, and Grossman and Helpman, then there is always an incentive to start up new firms and introduce new products as long as $L > \sigma F$. If the learning-by-doing or knowledge-spillover effect is stronger ($\lambda > 1$), then the possibility of underdevelopment traps arises, but, again, the cumulative process of growth, once started, will never stop.

5   The Logic of Coordination Failures

The models with complementarity discussed above often have Pareto-rankable multiple equilbria, which naturally raises many methodological questions. For those who work in this area, there is a familiar set of closely related criticisms and objections they encounter repeatedly when presenting their research. In this section, I address some of these questions, particularly, concerning the logic of coordination failures.[9]

Once objection to the analysis of coordination failures based on complementarity is that, with huge gains from coordination, people should eventually manage to find a way of coordinating complementary activities, hence the inefficiency due to such a failure would not be relevant in practice. Some would even suggest that mergers can solve the problem entirely.

There are several ways of responding to this objection. First, unlike the couple rowing a boat together, or the two producers manufacturing the nuts and bolts, complementarities in the models discussed here arise as an outcome of market interactions among a large number of producers and consumers. Second, finding out which activities are complementary and can be combined most profitably is an enormously demanding problem in practice. In the models discussed above, this problem is made artificially simple, because there are at most two sets of complementary products and all products enter symmetrically within each set. But these assumptions, made for the sake of analytical simplicity, are not realistic features of the models. (And we know that these assumptions are "true," having set up the models, but the agents living in these environments may not be so fortunate.) In reality, one has to overcome enormous information problems. The set of all products, both existing and potential, is huge. Products are not generally symmetric. One has to find out which combination of products is complementary, and the number of possible combinations grows exponentially with the number of products. This is not to deny that there are isolated instances in which coordination problems have been identified and solved. Successful businesses are introduced regularly by those who discover (or stumble upon) a new way of combining complementary products: business books are full of such stories. But the very fact that these innovators can get fabulously rich in the process and yet, new ways of doing businesses are introduced year after year suggests that a large number of coordination problems are waiting to be discovered.

Third, even when the agents know which activities need to be coordinated, the problem is far from being solved. Explicit coordination, such as the merger, is itself an activity that requires the use of resources. The important assumption in monopolistic competition models, though not always explicitly stated, is that firms achieve superior production technologies by specialization. An entrepreneur who attempts to manage many activities at the same time may face a production technology that is considerably less efficient than when these activities are managed by independent entrepreneurs.

Fourth, if mergers were costless, they would take place not only for the purpose of coordinating complementary activities, but also for restricting competition and enhancing monopoly power. In this case, other assumptions of the models studied in this paper—that the actions taken by an individual firm are negligible in the aggregate economy and there is no strategic interaction between firms—lose much of their plausibility. Of course, this is not to deny that multi-product firms can sometimes overcome coordination problems: introducing explicit costs of coordination, and hence endogenizing the range of activities undertaken by a firm in monopolistic competition models, would be a desirable direction for future research. However, it is optimistic to suppose that entrepreneurial efforts can eventually solve all important coordination problems.

The second line of criticism against the analysis of coordination failures questions its logical consistency with the equilibrium analysis. For the equilibrium analysis to be valid, there must be some reason for all agents to come to expect simultaneously that a particular equilibrium should prevail. Some may argue that the agents, if capable of coordinating their expectations, can equally well coordinate a change in their expectations, and move away from a Pareto-dominated equilibrium to the Pareto-dominant one.

One possible response is that coordinating expectations is much easier than coordinating changes in expectations. The former can be achieved historically through conventions, customs, cultural beliefs, ideologies, or other processes of learning (or some may say, assimilation or indoctrination). The formation of stable expectations indeed has an important social dimension, and many institutions can be viewed as responses to this problem. On the other hand, coordinating changes in expectations, and thereby initiating a concerted change in actions, requires a break from tradition and the institutional framework that helped agents to share the same expectations in the first place. These arguments, of course, have to be represented in an explicit dynamic setting, but many economists find them convincing, at least in the context of economic development and regional disparities.

The above response may not be convincing in the context of economic fluctuations, which is probably why many economists remain skeptical about the macroeconomics of coordination failures. In the unabridged version of this paper, I suggested a way of making it more plausible, by showing how agents naturally come to move in unison in the presence of intertemporal substitution. However, an altogether different response to the criticism may be more appropriate. The presence of Pareto-rankable multiple equilibria invalidates equilibrium analysis of business cycles; agents cannot coordinate their expectations, having a difficult time in forecasting the forecast of others, which may be why business cycles are unpredictable and why there is so much demand for business forecasting.

6 Concluding Remarks

In recent years, monopolistic competition models have frequently been applied in macroeconomics, international and interregional economics, as well as growth and development. The three features of monopolistic competition, the monopoly power of differentiated goods producers, the lack of strategic interaction, and the explicit analysis of entry and exit, make it a useful framework to examine the aggregate implications of monopoly distortions, increasing returns and expanding product variety. In this paper, I have presented a highly selective review in this area, with special emphasis on complementarity and its role in generating multiplier processes, business cycles, clustering, underdevelopment traps, regional disparities, and sustainable growth, or more generally, what Myrdal (1957) called the "principle of circular and cumulative causation."

I should point out that monopolistic competition is not the only way of modeling complementarity. As the self-adjusting nature of market forces in the standard neoclassical paradigm is due to efficient resource allocation, any departure from the standard paradigm would increase the chance of generating complementarities, thereby introducing instability and cumulative processes. For example, it is well known that more decentralized trading processes, instead of well-organized Walrasian markets, create complementarities, which have been used to explain underemployment (Peter Diamond 1982) and business cycles (P. Diamond and Drew Fudenberg 1989), and the universal adoption of a single medium of exchange (Kiyotaki and Randall Wright 1989; Matsuyama, Kiyotaki, and Akihiko Matsui 1993). In macroeconomics, the lack of complete enforceable contingent contracts is emphasized as the mechanism of generating coordination failure in financial and investment decisions (Douglas Diamond and Phlip Dybvig 1983; Marco Pagano 1989; Douglas Gale 1992; Daron Acemoglu 1993), as well as complementarity between real and financial sectors (Ben Bernanke and Mark Gertler 1989; Abhijit Banerjee and Andrew Newman 1993; Kiyotaki and John Moore 1993; Jeremy

Greenwood and Bruce Smith, forthcoming). Information externalities also generate complementarities and cumulative processes, which are used to explain a variety of phenomena, such as custom, fashion, and fads (Banerjee 1992; Sushil Bikhchandani, David Hirshleifer, and Ivo Welch 1992), and business cycles and market crashes (Andrew Caplin and John Leahy 1994; Christophe Chamley and Gale 1994; Joseph Zeira 1994). Recent work on political economy also demonstrates that political constraints may lead to an inefficiency trap (Kevin Roberts 1989; Raquel Fernandez and Rodrik 1991; Torsten Persson and Guido Tabellini 1994).

For that matter, pure technological externalities, either static Marshallian external economies or dynamic learning-by-doing effects, would be enough to generate complementarities. Many existing studies (including my own) used external economies to model the phenomena discussed in this paper, while maintaining the other assumptions of the neoclassical paradigm; see, for example, Brian Arthur (1990), Ethier (1982b), Krugman (1981, 1987), Matsuyama (1992d), and Alwyn Young (1991) for international and interregional inequalities and industrial localization; Costas Azariadis and Allan Drazen (1990), Steven Durlauf (1993) and Matsuyama (1991) for underdevelopment traps; Robert Lucas (1988, 1993), Romer (1986), and Nancy Stokey (1991) for sustainable growth. Peter Howitt and Preston McAfee (1992) and Dale Mortensen (1989, 1991) also rely on pure externalities to generate business cycles in their search models. Even some monopolistic competition models, such as the knowledge-driven models of sustainable growth discussed in Section 4.C, rely on pure technological externalities. Pure technological externalities resulting from knowledge spillovers are surely important in explaining some of these phenomena. But at the same time, assuming externalities in the standard paradigm would be viewed as a cheap way of generating complementarities. Krugman (1991), for example, argues against relying too much on assuming pure externalities. My own view on this matter is that models with pure externalities are often useful and convenient for exploring the consequences of complementarities, but should be taken at most as a reduced form that is meant to capture some underlying mechanism generating complementarities. Any result, particularly on the effects of policies, needs to be interpreted with great caution. For any change in the environment might also affect the nature of complementarities itself, as illustrated by a couple of examples in this chapter.

Notes

1. I should emphasize that this chapter surveys the literature in which complementarities arise as an outcome of equilibrium interaction in models of monopolistic competition. Many studies, both in industrial organization and in macroeconomics, analyze the performance of imperfect competitive markets in the presence of assumed technological complementarities. An extreme example would be the problems of two producers, each supplying a good to the customer that is a perfect complement to the other, such as "nuts and bolts." The most successful application of this framework is the literature on the organization of firms, exemplified by Paul Milgrom and John Roberts (1992). Many economists find the macroeconomic applications of this framework unconvincing, because there would be a strong incentive to internalize this kind of complementary activities, as rightly pointed out by Milgrom and J. Roberts, and hence the aggregate implications would be, at best, dubious. In the models discussed here, on the other hand, complementarities arise as an outcome of the internal mechanism of the market system: anything short of taking over the entire economy would not internalize them.

2. Alternatively, one can assert that some specific factors, such as entrepreneurial capital, are required to operate firms, and their services can be purchased in the competitive market, but they are fixed in supply. According to this interpretation, no firm earns monopoly profits and all rents are captured by the owners of competitively supplied factors. Whether one should describe this situation as "free entry" or "restricted entry" is a matter of semantics.

3. It should be noted that the primary goal of this literature is to explain the rigidity of nominal prices. Monopolistically competitive market structures are adopted out of necessity of modeling price-setting firms. Complementarities due to aggregate demand spillovers are rather by-products in this literature.

4. As the analysis above suggests, a small modification of the basic model can easily generate Pareto-rankable multiple equilibria. For example, incorporating nonhomothetic preferences (Walter Heller 1986), decreasing marginal costs (Kiyotaki 1988), or endogenizing the markup (Jordi Galí 1994), could magnify the multiplier to such an extent that the modified models have both good and bad equilibria. The so-called "coordination failure" literature, surveyed by Russell Cooper and Andrew John (1988), argues that such models with Pareto-rankable multiple equilibria describe the essence of business cycles with the interpretation of a good equilibrium as a boom and a bad one as a recession. Unfortunately, the static nature of most models in this literature leaves many skeptical of its usefulness as a foundation of business cycle theories. There are two ways of using a static model of complementarities as a building block of a dynamic model of endogenous business cycles. In the first approach, used by Shleifer (1986), Hall (1991) and Murphy, Shleifer, and Vishny (1989b), agents face some intertemporal substitution restrictions, so that they are concerned with the timing of their actions. When combined with intratemporal complementarities, such restrictions provide an incentive for temporal agglomeration. The second approach is based on "sunspots," used, for example, by Satyajit Chatterjee, Cooper, and B. Ravikumar (1993). In the unabridged version of this paper, I sketch these two approaches and discuss their relative merits.

5. It would be interesting to extend such a model to incorporate public goods, highways, and railroads. Once more people have chosen to drive and more shops have

established along highways, there would be a stronger political support to invest more on highways. Such a political process should further accentuate complementarities.

6. Of course, it is possible that some commodities are not produced in equilibrium in a model with complete competitive markets. However, the equilibrium allocation is still efficient, as markets are open even for these nonproduced commodities. There are publicly quoted equilibrium prices, to which consumers submit zero demand and producers submit zero supply. The equilibrium quantity is zero for these commodities precisely because there are no gains from trade. Another way of saying this is that the open but inactive market is fundamentally different from the closed market.

7. This is because markets exist for all the commodities actually produced and consumed. This is different from the literature of incomplete security markets, surveyed by Darrell Duffie (1992), or from the sunspot literature surveyed by Pierre-Andre Chiappori and Roger Guesnerie (1991), in which trading opportunities are restricted even for commodities that are a part of endowment bundle. The critical difference is that, unlike in these literatures, the set of goods consumed is determined endogenously in models of monopolistic competition.

8. Indeed, there is much broader argument why this kind of analysis cannot be interpreted as justification for policy activism (Matsuyama 1994).

9. In the unabridged version of this paper, I also offer counterarguments for general objections to models with multiple equilibria. My view on these methodological issues is far from original. Yet, it has been shaped so gradually over the years through conversations as well as readings that I cannot attribute it to particular sources. In writing this section, however, I found it useful re-reading some of the articles, including Guesnerie (1993), Romer (1994) and Michael Woodford (1987). Matsuyama (1993b, 1994) also discuss some issues in more detail.

References

Acemoglu, Daron. "Labor Market Imperfections, Innovation Incentives and the Dynamics of Innovation Activity." Unpublished paper, MIT, 1993.

Arrow, Kenneth J. and Hahn, Frank H. *General competitive analysis*. San Francisco: Holden-Day, 1971.

Arthur, W. Brian. "'Silicon Valley' Locational Clusters: When Do Increasing Returns Imply Monopoly?" *Math. Soc. Sci.*, June 1990, *19*(3), pp. 235–51.

Azariadis, Costas and Drazen, Allan. "Threshold Externalities in Economic Development," *Quart. J. Econ.*, May 1990, *105*(2), pp. 501–26.

Baran, Paul A. *The political economy of growth*. New York: Monthly Review Press, 1957.

Banerjee, Abhijit V. "A Simple Model of Herd Behavior," *Quart. J. Econ.*, Aug. 1992, *107*(3), pp. 797–817.

Banerjee, Abhijit V. and Newman, Andrew F. "Occupational Choice and the Process of Development," *J. Polit. Econ.*, Apr. 1993, *101*(2), pp. 274–98.

Barro, Robert J. and Sala-i-Martin, Xavier. "Public Finance in Models of Economic Growth," *Rev. Econ. Stud.*, Oct. 1992, *59*(4), pp. 645–61.

Beath, John and Katsoulacos, Yannis. *The economic theory of product differentiation.* Cambridge: Cambridge U. Press, 1991.

Benassy, Jean-Pascal. "A Neo-Keynesian Model of Price and Quantity Determination in Disequilibrium," in *Equilibrium and disequilibrium in economic theory.* Ed.: Gerhard Schwödiauer. Boston: Reidel, 1978, pp. 511–44.

———. "Monopolistic Competition," in *Handbook of mathematical economics,* Vol. IV. Eds.: Werner Hildenbrand and Hugo Sonnenschein. Amsterdam: North-Holland, 1991, ch. 37, pp. 1997–2048.

Bernanke, Ben S. and Gertler, Mark. "Agency Costs, Net Worth, and Business Fluctuations," *Amer. Econ. Rev.,* Mar. 1989, *79*(1), pp. 14–31.

Bikhchandani, Sushil; Hirshleifer, David and Welch, Ivo. "A Theory of Fads, Fashion, Custom, and Cultural Change as Informational Cascades," *J. Polit. Econ.,* Oct. 1992, *100*(5), pp. 992–1026.

Blanchard, Olivier J. and Kiyotaki, Nobuhiro. "Monopolistic Competition and the Effect of Aggregate Demand," *Amer. Econ. Rev.,* Sept. 1987, *77*(4), pp. 647–66.

Caplin, Andrew S. and Leahy, John. "Business as Usual, Market Crashes, and Wisdom after the Fact," *Amer. Econ. Rev.,* June 1994, *84*(3), pp. 548–65.

Chamberlin, Edward. *The theory of monopolistic competition.* Cambridge: Harvard U. Press, 1933.

Chamley, Christophe and Gale, Douglas. "Information Revelation and Strategic Delay in a Model of Investment," *Econometrica,* Sept. 1994, *62*(5), pp. 1065–85.

Chatterjee, Satyajit; Cooper, Russell W. and Ravikumar, B. "Strategic Complementarity in Business Formation: Aggregate Fluctuations and Sunspot Equilibria," *Rev. Econ. Stud.,* Oct. 1993, *60*(4), pp. 795–811.

Chiappori, Pierre-Ander and Guesnerie, Roger. "Sunspot Equilibria in Sequential Markets Models," in *Handbook of mathematical economics,* Vol. IV. Eds.: Werner Hildenbrand and Hugo Sonnenschein. Amsterdam: North-Holland, 1991, ch. 32, pp. 1683–762.

Ciccone, Antonio and Matsuyama, Kiminori. "Start-up Costs and Pecuniary Externalities as Barriers to Economic Development." Working Papers in Economics, E-92-14, Hoover Institution, Stanford U., 1992.

Cooper, Russell and John, Andrew. "Coordinating Coordination Failures in Keynesian Models," *Quart. J. Econ.,* Aug. 1988, *103*(3), pp. 441–63.

Diamond, Douglas W. and Dybvig, Phlip H. "Bank Runs, Deposit Insurance, and Liquidity," *J. Polit. Econ.,* June 1983, *91*(3), pp. 401–19.

Diamond, Peter A. "Aggregate Demand Management in Search Equilibrium," *J. Polit. Econ.,* Oct. 1982, *90*(5), pp. 881–94.

Diamond, Peter A. and Fudenberg, Drew. "Rational Expectations Business Cycles in Search Equilibrium," *J. Polit. Econ.,* June 1989, *97*(3), pp. 606–19.

Dixit, Avinash K. and Norman, Victor. *Theory of international trade.* Cambridge: Cambridge U. Press, 1980.

Dixit, Avinash K. and Stiglitz, Joseph E. "Monopolistic Competition and Optimum Product Diversity," *Amer. Econ. Rev.,* June 1977, *67*(3), pp. 297–308.

Domowitz, Ian; Hubbard, R. Glenn and Petersen, Bruce C. "Market Structure and Cyclical Fluctuations in U.S. Manufacturing," *Rev. Econ. Statist.*, Feb. 1988, *70*(1), pp. 55–66.

Duffie, Darrell. "The Nature of Incomplete Security Markets," in *Advances in economic theory: Sixth World Congress*, Vol. II. Ed.: Jean Jacques Laffont. Cambridge: Cambridge U. Press, 1992, ch. 4, pp. 214–62.

Durlauf, Steven D. "Nonergodic Economic Growth," *Rev. Econ. Stud.*, Apr. 1993, *60*(2), pp. 349–66.

Eaton, B. Curtis and Lipsey, Richard G. "Product Differentiation," in *Handbook of industrial organization*, Vol. I. Eds.: Richard Schmalensee and Robert D. Willig. Amsterdam: North-Holland, 1989, ch. 12, pp. 723–70.

Ellison, Glenn and Glaeser, Edward L. "Geographic Concentration in U.S. Manufacturing Industries: A Dartboard Approach." Working Paper, Harvard U., 1994.

Ethier, Wilfred J. "National and International Returns to Scale in the Modern Theory of International Trade," *Amer. Econ. Rev.*, June 1982a, *72*(3), pp. 389–405.

———. "Decreasing Costs in International Trade and Frank Graham's Argument for Protection," *Econometrica*, Sept. 1982b, *50*(5), pp. 1243–68.

Faini, Riccardo. "Increasing Returns, Nontraded Inputs and Regional Development," *Econ. J.*, June 1984, *94*(374), pp. 308–23.

Fernandez, Raquel and Rodrik, Dani. "Resistance to Reform: Status Quo Bias in the Presence of Individual-Specific Uncertainty," *Amer. Econ. Rev.*, Dec. 1991, *81*(5), pp. 1146–55.

Fujita, Masahisa. *Urban economic theory: Land use and city size*, Cambridge: Cambridge U. Press, 1989.

Gale, Douglas. "Standard Securities," *Rev. Econ. Stud.*, Oct. 1992, *59*(4), pp. 731–55.

Galí, Jordi. "Monopolistic Competition, Business Cycles, and the Composition of Aggregate Demand," *J. Econ. Theory*, June 1994, *63*(1), pp. 73–96.

Gordon, Robert J. "What Is New-Keynesian Economics?" *J. Econ. Lit.*, Sept. 1990, *28*(3), pp. 1115–71.

Greenwood, Jeremy and Smith, Bruce D. "Financial Markets in Development and the Development of Financial Markets," *J. Econ. Dynam. Control*, forthcoming.

Grossman, Gene M. and Helpman, Elhanan. *Innovation and growth in the global economy.* Cambridge: The MIT Press, 1991.

Guesnerie, Roger. "Successes and Failures in Coordinating Expectations," *Europ. Econ. Rev.*, Apr. 1993, *37*(2/3), pp. 243–68.

Hall, Robert E. "The Relation Between Price and Marginal Cost in U.S. Industry," *J. Polit. Econ.*, Oct. 1988, *96*(5), pp. 921–47.

———. *Booms and recessions in a noisy economy.* New Haven: Yale U. Press, 1991.

Hart, Oliver D. "Perfect Competition and Optimal Product Differentiation," *J. Econ. Theory*, Apr. 1980, *22*(2), pp. 279–312.

———. "A Model of Imperfect Competition with Keynesian Features," *Quart. J. Econ.*, Feb. 1982, *97*(1), pp. 109–38.

———. "Imperfect Competition in General Equilibrium: An Overview of Recent Work," in *Frontiers of economics.* Eds.: Kenneth J. Arrow and Seppo Honkapohja. Oxford: Blackwell, 1985, ch. 2, pp. 100–49.

Heller, Walter P. "Coordination Failure under Complete Markets with Applications to Effective Demand," in *Equilibrium analysis: Essays in honor of Kenneth J. Arrow*, Vol. II. Eds.: Walter P. Heller, Ross M. Starr, and David A. Starrett. Cambridge: Cambridge U. Press, 1986, pp. 155–75.

Helpman, Elhanan. *Monopolistic competition in trade theory.* Special Papers in International Finance, No. 16. Dept. of Economics, Princeton U., 1990.

Helpman, Elhanan and Krugman, Paul R. *Market structure and foreign trade.* Cambridge: The MIT Press, 1985.

Hicks, John R. *A contribution to the theory of the trade cycle.* Oxford: Oxford U. Press, 1950.

Hicks, John R. and Allen, R. C. D. "A Reconsideration of the Theory of Value, Parts I and II," *Economica*, N.S., Feb. 1934, pp. 52–76; May 1934, pp. 196–219.

Hirschman, Albert O. *The strategy of economic development.* New Haven: Yale U. Press, 1958.

Hotelling, Harold. "Stability in Competition," *Econ. J.*, Mar. 1929, *39*, pp. 41–57.

Howitt, Peter and McAfee, R. Preston. "Animal Spirits," *Amer. Econ. Rev.*, June 1992, *82*(3), pp. 493–507.

Judd, Kenneth L. "On the Performance of Patents," *Econometrica*, May 1985, *53*(3), pp. 567–85.

Kaldor, Nicholas. *Economics without equilibrium.* New York: M.E. Sharpe, 1985.

Kalecki, Michal. *Essays in the theory of economic fluctuations.* London: Allen & Unwin, 1939.

Kiyotaki, Nobuhiro. "Multiple Expectational Equilibria under Monopolistic Competition," *Quart. J. Econ.*, Nov. 1988, *103*(4), pp. 695–713.

Kiyotaki, Nobuhiro and Moore, John. "Credit Cycles." Unpub., U. of Minnesota and London School of Economics, 1993.

Kiyotaki, Nobuhiro and Wright, Randall. "On Money as a Medium of Exchange," *J. Polit. Econ.*, Aug. 1989, *97*(4), pp. 927–54.

Krugman, Paul R. "Increasing Returns, Monopolistic Competition, and International Trade," *J. Int. Econ.*, Nov. 1979, *9*(4), pp. 469–79.

———. "Trade, Accumulation, and Uneven Development," *J. Devel. Econ.*, Apr. 1981, *8*(2), pp. 149–61.

———. "The Narrow Moving Band, the Dutch Disease, and the Competitive Consequences of Mrs. Thatcher: Notes on Trade in the Presence of Dynamic Scale Economies," *J. Devel. Econ.*, Oct. 1987, *27*(1/2), pp. 41–55.

———. *Geography and trade.* Cambridge: The MIT Press, 1991.

Krugman, Paul R. and Venables, Anthony J. "Integration and the Competitiveness of Peripheral Industry," in *Unity with diversity in the European Community*. Eds.: Christopher Bliss and Jorge Braga de Macedo. Cambridge: Cambridge U. Press, 1990.

Lancaster, Kevin J. *Variety, equity, and efficiency*. New York: Columbia U. Press, 1979.

Lucas, Robert E., Jr. "On the Mechanics of Economic Development," *J. Monet. Econ.*, July 1988, *22*(1), pp. 3–42.

———. "Marking a Miracle," *Econometrica*, Mar. 1993, *61*(2), pp. 251–72.

Maddison, Angus. *Phases of capitalist development*. Oxford: Oxford U. Press, 1982.

Makowski, Louis. "Perfect Competition, the Profit Criterion, and the Organization of Economic Activity," *J. Econ. Theory*, Apr. 1980, *22*(2), pp. 222–42.

Markusen, James R. "Trade in Producer Services and in Other Specialized Inputs," *Amer. Econ. Rev.*, Mar. 1989, *79*(1), pp. 85–95.

———. "First Mover Advantages, Blockaded Entry, and the Economics of Uneven Development," in *International trade and trade policy*. Eds.: Elhanan Helpman and Assaf Razin. Cambridge: MIT Press, 1991, pp. 245–69.

Matsuyama, Kiminori. "Increasing Returns, Industrialization, and Indeterminacy of Equilibrium," *Quart. J. Econ.*, May 1991, *106*(2), pp. 617–50.

———. "Imperfect Competition, Foreign Trade, and the Multipliers: Machlup-Metzler Fifty Years Later." Working Papers in Economics, E-92-4, Hoover Institution, Stanford U., 1992a.

———. "The Market Size, Entrepreneurship, and the Big Push," *J. Japanese Int. Econ.*, Dec. 1992b, *6*(4), pp. 347–64.

———. "Making Monopolistic Competition More Useful." Working Papers in Economics, E-92-18, Hoover Institution, Stanford U., 1992c.

———. "Agricultural Productivity, Comparative Advantage, and Economic Growth," *J. Econ. Theory*, Dec. 1992d, *58*(2), pp. 317–34.

———. "Modelling Complementarity in Monopolistic Competition," *Bank Japan Monet. Econ. Stud.*, July 1993a, *11*(1), pp. 87–109.

———. "Comments on Paul Krugman's 'Complexity and Emergent Structure in the International Economy'" 1993b; forthcoming in Alan V. Deardorff, James A. Levinson, and Robert M. Stern, eds., *New directions in trade theory*. Ann Arbor: U. of Michigan Press.

———. "Economic Development as Coordination Problems." presented at the World Bank Conference on the Role of Government in the Evolution of System Change, 1994.

Matsuyama, Kiminori; Kiyotaki, Nobuhiro and Matsui, Akihiko. "Toward a Theory of International Currency," *Rev. Econ. Stud.*, Apr. 1993, *60*(2), pp. 283–307.

Matsuyama, Kiminori and Takahashi, Takaaki. "Self-Defeating Regional Concentration." Center for Mathematical Studies in Economics and Management Sciences Discussion Paper, No. 1086, Northwestern U., 1994.

Milgrom, Paul R. and Roberts, John. *Economics, organization, and management*. New Jersey: Prentice-Hall, 1992.

Mortensen, Dale T. "The Persistence and Indeterminacy of Unemployment in Search Equilibrium," *Scand. J. Econ.*, 1989, *91*(2), pp. 347–70

———. "Equilibrium Unemployment Cycles." Center for Mathematical Studies in Economics and Management Sciences Discussion Paper, #939, Northwestern U., 1991.

Murphy, Kevin M.; Shleifer, Andrei and Vishny, Robert W. "Industrialization and the Big Push," *J. Polit. Econ.*, Oct. 1989a, *97*(5), 1003–26.

———. "Building Blocks of Market Clearing Business Cycle Models," *NBER macroeconomics annual: 1989*. Eds.: Olivier Jean Blanchard and Stanley Fischer. Cambridge, MA and London: MIT Press, 1989b, pp. 247–87.

Myrdal, Gunnar. *Economic theory and underdeveloped regions*. London: Duckworth, 1957.

Negishi, Takashi. *General equilibrium theory and international trade*. Amsterdam: North-Holland, 1972.

———. "Existence of an Under-Employment Equilibrium," in *Equilibrium and disequilibrium in economic theory*. Ed.: Gerhard Schwödiauer. Boston: Reidel, 1978, pp. 497–510.

———. *Microeconomic foundations of Keynesian macroeconomics*. Amsterdam: North-Holland, 1979.

Nurkse, Ragnar. *Problems of capital formation in underdeveloped countries*. New York: Oxford U. Press, 1953.

———. *Equilibrium and growth in the world economy: economic essays*. Eds.: Gottfried Haberler and Robert M. Stern. Cambridge: Harvard U. Press, 1961.

Pagano, Marco. "Endogenous Market Thinness and Stock Price Volatility," *Rev. Econ. Stud.*, Apr. 1989, *56*(2), pp. 269–87.

Persson, Torsten and Tabellini, Guido. "Is Inequality Harmful for Growth?" *Amer. Econ. Rev.*, June 1994, *84*(3), pp. 600–21.

Prebisch, Raul. *The economic development of Latin America and its principal problems*. The Economic Commission for Latin America, United Nations, 1950.

Rivera-Batiz, Francisco L. "Increasing Returns, Monopolistic Competition, and Agglomeration Economies in Consumption and Production," *Reg. Sci. Urban Econ.*, Feb. 1988, *18*(1), pp. 125–53.

Rivera-Batiz, Luis A. and Romer, Paul M. "Economic Integration and Endogenous Growth," *Quart. J. Econ.*, May 1991, *106*(2), pp. 531–55.

Roberts, Kevin W. S. "The Theory of Union Behavior: Labor Hoarding and Endogenous Hysteresis." Unpub., London School of Economics, 1989.

Robinson, Joan. *The economics of imperfect competition*. London: MacMillan, 1993.

Rodríguez-Clare, Andres. "The Division of Labor, Agglomeration Economies and Economic Development." Ph.D. dissertation, Stanford U., 1993.

Rodrik, Dani. "Coordination Failures and Government Policy: A Model with Applications to East Asia and Eastern Europe," *J. Int. Econ.*, forthcoming.

Romer, Paul M. "Increasing Returns and Long-run Growth," *J. Polit. Econ.*, Oct. 1986, *94*(5), pp. 1002–37.

———. "Growth Based on Increasing Returns Due to Specialization," *Amer. Econ. Rev.*, May 1987, *77*(2), pp. 56–62.

———. "Endogenous Technological Change," *J. Polit. Econ.*, Oct. 1990, *98*(5, Part 2), pp. S71–102.

———. "New Goods, Old Theory, and the Welfare Costs of Trade Restrictions," *J. Devel. Econ.*, Feb. 1994, *43*(1), pp. 5–38.

Rosenstein-Rodan, Paul N. "Problems of Industrialisation of Eastern and South-Eastern Europe," *Econ. J.*, June/Sept. 1943, *53*, pp. 202–11.

Rotemberg, Julio J. "The New Keynesian Microfoundations," *NBER macroeconomics annual: 1987*. Ed.: Stanley Fischer. Cambridge, MA and London: MIT Press, 1987, pp. 69–104.

Scitovsky, Tibor. "Two Concepts of External Economies," *J. Polit. Econ.*, Apr. 1954, *62*(2), 143–51.

Shleifer, Andrei. "Implementation Cycles," *J. Polit. Econ.*, Dec. 1986, *94*(6), pp. 1163–90.

Silvestre, Joaquim. "The Market-Power Foundations of Macroeconomic Policy," *J. Econ. Lit.*, Mar. 1993, *31*(1), pp. 105–41.

Startz, Richard. "Monopolistic Competition as a Foundation for Keynesian Macroeconomic Models," *Quart. J. Econ.*, Nov. 1989, *104*(4), pp. 737–52.

Stiglitz, Joseph E. "Towards a More General Theory of Monopolistic Competition," in *Prices, competition, and equilibrium*. Eds.: Maurice H. Peston and Richard E. Quandt. Oxford: Phillip Allan/Barnes & Noble Books, 1986, ch. 3, pp. 22–69.

Stokey, Nancy L. "Human Capital, Product Quality, and Growth," *Quart. J. Econ.*, May 1991, *106*(2), pp. 587–616.

Tirole, Jean. *The theory of industrial organization*, Cambridge: MIT Press, 1988.

Weitzman, Martin L. "Increasing Returns and the Foundations of Unemployment Theory," *Econ. J.*, Dec. 1982, *92*(368), pp. 787–804.

———. "Monopolistic Competition with Endogenous Specialization," *Rev. Econ. Stud.*, Jan. 1994, *61*(1), pp. 45–56.

Wolinsky, Asher. "Retail Trade Concentration Due to Consumers' Imperfect Information," *Bell. J. Econ.*, Spring 1983, *14*(1), pp. 275–82.

Woodford, Michael. "Three Questions about Sunspot Equilibria as an Explanation of Economic Fluctuations," *Amer. Econ. Rev.*, May 1987, *77*(2), pp. 93–98.

Young, Allyn A. "Increasing Returns and Economic Progress," *Econ. J.*, Dec. 1928, *38*, pp. 527–42.

Young, Alwyn. "Learning by Doing and the Dynamic Effects of International Trade," *Quart. J. Econ.*, May 1991, *106*(2), pp. 369–405.

Zeira, Joseph. "Informational Cycles," *Rev. Econ. Stud.*, Jan. 1994, *61*(1), pp. 31–44.

9

Making a Miracle

Robert E. Lucas, Jr.

1 Introduction

In 1960, the Philippines and South Korea had about the same standard of living, as measured by their per capita GDPs of about $640 U.S. 1975. The two countries were similar in many other respects. There were 28 million people in the Philippines and 25 million in Korea, with slightly over half of both populations of working age. Twenty seven percent of Filippinos lived in Manila, 28 percent of South Koreans in Seoul. In both countries, all boys of primary school age were in school, and almost all girls, but only about a quarter of secondary school age children were in school. Only 5 percent of Koreans in their early twenties were in college, as compared to 13 percent in the Philippines. Twenty six percent of Philippine GDP was generated in agriculture, and 28 percent in industry. In Korea, the comparable numbers were 37 and 20 percent. Ninety six percent of Philippine merchandise exports consisted of primary commodities and 4 percent of manufactured goods. In Korea, primary commodities made up 86 percent of exports, and manufactured goods 14 (of which 8 were textiles).

From 1960 to 1988, GDP per capita in the Philippines grew at about 1.8 percent per year, about the average for per capita incomes in the world as a whole. In Korea, over the same period, per capita income grew at 6.2 percent per year, a rate consistent with the doubling of living standards every 11 years. Korean incomes are now similar to Mexican, Portuguese, or Yugoslavian, about three times incomes in the Philippines, and about one third of incomes in the United States.[1]

I do not think it is in any way an exaggeration to refer to this continuing transformation of Korean society as a miracle, or to apply this term to the very similar transformations that are occurring in Taiwan, Hong Kong, and Singapore. Never before have the lives of so many people (63 million in these four areas in 1980) undergone so rapid an improvement over so long a period, nor (with the tragic exception of Hong Kong) is there any sign that this progress is near its end. How did it happen? Why did it happen in Korea and Taiwan, and not in the Philippines?

Questions like these can be addressed at many levels. It is useful to begin simply by listing some of the features of these transformations in addition to their income growth rates. All of the East Asian miracle economies have become large scale exporters of manufactured goods of increasing sophistication. They have become highly urbanized (no problem for Singapore and Hong Kong!) and increasingly well-educated. They have high savings rates. They have pro-business governments, following differing mixes of laissez faire and mercantilist commercial policies. These facts—or at least some of them—must figure in any explanation of the growth miracles, but they are additions to the list of events we want to explain, not themselves explanations.

We want to be able to use these events to help in assessing economic policies that may affect growth rates in other countries. But simply advising a society to "follow the Korean model" is a little like advising an aspiring basketball player to "follow the Michael Jordan model." To make use of someone else's successful performance at any task, one needs to be able to break this performance down into its component parts so that one can see what each part contributes to the whole, which aspects of this performance are imitable and, of these, which are worth imitating. One needs, in short, a theory.

There has been a great deal of interesting new theoretical research on growth and development generally in the last few years, some of it explicitly directed at the Asian miracles and much more that seems to me clearly relevant. I will use this lecture to try and see what recent research offers toward an explanation for these events. My review will be sharply focused on neoclassical theories that view the growth miracles as *productivity* miracles. What happened over the last 30 years that enabled the typical Korean or overseas Chinese worker to produce 6 times the goods and services he could produce in 1960? Indeed, my viewpoint will be even narrower than the neoclassical theories on which I draw, since I intend to focus on issues of *technology*, with only cursory treatment of consumer preferences and the nature of product market competition. There is no doubt that the issue of who gets the rewards from innovation is a central one, and it is not one that can be resolved on the basis of technological considerations alone, so this narrow focus will necessarily restrict the conclusions I will be able to draw. But there is no point in trying to think through hard questions of industrial organization and general equilibrium without an adequate description of the relevant technology, so this seems to me the right place to start.

I will begin in Section 2, with a brief sketch of some recent theoretical developments and of the image of the world economy these developments offer. This image does not, as I see it, admit of anything one could call a miracle, but it will be useful in motivating my subsequent emphasis on the accumulation of human capital, and in particular on human capital accumulation on the job: learning by doing. In Section 3, I will review a piece of microeconomic evidence on learning and productivity, just to remind you how solid the evidence is and how promising, quantitatively, for the theory of growth. Yet establishing the importance of learning by doing for productivity growth on a specific production process is very different from establishing its importance for an entire economy as a whole, or even for an entire sector. This connection is much more problematic than I once believed. But it has been made, in research by Nancy Stokey and Alwyn Young, and I will sketch the main technological implications of their work in Section 4. There is good reason to believe, I will argue, that something like this technology provided the means for the productivity miracles to occur. Section 5 discusses some of the issues involved in developing market equilibrium theories in which differential learning rates account for observed growth rate differences, and offers some speculations about the implications of such a theory for the development prospects of poor countries. Conclusions are in Section 6.

2   Theoretical Background

There has been a rebirth of confidence—stimulated in large part by Romer's (1986) contribution—that explicit neoclassical growth models in the style of Solow (1956) can be adapted to fit the observed behavior of rich and poor economies alike, interacting in a world of international trade. I do not believe we can obtain a theory of economic miracles in a purely aggregative set-up in which every country produces the same, single good (and a rich country is just one that produces more of it) but such a framework will be useful in stating the problem and in narrowing the theoretical possibilities.

Consider, to begin with, a single economy that uses physical capital, $k(t)$, and human capital, $h(t)$, to produce a single good, $y(t)$:

$$y(t) = Ak(t)^{\alpha}[uh(t)]^{1-\alpha}. \tag{2.1}$$

Here I multiply the human capital input by u, the fraction of time people spend producing goods.[2] The growth of physical capital depends on the savings rate s:

$$\frac{dk(t)}{dt} = sy(t), \tag{2.2}$$

while the growth of human capital depends on the amount of quality-adjusted time devoted to its production:

$$\frac{dh(t)}{dt} = \delta(1 - u)h(t). \tag{2.3}$$

Taking the decision variables s and u as given, which I will do for this exposition, the model (2.1)–(2.3) is just a reinterpretation of Solow's original model of a single, closed economy, with the rate of technological change (the average Solow residual) equal to $\mu = \delta(1 - \alpha)(1 - u)$ and the initial technology level equal to $Ah(0)^{1-\alpha}$. In this system, the long run growth rate of both capital and production per worker is $\delta(1 - u)$, the rate of human capital growth, and the *ratio* of physical to human capital converges to a constant. In the long run, the level of income is proportional to the economy's initial stock of human capital.[3]

To analyze a world economy made up of countries like this one, one needs to be specific about the mobility of factors of production. A benchmark case that has the virtues of simplicity and, I think, a decent degree of realism is obtained by assuming that labor is completely immobile, while physical capital is perfectly mobile. That is, if there are n countries indexed by i, assume that the world stock of physical capital, $K = \sum_{i=1}^{n} k_i$, is allocated across countries so as to equate the marginal product in each country to a common world return, r. Then if each country has the technology (2.1) with a common intercept A, this world return is $r = \alpha A(K/H)^{\alpha-1}$, where $H = \sum_i u_i h_i$ is the world supply of effective labor devoted to goods production. Net domestic product in each country is proportional to its effective workforce:

$$y_i = A\left(\frac{K}{H}\right)^\alpha u_i h_i. \tag{2.4}$$

If everyone has the same constant savings rate s, the dynamics of this world economy are essentially the same as those of Solow's model. The world capital stock follows $(dk/dt) = sAK^\alpha H^{1-\alpha}$, and the time path of H is obtained by summing (2.2) over countries, each multiplied by its own time allocation variable u_i. The long run growth rate of physical capital and of every country's output is equal to the growth rate of human capital. Each country's income level will be proportional to its initial human capital, not only in the long run but all along the equilibrium path. The theory is thus consistent with the permanent maintenance of any degree of income inequality.

It would be hard to think of another theory as simple as this one that does a better job of fitting the postwar statistics in the back of the *World Development Report*. By reinterpreting Solow's technology variable as a country-specific stock of human capital, a model that predicts rapid convergence to common income levels is converted into one that is consistent with permanent income inequality. But the key assumption on which this prediction is based—that human capital accumulation in any one economy is independent of the level of human capital in other economies—conflicts with the evident fact that ideas developed in one place spread elsewhere, that there is one frontier of human knowledge, not one for each separate economy. Moreover, as Parente and Prescott (1991) observe, if the model above is realistically modified to permit each economy to be subject to shocks that have some independence across countries, the assumption that each economy undergoes sustained growth due to its own human capital growth *only* would imply ever-growing inequality within any subset of countries. Relative income levels would follow random-walk-like behavior. I do not see how this prediction can be reconciled with the postwar experience of, say, the OECD countries or the EEC. The countries of the world are tied together, economically and technologically, in a way that the model (2.1)–(2.3) does not capture.[4]

One way to introduce some convergence into the model I have sketched, proposed and studied by Parente and Prescott (1991), is to modify the human capital accumulation technology (2.2) so as to permit any one country's rate of human capital growth to be influenced by the level of human capital elsewhere in the world. For example, let $H(t)$ be the world effective labor variable defined above, and let $Z(t) = H(t)/\sum_i u_i$ be the world average human capital level. Replace the human capital accumulation equation (2.2) with:[5]

$$\frac{dh(t)}{dt} = \delta(1-u)h(t)^{1-\theta}Z(t)^{\theta}. \tag{2.5}$$

With this modification, the dynamics of the world stocks of physical and human capital are essentially unchanged, but now an economy with a human capital stock lower than the world average will grow faster than an above average economy. For example, if the time allocation is equal across countries, so that $H(t)$ and $Z(t)$ grow at the rate $\delta(1-u)$, a country's *relative* human capital, $z_i = h_i/Z$, follows

$$\frac{d}{dt}z_i(t) = \delta(1-u)z(t)[z(t)^{-\theta} - 1]. \tag{2.6}$$

Evidently, $z_i(t)$ converges to one, and from (2.4), this means that relative incomes converge to one at the same rate.

In the world as a whole in the postwar period, income dispersion across all countries appears to be increasing. But, of course, there are many reasons to believe that the assumption of free world trade that leads to (2.6) is a very bad approximation for much of the world, and there are certainly differences across countries in the incentives people have to accumulate both kinds of capital, implying differences in savings rates and the allocation of time. Yet over subsets of countries, or regions of countries, where factor and final goods mobility is high (like the EEC or the 50 U.S. states) convergence can be observed.[6]

Barro and Sala-i-Martin (1992) obtain a regression estimate of an average convergence rate of relative incomes, conditioned on variables that may be interpreted as controlling for a country's adherence to the above assumptions, of slightly less than .02 (Table 3, p. 242). As they observe, if one interprets this coefficient as reflecting differential rates of physical capital accumulation in a world in which income differences reflect mainly differences in capital per worker, this rate of convergence is much too low to be consistent with observed capital shares. Alternatively, interpreting this figure as an estimate of $(1/z)(dz/dt)$ in (2.6), their estimate implies $\theta\delta(1-u) = .02$. Since $\delta(1-u)$ is the average rate of human capital growth, also about

.02 in reality, this interpretation yields an estimated θ of unity, which from (2.5) would mean that human capital accumulation in any country depends on local effort together with worldwide knowledge, independent of the local human capital level. From this viewpoint, the Barro-Sala-i-Martin estimate seems high.

All of this is by way of a prelude to thinking about growth miracles—about deviations from average behavior. I have described a model of a world economy—reasonably realistic in its description of average behavior of countries at different income levels—in which everyone has the same savings rate and allocates time in the same way. What are the prospects for using the same theory to see how variations across economies in the parameters s and u can induce variation in behavior of the magnitude we seek to explain? Here the exercise begins to get hard.

The East Asian economies do indeed have high investment rates. The current ratio of gross domestic investment to GDP in Korea is about .29, as compared to average behavior of around .22. In Taiwan and Hong Kong, the investment ratios are .21 and .24 respectively. In Singapore, it is a remarkable .47. In the Philippines, for comparison it is .18.[7] In a world with the perfect capital mobility used in my illustration above, these differences in investment rates would have *no* connection with savings rates: any country's higher than average savings would simply be invested abroad. Even with no international capital mobility, to translate a given difference in savings rates into a differences in output growth rates one must multiply by the return on capital (since

$$\frac{\partial}{\partial s}\left(\frac{1}{y}\frac{dy}{dt}\right) = \frac{\partial}{\partial s}\left(\frac{1}{y}\frac{\partial y}{\partial k}\frac{dk}{dt}\right) = \frac{\partial y}{\partial k},$$

from (2.2)). If the return on capital were ten percent, then, the Korea-Philippines investment rate difference of .11 can account for a difference of .011 in output growth rates, or about one percentage point. Even this effect is only transient, since in the long run differences in savings rates are level effects only.

Now applying the same rough calculation to the Singapore-Philippines investment rate difference of .29, one can account for a difference in output growth rates of nearly three percentage points (and more, if a higher and still defensible return on capital is used) which is close to the differentials I am calling "miraculous." Indeed, Young (1992) demonstrates that output growth in Singapore since the 1960's can be accounted for *entirely* by growth in conventionally measured capital and labor inputs, with nothing left over to be attributed to technological change. But Young's point, underscored by his parallel treatment of Singapore and Hong Kong, is the exceptional character of growth in Singapore, and not that the Asian miracles in general can be attributed to capital accumulation.

Growth accounting methods, applied country-by-country as in Young's study, can quantify the role of investment differentials in accounting for growth rate differences. In general, these differentials leave most measured output growth to be explained by other forces. This conclusion, which seems to me so clear, remains controversial. Correlations between investment ratios and growth rates, which tend to be positive, are frequently cited but do not settle anything. If growth is driven by rapid accumulation of human capital, one needs rapid growth in physical capital just to keep up: look at equation (2.4)! It may be that by excluding physical capital from the human capital accumulation equation (2.3) or (2.5) I have ruled out some interesting possibilities: One cannot accumulate skill as a computer programmer without a computer. Perhaps physical capital will assume a more important role when the technology for accumulating human capital is better understood, but if so, it will be at best a supporting part. Let us look elsewhere.

In the framework I am using, the other possible source of growth rate differentials is differential rates of human capital accumulation, stemming from differences in societies' time-allocation decisions. But human capital takes many forms and its accumulation occurs in many ways, so there are decisions in emphasis to be made here as well. The key choice, I think, is whether to stress human capital accumulation at school, or on the job.

If one interprets (2.3) or (2.5) as describing knowledge accumulation through schooling, these equations imply that doubling the fraction in school would double the human capital growth rate, adding only another .02 to the average rate of .02. And, of course, the linearity of (2.3) probably leads to an *overstatement* of the effect of so large a change. As I remarked in my introduction, the fast growing Asian economies are not, in general, better schooled than some of their slow growing neighbors. Emphasis on formal schooling, then, seems to involve the application of a modest multiplier to very slight differences in behavior, leading to the same discouraging conclusion for human capital that I arrived at in the case of physical capital.

This conclusion may seem an inappropriate inference from an over-simplified model, but I think it is in fact reinforced by thinking more seriously about the effects of schooling. Actual schooling decisions take place in a life-cycle context, with school preceding work and each individual deciding on the length of these two career phases. (This is a simplification, too, but a better one than thinking of a representative agent dividing his time in perpetuity.) Now in a steady state or balanced path of an economy in which everyone spends a fraction $1 - u$ of his working life in school, workers with schooling level $1 - u$ are retiring from the labor force at exactly the same rate as new workers with the same education level are entering. No matter what the value of u is in such a steady state, *all* of this investment is replacement investment and there is *no* increase in the average skill level of the workforce. Since (2.3) is an hypothesis about *net* investment, one cannot then identify the variable $1 - u$ with time spent in school. One is left with two choices. We can identify *increases* in average schooling levels with net human capital investment. Since schooling levels are increasing in virtually all societies today, this is a possibility worth developing, but it cannot be pursued within a steady state framework. This is an important and neglected respect in which neither advanced nor most backward economies can be viewed as moving along balanced growth paths.

Alternatively, we can think of a balanced path on which time spent in school is constant but the *quality* of schooling is improving due to increases in general knowledge. This possibility is analyzed in Stokey (1991a), from which the argument of the last paragraph is taken. In this paper, the rate of expansion of knowledge is taken to be an external effect of the time spent in school, the hypothesis that transforms a level effect into the needed growth effect. But this hypothesis does not salvage the multiplier arguments I applied above, unless one is willing to assume that increases in general knowledge accrue equally from time spent in primary schools and universities. To quantify a model like Stokey's, one would need a much sharper empirical identification of the set of activities that lead to new knowledge—to net investment in a society's human capital—than is provided by any aggregate index of total schooling time. This would be a most interesting avenue to explore but I am not prepared to do so here, so I will end this digression and move on.

Human capital accumulation also occurs at work, as we know from the fact the experienced workers and managers earn more than inexperienced ones. This aspect of human capital accumulation—on the job training—could also be (and has been) modeled as a time-allocation decision. Alternatively, in a multiple good world, one could think of on the job accumulation—learning by doing—as associated with the type of process one is engaged in. That is, one might think of some activities as carrying with them a high rate of skill acquisition and others, routine or traditional ones, as associated with a low rate. If so, the mix of goods a society produces will affect its overall rate of human capital accumulation and growth. For understanding diversity, I think this route has promise: The variation across societies, or at least those engaged in international trade, in the mix of goods produced is enormous. In this section, I have tried to motivate a focus on this source of diversity by a process of elimination: Neither physical capital accumulation nor human capital accumulation through schooling seems to have much potential, at least within the framework I have adopted. In this next section, I turn to much more direct, microeconomic evidence on the same point.

3   The Liberty Ship Miracle

In Lucas (1988) I used a multi-good model, adapted from Krugman (1987), in which different goods were associated with different learning rates to capture the idea that the choice of which goods to produce can be viewed as an implicit choice of a human capital accumulation rate. In a world of open economies, comparative advantage—previously accumulated, good-specific human capital holdings—will determine who produces what, and the mix of goods that this process assigns to a particular economy will determine its rates of human capital growth. This kind of formulation has been taken in interesting directions by Boldrin and Scheinkman (1988) and Matsuyama (1992). It is attractive, for present purposes, because there are such wide differences in product mix across countries and because the fast growing Asian economies have undergone such dramatic changes in the goods they produce.

But the hypothesis that different goods are associated with *permanently* different learning potentials conflicts sharply with available evidence in two respects. First, examination of growth in total factor productivity (Solow residuals) across both industries and time (as conducted, for example, by Harberger (1990)), shows no decade-to-decade stability in the high productivity growth industries. Lumber and wood products can rank 14th in the 1950's, first in the 1960's, and disappear from the list of leaders altogether in the 1970's.[8] Second, evidence we have on learning on narrowly defined product lines invariably shows high initial learning rates, declining over time as production cumulates. These two kinds of evidence reinforce each other, and seem decisive against the formulation Krugman proposed. These observations have led Stokey (1988) and Young (1991a) to a very different formulation, one that is much more tightly grounded in microeconomic evidence. I will review this formulation in Section 4, but before doing so I want to reinforce the motivation with a reminder of just how impressive the evidence on the productivity effects of learning by doing can be.

The best evidence I know of that bears on on-the-job productivity change in a single, large scale production process, was utilized in studies by Allan D. Searle (1945) and Leonard A. Rapping (1965). Both studies used data on the production of a single type of cargo vessel—the Liberty Ship—in 14 U.S. shipyards during World War II. From December, 1941, through December, 1944, these yards produced a total of 2458 Liberty Ships, all to the same standardized design. For several individual yards, Searle plotted man-hours per vessel against number of vessels completed to date in that yard on log-log paper. His results for two yards are reproduced here as Figure 9.1. Average results over ten yards are given in Figure 9.2, along with results for three other vessel types. For Liberty Ships, "the reductions in man-hours per ship with each doubling of cumulative output ranged from 12 to 24 percent."[9]

Stimulated in part by Kenneth Arrow's (1961) theoretical suggestion that learning-by-doing might serve as the key factor in growth for an economy as a whole, Rapping incorporated Searle's and other evidence within a neoclassical production framework. He pooled the data for all yards and estimated a Cobb-Douglas production function, controlling for changes in capital per yard, with cumulated yard (not industry) production as an added regressor. He obtained estimates of the learning effect, comparable to Searle's, ranging from 11 to 29 percent. He also showed that the inclusion of calendar time added nothing (the trend came out slightly negative!) to these results.

I do not think there is anything unique to shipbuilding in the findings that Searle and Rapping obtained. The Boston Consulting Group (1972) has obtained fairly clean learning curves, with slopes similar to those estimated by Searle and Rapping, for a variety of industries,

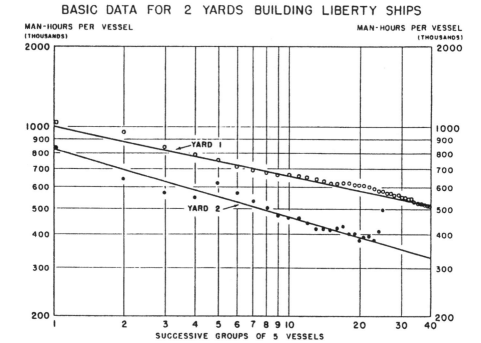

Figure 9.1
Reductions in man-hours per vessel with increasing production. Merchant shipyards.

and other researchers have done so as well. What is unique about the
Liberty ship data is that the ships were built according to exactly the
same blueprints over a period of several years and that data were
available yard by yard. Figure 9.2, which gives Searle's learning curve
for the industry as a whole, is not nearly as sharp as the curves in
Figure 9.1 for individual yards, presumably because industry expansion is a mix of increased production by existing yards and the entry
of new, inexperienced yards. Production data even from narrowly
defined industries mask continual model and other product mix
changes over time, which makes it difficult to use them to identify
even strong learning effects. What is exceptional about the Liberty
ship evidence, I think, is the cleanness of the experiment, not the behavior it documents so beautifully.

Quantitatively, these results are interesting to an economist looking for possible sources of miracles. For the three year period covered
by Rapping's study, industry output per manhour increased at a 40
percent annual rate! There is also considerable ambiguity about what

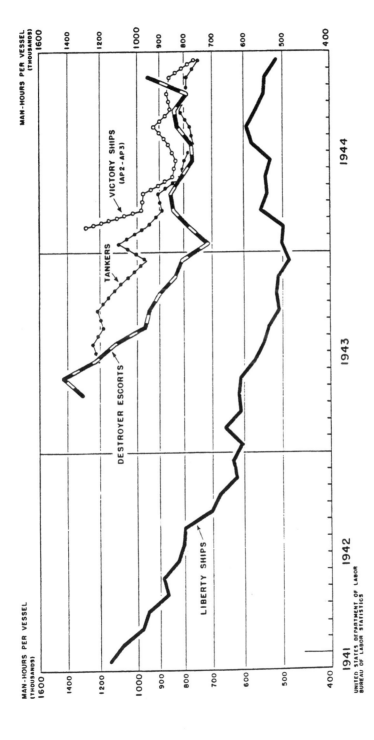

Figure 9.2
Unit man-hour requirements for selected shipbuilding programs. Vessels delivered December 1941–December 1944. United States Department of Labor, Bureau of Labor Statistics

this evidence means. Is it the individual worker who is doing the learning? The managers? The organization as a whole? Are the skills being learned specific to the production process on which the learning takes place, or more general? Does learning accrue solely to the individual worker, manager, or organization that does the producing, or is some of it readily appropriable by outside observers? These are questions that the theory of growth needs to address, but I will pass over them here.

A more urgent question, I think, is whether the kind of behavior Rapping and Searle documented, for one product line for one brief period, can be linked to productivity growth for an entire economy over periods of thirty or forty years. This is the topic of the next section.

4   Learning Models: Technology

In order to examine the possible connection between evidence of learning on individual product lines and productivity growth in an economy as a whole, consider the labor-only technology:

$$x(t) = kn(t)z(t)^{\alpha}, \tag{4.1}$$

where $x(t)$ is the rate of production of a good, k is a productivity parameter that depends on the units in which labor input and output are measured, $n(t)$ is employment, and $z(t)$ represents cumulative experience in the production of this good. Cumulative experience is in turn defined by the differential equation:

$$\frac{dz(t)}{dt} = n(t)z(t)^{\alpha}, \tag{4.2}$$

and the initial value $z(t_0)$, assumed to be greater than or equal to one, of the experience variable on the date t_0 when production was begun. The general solution to (4.2) is

$$z(t) = \left[(z(t_0))^{1-\alpha} + (1 - \alpha) \int_{t_0}^{t} n(u)\, du \right]^{1/1-\alpha}. \tag{4.3}$$

The implications of this model for the dynamics of production of a single good are familiar enough. Suppose, to take the simplest case, that employment is constant at $\bar{n}$ over time. Then (4.1) and (4.3) imply that production follows

$$x(t) = k\bar{n}[z(t_0)^{1-\alpha} + (1 - \alpha)\bar{n}(t - t_0)]^{\alpha/1-\alpha}.$$

Production grows without bound, and the rate of productivity growth declines monotonically from $\alpha\bar{n}(z(t_0))^{\alpha-1}$ to zero. For any initial productivity level $z(t_0) \geq 1$ and any employment level (or path) productivity at date t is an increasing function of the learning rate α.

Notice that the technology (4.2) implies a scale effect: a link between the level of employment and the rate of growth of productivity. This carries the unwelcome implication that a country like India should have an enormous growth advantage over a small country like Singapore. This is a feature of any learning by doing theory, but I agree with Matsuyama (1992) that if one is thinking about an entire economy or sizeable sector of an economy, it is a nuisance implication that we want to dispose of.[10] Matsuyama proposes thinking of a population as containing a fixed fraction of entrepeneurs, and of a technology that requires that each enterprise be headed by one of them. Then doubling the population means doubling the number of enterprises that are subject to the learning technology, keeping the size of each fixed, and has no growth effects. Insofar as learning effects are partly external to the firm, as I think they are, this device doesn't quite work, and one needs to think of some other limitation on scale—city size, say. I will simply ignore these scale economies in what follows, assuming that some explanation along the lines of Matsuyama's will be discovered to rationalize this neglect.

With the technology (4.1)–(4.3), one can obviously obtain miraculous rates of productivity growth by shifting a large amount of labor onto a single, new product line. Provided that $\bar{n}(t - t_0)$ is large relative to initial experience (which is the way most people interpret statistical learning curves), the rate of productivity growth t years after production is initiated is approximately $\alpha/((1 - \alpha)t)$. Using the value $\alpha = 0.2$ estimated by Rapping and Searle, productivity growth one year after a product is introduced is $\alpha/(1 - \alpha) = 0.25$. After two years, the growth rate is reduced by half to 0.125, and so on. A growth miracle sustained for a period of decades clearly must thus involve the continual introduction of new goods, not merely continued learning on a fixed set of goods. Even if new goods are introduced, a shift of workers from old goods with low learning rates to new goods with high rates involves an initial drop in productivity: people are better at familiar activities than they are at novel ones. It is not even clear how these factors balance out.

To pursue this question, I follow Stokey (1988) and consider an economy in which a variety of goods, indexed by s, is produced, where a higher index s means a better good. In Stokey (1988) and, in different ways in Young (1991a) and Grossman and Helpman (1991b), specific assumptions on consumer preferences or the technology give a precise meaning to the sense in which one good is better than another. For my immediate objectives, it will be adequate to consider a small, open economy and to use an assumed schedule $p(s, t) = e^{\mu s}$ of world prices to summarize the quality of goods: a better good means a good with a higher price on world markets. Assume that the economy progresses by introducing better quality (higher s) goods into production over time, and let $S(t)$ be the index of the good that is first produced at date t. (I will also use $\tau(s)$, where τ is the inverse function of the increasing function S, to denote the date on which good s is first produced.) Then if $x(s, t)$ is production of good s at date t, the value of the economy's total production is

$$y(t) = \int_0^{S(t)} e^{\mu s} x(s, t)\, ds. \tag{4.4}$$

Let $n(s, t)$ be employment on good s at t, and $z(s, t)$ be cumulated experience. Then if learning proceeds independently, good by good, (4.1) and (4.3) imply

$$x(s, t) = kn(s, t)\left[(z(s, \tau(s)))^{1-\alpha} + (1 - \alpha) \int_{\tau(s)}^{t} n(s, u)\, du \right]^{\alpha/1-\alpha}. \tag{4.5}$$

Equations (4.4) and (4.5) together describe the implications for total production of a given way of allocating labor across product lines through time.

Consider the following specific labor allocation. Let the rate of new product introduction be a constant λ, so that $S(t) = \lambda t$ and $\tau(s) = s/\lambda$. Let φ be a density function with cdf Φ, and suppose that for all $s \in (0, \lambda t]$, $n(s, t) = \varphi(t - s/\lambda)$ (that $\varphi(t - s/\lambda)$ workers are assigned to produce the goods of age $t - s/\lambda$) and that the remaining $1 - \Phi(t)$ workers produce a good 0 on which no learning occurs. Assume that initial productivity is the same for all goods, at the level $z(s/\lambda, s) = \xi \geq 1$. Under these assumptions, (4.4) and (4.5) imply that the value of total production is

$$y(t) = 1 - \Phi(t) + k\lambda e^{\mu \lambda t} \int_0^t e^{-\mu \lambda u} \varphi(u)[\xi^{1-\alpha} + (1 - \alpha)\Phi(u)]^{\alpha/1-\alpha}\, du. \tag{4.6}$$

The asymptotic growth rate for this economy is evidently $\mu\lambda$. This rate does not depend either on the learning parameter α or on the distribution φ of the workforce over goods of different vintages. Changes in either of these factors are simply level effects. To obtain sustained growth at all in this framework, it is necessary to assume that better goods become producible at some exogenously given rate λ, which then along with the quality gradient μ dictates the long run growth rate of the system, independent of learning behavior.

Though the production of new goods is continuously initiated in this example, the rate at which this occurs through time is fixed. In Stokey (1988) this rate is made endogenous through the assumption that the experience accumulated in producing good s reduces the cost of producing good $s' > s$. (It may reduce the cost of producing $s' < s$, too, but the spillover effect is assumed to be loaded in the direction of improving productivity on the more advanced good.) As a specific instance of Stokey's hypothesis, very close to that proposed by Young (1991a), let us modify the last example by postulating that the initial value $z(s, \tau(s))$ in the learning curve (4.3) depends on the experience that has been accumulated on less advanced goods. Suppose that an economy at some fixed date t has experience summarized by $z(s, t)$ for $s < S(t)$, but has yet to produce any good with index above $S(t)$. Assume that if production of a good $s \geq S(t)$ is initiated at t (if $\tau(s) = t$) then its initial z-value is proportional to an average of the economy's experience on previously produced goods:

$$z(s, \tau(s)) = \theta\delta \int_0^s e^{-\delta(s-u)} z(u, \tau(s)) \, du. \tag{4.7}$$

Equation (4.7) expresses the initial productivity on good s as an average of experience on lower quality goods. Equivalently, we can express the initial productivity on the good introduced at t, good $S(t)$, as an average of experience on goods introduced earlier:

$$z(S(t), t) = \theta\delta \int_0^t e^{-\delta[S(t)-S(t-v)]} z(S(t-v), t) S'(t-v) \, dv, \tag{4.8}$$

integrating over ages v instead of goods s.

Assume, next, that production on a new good is initiated whenever the expressions (4.7) and (4.8) reach a trigger value $\xi \geq 1$, taken as a given constant. Under this assumption, the left side of (4.8) is replaced with this constant ξ, implying that the function $S(t)$ whose derivative is the rate at which new goods are introduced must satisfy

$$\xi = \theta \delta \int_0^t e^{-\delta[S(t)-S(t-v)]} z(S(t-v), t) S'(t-v) \, dv. \tag{4.9}$$

As in the previous example, we continue to assume that the allocation of employment at any date is described by a density φ and cdf Φ, where $\Phi(u)$ is the fraction of people employed producing goods that were introduced less than u years earlier. In the present case, each good has the initial productivity level ξ, so inserting the solution (4.3) for $z(S(t-v), t)$ with this initial value into (4.9) yields a single equation in the function $S(t)$. For large values of t, the solution $S(t)$ to this equation will behave like $S(t) = \lambda t$, where the constant λ satisfies

$$\xi = \theta \delta \lambda \int_0^\infty e^{-\delta \lambda v} [\xi^{1-\alpha} + (1-\alpha)\Phi(v)]^{1/1-\alpha} \, dv. \tag{4.10}$$

The right side of (4.10) is just an average of the positive, increasing function $\theta[\xi^{1-\alpha} + (1-\alpha)\Phi(v)]^{1/(1-\alpha)}$, taken with respect to an exponential distribution with parameter $\delta \lambda$. Hence it is a positive, decreasing function of $\delta \lambda$, tending toward the value $\theta \xi$ as $\delta \lambda \to \infty$ and toward the value $\theta[\xi^{1-\alpha} + 1 - \alpha]^{1/(1-\alpha)}$ as $\delta \lambda \to 0$. (If the latter expression is less than ξ at $\lambda = 0$, then the economy does not accumulate relevant experience fast enough to introduce new goods in the steady state.) For fixed $\delta \lambda$, the right side of (4.10) is an increasing function of θ, α, and k, and it also increases as the distribution of labor $\varphi(v)$ becomes more concentrated on lower values of v (on newer goods). Hence if a positive solution λ exists, it is inversely proportional to the decay rate of spillover experience, an increasing function of the spillover parameter θ and the learning rate α, and increases as employment is more heavily concentrated on goods that are closer to the economy's production frontier.

The formula (4.6) for the value of total production continues to hold in this second example, and the economy's long run growth rate is $\lambda \mu$, as before. But under this second, spillover, technology, economies that distribute workers across goods of different ages in different ways will grow at different rates. Of course, this conclusion is not based purely on technological considerations: The value ξ of initial productivity that is assumed to trigger the initiation of production of a new good is of central importance, and needs an economic rationale.

One might view the spillover technologies of Stokey and Young as reconciling the Krugman hypothesis of a manufacturing sector with a constant rate of productivity growth, based on learning, with the fact that learning rates on individual production processes decline over time to zero. For example, one could interpret either of the examples in this section as describing a sector of an economy with a positive asymptotic rate of productivity growth. On this view, the contribution of Stokey and Young is to break down an assumed sectoral learning rate into its components, α, θ, and δ (in my notation), and to relate this rate to the way workers are distributed over goods of different vintages.

This interpretation seems fine to me as long as one is discussing the consequences of a *given* workforce distribution, but if one has in mind applying the theory of comparative advantage to *determining* the way workers in each country are allocated to the production of different goods it ceases to make sense. In Krugman's theory (as in Lucas (1988)) it is a sector *as a whole* that either has or does not have a comparative advantage. In a sectoral interpretation of Stokey and Young's theories, each sector consists of many goods and comparative advantage must be determined good by good. No country can be expected to have a comparative advantage in manufacturing in general, or even in crude aggregates like Chemicals and Allied Products or Printing and Publishing. Comparative advantage will be associated with categories, like acetylene or paperback editions of English poetry, that are invisible even in the finest industrial statistics. As we shall see in the next section, this feature—besides being a step towards greater realism—leads to an entirely different view of trade and growth than is implied by the Krugman technology, the superficial similarity of the two notwithstanding.

The main attraction of a learning spillover technology such as that described in the second example of this section is that it offers the potential of accounting for the great difference in productivity growth rates that are observed among low and middle income economies. Of course, little is known about the crucial spillover parameters δ and θ—on which the learning curve evidence described in Section 3 provides no information—but surely an essential first step is to find a formulation that is capable, under *some* parameter values, of generating the behavior we are trying to explain.

5   Learning and Market Equilibrium

The objective of the last section was to set down on paper a *technology* that is consistent with a growth miracle, which is to say, consistent with wide differences in productivity growth among similarly endowed economies. This has been done, following Stokey and Young, in a way that I think is consistent with the main features of the East Asian miracles, all of which have involved sustained movement of the workforce from less to more sophisticated products. A fast growing economy or sector under this technology is one that succeeds in concentrating its workforce on goods that are near its own quality frontier, and thus in accumulating human capital rapidly through the high learning rates associated with new activities and through the spillover of this experience to the production of still newer goods. These hypotheses are consistent with commonly known facts, and have testable implications for many more. As yet, however, I have said nothing about the *economics* that determine the mix of production activities in which an economy or sector of an economy in fact engages.

The papers of Stokey (1988), (1991b) and Young (1991a) develop models of market equilibrium with learning technologies under the assumption the effects of learning are external—that all human capital is a public good. In this case, labor is simply allocated to the use with the highest current return, independent of learning rates. With the constant returns technology these authors assume, the competitive equilibrium is Ricardian and straightforward to calculate. This is the simplest case, so I will begin with it too.

In such a setting, Stokey (1991b), studies north-south trade, where "north" means relatively well-endowed with human capital. Under specific assumptions about consumer preferences for goods of different qualities, she obtains a unique world equilibrium in which the south produces an interval of low quality goods, the north produces an interval of high quality goods, and there is an intermediate range of goods that are produced in neither place. With free trade (as opposed to autarky) learning-by-doing is depressed in the poor country, which now imports high-quality goods from the rich country rather than attempting to produce them at home. One can see that with dynamics as assumed in Stokey (1988), both countries will enjoy growth but the poor country will remain forever poorer.

A similar equilibrium is characterized in Young (1991a), using a parameterization of preferences and the learning technology that permits the explicit calculation of the north-south equilibrium, including a full description of the equilibrium dynamics. There are many possible equilibrium evolutions of his north-south system, depending on the populations of the two regions and on their relative human capital holdings at the time trade is initiated. As in Stokey's (1991b) analysis, the advanced country produces high quality goods and the poor country produces low quality goods. Free trade slows learning and growth in the poor country and speeds it in the rich one. In Young's framework, there are equilibria in which the poor catch up to the rich, but only when their larger population lets them enjoy greater scale economies. Young does not emphasize this possibility and, as I have said earlier, I do not wish to either.

The equilibria of Stokey and Young, then, involve sustained growth of both rich and poor, at possibly different rates, and the continuous shifting of production of goods introduced in the north to the lower wage south. Initial comparative advantage is not permanent, as in Krugman's formulation, since a rich country's experience in producing any given good will eventually be offset by the fact that the good can be produced more cheaply in a less experienced but lower wage environment. Yet there are no growth miracles in these theories. Though these equilibria could readily be modified to include cross-country external effects, and hence catching up (for reasons unrelated to economies of scale), as I have done with the Solow model, there would be nothing one would wish to call miraculous about this process.

In the models of Stokey and Young, all human capital benefits are assumed to be external. The learning and growth that occurs is always, in a sense, accidental. Other models contain aspects of privately held knowledge, so that individual agents fact the capital-theoretic problem of balancing current returns against the future benefits of learning of some kind. Matsuyama (1991) studies a two-sector system in which workers compare the present value of earnings in a traditional sector to the value of earnings in a manufacturing sector in which production is subject to external increasing returns. Young (1991b) augments learning with a research activity that yields patentable new products. Grossman and Helpman (1991a) postulate two R and D activities—innovation, done only in advanced economies, and imitation, done by poor economies too—with lags that let the discoverer or successful low-cost imitator enjoy a period of supernormal profits in a Bertrand-type equilibrium. Whether one calls the decision problems that arise in these analyses occupational choice, or research and development, or learning, all involve a decision on the allocation of time-at-work that involves balancing current returns against the benefits of increased future earnings, and all have a similar capital-theoretic structure.

Dropping the assumption that learning has external effects only is certainly a step toward realism, one that raises many interesting theoretical possibilities yet to be explored. It is thus only conjecture, but I would guess that the main features of the equilibria that have been worked out by Stokey and Young will turn out to stand up very well under different assumptions about the ownership, if I can use that term, of human capital. A learning spillover technology gives those who operate near the current goods frontier a definite advantage in moving beyond it. This advantage is decisive when decisions are taken myopically; I do not see why it should disappear when some of the returns from doing so are internalized and workers and firms look to the future in their individual decision problems.

In short, available general equilibrium models of north-south trade do not predict miraculous economic growth for the poor countries taken as a group, nor do I see any reason to expect that the equilibria of more elaborate theories will have this feature. This is a disappointment, perhaps, but it does not seem to me to be a deficiency of these models. These are theories designed to capture the main interactions between the advanced economies taken as a group and the backward economies as a whole, within a two-country world equilibrium framework. Since it is a fact that the poor are either not gaining on the rich or are gaining only very slowly, one wants a theory that does not predict otherwise.

A successful theory of economic miracles should, I think, offer the *possibility* of rapid growth episodes, but should not imply their occurrence as a simple consequence of relative backwardness. It should be as consistent with the Philippine experience as with the Korean. For the purpose of exploring these possibilities, the conventions of small, open economy trade theory are more suitable (as well as simpler to apply) than those of the theory of a closed, two-country system. If the technology available to individual agents facing world prices has constant returns, then anything is possible. Some allocations will yield high external benefits and growth in production and wages; others will not. There will be a large number of possibilities, with individual agents in equilibrium indifferent between courses of action that have very different aggregative consequences. Theoretically, one can shut off some of these possibilities by introducing diminishing returns in the right places, but I am not sure that these multiplicities should be viewed as theoretical defects, to be patched up. If our objective is to understand a world in which similarly situated economies follow very different paths, these theoretical features are advantageous. A constant returns (at the level of individual producing units) learning spillover technology is equally consistent with fast and slow growth. If our task is to understand diversity, this is an essential feature, not a deficiency.

A second attraction of the learning spillover technology is that it is consistent with the strong connection we observe between rapid productivity growth and trade or openness. Consider two small economies facing the same world prices and similarly endowed, like Korea and the Philippines in 1960. Suppose that Korea somehow shifts its workforce onto the production of goods not formerly produced there, and continues to do so, while the Philippines continues to produce its traditional goods. Then according to the learning spillover theory, Korean production will grow more rapidly. But in 1960, Korean and Philippine incomes were about the same, so the mix of goods their consumers demanded was about the same. For this scenario to be possible, Korea needed to open up a large difference between the mix of goods produced and the mix consumed, a difference that could widen over time. Thus a large volume of trade is essential to a learning-based growth episode.

One can use the same reasoning to see why import-substitution policies fail, despite what can initially appear to be success in stimulating growth. Consider an economy that exports, say, agricultural products and imports most manufactured goods. If this economy shifts toward autarky through tariff and other barriers, its workforce will shift to formerly imported goods and rapid learning will occur. But this is a one-time stimulus to productivity, and thereafter the mix of goods produced in this closed system can change only slowly, as the consumption mix changes. Note that this argument has to do only with the pace of *change* in an economy's production mix and does not involve scale, though it can obviously be reinforced by scale economies.

I do not intend these conjectures about the implications of a learning spillover technology for small countries facing given world prices to be a substitute for the actual construction of such a theory. To do this, one would need to take a realistic position on these issues touched on in my discussion of Rapping's and Searle's evidence. What is the nature of the human capital accumulation decision problems faced by workers, capitalists, and managers? What are the external consequences of the decisions they take? The papers cited here consider a variety of possible assumptions on these economic issues, but it must be said that little is known, and without such knowledge there is little we can say about the way policies that affect incentives can be expected to influence economic growth.

6 Conclusions

I began by asking what current economic theory has to say about the growth miracles of East Asia. The recent literature on which I have drawn to answer this question is fragmentary, and my survey of it more fragmentary still. Even so, the image of the growth process and the role of these remarkable economies within this process that emerges is, I think, surprisingly sharp, certainly compared to what could have been said on this subject ten years ago. I will conclude by summarizing it.

The main engine of growth is the accumulation of human capital—of knowledge—and the main source of differences in living standards among nations is differences in human capital. Physical capital accumulation plays an essential but decidedly subsidiary role. Human capital accumulation takes place in schools, in research organizations, and in the course of producing goods and engaging in trade. Little is known about the relative importance of these different modes of accumulation, but for understanding periods of very rapid growth in a single economy, learning on the job seems to be by far the most central. For such learning to occur on a sustained basis, it is necessary that workers and managers continue to take on tasks that are new to them, to continue to move up what Grossman and Helpman call the "quality ladder." For this to be done on a large scale, the economy must be a large scale exporter.

This picture has the virtue of being consistent with the recent experience of both the Philippines and Korea. It would be equally consistent with post-1960 history with the roles of these two economies switched. It is a picture that is consistent with any individual small economy following the East Asian example, producing a very different mix of goods from the mix it consumes. It does not appear to be consistent with the third world as a whole beginning to grow at East Asian rates: There is a zero-sum aspect, with inevitable mercantilist overtones, to productivity growth fueled by learning by doing.

Can these two paragraphs be viewed as a summary of things that are *known* about economic growth? After all, they are simply a sketch of some of the properties of mathematical models, purely fictional worlds, that certain economists have invented. How does one acquire knowledge about reality by working in one's office with pen and paper? There is more to it, of course: Some of the numbers I have cited are products of decades-long research projects, and all of the models I have reviewed have sharp implications that could be, and have not been, compared to observation. Even so, I think this inventive, model-building process we are engaged in is an essential one, and I cannot imagine how we could possibly organize and make use of the mass of data available to us without it. If we understand the process of economic growth—or of anything else—we ought to be capable of demonstrating this knowledge by *creating* it in these pen and paper (and computer-equipped) laboratories of ours. If we know what an economic miracle is, we ought to be able to *make* one.

Notes

1. The figures in the first paragraph are taken from the 1984 *World Development Report*. The income and population figures in this paragraph and the next are from Summers and Heston (1991).

2. One of the referees for this paper found my use of the term "human capital" in this aggregate context idiosyncratic, and I agree that aggregate theorists tend to use terms like "technology" or "knowledge capital" for what I am here calling "human capital." But the cost of having two terminologies for discussing the same thing, one used by microeconomists and another by macroeconomists, is that it makes it too easy for one group to forget that the other can be a source of relevant ideas and evidence.
   It was the explicit theme of Schultz (1962) that the theory of human capital, then in its infancy, would prove central to the theory of economic growth, and Schultz included the stock of human capital accumulated on the job in his Table 1 (p. S6). His figures were based on estimates provided in Mincer (1962), whose estimation method "treats 'learning from experience' as an investment in the same sense as are the more obvious forms of on-the-job training, such as, say, apprenticeship programs" (p. S51). My usage in this paper is, I think, consistent with 30 years of practice in labor economics.

3. Of course, essentially the same economics can be obtained from a model in which consumer preferences are taken as given and savings and time allocation behavior are derived rather than assumed. See Uzawa (1965), Lucas (1988), and Caballe and Santos (1991). The particular model sketched in the text is simply one rather arbitrarily selected example from the large number of similarly motivated models that have recently been proposed. See, for example, Jones and Manuelli (1990), King and Rebelo (1990), and Becker, Murphy, and Tamura (1990).

4. An informative recent debate on income convergence has been stimulated by the exchange between Baumol (1986), De Long (1988), and Baumol and Wolff (1988). My statement in the text simply echos the shared conclusion of these authors.

5. This external effect might better be captured through the human capital level of the most advanced countries, rather than the world average $Z(t)$. But the use of the latter variable keeps the algebra simple, and I don't think the distinction is critical for any conclusions I wish to draw here.

6. See, for example, Ben-David (1991).

7. All the figures cited are for 1984. The ratio for Taiwan is from the 1987 Taiwan *National Income*. The others are from the 1986 *World Development Report*.

8. Harberger (1990), Table 3.

9. Searle (1945), p. 1144.

10. Backus, Kehoe, and Kehoe (1991) is an empirical examination of scale effects on growth rates, formulated in a variety of ways. They find some evidence of such effects in manufacturing, and none for economies as a whole.

References

Arrow, Kenneth J. (1961): "The Economic Implications of Learning by Doing." *Review of Economic Studies*, 29, 155–173.

Backus, David K., Patrick J. Kehoe, and Timothy J. Kehoe (1991): "In Search of Scale Effects in Trade and Growth," Federal Reserve Bank of Minneapolis Working Paper.

Barro, Robert J., and Xavier Sala-i-Martin (1992): "Convergence," *Journal of Political Economy*, 100, 223–251.

Baumol, William J. (1986): "Productivity Growth, Convergence, and Welfare," *American Economic Review*, 76, 1072–1085.

Baumol, William J., and Edward N. Wolff (1988): "Productivity Growth, Convergence, and Welfare: Reply," *American Economic Review*, 78, 1155–1159.

Becker, Gary S., Kevin M. Murphy, and Robert Tamura (1990): "Capital, Fertility, and Economic Growth," *Journal of Political Economy*, 98, S12–S37.

Ben-David, Dan (1991): "Equalizing Exchange: A Study of the Effects of Trade Liberalization," National Bureau of Economic Research Working Paper No. 3706.

Boldrin, Michele, and Jose A. Scheinkman (1988): "Learning-by-Doing, International Trade and Growth: A Note," in Santa Fe Institute Studies in the Sciences of Complexity, *The Economy as an Evolving Complex System*, 285–300.

Boston Consulting Group (1968): *Perspectives on Experience*. Boston: Boston Consulting Group.

Caballe, Jordi, and Manuel S. Santos (1991): "On Endogenous Growth with Physical and Human Capital," Working Paper.

De Long, J. Bradford (1988): "Productivity Growth, Convergence, and Welfare: Comment," *American Economic Review*, 78, 1138–1154.

Directorate-General of Budget, Accounting and Statistics, Executive Yuan (1987): *National Income in Taiwan Area. The Republic of China*. Taipei: Veterans Printing Works.

Grossman, Gene M., and Elhanan Helpman (1991a): "Quality Ladders and Product Cycles," *Quarterly Journal of Economics*, 106, 557–586.

——— (1991b): *Innovation and Growth in the Global Economy*. Cambridge: MIT Press.

Harberger, Arnold C. (1990): "Reflections on the Growth Process," Working Paper, U.C.L.A.

Jones, Larry E., and Rodolfo E. Manuelli (1990): "A Convex Model of Equilibrium Growth: Theory and Policy Implications," *Journal of Political Economy*, 98, 1008–1038.

King, Robert G., and Sergio Rebelo (1990): "Public Policy and Economic Growth: Developing Neoclassical Implications," *Journal of Political Economy*, 98, S126–S150.

Krugman, Paul R. (1987): "The Narrow Moving Band, the Dutch Disease, and the Consequences of Mrs. Thatcher: Notes on Trade in the Presence of Scale Economies," *Journal of Development Economics*, 27, 41–55.

Lucas, Robert E., Jr. (1988): "On the Mechanics of Economic Development," *Journal of Monetary Economics*, 22, 3–42.

Matsuyama, Kiminori (1991): "Increasing Returns, Industrialization, and Indeterminacy of Equilibrium," *Quarterly Journal of Economics*, 106, 617–650.

——— (1992): "Agricultural Productivity, Comparative Advantage and Economic Growth," *Journal of Economic Theory*, 58, 317–334.

Mincer, Jacob (1962): "On-the-Job Training: Costs, Returns, and Some Implications," *Journal of Political Economy*, 70, S50–S79.

Parente, Stephen L., and Edward C. Prescott (1991): "Technology Adoption and Growth," NBER Working Paper.

Rapping, Leonard A. (1965): "Learning and World War II Production Functions," *Review of Economics and Statistics*, 47, 81–86.

Romer, Paul (1986): "Increasing Returns and Long-Run Growth," *Journal of Political Economy*, 94, 1002–1037.

Schultz, Theodore W. (1962): "Reflections on Investment in Man," *Journal of Political Economy*, 70, S1–S8.

Searle, Allan D. (1945): "Productivity Changes in Selected Wartime Shipbuilding Programs," *Monthly Labor Review*, 61, 1132–1147.

Solow, Robert M. (1956): "A Contribution to the Theory of Economic Growth," *Quarterly Journal of Economics*, 70, 65–94.

Stokey, Nancy L. (1988): "Learning by Doing and the Introduction of New Goods," *Journal of Political Economy*, 96, 701–717.

——— (1991a): "Human Capital, Product Quality, and Growth," *Quarterly Journal of Economics*, 106, 587–616.

——— (1991b): "The Volume and Composition of Trade Between Rich and Poor Countries," *Review of Economic Studies*, 58, 63–80.

Summers, Robert, and Alan Heston (1991): "The Penn World Table (Mark 5): An Expanded Set of International Comparisons, 1950–1988," *Quarterly Journal of Economics*, 106, 327–368.

The World Bank (1984, 1986): *World Development Report*. Oxford: Oxford University Press.

Uzawa, Hirofumi (1965): "Optimum Technical Change in an Aggregative Model of Economic Growth," *International Economic Review*, 6, 18–31.

Young, Alwyn, (1991a): "Learning by Doing and the Dynamic Effects of International Trade," *Quarterly Journal of Economics*, 106, 369–406.

―――― (1991b): "Invention and Bounded Learning by Doing," MIT Working Paper.

―――― (1992): "A Table of Two Cities: Factor Accumulation and Technical Change in Hong Kong and Singapore," NBER *Macroeconomics Annual 1992*, forthcoming.

10 Agglomeration and Economic Development: Import Substitution vs. Trade Liberalisation

Diego Puga and
Anthony J. Venables

The key determinants of a country's economic development are usually taken to be some combination of its factor endowment, technology, institutional structure and policy stance. While not denying the importance of these considerations, in this paper we explore a radically different view of economic development and underdevelopment, based on the idea that economic activity may agglomerate spatially. In this case it is possible that countries with similar, or even identical, underlying characteristics may nevertheless have different economic structures and income levels. Economic underdevelopment is a manifestation of the spatial pattern of agglomeration, and development occurs as this pattern changes, with industry spreading from existing concentrations to new ones.

Analysis of spatial agglomeration of industry has been formalised in recent work in economic geography (see for example Krugman and Venables (1995), Puga (1998)), and the goal of the present paper is to draw out the implications of this approach for economic development. What forces are conducive to the spatial concentration of industry, and what to its spread from country to country? If industrialisation does spread, what form does development take? What is the role of policy—in particular trade policy—in promoting industrialisation?

The basis of our analysis is a model in which there are forces which may cause industry to concentrate in a few locations. We create these forces from three main ingredients. First, there are transport costs or other trade barriers, and these create incentives for firms to locate close to customers and to suppliers. Second, firms have increasing returns to scale, which play the role of forcing firms to choose where to produce;[1] of course, with increasing returns we must handle the problem of market structure, and this we do by assuming monopolistic competition. The third ingredient is the presence of input-output linkages between firms. These linkages create an incentive for firms to locate close to other firms—their suppliers and customers. Krugman and Venables (1995) showed how this combination of forces creates the possibility that industry concentrates in one country, and established the dependence of the equilibrium on transport costs. Here we use the framework to study two issues which we think illuminate the process of economic development.

The first is to consider the spatial implications of growth in world manufacturing relative to other tradeable sectors. This growth increases demand for labour in established manufacturing countries, opening up a larger and larger wage gap between these and other countries. At some point this wage gap becomes unsustainable, and industry starts to spill over to low wage economies. We analyse this process and establish that it does not lead to steady development of all low wage economies, but instead to rapid industrialisation of countries in turn. The logic of spatial agglomeration implies that development cannot proceed simultaneously in all countries. Instead there is a group of rich countries and a group of poor ones, and development takes the form of countries being drawn in turn out of the poor group, and taken through a process of rapid development into the rich group. We think that this is an insightful way of thinking about the spread of industry in a number of contexts, for example from Japan to its East Asian neighbours.

The second issue we address is the role of developing country trade policy in promoting or hindering industrialisation. While recent papers in economic geography have focussed on the location effects of reciprocal reductions in trade costs, in this chapter we look at the effects of unilateral changes in trade barriers. We show that either unilateral trade liberalisation or import substitution policies may be used by the low wage economy to attract industry, but these two policies work through very different mechanisms. Although they are both superficially "successful" in attracting industry, they have different effects on economic welfare, with trade liberalisation yielding higher welfare than import substitution policies. We analyse this in an aggregate model, and then in a multi-industry variant of the model calibrated to South Korean input-output and demand data. We use the calibration to show the different sectoral impacts of trade liberalisation and import substitution, and to confirm the different welfare outcomes generated by the two policies.

Our approach in this chapter can be thought of as a formalisation of earlier ideas in development economics, in particular the role of forward and backward linkages, as emphasised by Hirschman (1958) and others. These linkages are of no particular economic significance in a perfectly competitive environment, but combined with the other ingredients sketched out above, they create pecuniary externalities between the location decisions of firms, and it is this that creates the incentives for agglomeration of industry. To see how this works, suppose that there is expansion of a downstream industry. This creates a backward linkage, expanding demand for intermediate goods, raising profits in an upstream industry, and attracting entry of upstream firms, which in turn may *decrease* the price of intermediates. How does this perverse price response occur? Entry of firms may make the industry more competitive, squeezing price cost margins and reducing price, or may lead to entry of more varieties, reducing a price index of industry output as a whole. This perverse price response constitutes a forward linkage—expanding the upstream industry reduces the costs of the downstream. Putting this together, we see a positive feedback, such that an expansion of the downstream industry makes the industry more profitable, encouraging further expansion.

The process described above is also suggestive of "cumulative causation"—the presence of more downstream firms attracts more upstream firms which in turn attract downstream firms and so on. Again this is reminiscent of old traditions in development and regional economics (for example in the work of Perroux (1955), Myrdal (1957), Hirschman (1958), Harris (1954), and Pred (1966)), as well as some newer approaches to development economics.[2]

1 The Model

We set out the model for the case of two countries and two sectors— manufacturing and agriculture—relegating a statement of the full multi-country and multi-industry model to the Appendix.

Agriculture

Each country is endowed with quantities L_i and K_i of labour and arable land (for countries $i = 1, 2$), both of which are internationally immobile. Agriculture is perfectly competitive and produces a homogenous output, which we choose as *numéraire*, and assume costlessly tradeable.[3] Its production function, F, is defined over labour and land, and has constant returns to scale. If manufacturing employment in country i is denoted m_i and the labour market clears, then agricultural output is $F(L_i - m_i, K_i) = K_i f[(L_i - m_i)/K_i]$. The country i wage is

$$w_i = f'[(L_i - m_i)/K_i].   \tag{1}$$

Manufacturing Industry

The industrial sector is monopolistically competitive, producing differentiated manufactures under increasing returns to scale. As in Krugman and Venables (1995), we assume that the output of firms in the industry is used both as a final consumption good and as an intermediate good for use in the same industry. The set of firms in each country is endogenously determined by free entry and exit, and denoted by N_i. The cost function for an industrial firm (firm k) in country i is

$$C_i(k) = q_i^{\mu} w_i^{(1-\mu)} [\alpha + \beta x_i(k)].   \tag{2}$$

$x_i(k)$ is the firm's output, and the fixed and marginal input requirements, α and β, are the same for all varieties and all countries. The input is a Cobb-Douglas composite of labour, with share $(1 - \mu)$, and an aggregate of the differentiated industrial goods, with price index q_i and share μ.[4] This price index takes a CES form, so is defined by

$$q_i \equiv \left\{ \int_{k \in N_i} [p_i(k)]^{(1-\sigma)} \, dk + \int_{k \in N_j} [\tau_i p_j(k)]^{(1-\sigma)} \, dk \right\}^{1/(1-\sigma)}, \qquad j \neq i,   \tag{3}$$

where $p_j(k)$ is the producer price of variety k produced in country j. Shipment of these products is subject to iceberg trade costs: (τ_i units must be shipped from country j in order that one unit arrives in i). Product differentiation is measured by the elasticity of substitution between varieties of good, σ, and captures the idea that firms benefit from access to a wider range of intermediate goods (following Ethier (1982)).

Demand

There is a single representative consumer in each country, who has quasi-homothetic preferences over agriculture (the *numéraire*) and the

CES aggregate of industrial goods. Hence there is a 'love for variety' on the consumer side, as in Dixit and Stiglitz (1977). The indirect utility of the consumer in country i is

$$V_i = q_i^{-\gamma}1^{-(1-\gamma)}(y_i - e_0). \tag{4}$$

where y_i is income, and e_0 is the subsistence level of agricultural consumption. Notice that we use the same price index for varieties of industrial goods in consumption as in production. This is not necessary for our results, but does much to simplify analysis.

Each product is sold in each country, and the demand for variety k produced in country $i, x_i(k)$, can be derived from (3) and (4) as

$$x_i(k) = [p_i(k)]^{-\sigma}[e_i q_i^{(\sigma-1)} + e_j q_i^{(\sigma-1)}\tau_j^{(1-\sigma)}], \tag{5}$$

where e_i is total expenditure on manufactures in country i. Since manufactures are used both as final consumer goods and as intermediates, e_i is given by;

$$e_i = \gamma\{w_i m_i + K_i f[(L_i - m_i)/K_i] - e_0\} + \int_{k \in N_i} C_i(k)\,dk. \tag{6}$$

The first term in (6) is the value of consumer expenditure on manufactures, and the second the value of intermediate demand. In the braces, the first term is wage income in manufacturing, and the second is income generated in agriculture; the consumer devotes the first e_0 of income to agriculture, and proportion γ of income above this level to expenditure on industrial products. The final term in (6) is intermediate demand, generated as firms spend fraction f of their costs on intermediates.

Supply

Each variety is produced by at most one firm, so the firm producing variety k faces demand curves (5) and cost function (2). Since all products produced in location i are symmetric (they have the same technology and demand curves) we drop the label for individual varieties. The profits of a single representative country i firm are therefore

$$\pi_i = p_i x_i - q_i^{\mu} w_i^{(1-\mu)}(\alpha + \beta x_i). \tag{7}$$

Each firm's perceived elasticity of demand is σ, so the equality of marginal revenue to marginal cost necessary for profit maximisation takes the form

$$p_i(1 - 1/\sigma) = \beta q_i^{\mu} w_i^{(1-\mu)}. \tag{8}$$

We choose units of measurement for output such that $\beta\sigma = \sigma - 1$, giving an equilibrium price of $p_i = q_i^{\mu} w_i^{(1-\mu)}$. Using this pricing rule in the definition of profits, it follows that firms break even if their sales are equal to level x^* given by

$$x^* = \alpha/\sigma. \tag{9}$$

If a firm were to sell less than x^* then it would make a loss, and more than x^*, a profit. At equilibrium profits are exhausted by free entry and exit. Denoting the number (mass) of firms in region i by $n_i \equiv \#N_i$, we therefore have

$$(x_i - x^*)n_i = 0, \quad x_i \leq x^*, \quad n_i \geq 0. \tag{10}$$

To complete characterisation of equilibrium we need only specify manufacturing labour demand. The manufacturing wage bill, $m_i w_i$, is fraction $(1 - \mu)$ of costs (equal, in equilibrium, to the value of output), so

$$m_i w_i = (1 - \mu)n_i C_i = (1 - \mu)n_i p_i x^*. \tag{11}$$

We have already seen how labour market clearing determines the wage rate (1).

Equilibria

Equilibria of the model are given by (1)–(11). What can be said about them? This question is most easily answered if we assume that the two economies have the same factor endowments. We therefore set

$$L_1 = L_2 = A, \quad K_1 = K_2 = A, \tag{12}$$

(where the fact that the quantities of L and K are the same is just a choice of units).

There is certainly now a symmetric equilibrium in which industry is equally divided between countries, although this equilibrium may not be stable. More interestingly, there may also be equilibria in which manufacturing is concentrated in a single country. To establish whether or not such an equilibrium exists, we *assume* that all manufacturing is concentrated in one country (say country 1) and then see if it is profitable for any firm to start production in country 2. If not, then the hypothesised concentration of manufacturing in country 1 is an equilibrium.

Let us assume then that $n_2 = 0$. The price indices of (3) reduce to

$$q_1 = n_1^{1/(1-\sigma)} p_1, \quad q_2 = n_1^{1/(1-\sigma)} p_1 \tau_2. \tag{13}$$

Sales of each firm in country 1 are,

$$x_1 = p_1^{-\sigma} q_1^{(\sigma-1)} (e_1 + e_2) = x^*,$$

where the first equation comes from using (13) in (5), and the second from the fact that country 1 industry equilibrium occurs when n_1 has adjusted to gives zero profits, so each firm sells output level $x_1 = x^*$.

Suppose now that a firm starts producing in country 2. Its sales are (from (5) and (13)),

$$x_2 = p_2^{-\sigma} q_1^{(\sigma-1)} [e_1 \tau_1^{(1-\sigma)} + e_2 \tau_2^{(\sigma-1)}]. \tag{15}$$

Relative goods price can be derived from (7) and (13) as

$$\left(\frac{p_2}{p_1}\right) = \tau_2^{\mu} \left(\frac{w_2}{w_1}\right)^{(1-\mu)}, \tag{16}$$

so taking the ratio of the sales equations (14) and (15) we obtain,

$$\frac{x_2}{x^*} = \left(\frac{w_1}{w_2}\right)^{\sigma(1-\mu)} \tau_2^{-\sigma\mu} \left[\frac{e_1}{e_1 + e_2} \tau_1^{(1-\sigma)} + \frac{e_2}{e_1 + e_2} \tau_2^{(\sigma-1)}\right]. \tag{17}$$

This expression provides the criterion that determines whether or not agglomeration of industry in country 1 is an equilibrium. If the expression has value greater than unity then an entrant in 2 can sell more than is required to break even ($x_2 > x^*$), so agglomeration in 1 is not an equilibrium. Conversely, if the expression is less than unity then concentration in 1 is sustainable—it is not profitable for any firm to produce in country 2.

The magnitude of this expression is determined by three forces. First, the factor market. The larger is w_1/w_2 the higher is x_2 and hence the less likely it is that agglomeration can be sustained.[5] Unsurprisingly, the larger are the wage differences associated with agglomeration, the more likely it is that production in country 2 will be profitable.

Second, forward linkages. The term $\tau_2^{-\sigma\mu}$ captures the fact that a firm setting up in country 2 would have to import all its intermediate goods, and pay τ_2 more for them than do firms in country 1. Transport costs or other barriers to country 2 imports ($\tau_2 > 1$) make this term less than unity, reducing x_2, and making it less profitable for a firm to start producing in country 2. Essentially, the term captures the forward linkages foregone by locating in country 2, away from intermediate suppliers.

The third force is backward linkages, and these are captured by the term in square brackets. To interpret this, suppose that $\tau_1 = \tau_2 > 1$ and that $e_1 + e_2$ is constant. Since $\tau_1^{(1-\sigma)} < \tau_2^{(\sigma-1)}$, an increase in e_1 and reduction in e_2 reduces the size of this term, meaning simply that a transfer of expenditure from market 2 to market 1 reduces the sales of a firm in 2. With manufacturing concentrated in country 1 we have $e_1 > e_2$, making for a relatively small value of this term. The effect therefore captures the backward linkages foregone by not being close to industrial consumers.

Equation (17) has endogenous variables on the right hand side, but these can be found as follows. By construction, all of country 2's labour force is in agriculture, so $m_2 = 0$. Country 1's agricultural labour force must therefore adjust to equate world supply and demand for agriculture, that is to satisfy,

$$2e_0 + (1 - \gamma)[m_1 f'(1 - m_1/A) + Af(1 - m_1/A) + Af(1) - 2e_0]$$
$$= Af(1 - m_1/A) + Af(1). \tag{18}$$

The right hand side of this expression is food production and the left hand side is demand, coming from the subsistence requirement of the representative consumer in each country, e_0, plus proportion $(1 - \gamma)$ of world income in excess of this subsistence requirement. This equation gives m_1 as a function of parameters of the model. We can then find the wage rates from (1)

$$w_1 = f'(1 - m_1/A), \quad w_2 = f'(1), \tag{19}$$

and manufacturing expenditure levels,

$$e_1 = \gamma[w_1 m_1 + Af(1 - m_1/A) - e_0] + \mu(e_1 + e_2), \quad e_2 = \gamma[Af(1) - e_0]. \tag{20}$$

(Derived from (6), noting that manufacturing costs equal total expenditure on manufactures, and all are incurred in country 1).

The dependence of x_2/x^* on some of the parameters of the model is illustrated by the lines in Fig. 10.1, in which the vertical axis gives A/e_0 and the horizontal the country 2 import barrier, τ_2.[6] Lines correspond to different values of the input-output linkage, μ, and each line

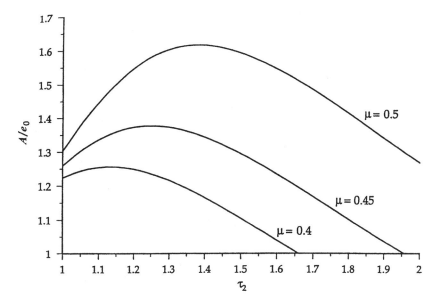

Figure 10.1
Sustainable agglomeration.

is the locus along which $x_2/x^* = 1$. We call this relationship the sustain curve, because it delimits the region of parameter space where agglomeration is sustainable. Below the sustain curve $x_2/x^* < 1$, so that concentration of manufacturing in country 1 is an equilibrium, while above it we know that concentration is not an equilibrium (it is profitable for a firm to start production in country 2). As the economy passes through this line a bifurcation occurs—the qualitative structure of equilibria changes—and in remaining sections of the chapter we explore this transition.

Fig. 10.1 provides a framework for the analysis of the rest of the chapter, and in subsequent sections we shall discuss the shape of the $x_2/x^* = 1$ curve in greater detail. In the next section we consider the effects of increasing A/e_0, and show what happens as we move upwards through the bifurcation set. In Section 4 we look at developing country trade policy—that is, at horizontal movements across the figure. In both these sections we shall at various points move to a more general model, with more countries and more industries. However, much of the intuition for our results comes from (17) and its illustration on Fig. 10.1.

3   Growth and the Spread of Industry

We now turn to investigating the implications of growth in the world economy as a whole for the spatial location of economic activity. Since we do not seek to explain growth, we simply assume that exogenous technical progress augments the productivity of all primary factors in all countries equally. What are the implications of such technical progress for the location of manufacturing production?

A completely homogenous process of economic growth—raising supply and demand for each sector in each country in the same proportion—will not have any spatial effects. But if demand for manufactures rises faster than demand for agriculture, then relative price changes will occur and, as we shall see, this can trigger industrial relocation.[7] We capture a relatively rapid growth of demand for manufactures by using the linear expenditure system with a positive level of subsistence expenditure on agriculture, e_0, so that growth of household income is associated with proportionately faster growth of demand for manufactures.[8]

In terms of the model, we assume then that A increase through time, and reinterpret w_i and m_i as wages and employment of efficiency units of labour. Starting from a situation in which manufacturing is concentrated in country 1, we see from the expression for country 1 manufacturing employment, (18), that such growth causes an equiproportionate increase in m_1 only if $e_0 = 0$, while if $e_0 > 0$, then m_1 increases more than proportionately with A. Turning to the wage equations (19), if m_1/A increases, then so too does the country 1 wage per efficiency unit, both absolutely and relatively to the country 2 wage.

The implications of this for the location of industry can be seen from (17). The increase in w_1/w_2 raises x_2, working against sustainability of the agglomeration in country 1. But as the wage in country 1 increases, so does country 1's share of world expenditure on manufactures, $e_1/(e_1 + e_2)$, tending to decrease x_2 and make 1 a relatively more profitable location. The net effect depends on parameters of the model. If the share of manufactures in consumption, γ, is very small then the effect on wages will be small and the agglomeration will always be sustainable. However, if γ is large enough then the wage effect will come to dominate, and at a high enough value of A the agglomeration will become unsustainable.[9] This corresponds to the

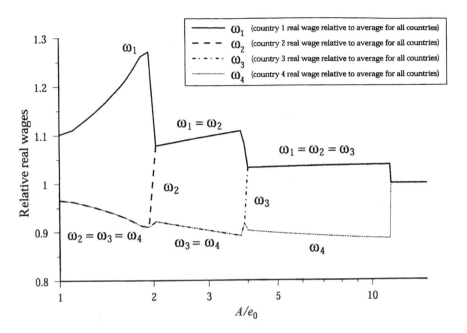

Figure 10.2
Waves of industrialisation.

case illustrated in Fig. 10.1, where as A increases so the economy crosses the $x_2/x^* = 1$ locus.

When $x_2/x^* = 1$, entry of a manufacturing firm in country 2 is profitable. What then happens as A increases further? The presence of some manufacturing in country 2 creates forward and backward linkages (reduces q_2 and increases e_2), but also has the effect of narrowing the wage gap between the countries (raising w_2/w_1). If the linkage effects are very powerful compared to the wage effects then there may be discontinuous change—production in country 2 becomes profitable enough that the two economies jump to the symmetric equilibrium. Discontinuities are avoided if the wage effects are relatively strong, in which case as A increases further so the two economies converge smoothly to the symmetric equilibrium.[10]

To draw out the economics of the process we illustrate it not for our two country example, but by numerical simulation of the model for a world of four identical countries. Fig. 10.2 plots real wages per efficiency unit of labour in each economy relative to the average for all economies as A increases. The vertical axis is this relative real wage per efficiency unit, ω_i, and the horizontal axis the exogenous technological progress parameter A.

At low A, all industry is in country 1, but growth in A causes an increase in demand for manufactures and hence a divergence of wages—the country 1 wage reaching, for our parameter values, nearly one and a half times the level of wages elsewhere in the world. Despite this wage gap it is not profitable for any firm to move out—the forward and backward linkages received by being in country 1 compensate for the higher wage. But as pressure builds up in country 1, so A reaches the bifurcation point at which production in the other countries becomes profitable. Industrialisation commences in all of them, but as their volume of manufacturing increases so do the associated linkages and pecuniary externalities. There comes a point at which simultaneous industrialisation in *all* of them ceases to be a stable equilibrium—if one got slightly ahead of the others then its lead would cumulate.[11] This means that just one of the countries (call it country 2) gains manufacturing; this country's wage path is illustrated by the first dashed line, and we see very rapid convergence with country 1. Country 1 suffers both a relative and absolute real wage decline, as it loses a share of its manufacturing to the newly industrialised country.

The other countries remain specialised in agriculture following this first transition, but continuing growth now starts to raise real wages in 1 and 2 relative to these countries. This continues until another critical value is reached at which point industry spreads to a third country, and so on. What we see then is industrialisation spreading, in a series of waves, from country to country. The model predicts that economic development is not a smooth process of many countries catching up with the rich. It is instead the coexistence of a rich and a poor group of nations, but with growth of world demand for manufactures causing successive poor countries to join the rich club.

This, we think, provides a useful way of thinking about the spread of industry from Japan to several of its East Asian neighbours over the last three decades. Fig. 10.3 plots the share of manufacturing in total employment in Japan, Taiwan, South Korea, Malaysia and Philippines between 1965 and 1995. Throughout this period about 25% of Japanese workers have been employed in manufacturing; Taiwan, South Korea and Malaysia have gained industrial employment in that sequence, while the fraction of workers in manufacturing has remained below 12% in Philippines.

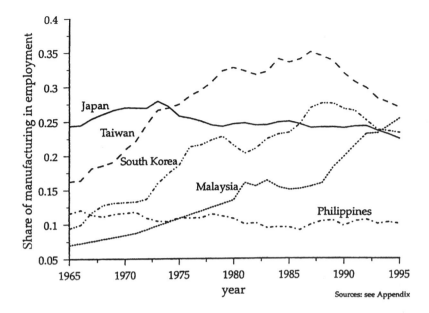

Figure 10.3
Waves of industrialisation in East Asia.

3   Import Substitution vs. Trade Liberalisation

Can the less developed country use trade policy to attract industry? Fig. 10.1 suggests that the answer is affirmative—changing τ_2 can move the economy out of the region in which country 2 has no industry—and we now investigate this in more detail.[12]

Consider first the effects of an import substitution policy, raising trade barriers. τ_2 effects x_2/x^* in two ways. An increase in τ_2 makes imported inputs more expensive, this reducing the term $\tau_2^{-\sigma\mu}$ and making it less attractive for a firm to establish production in country 2. But pulling in the opposite direction, an increase in τ_2 switches country 2 expenditure on manufactures towards production in country 2 (the term $e_2\tau_2^{(\sigma-1)}$).[13] Which of these effects is more powerful? Letting $\tau_2 \to \infty$ we see that $x_2 \to \infty$ providing that there is some manufacturing expenditure in country 2 ($e_2 > 0$) and that $(\sigma - 1)/\sigma > \mu$. We shall assume that this restriction on parameters is satisfied—without it we have the curious result that even under autarky it is not profitable to set up production to meet local demand.[14] In this case then, raising trade barriers can always be successful in attracting industry (we return in a moment to seeing how much industry and of what type).

What about trade liberalisation? Can a reduction in τ_2 cause industrialisation to commence? We see from Fig. 10.1 that the answer depends on the values of A/e_0 and other parameters. We can get some more information on this by looking at the derivative $dx_2/d\tau_2$. Differentiating (17) this is,

$$\frac{dx_2}{d\tau_2} \cdot \frac{\tau_2}{x_2} = \left[\frac{(\sigma - 1 - \sigma\mu)e_2\tau_2^{(\sigma-1)} - \sigma\mu e_1\tau_1^{(1-\sigma)}}{e_1\tau_1^{(1-\sigma)} + e_2\tau_2^{(\sigma-1)}} \right]. \tag{21}$$

The derivative is positive for large enough τ_2 (providing $(\sigma - 1 - \sigma\mu)e_2 > 0$), reflecting our earlier discussion about import substitution. The numerator switches sign as τ_2 becomes small enough, and it is this that generates the hump of the sustain curve illustrated on Fig. 10.1, and suggests that reducing τ_2 will attract industry. However, it is not necessarily the case that this change in the sign of $dx_2/d\tau_2$ occurs at $\tau_2 > 1$. From inspection of (21) we see that this is more likely the stronger are linkages (larger μ, increasing the forward linkage benefits from trade liberalisation), and the larger is e_1/e_2 (reducing the value of protecting the country 2 domestic market).

Although both import substitution and unilateral liberalisation can be effective in attracting industry, they have different welfare implications. This is explored in Fig. 10.4, which plots country 2 welfare as a function of its import barrier, τ_2. The figure is computed from a two country numerical example, details of which are given in the Appendix, but two aspects of which need to be explained here. First we assume that country 2 is quite small—one third of the size of country 1 in endowments (and less in income); the reason is that we want to think in terms of a developing country importing from the rest of the world. Second, we split the trade barriers into natural and tariff barriers, and set the natural trade barriers at 15%, so define $\tau^* = 1.15$. Country 1 has no further barriers, so $\tau_1 = \tau^*$, but country 2 has tariff barriers over and above τ^*. The horizontal axis on Fig. 10.4 is this extra country 2 barrier, $\tau_2 - \tau^*$, and the vertical is country 2 real income.[15]

In the interval $\tau_2^- - \tau^*$ to $\tau_2^+ - \tau^*$ there is no manufacturing in country 2, and these values of τ_2 are the two solutions of $x_2/x^* = 1$ from the sustain curve. Import substitution draws industry in when $\tau_2 > \tau_2^+$, as does trade liberalisation when $\tau_2 < \tau_2^-$.

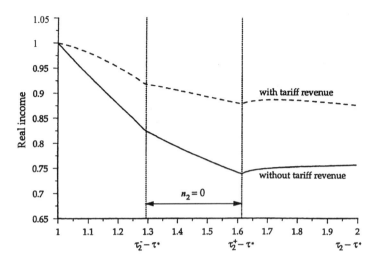

Figure 10.4
Import substitution vs trade liberalization.

The two curves illustrated on the figure plot country 2 welfare under different assumptions about the social value of tariff revenue. The lower solid line gives the case when its social value is zero, and in the upper line we suppose that the tariff revenue accrues to country 2 citizens and is added into the welfare measure.[16]

Looking first at the case in which tariff revenue is included in welfare (the upper curve), we see four main points. First, there is a range of tariffs within which import substituting industrialisation raises welfare, but this range is of limited width (between τ_2^+ and approximately $\tau_2 = 1.73$), and higher tariffs lead to welfare reduction. This arises from the trade-off between the beneficial linkages created by industry, and the loss of gains from trade. Second, in the region in which there is no manufacturing, $\tau_2 \in (\tau_2^-, \tau_2^+)$, reducing the tariff raises welfare. This is simply because it reduces the distortion on imported manufactures. Third, reducing the tariff further, into the region in which country 2 gains industry ($\tau_2 < \tau_2^-$), increases the rate at which welfare increases, because of the linkage benefits that are being achieved. The overall message is therefore clear. While import substitution may be locally welfare raising, it yields lower welfare levels than industrialisation via unilateral trade liberalisation.

If the tariff does not generate income for domestic consumers, then the lower line applies. The qualitative conclusions of the previous paragraph apply, with two quantitative qualifications. The gains from attracting industry by unilateral liberalisation are now larger—simply because of the real trade costs now being saved. However, at trade barriers above τ_2^+ welfare is increasing in τ_2. And essentially trade barriers are so costly that—within this interval—the best a country can do is go on raising the trade barriers to create further import substitution and drive imports to zero.

Fig. 10.4 is, of course, just from a numerical example. How are things changed as parameters of the model change? The effects of stronger industrial linkages (higher μ) can be seen from Fig. 10.1. Higher μ has the effect of increasing the interval of trade barriers within which agglomeration occurs (for a given value of A/e_0) raising the point at which import substitution commences, τ_2^+, and reducing the point at which unilateral liberalisation causes industrialisation, τ_2^-. However, it is noteworthy that the upwards shift of τ_2^+ is much larger than the downwards shift of τ_2^-, indicating that strong linkages make inward-looking industrialisation more difficult. Reducing the size of country 2 has a similar effect, again with τ_2^+ rising more than τ_2^- falls; in other words an import substitution policy is more difficult to implement the smaller is the economy. Raising developed country import barriers also shifts τ_2^+ up and τ_2^- down, but the relative magnitude of the shift is now reversed; the fall in τ_2^- is large, reflecting the difficulty that developed country trade barriers create for an outward looking development strategy.[17]

4   Trade Policy and Industrial Structure

So far we have assumed a single manufacturing sector. We now dis-aggregate this in order to see how import substitution and trade liberalisation policies affect the industrial structure of the developing economy.

We base our investigations on a five sector model, with input-output structure aggregated from a South-Korean input-output matrix. Sector 1 is the aggregate of all primary sectors and is assumed to be perfectly competitive and tradeable. Sectors 2–4 are manufacturing sectors, all of them monopolistically competitive. Sector 2 gathers all labour intensive manufacturing activities (those with an above average labour share). Labour un-intensive manufacturing sectors are split by consumer (sector 3) versus industry (sector 4) orientation (consumer oriented being those with an above-average ratio of final to total demand). Finally, Sector 5 is made up of services and is assumed to be monopolistically competitive and non-tradeable. (The mapping from the 19-sector transaction table in the 1980 input-output tables for South Korea to our five sectors is detailed in the Appendix).

To implement the linear expenditure system we combine the "subsistence" levels of consumer expenditure calculated for South Korea by Lluch and Powel (1975) and the consumer expenditure shares in the South Korean input-output tables, as detailed in the Appendix. In all respects other than technical coefficients and demand parameters, we leave the manufacturing sectors identical. Thus, we do not attempt to estimate how product differentiation varies across industries, instead leaving $\sigma = 6$ in all imperfectly competitive sectors.

We assume that there are three primary factors, arable land, internationally mobile capital and labour. There are three countries, one (on which we shall focus) having one quarter of the world endowment, and the other two having the rest divided equally between them. We continue to abstract from traditional sources of comparative advantage, so relative endowments of each factor are the same in all countries.

Trade barriers and tariffs are the same for all manufacturing sectors, with developed country import barriers for manufactures set at 20%. Our experiment is to change the less developed country's trade barriers, but we keep these barriers equal across sectors in order to show how the same trade policy affects different sectors differently, and to reflect the evidence that both Korea and Taiwan shows "relatively low variances in protection across sectors" (Pack, 1992).

Figs. 10.5 and 10.6 give, for the less developed economy on which we focus, the simulated shares of the labour force in each manufacturing industry, and the associated level of welfare.

We see from Fig. 10.5 that manufacturing employment as a whole is lowest at intermediate levels of the country's trade barriers, although at no point is manufacturing employment zero. At these intermediate trade barriers the country has a small presence in labour intensive manufactures (Sector 2), and also in labour un-intensive but consumer oriented manufactures (Sector 4). Sector 2 is active because of low wages, and Sector 4 because of consumer demand. However, the developing country is a net importer of all manufacturing products.

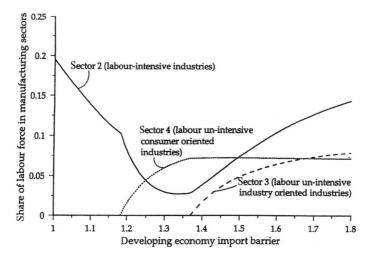

Figure 10.5
Shares of developing economy labour force in manufacturing.

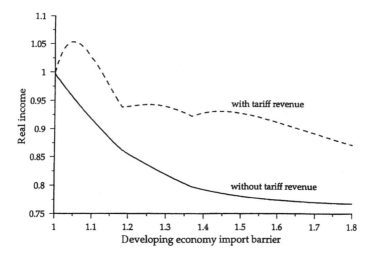

Figure 10.6
Import substitution vs trade liberalisation with several manufacturing sectors.

Raising import barriers leads to import substituting industrialisation. There is expansion of consumer oriented manufactures (Sector 4) in order to meet final demand, and beyond some level the labour industry oriented Sector 3 becomes active, driven by intermediate demand from the other sectors. As we raise import barriers at no point does the country become a net exporter in any of these sectors.

Trade liberalisation leads to a quite different industrial structure, as would be expected. The low wages of the developing country lead to rapid expansion of labour intensive industries, which become significant net exporters. This employment expansion starts to raise wages, forcing out the other two sectors.

In interpreting these results it is important to bear in mind that we have assumed that there are no differences in relative factor endowments, and that the trade liberalisation is a unilateral import liberalisation by the developing country. How then does this import liberalisation lead to such a dramatic expansion of the labour intensive sector? The reason is that import barriers make intermediate goods expensive in the developing country, and this is one of the factors inhibiting industrial development. Reducing import barriers removes this obstacle. All sectors benefit from this effect but, since wages are low in the developing country, it is the labour intensive sector that is best placed to expand output in response to the change. Interestingly then, even without assuming comparative advantage differences, open developing countries will export labour intensive products.

All this conforms with the empirical evidence from the newly industrialising East Asian economies which have liberalised trade over the last 20 years. For example, Korea reduced its average tariffs from about 32% in 1982 to 22% in 1985 and to about 10% in 1992 (World Bank, 1994). These countries have seen labour intensive products grow most as exports have exploded. Little (1994) looks at the sectoral detail of this process, comparing the patterns of industrial development of newly industrialising East Asian economies with the standard norms for less developed economies calculated by Syrquin and Chenery (1989). He finds that textiles, clothing, and metal products and machinery (all of them included in Sector 2 in our numerical example) have grown much faster than normal in these economies, while chemicals and primary metal manufactures (aggregated into Sector 3 in our example) remained well below normal in their shares of GDP.

The real income effects in this case confirm those that we saw in the aggregate case. Results are in Fig. 10.6 and as before the solid line is with real trade barriers, and the dashed line gives the case in which barriers create tariff revenue. Concentrating on the dashed line we see that real income is higher with trade liberalisation than with import substitution. The welfare maximum at low tariffs derives from the optimal tariff argument. This arises primarily for exports of labour intensive products, in which the developing country has a significant share of world production. (It is absent in Fig. 10.4 because with a single manufacturing sector the less developed economy never achieves a large enough world market share for terms of trade effects to be significant).

5 Conclusions

In the analysis of this paper we have abstracted from many of the differences between countries which are the focus of traditional development economics—for example, we have assumed that all countries have the same amounts of capital and land per unit labour. Clearly, we do not think that international differences in these factors are unimportant, but our objective is to see how much can be explained without them.

We think the answer is a great deal. Industrial linkages create agglomeration of manufacturing sectors, and this results in substantial real income differences between countries.[18] Yet firms do not move to the low wage economy, because if they were to do so they would forego the benefits of proximity to suppliers of intermediate goods and to their industrial customers.

Industrial centres may however become too large to be constricted in their initial set of locations. Rising relative demand for manufactures will widen the wage gap between those countries that have industry and those that do not, and at some point industry will spread to other locations. But the logic of agglomeration dictates that this is not spread evenly over developing countries. Instead industry spreads from one country to the next in a series of steps. Development takes place not as a process of smooth convergence of countries, but instead by countries in turn making the transition from a low level of development to the rich country club.

The approach also provides insights into the effects of trade policy. Unilateral trade policy can be used to attract industry by import substitution. More surprisingly, unilateral trade liberalisation can also be successful in attracting industry, as lower cost intermediate goods remove a barrier to industrial development. Comparison of import substitution and trade liberalisation indicates that while the former leads to a presence in a wider range of sectors, the latter yields higher levels of welfare. And a simple calibrated example of the model indicates a sectoral development pattern that fits well with that observed in many newly industrialising countries. Even though we abstract from comparative advantage, we see that an open newly industrialising country will tend to export labour intensive manufactures.

Appendix

The Multi-Industry Model

To the two internationally immobile primary factors of the single sector model, labour and arable land, we add capital which is perfectly mobile across the M countries. There is a perfectly competitive primary sector and a number of monopolistically competitive tradeable manufacturing and non-tradeable service sectors. The price index for sector s in the set of industrial sectors I takes the form:

$$q_i^s = \left[\sum_{j=1}^{M} n_j^s (p_j^s \tau_i)^{(1-\sigma)} \right]^{1/(1-\sigma)}, \qquad s \in I, \tag{A.1}$$

where the superscript s denotes the sector. The price index for sector s in the set of service sectors S is:

$$q_i^s = [n_i^s (p_i^s)^{(1-\sigma)}]^{1/(1-\sigma)}, \qquad s \in S. \tag{A.2}$$

The cost function of a single firm in sector s at location i is:

$$C_i^s = (\alpha + \beta x_i^s) r^{\rho^s} w_i^{\left(1-\eta^s-\rho^s-\sum_{k \in I \cup S} \mu^{k,s}\right)} 1^{\eta^s} \prod_{k \in I \cup S} (q_i^k)^{\mu^{k,s}}, \qquad s \in I \cup S, \tag{A.3}$$

where the share of primary sector output in the s industry is η^s, the share of industry k in the s industry is $\mu^{k,s}$, r is the rate of return on capital, ρ^s is the share of capital in costs and η^s is the share of primary sector output, and other parameters and variables are as in the single-industry version of the model. The cost function in the perfectly competitive primary sector P is:

$$C_i^P = z_i r^{\rho^P} t^{\theta} w_i^{\left(1-\eta^P-\rho^P-\sum_{k \in I \cup S} \mu^{k,P}\right)} 1^{\eta^P} \prod_{k \in I \cup S} (q_i^k)^{\mu^{k,P}}, \tag{A.4}$$

where z_i is primary sector production in country i, t is the rental price of arable land, and θ is land share in agriculture. Preferences are given by the following indirect utility function:

$$V_i = 1^{-\left(1-\sum_{s\in I\cup S}\gamma^s\right)} \prod_{s\in I\cup S} (q_i^s)^{-\gamma^s} \left(y_i - \sum_{s\in\{P\}\cup I\cup S} e_0^s \right). \tag{A.5}$$

Demand for primary factors comes from the cost functions in the usual way, and their prices are determined by market clearing. Final and derived demands for output come from cost functions and indirect utility functions. Given these demand functions and cost functions (A3) firms maximise profits, and the number of firms in each sector is determined by free entry and exit.

Simulation Parameters

Section 1: $\sigma = 5, \tau_1 = 1.1, \gamma = 0.5$, and $\theta = 0.3$, where θ is the land share in the Cobb-Douglas agricultural production function.

Section 2: $\sigma = 5, \tau_1 = \tau_2 = 1.3, \gamma = 0.5, \mu = 0.4$, and $\theta = 0.1$.

Section 3: $\sigma = 5, \tau_1 = \tau^* = 1.15, \gamma = 0.5, \mu = 0.5$, and $\theta = 0.3$.

Section 4: Sectors are the aggregate of the following sectors from the 19-sector 1980 Korean input-output tables (pp. 56–7 in Bank of Korea (1983)):

Sector 1 (primary sectors): agriculture, forestry and fishing; and mining.

Sector 2 (labour intensive manufactures): textiles and leather; lumber and wood products; paper, printing and publishing; non-metal mineral products; metal products and machinery; and miscellaneous manufactures.

Sector 3 (labour un-intensive and industry oriented manufactures): chemicals and chemical products; and primary metal manufacturing.

Sector 4 (labour un-intensive and consumer oriented manufactures): food and beverages.

Sector 5 (services): all service sectors.

The input output matrix takes the following form:

η^s		0.085	0.058	0.268	0.498	0.010
$\mu^{2,s}$		0.018	0.340	0.041	0.030	0.111
$\mu^{3,s}$		0.093	0.201	0.397	0.029	0.116
$\mu^{4,s}$	$=$	0.056	0.005	0.004	0.145	0.016
$\mu^{5,s}$		0.050	0.135	0.102	0.070	0.203
θ		0.373	—	—	—	—
ρ^s		0.192	0.125	0.129	0.177	0.281
$1 - \eta^s - \rho^s - \Sigma\mu^{r,s}(-\theta)$		0.132	0.135	0.059	0.050	0.262

"Subsistence" consumer expenditure shares are adapted from those calculated for South Korea by Lluch and Powel (1975):

$e_0^s/\Sigma e_0^s$	0.308	0.198	0.000	0.308	0.186

Marginal consumer expenditure shares are calculated from the subsistence levels of expenditure and the actual consumer expenditure shares in the South Korean input-output tables:

| γ^s | 0.060 | 0.190 | 0.057 | 0.215 | 0.477 |

$\sigma = 6$, $\tau_1 = 1.2$.

Data Sources for Fig. 10.3

International Labour Office. Annual issues. *Year Book of Labour Statistics.*
  Geneva: International Labour Office.
Republic of China, Directorate General of Budget, Accounting and Statistics.
  Annual issues. *Year Book of Statistics.*

Notes

1. Without increasing returns, if factors are uniformly distributed, every location can become an autarkic economy producing all goods at an arbitrarily small scale (Scotchmer and Thisse (1992)).

2. Murphy *et al.* (1989) model a 'big push' in which increasing modern sector employment raises aggregate demand, thereby increasing the profitability of modern sector firms. Their model works through aggregate demand, rather than intermediate goods, so has no forward linkages. It also assumes a closed economy.

3. Adding a trade cost in agriculture does not change the qualitative results of the model providing that trade in agriculture occurs in equilibrium. For details of this see Fujita *et al.* (1999).

4. In the full multi-industry model given in the Appendix each industry uses inputs from all other industries, with value shares given by the input-output matrix of the economy.

5. The relative wage term enters with exponent $\sigma(1 - \mu)$ because labour accounts for $(1 - \mu)$ of costs, and a price increase reduces sales according to elasticity σ. Relative wages are endogenous, and determined in (18) and (19) below.

6. The figure is computed using solutions of (18)–(20) in (17). Key parameters are μ, and σ which we set at 5, corresponding to a price–marginal cost mark up of 25%. Full details of parameters used in this and subsequent figures are given in the Appendix.

7. Between 1960 and 1990 world value added in manufacturing increased fourfold while world GDP increased threefold.

8. Econometrically estimated values of e_0 are positive, see for example Lluch and Powell (1975).

9. In the former case the curve is unbounded for some intermediate values of τ_2. Puga (1998) investigates further.

10. Details of the nature of the bifurcation (whether or not it is discontinuous) are examined by Puga (1998) and Fujita *et al.* (1999) in similar models, and we do not pursue them here.

11. Entry and exit of firms occurs in response to instantaneous profits, so the dynamic system is $dn_i/dt = k\pi_i$, and stability is defined with respect to this system. Analysis of the stability of models of this type is undertaken in Fujita *et al.* (1999), and analytical

results on the instability of simultaneous development by two economies are available on request from the authors.

12. We look only at unilateral changes in trade costs. A multilateral reduction in trade costs can cause relocation of industry to non-industrialised economies, as shown in Krugman and Venables (1995). In a three country set up, the relocation might not be to all countries simultaneously (see Puga and Venables (1997), who also study the effects of regional integration).

13. None of the endogenous variables in (17) depend directly on τ_2, as may be seen by inspection of (18)–(20).

14. This condition is standard in models of this type, and rules out unbounded agglomeration. Fujita et al. (1999) have labelled it the 'no-black-hole' condition.

15. Welfare is the long run equilibrium utility V_i as defined in (4).

16. Tariff revenue is of no value if all rents are dissipated, or accrue to foreigners. When we add tariff revenue back we assume that it is all spent on agriculture or on leisure, and do not allow it to change manufacturing expenditure levels e_1 or e_2.

17. This point suggests that if developed countries reacted to import substituting policies by raising their own tariffs, then the effectiveness of these policies would be reduced.

18. Of course, the real wage differentials suggested by our simulations are nothing like as large as real world income differentials, presumably reflecting the fact that we have assumed the same labour quality and levels of social capital in all countries.

References

Bank of Korea. (1983). *1980 Input-Output Tables of Korea*. Seoul: The Bank of Korea.

Dixit, Avinash K. and Stiglitz, Joseph E. (1977). "Monopolistic competition and optimum product diversity." *American Economic Review*, vol. 67, pp. 297–308.

Ethier, Wilfred J. (1982). "National and international returns to scale in the modern theory of international trade." *American Economic Review*, vol. 72, pp. 389–405.

Fujita, Masahisa, Krugman, Paul R. and Venables, Anthony J. (1999). *The Spatial Economy: Cities, Regions and International Trade*, Cambridge MA: MIT Press.

Harris, C. (1954). "The market as a factor on the localization of industry in the United States." *Annals of the Association of American Geographers*, vol. 64, pp. 640–56.

Hirschman, Albert O. (1958). *The Strategy of Economic Development*. New Haven: Yale University Press.

Krugman, Paul R. and Venables, Anthony J. (1995). "Globalization and the inequality of nations." *Quarterly Journal of Economics*, vol. 110, pp. 857–80.

Little, Ian. (1994). "Trade and industrialisation revisited." *Pakistan Development Review*, vol. 33, pp. 359–89.

Lluch, Constantino and Powel, Alan (1975). "International comparisons of expenditure patterns." *European Economic Review*, vol. 5, pp. 275–303.

Murphy, Kevin M., Shleifer, Andrei and Vishny, Robert W. (1989). "Industrialization and the big push." *Journal of Political Economy*, vol. 97, pp. 1003–26.

Myrdal, Gunnar (1957). *Economic Theory and Under-developed Regions*. London: Duckworth.

Pack, Howard (1992). "New perspectives on industrial growth in Taiwan." In (Gustav Ranis, ed.). *Taiwan, from Developing to Mature Economy*. Boulder, Colorado: Westview Press.

Perroux, François (1955). "Note sur la notion de pôle de croissance." *Economique Appliquée*, vol. 1–2, pp. 307–20.

Pred, Alan R. (1966). *The Spatial Dynamics of US Urban-Industrial Growth, 1800–1914: Interpretive and Theoretical Essays*. Cambridge: MIT Press.

Puga, Diego (1998). "The rise and fall of regional inequalities." *European Economic Review*, (forthcoming).

Puga, Diego and Venables, Anthony J. (1997). "Preferential trading arrangements and industrial location." *Journal of International Economics*, vol. 43, pp. 347–68.

Scotchmer, Susan and Thisse, Jacques-François (1992). "Space and competition: a puzzle." *Annals of Regional Science*, vol. 26, pp. 269–86.

Syrquin, Moshe and Chenery, Hollis B. (1989). "Patterns of development: 1950–83." Discussion Paper 41, The World Bank.

World Bank (1994). *East Asia's Trade and Investment: Regional and Global from Liberalization*. Washington, DC.

11 North-South Trade and the Environment

Brian R. Copeland and
M. Scott Taylor

I Introduction

One of the most interesting developments in trade policy in recent years has been the emergence of trade liberalization as an environmental issue.[1] In addition to facing traditional protectionist pressures, recent initiatives such as the North American Free Trade Agreement and the Uruguay Round of GATT negotiations have been questioned on the grounds that they might increase pollution. This has led to much debate about the environmental consequences of free trade.

Proponents of freer trade argue that environmental quality is a normal good, and hence trade-induced income gains should create political demands for tougher environmental standards. Tougher standards should in turn bring forth cleaner *techniques* of production. Skeptics, however, point out that if production methods do not change, then pollution must rise as trade increases the *scale* of economic activity. Moreover, if environmental quality is a normal good, then less developed countries will adopt relatively low environmental standards. As a result, because of asymmetries in the world distribution of income, free trade may affect the *composition* of national output with many developing countries turning toward relatively pollution-intensive activities. Grossman and Krueger [1991] and others have recently begun to investigate the empirical significance of each of these effects, but the issue has received relatively little attention in the theoretical literature.

This chapter takes a first step toward clarifying the theoretical issues by developing a simple static two-country general equilibrium model in which income-induced differences in environmental policy create incentives to trade. Using this framework, we first define the scale, technique, and composition effects,[2] and link their magnitudes to tastes, technologies, and endowments. We then use this decomposition to examine how pollution levels are affected by trade liberalization, exogenous increases in production capacity (scale-induced increases in income), and international transfers (redistributions of world income). We emphasize income effects because they determine the strength of the technique effect mentioned above, are tied to the scale of economic activity, and can determine how free trade affects the composition of national outputs and overall pollution levels.

Since the primary objective of the paper is to investigate factors determining the level and international incidence of pollution, we focus on positive rather than normative issues. As well, we simplify the analysis by assuming that the damage caused by pollution is confined to the country of emission.[3] As a consequence, it is perhaps wise to remind the reader at the outset that increases in pollution levels should *not* be viewed as equivalent to decreases in welfare. In fact, trade is always welfare-improving in our model, even when it raises pollution levels.

Our results indicate that increases in economic activity per se need not lower environmental quality because income effects can lead to the adoption of cleaner techniques of production. However, this conclusion must be tempered when we move to an open economy: we find that openness to international markets fundamentally alters the way in which income effects determine pollution levels. For example, in our model, economic growth[4] in autarky has no effect on pollution levels, but economic growth in a trading environment can raise pollution levels. Moreover, the distribution of growth across countries matters: growth in the rich North may increase pollution, while growth in the poor South lowers pollution. Freer trade, like growth, raises real incomes, but it also changes the composition of national output and hence alters both the incidence and level of pollution across countries. If the pattern of trade-induced specialization is driven only by differences in pollution policy, then aggregate world pollution may rise with trade.

The model that we develop has three key features designed to capture what we feel are the essentials. First, since most of the concern over the effect of international trade on environmental quality is motivated by international differences in pollution policy, we adopt a North-South framework in which there is a large income disparity across countries. To generate this disparity in income, we start with a model where countries differ only in the level of human capital per person.[5] As a result, income-induced differences in the level of pollution taxes are the sole determinant of trade flows. This permits an investigation of whether trade that is motivated by differences in environmental policy is inherently pollution-creating, and the simplicity thereby gained also allows us to decompose any change in pollution levels into scale, technique, and composition effects.

In reality, of course, trade is influenced by many conflicting factors. However, as a first step in understanding the interaction between trade and the environment, it is useful to isolate the impact of environment standards on the pattern of trade.[6] To make inferences about the actual pattern of trade, one would have to weigh the influences derived from environmental policy against other determinants of trade. Current estimates of environmental control costs are relatively small [Dean 1992]. However, marginal control costs are in many cases higher than average costs, and this suggests that environmental control costs are likely to become an increasingly important influence on trade in the future.

Second, to provide a link between income levels and environmental policy, we assume that benevolent planning authorities in each country set pollution taxes to offset the marginal damage from emissions. This assumption ensures that pollution is optimally provided in both autarky and trade and, moreover, that governments adjust pollution policy in response to changed economic circumstances such as growth or trade. While this may reflect an overly optimistic belief in the capabilities of government policy, it is the simplest way to capture the view that governments are responsive to the preferences of their citizens.

Finally, to capture the effect of differing standards of environmental protection on trade patterns, we adopt a many-good general equilibrium model based on Dornbusch, Fischer, and Samuelson [1977]. By adopting a general equilibrium approach, we ensure that the full impact of environmental policy can be traced through to its ultimate effects on factor markets, incomes, and trade flows. A many-good framework allows us to highlight composition effects. If, as we assume, industries differ in their pollution intensities, then changes in the composition of output arising from free trade will affect both national and world pollution levels.

Several previous studies [Baumol and Oates 1988; Pethig 1976; Siebert et al. 1980; McGuire 1982] have investigated the effects of pollution policy on the pattern of trade. Pethig [1976] extends the two-good Ricardian model to include pollution, and shows that if two countries are identical, except that they exogenously set different emission standards, then the country which allows a higher level of pollution emissions will export the pollution-intensive good. Siebert et al. [1980] and McGuire [1982] extend the analysis to the case of two primary factors. Pollution policy in all of these models, however, is exogenous. By endogenizing policy in the present paper, we explain the pattern of trade as a function of the underlying technology and endowments, rather than as merely reflecting exogenous policy differences. This allows us to examine explicitly the role that income differences may play in determining the pattern of trade. This issue, which is the subject of much policy debate, has not been addressed in previous formal models.[7]

Recent empirical work in the area is mixed. Grossman and Krueger [1991] examine data on air pollution levels in 43 developed and developing countries and conclude that pollution levels first rise and then fall with per capita income. Therefore, if trade liberalization raises incomes, it may also lower pollution levels. Low and Yeats [1992, p. 94] find that the share of world trade accounted for by pollution-intensive products has experienced a secular decline from 20.4 percent in 1965 to 15.9 percent in 1988; but the export share of such "dirty" goods has been increasing for many developing countries. In addition, Lucas, Wheeler, and Hettige [1992] find that although many developed countries are experiencing a fall in the pollution intensity of national product, this appears to be due to a change in the composition of output and *not* a movement toward cleaner production methods. These last two results suggest that international trade may be serving as a vehicle for dirty industry migration to less developed countries. While our model is highly stylized and abstracts from other important determinants of trade, it provides a useful starting point from which to interpret the earlier empirical work.

It is important, however, to recognize the limitations of our analysis. For example, openness to international markets may mean less developed countries gain access to better pollution abatement technology and to international capital markets. Our analysis limits the effects of openness to those arising from goods trade. As well, our conclusions follow from a decidedly stark model. While we are able to derive unambiguous answers to many questions and clearly identify the forces at work, there is much scope for future work aimed at relaxing some of our assumptions.

The remainder of the chapter is organized as follows. Section II sets out our assumptions on preferences and technologies. A simple diagrammatic framework to analyze the equilibrium is developed in Section III. Section IV explores the relation between international trade and the level of pollution; we also derive the scale, technique, and composition effects at this point. The effects of economic growth and international transfers on pollution are investigated in Sections V and VI. Section VII considers some extensions of the model, and Section VIII concludes.

II The Model

We consider a world with two countries: the highly developed North and the less developed South. Southern variables are indicated by an asterisk (*). There is a continuum of private consumption goods, indexed by $z \in [0, 1]$, and one primary input, effective labor (to be described in more detail below). Pollution is produced jointly with consumption goods. We assume that the output (y) of good z can be written as a function of pollution discharge (d) and effective labor input (l).[8] To keep the model simple, we adopt the following functional form:

$$y(d, l; z) = \begin{cases} l^{1-\alpha(z)} d^{\alpha(z)} & \text{if } d \leq \lambda l, \\ 0 & \text{if } d > \lambda l, \end{cases} \qquad (1)$$

where $\lambda > 0$ and $\alpha(z)$ is a parameter that varies across goods. We assume that $\alpha(z) \in [\underline{\alpha}, \bar{\alpha}]$, with $0 < \underline{\alpha} < \bar{\alpha} < 1$.

Isoquants for two typical goods z' and z'' are illustrated in Figure 11.1. For any given level of output of a good, a firm may choose among a continuum of production techniques, each of which generates different levels of pollution. By moving down and to the right along the isoquant, the firm adopts relatively cleaner technologies by abating pollution at the expense of more labor input. Note that the specification in (1) is analytically equivalent to treating pollution as an input that can be substituted for labor in the production of good z.[9] There is a limit to these substitution possibilities, however, because output must be bounded above for a given labor input. Hence points above the line $d = \lambda l$ are not feasible.[10]

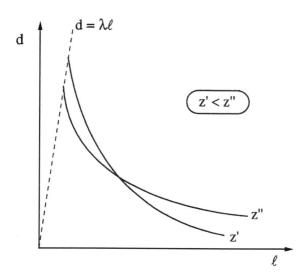

Figure 11.1
Unit isoquants for two industries, z' and z''. Industry z'' is more pollution intensive than industry z'.

If firms were unregulated, they would have no incentive to abate pollution and would always choose a point along the line $d = \lambda l$ in Figure 11.1. We assume throughout, however, that governments regulate pollution and that firms chose interior solutions where they engage in at least a small amount of abatement.[11] Consequently, if a pollution tax τ is imposed and w_e is the return to a unit of effective labor, the firm's labor/pollution combination that minimizes costs satisfy

$$\frac{w_e}{\tau} = \frac{1 - \alpha(z)}{\alpha(z)} \frac{d}{l}. \tag{2}$$

An implication of (2) is that the share of pollution charges in the cost of producing good z is always $\alpha(z)$. As a result, we can order the goods in terms of increasing pollution intensity to obtain $a'(z) > 0$.[12] Thus, in Figure 11.1, if $z'' > z'$, the isoquants for good z'' are flatter than those for good z' along any ray through the origin: good z'' is always more pollution intensive than good z'.

The technologies embodied in (1) are available to both countries. The North-South distinction arises only from an assumed higher level of human capital in the North. Each worker in the North has effectiveness $A(h)$, where h is the level of human capital, and $A' > 0$. Each

Southern worker has $h^* < h$ units of human capital, and hence supplies less effective labor than a Northern worker. For most of the paper we assume that each country has the same number of workers, L, so that the total supply of effective labor in the North is $A(h)L$, while that in the South is $A(h^*)L$.

Northern and Southern consumers have identical utility functions defined over consumption goods and pollution. To simplify matters, we assume that utility is strongly separable with respect to consumption and pollution, and we follow Dornbusch, Fischer, and Samuelson [1977] in assuming that the share of spending on each good is constant.

To specify how the damage caused by pollution affects utility, recall that we are concerned with pollution which has only localized effects. Suppose that individuals within a country live in identically sized communities, that pollution generated by one community affects only that community, and that sources of pollution are evenly spread throughout a community. Then pollution damage depends on both the pollution generated per individual, and the community's population density. If population density is very low, people are harmed mainly by their own pollution; but as communities get more crowded, individuals are affected by the pollution of others as well, and the harm caused by pollution rises. As well, if we increase population size but hold aggregate pollution and population density fixed (either by increasing the physical size of the country, or by creating another community distant from the others), then the harm caused by a given amount of aggregate pollution falls since each person is exposed to a smaller fraction of the total pollution.

A simple specification satisfying these requirements is given by

$$U = \int_0^1 b(z) \ln[x(z)]\, dz - \frac{\beta(L,\rho)D^\gamma}{\gamma}, \qquad (3)$$

where $x(z)$ is consumption of good z, $b(z)$ is the continuum counterpart to the many-commodity budget share, and $\int_0^1 b(z)\, dz = 1$. The impact of pollution on utility is captured by $\beta(L,\rho)D^\gamma/\gamma$, where D is the total amount of pollution generated by the country where the individual lives, ρ is the community population density, $\partial\beta/\partial L < 0$, $\partial\beta/\partial\rho > 0$, and $\gamma \geq 1$. The assumption on γ ensures that the marginal willingness to pay for pollution reduction is a nondecreasing function of pollution levels.

Since our main objective is to focus on the effects of income-induced differences in pollution policy on the pattern of trade and environmental quality, in most of the paper we consider the case where all countries are identical in size and population density, and differ only in their per capita endowment of human capital. In this case, β is constant across countries, and to economize on notation, we drop the reference to the arguments of β. In Section VII we examine the more general case where L and ρ differ across countries.

III   North-South Trading Equilibrium

A   Exogenous Pollution Taxes

As a first step toward determining the equilibrium, suppose that North and South have imposed pollution taxes of τ and τ^* per unit of discharge. For concreteness, assume that $\tau > \tau^*$ on the basis of North's higher income (we later show when this holds in equilibrium). Then the unit cost functions derived from (1) and (2) can be written as

$$c(w, \tau; h, z) = \kappa(z)\tau^{\alpha(z)}[w/A(h)]^{1-\alpha(z)}, \tag{4}$$

where $\kappa(z) \equiv \alpha^{-\alpha}(1-\alpha)^{-(1-\alpha)}$ is an industry-specific constant, and w is the wage rate for raw labor. For given Northern and Southern taxes and wages, good z will be produced in the North if $c(w, \tau; h, z) \leq c(w^*, \tau^*; h^*, z)$; that is, if

$$\omega \equiv \frac{w}{w^*} \leq \frac{A}{A^*}\left(\frac{\tau^*}{\tau}\right)^{\alpha(z)/(1-\alpha(z))} \equiv T(z). \tag{5}$$

Conversely, good z will be produced in the South if $\omega \geq T(z)$. With $\tau > \tau^*$ and $\alpha'(z) > 0$, T must be decreasing in z: because of North's relatively higher pollution taxes, its cost advantage in producing good z declines as pollution charges become a larger fraction of total costs.

For any given relative wage rate, ω, the $T(z)$ locus determines a critical industry $\tilde{z}(\omega)$ such that goods in the interval $[0, \tilde{z})$ are produced at least cost in the North, while goods over $(\tilde{z}, 1]$ are produced at least cost in the South. That is, with $\tau > \tau^*$, the North produces the least pollution-intensive goods, while the South produces the most pollution-intensive goods.

B   Endogenous Pollution Taxes

To determine τ and τ^*, first consider a representative Northern consumer's problem. All consumers own one unit of labor and receive an equal share of the pollution taxes collected by their government. Each consumer takes as given prices, aggregate pollution (D), and his or her share of national income (I/L). The indirect utility function corresponding to (3) for a representative consumer is given by

$$V = \int_0^1 b(z) \ln[b(z)] \, dz - \int_0^1 b(z) \ln[p(z)] \, dz + \ln\left(\frac{I}{L}\right) - \frac{\beta D^\gamma}{\gamma}. \tag{6}$$

The government's problem is then to choose its pollution tax τ to maximize V taking as given consumer and producer behavior. We also assume that governments treat world prices as given when choosing their environmental policy. This means that governments do not attempt to use pollution policy to manipulate their terms of trade. There are two reasons why we think that this is the most reasonable assumption. First, in many countries pollution policy is set at the local and state or provincial level, while international trade policy is set by national governments. Any individual local regulator is unlikely to perceive significant international market power. Second, Article XX of the General Agreement on Tariffs and Trade (GATT) requires that countries abstain from using domestic health or environmental policies as disguised trade barriers. Since we wish to focus on the pattern of trade, and not on strategic trade policy, we assume that governments honor their GATT commitments.

Maximizing indirect utility with respect to τ, treating $p(z)$ as given, yields

$$\tau = -LV_D/V_I = \beta D^{\gamma-1} I, \tag{7}$$

using (3). The government simply sets the pollution tax equal to the marginal damage caused by pollution emissions. Similarly, South's tax is given by $\tau^* = \beta D^{*\gamma-1} I^*$. Pollution taxes are increasing in income since environmental quality is a normal good, and nondecreasing in the aggregate pollution level since the marginal rate of substitution between consumption and pollution in nondecreasing.

We now replace the $T(\cdot)$ schedule, which depends on exogenous pollution taxes, with a new schedule $S(\cdot)$, which reflects endogenous choice of taxes. To do so, we obtain an expression for τ/τ^* in terms of $\tilde{z}$, which we then substitute into (5).

To begin, our optimal tax rate calculations imply that

$$\frac{\tau^*}{\tau} = \frac{I^*}{I} \left(\frac{D^*}{D}\right)^{\gamma-1},\tag{8}$$

which means that we now must solve for both income and pollution in terms of $\tilde{z}$. Let $\varphi(\tilde{z}) \equiv \int_0^{\tilde{z}} b(z)\,dz$ denote the share of world spending on Northern goods. Then balanced trade requires that

$$I = \varphi(\tilde{z})(I + I^*).\tag{9}$$

Aggregate Northern pollution, D, is the sum of pollution generated by the production of Northern output:

$$D = \int_0^{\tilde{z}} d(z)\,dz = \int_0^{\tilde{z}} \frac{[\alpha(z)p(z)y(z)]}{\tau}\,dz = \int_0^{\tilde{z}} \left[\frac{\alpha(z)b(z)(I + I^*)}{\tau}\right]\,dz.\tag{10}$$

The second equality follows from our Cobb-Douglas production functions (recall that $\alpha(z)$ is the share of pollution charges in the cost of good z) and from the zero profit conditions. The third equality follows from the definition of $b(z)$. Combining (9) and (10), we obtain

$$D = I\theta(\tilde{z})/\tau\varphi(\tilde{z}),\tag{11}$$

where $\theta(\tilde{z}) \equiv \int_0^{\tilde{z}} \alpha(z)b(z)\,dz$ is the share of Northern pollution charges in world income.[13] Now use the optimal pollution tax formula (7) to eliminate τ from (11), and do the same for the South to obtain expressions for pollution:

$$D = \left(\frac{\theta(\tilde{z})}{\beta\varphi(\tilde{z})}\right)^{1/\gamma} \quad \text{and} \quad D^* = \left(\frac{\theta^*(\tilde{z})}{\beta\varphi^*(\tilde{z})}\right)^{1/\gamma},\tag{12}$$

where $\varphi^*(\tilde{z}) = 1 - \varphi(\tilde{z})$ is the share of world spending on Southern goods, and

$$\theta^*(\tilde{z}) = \int_{\tilde{z}}^1 \alpha(z)b(z)\,dz$$

is the share of Southern pollution charges in world income.

We can now return to (8) and use the balance of trade condition (9) and our expressions for pollution in (12) to obtain relative pollution taxes as a function of $\tilde{z}$:

$$\frac{\tau^*}{\tau} = \left(\frac{\theta^*(\tilde{z})}{\theta(\tilde{z})}\right)^{(\gamma-1)/\gamma} \left(\frac{\varphi^*(\tilde{z})}{\varphi(\tilde{z})}\right)^{1/\gamma} \equiv \zeta(\tilde{z}).\tag{13}$$

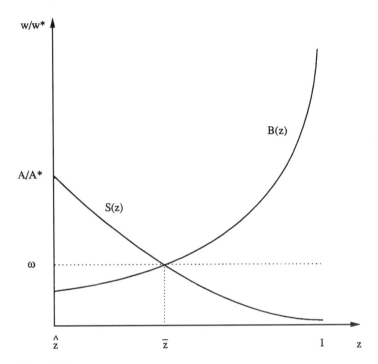

Figure 11.2
Trading equilibrium.

Finally, substituting (13) into (5) yields the result that North will produce all goods in the interval $[0, \tilde{z})$ if

$$\omega = \frac{A}{A^*} [\zeta(\tilde{z})]^{\alpha(\tilde{z})/(1-\alpha(\tilde{z}))} \equiv S(\tilde{z}), \tag{14}$$

provided that in equilibrium, $\tau > \tau^*$. The condition $\tau > \tau^*$ requires that $\zeta(\tilde{z}) < 1$. Thus, (14) is valid only for $\tilde{z} > \hat{z}$, where $\zeta(\hat{z}) \equiv 1$.[14] In this region S is decreasing in $\tilde{z}$;[15] we also have $S(\hat{z}) = A/A^*$, and $S(1) = 0$. The S schedule is plotted in Figure 11.2.

To determine the equilibrium critical industry $\tilde{z}$, we must combine $S(\tilde{z})$ with a balance of trade schedule that takes into account the resource constraints of the economy. Northern income is the sum of wages and pollution taxes (which are rebated to consumers). Hence

$$I = wL + \tau D. \tag{15}$$

Using (11) to eliminate D in (15), and rearranging yields

$$I = \frac{wL_\varphi(\tilde{z})}{\int_0^{\tilde{z}} b(z)[1 - \alpha(z)]\, dz}. \tag{16}$$

Following similar steps to obtain an expression for Southern income, and substituting into (9), we can solve for the balance of trade schedule:

$$\omega = \frac{\int_0^{\tilde{z}} b(z)[1 - \alpha(z)]\, dz}{\int_{\tilde{z}}^1 b(z)[1 - \alpha(z)]\, dz} \equiv B(\tilde{z}). \tag{17}$$

Note that $B(0) = 0, B(1) = \infty$, and $dB/d\tilde{z} > 0$. The $B(\tilde{z})$ schedule is positively sloped because an increase in the range of goods produced in the North raises exports and lowers imports, and must be met with an increase in North's relative wages to maintain balanced trade.

If $B(\tilde{z})$ and $S(\tilde{z})$ intersect at some $\tilde{z} = \bar{z} > \hat{z}$, as shown in Figure 11.2, they determine an equilibrium where North produces all of the relatively clean goods (i.e., all $z < \bar{z}$), and South produces all of the relatively pollution-intensive goods (all $z > \bar{z}$).[16] We now show that this pattern of trade must obtain if a Northern worker's human capital endowment is sufficiently large relative to that of a Southern worker.

PROPOSITION 1   There exists an equilibrium with $\tau > \tau^*$, where North produces all goods $z \in [0, \bar{z})$ and South produces all goods, $z \in (\bar{z}, 1]$ if and only if $A/A^* > \delta > 1$, where $\delta \equiv B(\hat{z})$.

Proof of Proposition 1   See Appendix.

The intuition for this result is straightforward. If North has a relatively high income, it chooses a higher pollution tax. Consequently, this forces all of the pollution-intensive industries to locate in the South. Conversely, all of the relatively clean industries locate in the North. However, as the statement of the proposition makes clear, this result is reliant on relative factor endowments being sufficiently different. If this is not the case, then B and S will not intersect over the range $z \in [\hat{z}, 1]$, and other outcomes are possible.

First, the roles of South and North may be reversed: if South is sufficiently well endowed with human capital relative to North (i.e., if $A/A^* < 1/\delta$), then $\tau^* > \tau$, and there will be an equilibrium where the pattern of trade is reversed and North produces all of the pollution-intensive goods. Second, if Southern and Northern human capital levels are similar (i.e., if $1/\delta \leq A/A^* \leq \delta$), then a factor-price equalization equilibrium will arise. The two countries will choose identical pollution taxes, and the returns to *effective* labor units will be equalized. The pattern of trade in goods will be indeterminate, but as long as $A/A^* > 1$, the North will be a net exporter of embodied labor services, while the South will be a net exporter of embodied pollution services. Since our primary interest in this paper is in the effect of significant income differences on linkages between trade and the environment, we limit our discussion to equilibria where North chooses a higher pollution tax than the South.

IV Trade and Pollution

One of the central questions raised by many of those concerned about linkages between trade and the environment is whether trade is inherently pollution-creating. Since trade in our model is driven entirely by income-induced international differences in pollution policy, it provides a useful framework in which to examine this question. By comparing free trade pollution levels with those in autarky, we obtain

PROPOSITION 2 If the assumptions of Proposition 1 hold, trade always lowers the pollution level in the North, increases the pollution level in the South, and increases worldwide pollution.

Proof of Proposition 2 See Appendix.

To investigate the intuition behind Proposition 2, it is useful to decompose the change in pollution levels into the scale, technique, and composition effects. Totally differentiating (11) (evaluated at the equilibrium) yields

$$dD = \frac{\partial D}{\partial I} \, dI + \frac{\partial D}{\partial \tau} \, d\tau + \frac{\partial D}{\partial \bar{z}} \, d\bar{z}. \tag{18}$$

Similar decompositions can be carried out for Southern and World pollution.

The *scale effect* reflects the increase in pollution created by an increase in the level of economic activity in the relevant jurisdiction, holding constant the techniques of production and the composition of final output. For the North it is represented by the first term in (18). This effect must be positive, and in fact, pollution must rise in direct proportion to income if tastes are homothetic (implying an equal percentage increase in the demand for all goods), and if technologies exhibit constant returns to scale (ensuring that these increases in output are met by an equal percentage increase in labor input and pollution discharge). This is confirmed by differentiating (11):

$$\frac{\partial D}{\partial I} = \frac{\theta(\bar{z})}{\tau\varphi(\bar{z})} > 0, \quad \text{and} \quad \frac{\partial D}{\partial I}\frac{I}{D} = 1. \tag{19}$$

Similarly, the scale effect in the South is positive and proportional to income.

The *technique effect* measures the change in aggregate pollution arising from a switch to less pollution-intensive production techniques, holding constant income and the range of goods produced. Since an increase in pollution taxes leads to the adoption of cleaner production methods, the technique effect, given by the second term in (18), must be negative:

$$\frac{\partial D}{\partial \tau} = -\frac{I\theta(\bar{z})}{\tau^2\varphi(\bar{z})} < 0. \tag{20}$$

Similarly, $\partial D^*/\partial \tau^* < 0$. Moreover,

$$\frac{\partial D}{\partial \tau}\frac{\tau}{D} = \frac{\partial D^*}{\partial \tau^*}\frac{\tau^*}{D^*} = -1.$$

This follows directly from our assumptions on the substitution possibilities in production and consumption which imply that τD is constant when both I and $\bar{z}$ are held constant:

$$\tau D = \int_0^{\bar{z}} \tau d(z)\, dz = \int_0^{\bar{z}} \alpha(z)p(z)y(z)\, dz$$

$$= \int_0^{\bar{z}} \alpha(z)b(z)[I + I^*]\, dz = \int_0^{\bar{z}} \frac{\alpha(z)b(z)I}{\varphi(\bar{z})}\, dz.$$

The second equality holds because the elasticity of substitution in production is one, and the third holds because the elasticity of substitution in consumption is one. (The final equality follows from the balance of trade condition.) The preceding suggests that if the elasticities of substitution in production or consumption exceed one, we expect a larger technique effect, and if they are less than one, we expect a smaller technique effect.

Finally, the *composition* effect measures the change in pollution due to a change in the range of goods produced by a country. For the North this effect is captured by the third term in (18). Differentiation of (11) yields

$$\frac{\partial D}{\partial \bar{z}} = D\left[\frac{\theta'(\bar{z})}{\theta(\bar{z})} - \frac{\varphi'(\bar{z})}{\varphi(\bar{z})}\right] = \frac{Ib(\bar{z})}{\tau\varphi(\bar{z})^2}\int_0^{\bar{z}}[\alpha(\bar{z}) - \alpha(z)]b(z)\,dz > 0, \tag{21}$$

since α is increasing in z. Thus, pollution rises in response to an increase in the range of goods produced in the North, if income and pollution taxes are held constant. This is because marginal goods added to Northern production are more pollution intensive than the original goods. Allocating a given Northern labor force across a group of industries that has become, on average, more pollution intensive must raise Northern pollution.

In the South we obtain

$$\frac{\partial D^*}{\partial \bar{z}} = \frac{I^*b(\bar{z})}{\tau^*\varphi^*(\bar{z})^2}\int_{\bar{z}}^1[\alpha(z) - \alpha(\bar{z})]b(z)\,dz > 0.$$

The composition effect for the South due to an increase in $\bar{z}$ is also positive. However, note that in this case, an increase in $\bar{z}$ corresponds to a *decrease* in the range of products produced by the South. As $\bar{z}$ increases, South loses its cleanest industries, leading to an increase in average pollution intensity. With a given production capacity, over-all pollution must rise. Conversely, the composition effect due to an *increase* in the range of industries produced by the South (*a fall in* $\bar{z}$) leads to a *decrease* in Southern pollution. Thus, the composition effect works to increase pollution in a country if it leads to an increase in the average pollution intensity of production (i.e., if dirty industries are attracted to a region or if clean industries leave), and it leads to a decrease in pollution if the average pollution intensity falls.

With these definitions in hand, we can now show that although international trade changes the range of goods produced in each country (a composition effect), increases real incomes (a scale effect), and creates incentives for governments to adjust their pollution taxes (a technique effect), the composition effect always dominates the other two effects. To examine the net result of these three effects, use (19)–(21) to rewrite (18) in percent change notation. Letting $\hat{D} = dD/D$, etc., this yields

$$\hat{D} = \hat{I} - \hat{\tau} + (\hat{\theta} - \hat{\varphi}), \tag{22}$$

where $\hat{I}$ is the scale effect, $-\hat{\tau}$ is the technique effect, and $\hat{\theta} - \hat{\varphi}$ is the composition effect.[17] The change in the pollution tax can be obtained from (7):

$$\hat{\tau} = (\gamma - 1)\hat{D} + \hat{I}. \tag{23}$$

Combining the above two expressions and rearranging yields

$$\hat{D} = -[(\gamma - 1)/\gamma](\hat{\theta} - \hat{\varphi}) + (\hat{\theta} - \hat{\varphi}). \tag{24}$$

The first term is the net result of the scale and technique effects. If $\gamma = 1$, this term disappears: the technique effect exactly offsets the scale effect. When $\gamma > 1$, pollution taxes respond more than proportionately to a change in income if pollution rises. As a result, the technique effect not only fully offsets the scale effect, but also offsets a fraction $(\gamma - 1)/\gamma$ of the composition effect. However, the composition effect must always dominate: from (24) we have

$$\hat{D} = (\hat{\theta} - \hat{\varphi})/\gamma. \tag{25}$$

Thus, while a larger γ dampens the magnitude of response of pollution to changes in the economy, the direction of the change is always determined by the sign of the composition effect $(\hat{\theta} - \hat{\varphi})$.

To understand why the composition effect dominates, it is useful to reinterpret trade in goods as implicit trade in factor services. The model behaves much like a two-factor Heckscher-Ohlin model with one factor in variable supply (pollution in our case) and one factor in inelastic supply (effective labor).[18] Hence by constructing pollution demand and supply, we can show that trade is driven by differences in relative factor supplies, and that when the South has an opportunity to trade, it can increase its gains from trade by accepting an increase in pollution.

Combining the optimal tax condition (7) and the economy's budget constraint (15) yields an expression for the inverse supply of pollution in the North:

$$\frac{\tau}{w_e} = \frac{\beta A(h)LD^{\gamma-1}}{1 - \beta D^\gamma}, \tag{26}$$

where $w_e = w/A(h)$ is the return to a unit of effective labor. This is plotted in Figure 11.3 and labeled N_s. The supply of pollution is increasing in τ/w_e since consumers are willing to accept increases in pollution if they are compensated with higher revenue from pollution taxes.

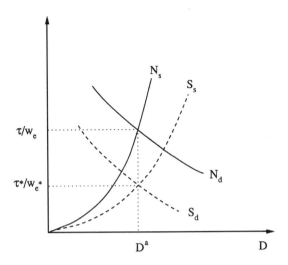

Figure 11.3
Pollution supply and demand.

The derived demand for pollution in autarky (i.e., the pollution implicit in the demand for consumer goods) can be obtained by setting $\bar{z} = 1$ in (11), and combining with the economy's budget constraint to obtain

$$\frac{\tau}{w_e} = \frac{A(h)L\theta(1)}{D[1 - \theta(1)]}. \tag{27}$$

This is plotted as N_d in Figure 11.3. As one would expect, the derived demand for pollution is decreasing in its relative price, τ/w_e.

Equating the demand and supply for pollution in the North yields the autarky factor price ratio (τ/w_e), and autarky pollution level,

$$D^a = \left(\frac{\theta(1)}{\beta}\right)^{1/\gamma}. \tag{28}$$

Note that a reduction in human capital shifts down both the demand and supply curves by the same proportion (as indicated by the two dashed lines S_s and S_d in Figure 11.3). This leaves the pollution level unchanged, but reduces τ/w_e.[19] Since the South differs from the North only in that it has less human capital, we conclude that pollution is a relatively scarce input in the North prior to trade ($D^a/AL < D^a/A^*L$), and consequently, that pollution is relatively more costly for firms in the North than in the South ($\tau/w_e > \tau^*/w_e^*$).

This provides a basis for trade. North is willing to export effective labor services (embodied in goods) in return for imports of pollution services, and South is willing to do the reverse. Since trade increases the demand for pollution services in the South, and reduces the demand in the North, it reduces the gap between factor prices by raising τ^*/w_e^* and reducing τ/w_e. Since the supply curves are valid both in trade and autarky, we see from Figure 11.3 that trade must therefore increase pollution in the South (a movement up its pollution supply curve) and reduce pollution in the North (a movement down its supply curve). Increases in γ make the supply curves more inelastic, but the direction of the response is not altered, since trade is driven by pressures to reduce the gap in factor prices across countries.

The last result in Proposition 2 is that total world pollution rises with trade. The change in world pollution is the net result of the scale, technique, and composition effects in both countries. We have already shown that the composition effect dominates the scale and technique effects; and therefore to understand how world pollution responds to trade, we need to consider the strength of the two opposing composition effects.

Trade shifts some of the Northern labor force from dirty industries into clean ones, and shifts some of the Southern labor force from clean industries into dirty ones. To examine the consequences of these reallocations, consider the movement of one unit of Southern effective labor from a clean industry in the South (z') to a dirty industry in the South (z''). At the same time, shift one unit of Northern effective labor from a dirty industry in the North (z'') to a clean industry in the North (z'). The change in pollution in each country can be deduced from the local $d(z)/l(z)$ ratio. Using (2), we can infer that the induced change in pollution in the North is

$$\Delta d_N = \frac{d(z')}{l(z')} - \frac{d(z'')}{l(z'')} = \frac{w_e}{\tau} \left[\frac{\alpha(z')}{1 - \alpha(z')} - \frac{\alpha(z'')}{1 - \alpha(z'')} \right] < 0,$$

since $\alpha(z') < \alpha(z'')$. A similar calculation for the South yields $\Delta d_S > 0$. Adding, to determine the net effect of this reallocation on world pollution, we obtain

$$\Delta d_N + \Delta d_S = \left[\frac{\alpha(z'')}{1 - \alpha(z'')} - \frac{\alpha(z')}{1 - \alpha(z')} \right] \left[\frac{w_e^*}{\tau^*} - \frac{w_e}{\tau} \right].$$

Since trade reduces but does not eliminate the gap between relative factor prices, we have $w_e^*/\tau^* > w_e/\tau$, and therefore $\Delta d_N + \Delta d_S > 0$. This combined world composition effect raises world pollution provided that factor prices are not equalized across countries.[20]

V Trade, Pollution, and Economic Development

The previous section showed that opening a country up to trade affects both the level and distribution of world pollution. These results were driven mainly by changes in the location of production since the output-enhancing effects of trade were offset by changes in pollution policy. In the present section we focus on the effects of changes in production capacity on pollution, by examining the consequences of increases in human capital.

Let us first consider the effects of growth on pollution in autarky. An increase in the level of human capital stimulates pollution directly through the scale effect. In Figure 11.3 this corresponds to an outward shift in the demand for pollution. Because of higher income, the pollution supply curve shifts inward. This increases the τ/w_e ratio, but since the demand and supply for pollution are proportional to the economy's endowment of effective labor, the scale and technique effects exactly offset each other, leaving the level of pollution unaffected by economic growth. Note that there is no composition effect in autarky since tastes are homothetic.[21] The result that growth has no effect on pollution in autarky is specific to our assumptions on substitution possibilities, but it nevertheless provides a very useful benchmark. Any change in pollution induced by trade or growth in the open economy version of our model must be driven entirely by the opportunity to trade, and not by the simple effects of increases in the level of economic activity.

We next consider symmetric growth in the world economy. Suppose that there is equiproportionate, labor-augmenting technological progress. With $dA/A = dA^*/A^* > 0$, neither the $S(z)$ nor the $B(z)$ schedule is affected, and hence (referring to Figure 11.2) ω and $\bar{z}$ are unchanged. Since $\bar{z}$ does not change, then from (12), pollution levels are unchanged. As in autarky, symmetric growth across countries increases the world's productive capacity and raises pollution through the scale effect, but this is just offset by the technique effect as pollution taxes respond to higher income levels. With equiproportionate growth in both countries the terms of trade remain constant

—there is no reallocation of industries across countries, and hence no composition effect. World pollution remains constant.

Now consider asymmetric growth. Suppose that there is an increase in the level of human capital in the North, holding the level of Southern human capital constant. This shifts the $S(z)$ schedule upwards, while leaving $B(z)$ unaffected. From Figure 11.2 it is apparent that North's relative wage rises $(d\omega/dh > 0)$, and the range of commodities produced in the North grows $(d\bar{z}/dh > 0)$. The effect on Northern pollution is obtained by differentiating (12):

$$\frac{dD}{dh} = \frac{1}{\gamma}\left[\frac{b(\bar{z})D}{\theta(\bar{z})\varphi(\bar{z})}\int_0^{\bar{z}} b(z)[\alpha(\bar{z}) - \alpha(z)]\,dz\right]\frac{d\bar{z}}{dh} > 0, \tag{29}$$

since α is increasing in z. Northern pollution increases, even though the government has an opportunity to adjust the pollution tax rate.

To understand this result, recall that North's government adjusts the pollution tax so that the technique effect fully offsets the scale effect, and partially offsets the composition effect. That is, if $\bar{z}$ were held constant, pollution levels in the North would be unaffected by the increase in output generated by the increase in human capital. However, $\bar{z}$ cannot remain constant since the North's production of exportables and its demand for importables both rise. A fall in North's terms of trade is required to maintain balanced trade. This induces Southern industries to migrate to the North. Thus, the effect of growth on pollution is determined by the composition effect. This can be confirmed by referring to (21), and noting that the term in brackets in (29) is simply $\partial D/\partial \bar{z}$. Because the marginal Southern industries that move northward are more pollution intensive than existing Northern industries, the composition effect is positive, and Northern pollution rises.

To determine the effect of Northern growth on Southern pollution, differentiate (12):

$$\frac{dD^*}{dh} = \frac{1}{\gamma}\left[\frac{b(\bar{z})D^*}{\theta^*(\bar{z})\varphi^*(\bar{z})}\int_{\bar{z}}^{1} b(z)[\alpha(z) - \alpha(\bar{z})]\,dz\right]\frac{d\bar{z}}{dh} > 0.$$

Once again, the composition effect determines the direction of the change in pollution. An increase in $\bar{z}$ shifts South's least pollution-intensive industries to the North. As a result, the average pollution intensity in the South rises, and with a given labor force, this increases total pollution.

In contrast, economic development in the South lowers pollution in both countries. An increase in Southern human capital shifts down the $S(z)$ schedule in Figure 11.2, and both ω and $\bar{z}$ fall. South's economy expands, but the marginal industries it attracts from the North are less pollution intensive than existing Southern industries. Hence the composition effect is negative, and Southern pollution falls. The composition effect in the North is also negative since the North loses its most pollution-intensive industries to the South; hence Northern pollution also falls.

To summarize, we have found that as rich countries get richer, world pollution increases, but as poor countries get richer, world pollution falls. The intuition for these surprising results can best be understood with the aid of Figure 11.3. Growth increases a country's supply of effective labor, which raises its autarky τ/w_e ratio. When growth occurs in the North, the differences between the two countries are magnified. This widens the gap between both pre- and posttrade factor prices. But recall that it is the gap between posttrade factor prices that determines the strength of the overall world composition effect. A greater gap between factor prices means a greater difference in techniques across countries, and a greater increase in pollution arising from concentrating dirty industries in the lower income country. When growth occurs in the South, the opposite occurs. Factor supply ratios move closer together, shrinking the gap between factor prices. The world composition effect is muted, and hence pollution falls. Therefore, our results here provide a corollary to Proposition 2.

COROLLARY The increase in pollution accompanying trade is greater, the greater are the differences across countries in human capital endowments.

VI Transfers, Trade, and Pollution

In this section we consider the impact of an income transfer from North to South. In the basic Dornbusch-Fischer-Samuelson [1977] model, transfers have no real effects because there are identical homothetic preferences and no public goods. In the present model, transfers have real effects since they alter relative income levels, and hence relative pollution taxes. The transfer case is important to consider because unlike the asymmetric growth experiments conducted above, a transfer provides us with an example of a change in the world distribution of income that is not accompanied by changes in production capacity. Consequently, it allows us to focus on pure income effects. The study of transfers is also of interest because a theme in the recent literature on trade and the environment is that tied aid can be used to reduce pollution in the South. In this section we show that untied aid can accomplish the same objective.

To proceed, we derive a modified $S(\cdot)$ schedule that incorporates transfers. Once this schedule is constructed, we can again use Figure 11.2 to generate comparative static results. Let T be the value of the transfer (measured in terms of Northern labor), and let I and I^* be the level of income (excluding transfers) generated within each country. Then it is straightforward to show that pollution taxes are given by

$$\tau = \beta D^{\gamma-1}(I - T) \quad \text{and} \quad \tau^* = \beta D^{*\gamma-1}(I^* + T). \tag{30}$$

Using a derivation analogous to that which led to (12), we obtain pollution levels:

$$D = \left(\frac{I\theta(\tilde{z})}{(I - T)\beta\varphi(\tilde{z})}\right)^{1/\gamma} \quad \text{and} \quad D^* = \left(\frac{I^*\theta^*(\tilde{z})}{(I^* + T)\beta\varphi^*(\tilde{z})}\right)^{1/\gamma}. \tag{31}$$

Combining (30) and (31) and letting

$$h(T, \tilde{z}) = \frac{T}{\varphi(\tilde{z})(I - T)} > 0, \tag{32}$$

we can obtain an expression for the ratio of pollution taxes:

$$\frac{\tau^*}{\tau} = \left(\frac{\theta^*(\tilde{z})}{\theta(\tilde{z})}\right)^{(\gamma-1)/\gamma} \left(\frac{\varphi^*(\tilde{z})}{\varphi(\tilde{z})} + h(T, \tilde{z})\right)^{1/\gamma} \equiv \zeta(\tilde{z}, T). \tag{33}$$

Note that (33) differs from (13) only by the presence of the term $h(T, \tilde{z})$. It is easy to show that $\partial h/\partial T > 0$, $\partial h/\partial \tilde{z} < 0$, and $h(0, \tilde{z}) = 0$; and hence (33) reduces to (13) when there is no transfer. Also note that with Northern labor as the numeraire, h is a function of $\tilde{z}$ and T, but not of ω.

A modified $S(\cdot)$ schedule is obtained by substituting (33) into (4):

$$\omega = \frac{A}{A^*}[\zeta(\tilde{z}, T)]^{\alpha(\tilde{z})/(1-\alpha(\tilde{z}))} \equiv S(\tilde{z}, T). \tag{34}$$

Since h is decreasing in $\tilde{z}$, $S(\tilde{z}, T)$ is also decreasing in z, provided that North remains the high income country after the transfer; i.e., provided that $I - T > I^* + T$. Also, since $h(0, \tilde{z}) = 0$, the modified $S(\tilde{z}, T)$ schedule coincides with the original $S(\tilde{z})$ schedule for $T = 0$.

A transfer has no effect on $B(\tilde{z})$, but $S(\tilde{z}, T)$ shifts up as T rises. Hence by interpreting the S schedule as a function of $\tilde{z}$ and T, we can use Figure 11.2 to conclude that a transfer raises both $\tilde{z}$ and ω. The reasoning is straightforward. A transfer from North to South reduces North's relative income, and hence its relative pollution tax falls, rendering Northern industries more competitive. As a result, North attracts marginal industries from the South ($\tilde{z}$ rises). This increases the relative demand for North's labor, pushing up its relative wage, but not by enough to offset the direct effect of the transfer.

Let us now consider the effects of the transfer on pollution. Define $\sigma(T) = (I - T)/(I + I^*)$ to be the share of income accruing to the North after the transfer is applied. We confine ourselves to the case where $\sigma(T) > 1$; that is, where North continues to be the relatively rich country. Note that a transfer must lower North's consumption share of world income; that is, $d\sigma/dT < 0$.[22] Using (31), Northern pollution can be written as

$$D(T) = \left(\frac{\theta(\tilde{z})}{\beta\sigma(T)} \right)^{1/\gamma}.$$

Differentiating with respect to T shows that the transfer leads to an increase in North's pollution:

$$\frac{dD}{dT} = \frac{D}{\gamma} \left[-\frac{\sigma'}{\sigma} + \frac{\alpha(\tilde{z})b(\tilde{z})}{\theta} \frac{d\tilde{z}}{dT} \right] > 0, \tag{35}$$

where $\sigma' \equiv d\sigma/dT$. North reduces its pollution tax in response to its lower disposable income, and this tends to increase pollution via the technique effect.[23] As well, the decline in North's pollution tax attracts marginal industries from the South, and since these new industries are relatively pollution intensive, the composition effect also tends to increase North's pollution.

Conversely, South's pollution falls in response to the transfer:

$$\frac{dD^*}{dT} = \frac{D^*}{\gamma} \left[\frac{\sigma'}{1 - \sigma} - \frac{\alpha(\tilde{z})b(\tilde{z})}{\theta^*} \frac{d\tilde{z}}{dT} \right] < 0. \tag{36}$$

In the South, disposable income increases, its pollution tax rises, and pollution falls from the technique effect. However, its marginal industries migrate to the North, and since these are relatively clean, the average pollution intensity of South's industries rises for given techniques. Consequently, Southern pollution should rise from the composition effect. However, as (36) shows, the direct effect of the pollution tax increase more than offsets this indirect composition effect: pollution falls in the South. Direct effects swamp indirect effects since the increase in the pollution tax affects the pollution intensity of all Southern industries, and all of these industries are more pollution intensive than the marginal ones given up.

Finally, we show that a small transfer must lower world pollution. Summing (35) and (36) and evaluating at $T = 0$ noting that at this point $\sigma(T) = \varphi(\bar{z})$ yields

$$\frac{d(D + D^*)}{dT}\bigg|_{T=0} = \left(\frac{\sigma'}{\gamma}\right)\left[\frac{D^*}{1 - \varphi(\bar{z})} - \frac{D}{\varphi(\bar{z})}\right]$$

$$+ \frac{\alpha(\bar{z})b(\bar{z})(I + I^*)}{\gamma}\left[\frac{1}{\tau} - \frac{1}{\tau^*}\right]\frac{d\bar{z}}{dT} < 0.$$

Putting the technique and composition effects from both countries together, world pollution must fall. This follows since the transfer raises pollution taxes in the most pollution-intensive country, and reduces the disparity in techniques used worldwide.[24]

VII Extensions

This section extends the model to examine the implications of cross-country differences in population density, climate, and other factors that affect the damage caused by pollution. These modifications would be an important preliminary step to empirically testing the model.

Consider the following specification for the utility function:

$$U = \int_0^1 b(z)\ln[x(z)]\,dz - \beta_0\left[\frac{D}{L}g(\rho)\right]^\gamma\bigg/\gamma \tag{37}$$

where $\beta_0 > 0$ is a constant, and $g'(\rho) > 0$. This corresponds to setting

$$\beta(L, \rho) = \beta_0[g(\rho)/L]^\gamma \tag{38}$$

in (3). In this specification, increases in either pollution per capita or in population density (for given pollution levels) reduce utility by increasing the exposure of a typical person to pollution.

Let us now reconsider autarky pollution. Substituting (38) into (28) yields

$$\frac{D^a}{L} = \frac{(\theta(1)/\beta_0)^{1/\gamma}}{g(\rho)}. \tag{39}$$

If two countries have the same population density, then pollution per capita is the same across countries. This means that if we scale up the size of a country, by increasing both land mass and population proportionately, then aggregate pollution rises. This is a reasonable prediction for pollution that has localized effects. On the other hand, as population density increases, pollution per capita falls, since a given unit of pollution causes more damage in a more crowded environment.

Let us now consider trade. First, suppose that two countries differ only with respect to labor force size, but are otherwise identical in terms of population density and human capital. In this case, there is no basis for trade. The larger country is just a scaled-up version of the smaller, and relative factor supplies are identical. Not surprisingly, in a constant returns to scale world with equal relative factor supplies, autarky prices are identical, and free trade is identical to autarky. This is confirmed by substituting (39) into (27) to obtain the autarky factor price ratio:

$$\frac{\tau}{w_e} = \frac{A(h)[\theta(1)^{\gamma-1}\beta_0]^{1/\gamma}g(\rho)}{1 - \theta(1)},$$

which is independent of L.

Next suppose that North and South are identical in all respects, except that North is more densely populated. Then from (26), (27), and (38), North's pollution supply curve will be to the left of South's, and hence the autarky τ/w_e ratio will be relatively higher in the North. Thus, in free trade the more densely populated country will export labor-intensive goods, while the less densely populated country will export pollution-intensive goods.

If countries differ both with respect to the level of human capital and population density, then the pattern of trade depends on the interaction between the two effects. If the human-capital-poor country is less densely populated than the rich country, then its tendency to specialize in pollution-intensive goods will be reinforced. However, if the poor country is more densely populated than the rich country, then its supply curve for pollution will shift inward, and the pattern of trade may be reversed, with the poor country exporting relatively clean goods.

Finally, suppose that two countries differ with respect to the carrying capacity of the environment, as determined by prevailing winds, ocean currents, soil conditions, and other factors. This may be captured by allowing the β function to differ across countries. Suppose that a given unit of pollution causes less damage at Home than abroad because of differences in the environment. Then for any given L and ρ, we have $\beta(L, \rho) < \beta^*(L, \rho)$. Consequently, if the countries are otherwise identical, Home's supply of pollution will be to the right of Foreign's, and hence Home exports pollution-intensive goods.

VIII Conclusion

This chapter has presented a simple model to examine how trade between two countries differentiated solely by income can affect environmental quality. Our most important results are that income gains arising from an opportunity to trade can affect pollution in a different way than income gains obtained through economic growth and, moreover, that economic growth has different effects on pollution in a free trade regime than in autarky.

If environmental policy is set optimally, then potential increases in pollution generated by economic growth in autarky can be prevented by a policy-induced switch to cleaner methods of production. Given our assumption on substitution possibilities in production and consumption, growth in autarky has a neutral effect on pollution: the technique effect fully offsets the scale effect.

However, international trade opens up a different channel that may nevertheless lead to an increase in world pollution. While trade, like growth, increases real incomes in both countries, it also creates a composition effect that is critical in determining the effect of trade on pollution. If differences in pollution taxes are the only motive for trade, and trade does not equalize factor prices, then a movement from autarky to free trade increases aggregate world pollution.

Composition effects also determine the impact of asymmetric economic growth on pollution in free trade. Even if, as in our model, the pollution-generating effects of symmetric growth across countries are exactly offset by stricter environmental policy, the migration of industries induced by asymmetric growth has important and interesting effects on pollution through the composition effect. Consequently, economic growth in the North has much different effects on the environment than economic growth in the South.

While our model is stylized and many of its particular results model-specific, much of the intuition springs from more general factor endowment considerations. Most of our results follow from just two suppositions: (1) trade has a tendency to reduce, but not fully eliminate, international differences in factor prices if countries are sufficiently different; and (2), in autarky, the relative price of pollution-intensive goods is higher in relatively high-income countries. The first of these suppositions is a quite general result. The second is much more tenuous, but it clearly holds in our simple model. In more general factor endowment models it may not. Nevertheless, the simple structure of our model is a virtue since it lays bare the basic relationships driving our results, and at once suggests extensions of the model that can only enhance our understanding of the relationship between pollution and international trade.

Appendix

A   Derivation of Equation (1) from a Joint Production Technology

The following is one way to motivate equation (1). Let l_y be the amount of effective labor used to produce good y. Since the analysis applies to any good, we suppress the index z to economize on notation. Assume that

$$y = \lambda^\alpha l_y, \tag{A1}$$

$$d_0(y) = \lambda^{(1-\alpha)} y = \lambda l_y, \tag{A2}$$

where d_0 is the amount of pollution produced in the absence of any abatement activity.

The firm has an abatement technology given by

$$A[l_a, d_0(y)] = d_0(y) - \left[\frac{\lambda^{\alpha-1} d_0(y)}{[d_0(y)/\lambda + l_a]^{1-\alpha}} \right]^{1/\alpha},$$

where l_a is the amount of effective labor assigned to abatement. Note that $A[0, d_0(y)] = 0$, and that $\partial A/\partial l_a > 0$, so that there is no abatement unless labor is allocated to it, and that an increase in labor assigned to abatement yields an increase in abatement. In addition, note that the abatement function is concave in l_a, and is asymptotic to $d_0(y)$, reflecting an assumption of diminishing returns to abatement activity.

Pollution discharged by the firm is equal to the unconstrained level of pollution, less the amount abated:

$$d(y, l_a) = d_0(y) - A[l_a, d_0(y)] = \left[\frac{\lambda^{\alpha-1} d_0(y)}{[d_0(y)/\lambda + l_a]^{1-\alpha}} \right]^{1/\alpha}.$$ (A3)

Using (A1) and (A2), we can rewrite (A3) as

$$d(y, l_a) = \left[\frac{y}{[l_y + l_a]^{1-\alpha}} \right]^{1/\alpha}.$$ (A4)

Letting $l = l_y + l_a$ be the total effective labor employed by the firm, we can rearrange (A4) to obtain

$$y = d^{\alpha} l^{1-\alpha}.$$ (A5)

Note that we require $l_a \geq 0$ and $l_y \geq 0$. Hence since $y = \lambda^{\alpha} l_y$, equation (A5) is valid only for $y \leq \lambda^{\alpha} l$, or equivalently, for $d \leq \lambda l$. Thus, output is not feasible for $d/l > \lambda$.

B   Conditions for an Interior Solution

To ensure an interior solution (i.e., that all firms engage in at least a small amount of abatement), we assume that $d/l < \lambda$ for all firms. Because Southern firms are the most pollution intensive, it is sufficient to ensure that this holds for the South. Using (2), we require that $\tau^*/w^* > \alpha(z)/[\lambda A^*(1 - \alpha(z))]$, for all z. Using the Southern version of (7) and (16) to eliminate τ^*/w^*, this is equivalent to requiring that

$$A^* L > \frac{\alpha(z)[\varphi^*(\bar{z}) - \theta^*(\bar{z})]}{\lambda \beta [1 - \alpha(z)] D^{*\gamma-1} \varphi^*(\bar{z})}, \qquad \text{for all } z.$$ (A6)

But from Proposition 2, $D^* > D^a$, which implies that $\theta^*(\bar{z}) > \varphi^*(\bar{z})\theta(1)$. Hence we have

$$\frac{\varphi^*(\bar{z}) - \theta^*(\bar{z})}{D^{*\gamma-1}\varphi^*(\bar{z})} < \frac{1 - \theta(1)}{[\theta(1)/\beta]^{(\gamma-1)/\gamma}}.$$ (A7)

Using (A7) in (A6), and noting that $\alpha(z) < \bar{\alpha}$, we conclude that the following condition is sufficient to ensure that $d/l < \lambda$ for all z (in either country):

$$AL > A^* L > \frac{\bar{\alpha}[1 - \theta(1)]}{\lambda \beta^{1/\lambda}(1 - \bar{\alpha})\theta(1)^{(\gamma-1)/\gamma}}.$$

The following make the condition more likely to be satisfied: (1) an increase in β, which corresponds to an increase in the disutility of pollution; (2) an increase in $A^* L$, which increases the willingness to pay to control pollution; (3) an increase in λ, which is the unregulated d/l ratio; and (4) an increase in $\theta(1)$, which is a weighted average of the pollution share parameters α.

C   Proofs of Propositions

The following inequalities are useful:

$$\theta(\bar{z}) < \alpha(\bar{z})\varphi(\bar{z}),$$ (A8)

$$\theta^*(\bar{z}) > \alpha(\bar{z})\varphi^*(\bar{z}). \tag{A9}$$

$$\varphi(\hat{z}) > 1/2. \tag{A10}$$

The first two follow since α is increasing in z. The third follows from the definition of $\hat{z}$.

Proof of Proposition 1 (i) Sufficiency. B and S are both continuous. Also B is strictly increasing, and S is strictly decreasing for $z > \hat{z}$. Hence if $B(\hat{z}) < S(\hat{z}) = A/A^*$, they must intersect at some $z \in (\hat{z}, 1)$. (ii) Necessity. If $B(\hat{z}) > A/A^*$, then (17) and (14) cannot be solved for $\bar{z} > \hat{z}$. But for $\bar{z} \le \hat{z}$, we have $I \le I^*$, which is inconsistent with $\tau > \tau^*$ (and hence the construction of B and S is not valid). (iii) Finally, to show that $\delta > 1$, note that using (A8)–(A10), we have $\delta > \varphi(\hat{z})/\varphi^*(\hat{z}) > 1$. QED

Proof of Proposition 2 Using a derivation similar to that which led to (12), we obtain an expression for autarky pollution levels:

$$D^a = D^{*a} = \left(\frac{\theta(1)}{\beta}\right)^{1/\gamma}.$$

Free trade pollution is given by (12). Subtracting yields

$$D - D^a = \beta^{-1/\gamma}\left[\left(\frac{\theta(\bar{z})}{\varphi(\bar{z})}\right)^{1/\gamma} - \theta(1)^{1/\gamma}\right]. \tag{A11}$$

Since $\theta(1) = \theta(\bar{z}) + \theta^*(\bar{z})$, and using (A8) and (A9), we have

$$\frac{\theta(\bar{z})}{\varphi(\bar{z})} - \theta(1) = \frac{\theta(\bar{z})\varphi^*(\bar{z}) - \varphi(\bar{z})\theta^*(\bar{z})}{\varphi(\bar{z})} < \frac{\alpha(\bar{z})\varphi(\bar{z})\varphi^*(\bar{z}) - \varphi(\bar{z})\alpha(\bar{z})\varphi^*(\bar{z})}{\varphi(\bar{z})} = 0.$$

Hence $\theta(\bar{z})/\varphi(\bar{z}) < \theta(1)$. But since the inequality is preserved by a monotonic transformation, we conclude that $[\theta(\bar{z})/\varphi(\bar{z})]^{1/\gamma} < [\theta(1)]^{1/\gamma}$, and hence $D < D^a$.

Turning now to the South, a similar analysis yields

$$D^* - D^{*a} = \beta^{-1/\gamma}\left[\left(\frac{\theta^*(\bar{z})}{\varphi^*(\bar{z})}\right)^{1/\gamma} - \theta(1)^{1/\gamma}\right]. \tag{A12}$$

Proceedings as above, we have

$$\frac{\theta^*(\bar{z})}{\varphi^*(\bar{z})} - \theta(1) = \frac{\theta^*(\bar{z})\varphi(\bar{z}) - \varphi^*(\bar{z})\theta(\bar{z})}{\varphi^*(\bar{z})} > \frac{\alpha(\bar{z})\varphi(\bar{z})\varphi^*(\bar{z}) - \varphi(\bar{z})\alpha(\bar{z})\varphi^*(\bar{z})}{\varphi^*(\bar{z})} = 0.$$

Using this inequality, it is straightforward to show that $D^* > D^{*a}$.

Finally, consider world pollution.[25] Define $r = 1/\gamma$, and $f(z) = [\theta(z)/\varphi(z)]^r + [\theta^*(z)/\varphi^*(z)]^r - 2[\theta(z) + \theta^*(z)]^r$. Summing (A11) and (A12), we see that proving that world pollution goes up is equivalent to showing that $f(\bar{z}) > 0$ for $\bar{z} > \hat{z}$, where, from (13), $\hat{z}$ is defined by

$$[\theta^*(\hat{z})/\theta(\hat{z})]^{1-r}[\varphi^*(\hat{z})/\varphi(\hat{z})]^r = 1. \tag{A13}$$

Using (A8) and (A9), one can show that f is increasing in z. Hence to prove our result, we need only show that

$$f(\hat{z}) \ge 0. \tag{A14}$$

Using (A13) to eliminate φ^*, (A14) is equivalent to (where unless otherwise indicated, all functions are evaluated at $\hat{z}$):

$$(\theta + \theta^*)/\varphi^r \theta^{1-r} \geq 2(\theta + \theta^*)^r. \tag{A15}$$

Rearranging (A15) yields

$$(1 + \theta^*/\theta)^{1-r} \geq 2\varphi^r. \tag{A16}$$

Using (A13) to eliminate θ^*/θ, (A16) is equivalent to

$$\varphi^{*s} + \varphi^s \geq 2\varphi^s \varphi^{*s}, \tag{A17}$$

where $s \equiv r/(1-r)$. Hence to show (A14), we must establish (A17). But since $\varphi^{*s} + \varphi^s - 2\varphi^{s/2}\varphi^{*s/2} = [\varphi^{s/2} - \varphi^{*s/2}]^2 \geq 0$, and since $s \geq 0$, we have

$$\varphi^{*s} + \varphi^s \geq 2\varphi^{s/2}\varphi^{*s/2} \geq 2\varphi^s \varphi^{*s},$$

where the latter inequality follows since $\varphi^s \varphi^{*s} < 1$. QED

Notes

1. See Anderson and Blackhurst [1992] and Dean [1992] for useful surveys of the literature on trade and the environment.

2. The "scale, technique, and composition effect" terminology has been employed by several authors, including Grossman and Krueger [1991], but explicit model-based definitions of these effects have yet to be presented.

3. Transboundary pollution is clearly an important issue, but its analysis is left to a companion paper [Copeland and Taylor 1993]. This allows us to abstract from problems of policy failure due to the lack of an international government, and frees us to concentrate on the transmission mechanisms linking trade and pollution.

4. By "growth" we mean the effect of once-for-all increases in technological capabilities or endowments.

5. In Section VII of the chapter we examine how differences in population density, country size, and physical carrying capacity of the environment can also affect trade flows.

6. This is a fairly standard methodology. For example, Staiger [1987] uses a similar model to investigate the effect of unionization on the pattern of trade, and assumes that differences in the scope of unionization are all that differentiate countries. Similarly, much of the early literature on increasing returns to scale abstracted from all other incentives to trade.

7. There is also a literature on optimal choice of pollution policy and trade policy in an open economy (see, for example, Markusen [1975], Baumol and Oates [1988], and Copeland [1994]). The focus of this literature is on the structure of the optimal policy for a single country, whereas in our paper we are concerned with how the choice of policies in two countries interact to determine the pattern of trade. Moreover, this literature has not examined how optimal pollution policy would differ systematically across countries that have different income levels.

8. This requires that the joint production technology satisfy certain regularity conditions. In the Appendix we show how equation (1) can be derived from a joint production technology.

9. The treatment of pollution as an input has been adopted by several others; see, for example, Pethig [1976], Siebert et al. [1980], and McGuire [1982].

10. To see that this assumption puts an upper bound on production for given labor input, note that with $d \leq \lambda l$, we have $y \leq l^{1-\alpha}(\lambda l)^{\alpha} = l\lambda^{\alpha}$. The Appendix describes in more detail how this constraint arises naturally from an underlying abatement technology.

11. If the South's endowment of effective labor is not too small, then an interior solution will always obtain. See the Appendix for further details.

12. For simplicity, we assume that α is *strictly* increasing in z.

13. To see this, note that the share of Northern pollution charges in world income is $\tau D/(I + I^*)$, and use (10).

14. Equation (14) is not valid outside this interval because the balance of trade condition (9) is constructed for the case where $\tau > \tau^*$. If $\bar{z} < \hat{z}$, we would have $\tau < \tau^*$, which is inconsistent with the pattern of trade implicit in (9). The case where $\tau \leq \tau^*$ is discussed briefly below.

15. $\dfrac{d \ln(S(\bar{z}))}{d\bar{z}} = \left[\dfrac{\alpha'}{(1-\alpha)^2} \right] \ln(\zeta) - \left[\dfrac{\alpha}{(1-\alpha)^2} \right] \left\{ \dfrac{(\gamma-1)\theta'\theta(1)}{\gamma\theta^*\theta + \varphi'/\varphi\varphi^*} \right\} < 0, \quad \text{since } \zeta < 1.$

16. The case where the two curves do not intersect to the right of $\hat{z}$ is discussed below.

17. Note that $\hat{\theta} = \theta' d\bar{z}/\theta$ and $\hat{\varphi} = \varphi' d\bar{z}/\varphi$. Also, note from (21) that $\hat{\theta} - \hat{\varphi} > 0$ for $d\bar{z} > 0$.

18. We are grateful to Alan Deardorff for suggesting this interpretation.

19. Pollution is not, however, independent of country size, since β depends on L. The effect of country size is discussed in Section VII.

20. As may be expected from our simple argument above, it is straightforward to show that if North and South are sufficiently similar so that pollution taxes are equalized by trade, then free trade has no effect on global pollution levels. However, trade will still alter the distribution of pollution across countries with the human-capital-rich country reducing its pollution level while the human-capital-poor country increases its pollution level.

21. If demand shifted to relatively clean goods (such as services) as income rose, then there would be a composition effect in autarky. We leave the investigation of non-homothetic preferences for future work.

22. Since $\tau^*/\tau = (1-\sigma)/\sigma$, we have $\sigma(T) = 1/(1 + \tau^*/\tau)$. Moreover, note that since $d\bar{z}/dT > 0$, we must have $d(\tau^*/\tau)/dT > 0$; and hence $\sigma'(T) < 0$. Note that this is not a partial derivative, as it includes both the direct and indirect effects of the transfer on σ.

23. Note that the technique effect is usually offsetting a scale effect, but that in this case there is no direct scale effect, since North's underlying production capacity is not affected by the transfer.

24. The effects of a transfer on pollution can be summarized by appealing to Figure 11.3 one last time. A transfer shifts out the donor's supply of pollution (since environmental quality is a normal good), and shifts in the recipient's supply function. This reduces the gap between autarky factor price ratios, reduces the incentives to trade to exploit differences in pollution policy, and thereby reduces world pollution. South to North transfers have opposite effects.

25. We are grateful to Michele Piccione and Guofu Tan for help with this proof.

References

Anderson, Kym, and Richard Blackhurst, eds., *The Greening of World Trade Issues* (London: Harvester Wheatsheaf, 1992).

Baumol, William J., and Wallace E. Oates, *The Theory of Environmental Policy* (Cambridge: Cambridge University Press, 1988; first edition: 1975).

Copeland, Brian R., "International Trade and the Environment: Policy Reform in a Polluted Small Open Economy," *Journal of Environmental Economics and Management*, XXVI (1994), 44–65.

Copeland, Brian R., and M. Scott Taylor, "Trade and Transboundary Pollution," Discussion Paper 93–46, Department of Economics, University of British Columbia, December 1993.

Dean, Judith M., "Trade and the Environment: A Survey of the Literature," in Patrick Low, ed., *International Trade and the Environment: World Bank Discussion Papers* (Washington, DC: World Bank, 1992).

Dornbusch, Rudiger, Stanley Fischer, and Paul A. Samuelson, "Comparative Advantage, Trade and Payments in a Ricardian Model with a Continuum of Goods," *American Economic Review*, LXVII (1977), 823–39.

Grossman, Gene M., and Alan B. Krueger, "Environmental Impacts of a North American Free Trade Agreement," NBER Working paper No. 3914, November 1991.

Low, Patrick, and Alexander Yeats, "Do 'Dirty' Industries Migrate?" in Patrick Low, ed., *International Trade and the Environment: World Bank Discussion Papers* (Washington, DC: World Bank, 1992).

Lucas, Robert E. B., David Wheeler, and Hermamda Hettige, "Economic Development, Environmental Regulation and the International Migration of Toxic Industrial Pollution: 1960–1988," in Patrick Low, ed., *International Trade and the Environment: World Bank Discussion Papers* (Washington, DC: World Bank, 1992).

Markusen, James R., "International Externalities and Optimal Tax Structures," *Journal of International Economics*, V (1975), 15–29.

McGuire, Martin C., "Regulation, Factor Rewards, and International Trade," *Journal of Public Economics*, XVII (1982), 335–54.

Pethig, Ruediger, "Pollution, Welfare, and Environmental Policy in the Theory of Comparative Advantage," *Journal of Environmental Economics and Management*, II (1976), 160–69.

Siebert, Horst, J. Eichberger, R. Gronych, and R. Pethig, *Trade and Environment: A Theoretical Enquiry* (Amsterdam: Elsevier/North-Holland, 1980).

Staiger, Robert W., "Organized Labor and the Scope of International Specialization," *Journal of Political Economy*, XCVI (1988), 1022–47.

12

Managing Local Commons: Theoretical Issues in Incentive Design

Paul Seabright

Growing interest in environmental economics has led to a great deal of work in recent years on the economics of local common property resources, but it would be a mistake to think that the topic is in any danger of being over-grazed. Local commons encompass a wide range of resources whose shared feature is the need for some form of collective management, and pose interesting problems in such disparate sub-fields as agricultural economics and the theory of the firm.

The definition of local common property resources must do two things: first, define common property resources, and secondly, distinguish local from other kinds of common property resources. Common property resources, as the name suggests, are resources in which there exist property rights, but property rights that are exercised (at least partly) collectively by members of a group. There must also be rivalry in consumption of the resource within the group; that is, an increase in the amount consumed by one individual reduces the amount remaining for others to consume. What makes the right of control collective, rather than individual, is simply the absence of a complete set of contractual relations governing which member of the group is entitled or required to do what. Like lawyers in a lifeboat, they find themselves obliged by circumstances to cooperate. However, membership of the group *is* limited by legally recognized and practically enforceable rights, and does not have to be concerned with the possibility of "open access," namely the risk that additional exploiters might have free entry to the resource.[1]

The typical examples of *local* commons, as opposed to other types of commons, are often assets owned by reasonably small communities, such as villages. These are distinguished from global commons in two main ways. Most importantly, the main members of the local community are few enough to be known to each other; some of their actions are observable; and consequently they have the ability and sometimes the incentive to build reputations for behaving in certain ways. By contrast, some global commons problems, like global warming, involve billions of us. However, sometimes global commons problems concern a limited set of known players, namely governments; what distinguishes these cases from classic local commons is a second feature, namely the absence of even the potential for intervention by a state that is more powerful than any of the individuals. In the case of governments making decisions about global warming, this simply means that no world government exists to tackle the issue. For the purposes of this chapter I shall define local commons problems as small-numbers problems, but I shall generally also make the empirical assumption that state intervention is one option among others for resolution of these problems.

So local commons certainly include the familiar *dramatis personae* of environmental microeconomics, like grazing lands and inshore fisheries (although since deep-sea fisheries are open to access by others, they fall into a separate category). They include collectively managed irrigation systems such as canals and tanks; subterranean aquifers and oil reserves; forests and many wildlife habitats.[2] But they also include many phenomena that should be analyzed in similar terms, and which typically appear in very different areas of the economics literature: partnerships and joint-stock companies, for example. Other situations that can be analyzed within this framework include households, research joint ventures, collective amenities in apartment buildings, pension funds, university departments.

Establishing Common Interests

The bulk of the literature on common property resources has taken the main analytical problem they raise to be one of resolving conflicts over the contribution of different members towards a common management policy. As a result, conflicts of interest over what is the optimal management of the resource have been largely ignored. At first, this distinction may sound merely semantic. After all, the difference in value to some member between the optimal management policy given the preferences of that member and a compromise management policy might be counted as part of the "contribution cost" paid by the member towards the compromise solution. However, the distinction is important for two reasons.

First, social choice theory points out that the very existence of an optimal collective management policy cannot be taken for granted, and that mechanisms to decide upon such a policy may be vulnerable to strategic manipulation. Secondly, the information required for commons management will be much reduced if it can be assumed that the management policy for the resource (for example, what its aggregate rate of depletion should be) can be determined separately from the way that policy should be implemented (for example, how the consumption made possible by the agreed-upon depletion rate should be shared out among members). Call these two aspects of the management problem the *production plan* and the *implementation plan*.

The separation of these tasks will be a reasonable assumption only when everyone can agree on what would be the optimal production plan, without knowing anything about the distribution plan. This may sound unlikely. But remember that a firm's shareholders will unanimously support attempts by that firm to maximize value (according to the Fisher separation theorem as described in Milne, 1974; DeAngelo, 1981), as long as the economy has complete risk-sharing opportunities. Consequently it is possible to determine the firm's optimum production plan (given a price system) without knowing anything about shareholders' preferences or constraints. It follows that, for there to be conflicts of interest between member-beneficiaries of a common property resource over the production plan, production decisions must make a significant difference to at least some members' risk-sharing opportunities, and must do so in different ways for different members.

An example should help to clarify the issue here. Consider a group of farmers who have conflicting interests regarding the use of common grazing land during periods of drought, according to whether or not they have access to irrigation. A strictly value-maximizing policy would restrict access to common grazing more during droughts than at other times because of the danger of erosion; but it is precisely during droughts that those engaged in rain-fed agriculture may find themselves most dependent upon livestock and therefore most in need of common grazing. Therefore, in the absence of other means to diversify away this risk they would prefer a policy that permitted them to react to a drought by *increasing* their demands on the common grazing land. Their conflict of interest with the farmers who have access to irrigation will in consequence concern not just how the limited grazing opportunities should be shared between them (the implementation plan), but will also extend to a basic conflict of interest over the production plan—that is, over how much grazing in total there should be when droughts occur.

Solving such conflicts of interest may be very difficult, and the absence of appropriate means of compensation for the missing risk-sharing mechanisms may lead to a breakdown of the management of the common property resource. In what follows, however, we shall be concerned mainly with the problems of implementing a known optimal production plan. These problems, as the empirical evidence shows, are quite serious enough.

Devising Incentives to Advance Common Interests

The central implementation problem for common property resources is that, in the absence of binding agreements to the contrary, consumption of the common resource by one agent will impose negative externalities on others. Since individuals do not take these externalities into account, aggregate consumption of the resource is typically inefficiently high. Deforestation, over-grazing and excessive mineral depletion are the standard instances. In a classic article, Garrett Hardin (1968) referred to this outcome as a "tragedy of the commons." Alternatively, the externalities may mainly affect investment, in that resources expended in the enhancement of the common property resource's value will typically confer external benefits on other members, and under-investment will result. Inadequate maintenance of irrigation systems and roads, and neglect of drainage, fencing and upkeep of public land are common examples.

The investment externality characterizes virtually all common property resources, including such non-standard examples as firms and research joint ventures: the tendency towards under-investment by shareholders in monitoring a firm's management is a classic example (Grossman and Hart, 1980). In fact, the distinction between consumption and investment externalities is practically useful but not analytically important: the optimal production plan for common property resources will typically involve most if not all members both consuming less of the resource than their private incentives would lead them to do, and investing more of their other resources in the maintenance and enhancement of the common property resource's value.

How might members be induced to implement such a plan? The next section will focus on informal mechanisms that may induce members of a common property resource to undertake collectively beneficial but individually costly actions. The following section will focus on more formal mechanisms: the privatization of property rights, the decentralization of incentives within common ownership and control, and the delegation of management responsibility to an agent so that participants are limited to a monitoring role. The value of these more formal mechanisms will depend significantly upon the success or lack of success of the informal mechanisms of collective management that they replace.

Informal Incentives for Cooperative Behavior

Mechanisms of collective management tend to look very different under the lenses of different social sciences. In particular, anthropologists and sociologists focus on the way in which individual behavior is governed by rules and codes of conduct, the genesis of which is often explained by how well such rules serve the interests of the group. Economists, by contrast, focus less upon rules than upon incentives. Recent work in game theory has devoted much effort to explaining cooperative behavior in terms of a more sophisticated understanding on the part of individuals about where their (individual) long-term interests really lie. In particular, individuals face problems of collective action not once but repeatedly. The knowledge that pursuit of their short-term interests can harm their long-term aims by affecting the reaction of others in future interactions may be a powerful inducement to behavior that displays apparent solidarity with the interests of the group. This does not mean that economics has undermined the validity of arguments that appeal to altruism or to social norms; these different explanations are complementary, although their relative importance will need careful empirical investigation.[3]

Economists who argue that cooperative behavior can grow out of self-interest usually draw heavily on the theory of repeated games (see the survey by Sabourian, 1990). Figure 12.1 displays a version of the familiar prisoners' dilemma. If the two players know that they are playing the game only once, then Player 1 reasons as follows: "Player 2 might either cooperate or defect. If 2 cooperates, than I am better off defecting, and receiving 5 rather than 4. If 2 defects, then I

Player 2

	Cooperate	Defect
Cooperate	1 receives 4 2 receives 4	1 receives − 10 2 receives 5
Defect	1 receives 5 2 receives − 10	both players receive zero

Player 1

Figure 12.1
A prisoner's dilemma.

am still better off defecting, since I receive 0 rather than −10." When both players reason this way, they both defect, and end up receiving 0. The problem is whether, if the game is repeated a number of times, the two players can find a way to cooperate.

The idea that repetition can sustain cooperation is based on the thought that individuals tempted to defect may be dissuaded from doing so from fear of losing the benefits of cooperation in the future. For this dissuasion to be effective, three conditions must hold. First, the future must matter enough to outweigh the immediate benefits to any individual of failing to cooperate; that is, other players must have at their disposal retaliatory strategies that "hurt" the deviator sufficiently in future periods, even when future payoffs are discounted.[4] So, for instance, excluding those who breach their fishing quotas from the fishing grounds in the future must be a sufficiently damaging prospect to outweigh any immediate gains from overfishing. In the prisoners' dilemma example in Figure 12.1, the benefits to and costs of cooperation are symmetric, but asymmetry of itself need not threaten cooperation so long as there exists, *for each player*, a retaliation strategy capable of outweighing the gains to that player of failing to cooperate.

Secondly, these retaliatory strategies must be credible, which means that, once an individual has defected, it must be in the others' interest to put the retaliation into effect. For example, excluding those who have breached their fishing quotas must not require an unreasonable level of effort on the part of others in policing the fishing grounds. Abandoning an agreement to restrict extraction rates of a mineral asset (as a punishment for free-riding by some parties to that agreement) must not reduce its stock so substantially as to damage the interests of the retaliators by more than the original free-riding did. So when will retaliation be credible? It may be credible naturally (retaliation may be what they would anyway do in the circumstances, as when it involves playing a Nash equilibrium of the prisoners' dilemma game). Alternatively, it may be true because of a credible agreement between the affected parties to put the retaliation into effect. In the latter circumstance, retaliation is itself a form of collective action, which must therefore be credible if the original collective action is to be credible. It is in this respect that one can think of the setting up of police forces, inspectorates and similar institutions as a central form of common property resource management. The formal mechanisms to be discussed in the next section are therefore special cases of the more general repeated game response to one-shot inefficiencies.

Thirdly, the benefits of cooperation in the future must themselves be sufficiently probable to act as an incentive to cooperation in the present. Sheer repetition of the game is not enough to ensure this. For example, if the game is to be played a fixed number of times, then both players will know before the last repetition of the game that defection in that last round cannot be punished and that therefore cooperation is unlikely in that round. But knowing that, they will each defect in the penultimate round. And knowing that, the argument by backward induction holds that they will defect even in the original round.

For future cooperation to be a sufficiently probable incentive, one of a number of conditions must hold. The game may be infinitely repeated, or there may be sufficient uncertainty about how many times it will be repeated. An alternative solution is "reputation;" even a very small probability that the player is of a type that intrinsically prefers to cooperate acts as an incentive to all types of players to behave cooperatively, so long as the game is sufficiently far from its final period for the loss of a reputation for cooperation to be costly.[5] Another is bounded rationality, where a small probability that the player is of a type to cooperate "irrationally" has much the same effect (Radner, 1980). Finally, the one-shot game may have multiple Nash equilibria over which all players have a strict preference ordering (Benoit and Krishna, 1985; Friedman, 1985; Fraysse and Moreaux, 1985). In all cases, the possibility of cooperation depends upon players' not discounting future payoffs too heavily (or equivalently, on their interacting at sufficiently frequent intervals); if they don't place much value on the future, the gains from short-term self-interested behavior may be too great for any future inducements to outweigh.[6] They must also be able to observe one another's behavior with sufficient reliability to observe whether agreements are being kept.

To this point, the considerations discussed in this section are all essentially forward-looking: people will cooperate if they expect to gain in the future from doing so. Much of the empirical literature on the management of common property resources, however, stresses that historical considerations also play an extremely important part in accounting for successful collective action. In particular, traditions and institutions of collective action can increase the likelihood of successful collective action in the future, and we often observe that cooperative institutions work more successfully when they are embedded in a context in which collective action has worked in the past. Alternatively put, cooperation can be habit-forming (Seabright, 1993).

What can the theory of repeated games say about this phenomenon? One possibility that immediately springs to mind is that all cooperative equilibrium strategies in repeated games must be to some extent history-dependent, if only in the simplest of ways: the possibility of retaliation depends on actions that are sensitive to what other players have done in previous periods.[7] So, a breakdown of cooperation in one period would be expected to lead to a failure of cooperation in a future period, by way of retaliation. Unfortunately, this suggestion is not every useful as a way of explaining a tendency for cooperation to be habit-forming. What it tells us is that the use of *threats* that are history-dependent can enable parties to achieve efficient outcomes; but if the outcomes are achieved, the threats do not need to be exercised, so we may never see any history-dependence in observed behavior. What we need to know is why cooperation sometimes works and sometimes doesn't, and whether the fact that there has been cooperation in the past should by itself make any difference to the prospects of cooperation in the future.

Another possibility is that, in the absence of effective means of communication between players, past history may act as a mechanism which enables them to coordinate in selecting between the multiplicity of potential equilibria to which we know repeated interactions give rise.[8] However, it is hard to believe that this is practically important for local commons. First of all, in the kinds of cooperative institutions that are typically established to mange local commons, there is no difficulty about communication. On the contrary, members may spend a long time communicating with each other (or squabbling, to put the matter less clinically), but may still fail to resolve their difficulties in implementing successful collective action. Secondly, if individuals are seeking to coordinate their actions, it is hard to understand why they should ever choose to coordinate on any but efficient outcomes. If we observe failures of cooperation in the past followed by failures of cooperation in the future, it seems perverse to imagine that the reason for this is that players have chosen to coordinate on an equilibrium with little cooperation (when they might have chosen to coordinate on one with more).

So if none of these arguments really explains the observation that cooperation does seem to be habit-forming, what sort of analysis does demonstrate the point? To begin, since cooperation often fails even when the opportunities for communication are good, we can infer that cooperation is hard to sustain. This suggests that most common property resource problems involve *either* high discount rates (relative to the frequency with which opportunities occur for repeated cooperation), *or* one-off benefits from defection that are high relative to the per period costs to the defector of retaliation. This accords with common sense. Suppose an institution is established to protect common grazing land in a village. It may take some time to discover that the rules of grazing are being flouted or that the officers have embezzled the funds set aside to put up fences. Even though the previously cooperative members may now withdraw their cooperation in retaliation, the dishonest officers or the uncooperative grazers may have benefitted by enough in the meantime for this retaliation to leave them no worse off than they would have been by cooperating.

In circumstances like these—namely, where the sustainability of cooperation is a marginal matter—the presence or absence of trust will affect the extent to which cooperation succeeds. By "trust" here I mean the expectation by members of a group that other members will cooperate. The very fact that the immediate benefits from defecting are large implies that it makes a significant difference to individuals whether they cooperate anticipating similar behavior on the part of others, or choose instead to defect without waiting for others to do so first. A good analogy is a cease-fire during a civil war: if each side expects the cease-fire to hold, it has less of an incentive to make a preemptive strike, and consequently the cease-fire is more likely to hold.

This presence or absence of trust may itself depend on past traditions and institutions; in short, institutions can channel trust. In Seabright (1993), I develop a model of "habit-forming" cooperation in which the frequency of past cooperation determines the probability of future cooperation. The basic idea of the model is that people's expectations about how cooperative others will be may fluctuate randomly. If people's moods are correlated, but not perfectly correlated, then any one person's expectation about the cooperativeness of others will amount to an expectation about how likely others are to be sufficiently optimistic about the prospects for cooperation to be willing to cooperate themselves. Cooperation is then induced by "optimism about the level of optimism," which is something that pre-existing institutions can channel and enhance. The same paper reports an econometric study of milk producers' cooperative societies in India, which are organizations requiring small farmers to sell milk at less than open market prices in return for the provision of a number of collective benefits such as access to finance and infrastructure. The study suggests that, controlling for directly economic variables, the presence of a prior history of cooperative institutions in the communities concerned was a positive predictor of cooperative society success.

What exactly does it mean to say that institutions can "channel" trust? One possibility is simply that certain institutions, by giving people the opportunity to undertake collective action, allow them to establish a reputation for cooperation that will serve them well in the future. So, for instance, in the study just reported, villages whose members had previously organized collective religious festivals (as opposed to those where festivals were organized by sub-groups such as caste), were more likely to make a success of milk-producers' cooperatives. Likewise, many voluntary organizations working in poor countries concern themselves with promoting plays, festivals and sporting activities among disadvantaged groups, not only because of these activities' intrinsic value but because they know of their value in "building trust."

A second possibility is more subtle, and appeals to the idea that institutions may allow the establishment of "collective reputation." For instance, Kreps (1990) discusses the way in which the reputation of individuals undertaking market transactions will be heavily influenced by the reputation of the firms to which they belong; indeed, one of the primary purposes of firms is to transmit reputation across cohorts of employees. Tirole (1993) proposes that the persistence of corruption in a society may partly be explained by the fact that younger generations "inherit" the reputation of their elders; those born to corrupt elders will in consequence have less incentive to be honest themselves. An unresolved theoretical question is why some institutions are more effective than others at transmitting reputation across cohorts of members; but given that they are effective, such institutions may then represent a mechanism whereby cooperation can be habit-forming.

Both these suggestions imply that trust is to be understood as a kind of capital good, embodied either in individuals or in the organizations to which they belong, and which acts as a state variable whose value influences the probability of future cooperation independently of the direct payoffs associated with such cooperation. In addition, informal institutions that enhance cooperative management of common property resources may also act in other more or less formal ways to change the direct payoffs. They may act as monitoring mechanisms, for example: by helping members to observe the behavior of others, they may make it easier to implement retaliation strategies. For instance, Indian cooperative societies with relatively educated officers were reported in Seabright (1993) to be more successful; closer investigation revealed this to be not because the more educated were intrinsically more trustworthy, but because they were more likely to have implemented mechanisms of quality control that diminished members' incentives to "cheat" by watering down their milk. An alternative, more subtle possibility is that in circumstances where it is unclear what kind of behavior is consistent with optimal resource management, institutions may help members to coordinate on relatively simple (and therefore more easily monitored) standards of acceptable behavior (Kreps, 1990, suggests this to be the main function of a corporate culture). A number of empirical studies have reported the successful evolution within relatively short periods of time of collective management institutions whose primary function is monitoring and the clarification of rules (Feeny et al., 1990, p. 10–11).[9]

Whatever the mechanisms invoked, many recent contributions to the literature have stressed that relatively informal collective management of common property resources can in the right circumstances avoid the severe resource degradation predicted by "the tragedy of the commons." Nevertheless, both empirical and theoretical arguments suggest that cooperative behavior may be only partial, and the incentives of short-term self-interest only partially held in check. Under what circumstances, then, can more formal implementation mechanisms make good the deficiency? And, given that formal incentives are typically stronger than informal ones, are there any reasons why informal incentives might nevertheless sometimes be preferred?

Formal Incentives for Cooperative Behavior

The distinction between formal and informal implementation mechanisms is itself only an informal one. Nevertheless, a useful pragmatic line can be drawn between cases where uncooperative behavior by individuals is met merely by a withdrawal of cooperation by others, and those where cooperation is enforced by rewards and punishments that are defined in law or in customary practice, and are enforceable by appeal to courts or other institutions of arbitration. This section considers the theoretical rationale for three kinds of formal inducement to cooperative behavior in the management of common property resources: the privatization of property rights; the decentralization of incentives within common ownership and control; and the delegation of management responsibility to an agent so that participants are limited to a monitoring role.

Privatization of Property Rights: Can Trade Destroy Trust?

The case for privatizing property rights in what have hitherto been common property resources rests on the view that having an individual or firm own the resource will lead to the resource being allocated in a more efficient way. Any private property right requires specifying enforceable and appropriate contractual relations. Sometimes the means of doing this (and especially the technology embodied in a modern legal system) have only recently become available in developing countries, so privatization is seen as a response to changing conditions rather than an adverse judgment on the appropriateness of collective management for previous conditions.

The desirability of privatization for any particular common property resource is, of course, an empirical matter. Stevenson (1991), for example, demonstrates econometrically the higher productivity of pasturing under private than under common property in Switzerland, while nevertheless accepting that transactions costs may make privatization infeasible in some circumstances. But in addition to the costs of specifying and enforcing rights, there are a number of things that can go wrong in attempting to introduce private property rights in what was once a common property resource; identifying these factors will help to describe in which situations privatization is more or less likely to succeed. All of the problems with privatization have their roots in the fact that private contractual rights can provide effective incentives for only some of the many individual actions that may be required for implementing an efficient production plan. Other necessary actions may remain unenforceable, either because they are unobservable by some of the affected parties or by the enforcing authorities, or because they are too complex to be specified in contractual form (actual contracts, in other words, are likely to be incomplete). As a result, the attempt to enforce private contractual rights may lead to a breakdown of whatever cooperative mechanisms may have evolved among those who shared implicit, non-contractual rights in the common property resource beforehand.

For example, the privatization of areas of forest for timber production may fail to internalize all the externalities involved (so there will still be excess production and inadequate replanting). It may also fail to respect some of the implicit entitlements of those who previously used the forest for food, fuelwood or medicine, in ways that are both inequitable and inefficient. They are inequitable because implicit entitlements are still entitlements; and they are inefficient because they fail to build on the fact that those who benefit from a resource may also be induced to contribute to its maintenance, and some of them may have a comparative advantage in doing so (those who live in the forest may be in a position more easily to monitor its rate of degradation, for instance).

Must private property make it more difficult to respect implicit entitlement? It might be thought that the breakdown of pre-existing cooperative mechanisms shows merely a failing in the particular system of private property rights introduced, and has no implications one way or the other for the merits or otherwise of private property in itself. But in fact there are two important reasons, intrinsic to the nature of (most) private property systems, that suggest how privatization may threaten implicit entitlements. First, privatization typically changes the relative bargaining power of those who depend upon the resource, giving more power to those who acquire the property rights and less to those who do not, in a way that may be

Player 2

		Cooperate	Defect
Player 1	Cooperate	1 receives 4 2 receives 4	1 receives − 10 2 receives 5
	Defect	1 receives 5 2 receives − 10	1 receives 3 2 receives − 3

Figure 12.2
The dilemma after privatisation.

sufficiently asymmetric to undermine the mutual dependence that was the incentive to cooperate originally. For example, privatizing grazing land may not completely prevent encroachment, but may reduce the incentives of those without private rights to prevent erosion on the land belonging to those who do. Privatizing forest land, by making forest dwellers unable to rely on traditional sources of food or fuelwood, may encourage more destructive practices (say of slash-and-burn) and discourage care of newly-planted saplings. In addition, it is difficult to frame formal contractual rights so as to safeguard traditional entitlements (a clause requiring landowners to grant "reasonable" access to "responsible" grazers or forest dwellers would be very hard to enforce).

In fact, it is quite possible than by diminishing incentives for informal cooperation, privatization may make both parties worse off—including the owner of the newly created property right! This possibility is suggested by the game in Figure 12.2. In this game, Player 1 has a property right, which means that if both players defect, Player 1 ends up better off than Player 2. Consequently the threat of retaliation by Player 2 can no longer hurt Player 1 sufficiently to induce him to cooperate. But notice that in spite of this, cooperation is still better for both players than defecting.[10] So there is a sense in which members of a common property resource can in some circumstances be made better off by being denied rights that appear superficially to be to their advantage.

There is an air of paradox about this conclusion, since it might seem that Player 1 could simply offer to relinquish his property right. But voluntary relinquishment may not be credible, since (if cooperation breaks down) there may be nothing to prevent him from reasserting it. Thus a promise by landowners not to prevent entry to their land by forest dwellers may not be credible given the fact that private property entitles them to bring actions for trespass; the only way for them to make this promise credible may be for there not to be privatization at all. And intermediate kinds of property (such as logging rights) may not give a credible mechanism of enforcement to the forest dwellers (as inhabitants of the Amazon basin have discovered).

This leads naturally to the second and more subtle reason why private property may make it difficult to respect implicit entitlements. This is that some of the mechanisms that sustain informal cooperation —like a reputation for cooperating or the threat of retaliation— require reasonably long time horizons, the reliability of which may be undermined by the tradeability of private property rights. For example, those who farm communally owned land may be prepared to invest in the soil's fertility by using organic fertilizer, may plant trees to prevent erosion and so on. But once ownership is privatized, even an assurance that *present* owners would continue to respect the implicit entitlements of farmers to the fruits of their investment may be inadequate if present owners are able at any time to sell their land to new owners without such a reputation.

Exactly this kind of argument has been advanced in the context of firms by Shleifer and Summers (1988), who point to the possible adverse consequences of highly liquid markets in the ownership of firms. Hostile takeovers, they suggest, may result in "breaches of trust" when incoming management teams cut wages or fire workers who had previously invested in firm-specific human capital for which existing management had promised adequate remuneration (but without being able to make such an understanding contractually binding). Even in the absence of an actual takeover, the knowledge that share markets are sufficiently liquid to make takeover possible is, they suggest, a serious disincentive to efficient levels of investment in firm-specific human capital.[11]

Intuitively appealing as this argument is, it is somewhat trickier than it sounds. The reputation model suggests that owners will be deterred from inadequately rewarding the specific human capital investments of workers by fear of the loss of their reputation. However, that reputation is itself a sunk cost; if owners sell the firm, the best price they can receive for it from new owners is the value of the firm under owners who lack a reputation for honoring implicit contracts; the price will discount the cost to them of the retaliation they may expect to face. Consequently, the incentive to sell the firm to new owners who will breach implicit contracts is no greater than the temptation to breach implicit contracts directly.[12] Or, to put it another way, selling the firm to disreputable owners is itself a disreputable act. *So the tradeability of property rights as such has no direct effect on the incentive properties of long-term relationships.*

This does not mean that there is nothing in the argument that tradeability of property rights can weaken incentives for relationship-specific investment. But such weakening, if it occurs, is not due to the intrinsic undermining of the credibility of reputation or the threat of retaliation by the tradeability of property rights alone. Something more must be added to the story. Suppose, for example, the new owners differ from the old in that breaching the implicit contract offers them a higher payoff. For instance, new owners may be less concerned about the anger and resentment of the existing workers or tenants on the common resource. Then they may be less deterred by the threat of retaliation and may consequently be willing to offer a price for the asset that does not discount for the expected retaliation by as much as the cost of such retaliation to the original owners.

What welfare consequences follow therefore from the tradeability of property rights? It may happen that the welfare of the owner of an asset is higher if the owner is prevented from selling than if the owner's rights are tradeable. This will be true in the case where the owner is unique in some way (perhaps through having enjoyed a long-standing relationship with workers or tenants), making it likely that any alternative owner will have more immediately to gain from breaching the implicit contracts. Given the possibility of a sale, this risk will dissuade cooperation with the present owner. Conversely, owners that can commit themselves not to sell, or to do so only subject to safeguarding the interest of workers and tenants, may thereby help themselves as well.

In many common property resources, there is no absolute prohibition on trading the right to membership, but typically the admission of new members requires the consent of (at least some of) the existing members, a stipulation that may be enough to mitigate the problem described above. Systems of private property, by contrast, often face difficulties, since it is impossible to specify formal incentives to safeguard the interests of existing members (indeed, that is typically the reason why there were implicit rather than explicit contracts in the first place).

Two caveats are in order. First, it has so far been assumed that the new owner differs from the old owner only in receiving higher pay-offs from choosing not to cooperate. If, however, the new owner is also more efficient at managing the firm in equilibrium, the costs of denying tradeable property rights would be correspondingly higher. There is a trade-off: private property may damage implicit contracts, but it is also likely to match owners more efficiently to their assets. Secondly, the welfare of the old owner is not the only important consideration, since that owner did not internalize the welfare of workers/tenants in decisions. So introducing tradeable property rights, even if it is in the interest of owners, may damage the interests of workers and tenants by enough to outweigh this benefit.

To summarize, it should be clear that private property rights not only may fail to solve the problems of externalities that bedevil common property resources. When contractual relations remain in important respects incomplete, private property may also weaken the mechanisms of cooperation that previously existed, either by shifting the bargaining power of the parties so that they no longer share enough interdependence to make cooperation credible, or by weakening the credibility of long-term contracts. However, we have also seen that the circumstances under which the latter problem occurs are somewhat special. Long-term implicit contracts are not weakened by the mere fact of tradeability of property rights in assets; it is tradeability plus a sufficient likelihood of the presence of potential new owners with different out-of-equilibrium payoffs that is the key factor. Establishing that such circumstances exist empirically may require quite careful examination of the evidence.

Decentralization of Incentives under Common Management

It often happens that the members of a local common property resource meet and decide on systems of rewards and penalties to implement a production plan. The most frequent means of doing so are production quotas, reinforced by systems of monitoring, with fines or the threat of exclusion from the common property resource altogether for those who breach the agreement. Such quotas have been evident in agreements over grazing land (see McCloskey, 1976, for the medieval English commons, and the contributions surveyed in Feeny et al., 1990); in control of fisheries (Berkes, 1986); and in the production agreements of the OPEC oil cartel. As the discussion to this point would imply, cooperation will be feasible in these situations only when the penalties for breaching quotas are sufficiently large relative to the gains from doing so.

One circumstance that favors the chances for cooperation is when members of the common property resource also share access to additional resources. Suppose the common property resource is grazing land or an irrigation system, but it is owned by a village; individuals who breach the agreed quotas can be punished by being denied access not merely to the common property resource but to some of the other benefits of village membership. When these additional benefits are sufficiently important, village leaders have the power to levy fines or impose other punishments that substantially enhance the credibility of the cooperative outcome.

Why are quantitative instruments, like quotas for enforcing production plans, so much more common than price-based instruments like taxes? One answer is that for many common property resources that involve renewable resources such as forests or fisheries, the damage done by misjudging the optimum utilization rate may be very much higher than that due to misjudging members' willingness to pay. For example, an unexpected surge in demand one year would under quotas lead to unexpectedly high prices; this may be preferable to the outcome under a tax system, namely unexpectedly high production which could leave the fishery seriously depleted and requiring several years of nursing back to optimum levels. In general, when the optimum use of a resource lies quite close to the level below which the resource's capacity for self-renewal is seriously damaged, and when some uncertainty is involved in how any control mechanism will work, a quota will pose lower risks than a price mechanism (Weitzman, 1974).

A second reason for the prevalence of quotas is the comparative ease with which they allow decentralization of the monitoring process. It is often easier for other members of the common property resource to observe whether a quota has been violated than to know whether a particular member is evading the terms of some (possibly non-linear) optimum schedule of Pigouvian taxes. The former can usually be monitored by observing production, which happens within the common resource, whereas the latter may require monitoring of market transactions, which can happen anywhere. This consideration may also account for the observed prevalence of systems of strict equality among members in production rights even when efficiency considerations might suggest otherwise: Feeny et al. (1990) report agreements to fish in rotation to ensure equal access to the best sites in Turkey; random assignment of harvest produce to households in meadow commons in Japan; and revenue pooling regardless of the productivity of individual members in a fishing cooperative in New Jersey. In all of these cases a visible commitment to equality of treatment, besides facilitating monitoring, may also have helped to build up mutual trust. When a group simply pools its output, it assures that the benefits of any excessive production are shared among its members, rather than privately appropriated.

Delegation of Management Responsibility to an Agent

All forms of collective management involve some asymmetry in the degree of involvement of different parties. At one end of the spectrum is the practice of delegating managerial responsibility to an agent charged with managing the asset on behalf of others; at the other, full participatory decision-making. In the middle of the range, a smaller group of agents are chosen by the larger group, which simply means that the collective management problem of the original owners of the common property resource is reproduced in miniature among the agents.

The delegation of responsibility to an agent does not, of course, leave the original members with nothing to do (otherwise they might as well just sell the asset); but it does limit their activities to a monitoring rather than a fully participatory role. So when is it desirable for members of a common property resource to specialize—some in management, some in monitoring—rather than all attempting a combination of the two? And what might be the source of gains from specialization? Another way to pose these questions is to inquire under what circumstances economies (or possibly diseconomies) of scope between the management and monitoring tasks are offset by diseconomies (or possibly economies) of scale in the management and monitoring tasks themselves.

Some jobs can be easily monitored using almost none of the skill or the effort that are required for the task's performance: someone who has never held a spade can tell fairly easily how fast someone else is digging. Others need much more: refereeing a scientific paper may require as much skill, as well as (notoriously) sometimes almost as much effort as writing it. Delegation of management responsibility is much more likely where the management of the resource resembles the first kind of task rather than the second, since those who delegate thereby save themselves a substantial amount of work.

But is is important not to confuse the ease with which management can be monitored and the ease with which management can itself monitor any resources it employs. For instance, suppose a community needs to dig an irrigation channel. It makes sense to delegate this job to a manager, since the main activity (digging) can be monitored by the manager, and it is easy for the rest of the community to see how fast the channel is progressing. By contrast, suppose the community wants to landscape some parkland. Again the main activity is digging, and it is just as easy for the manager to monitor this. But it now matters very much how and where this digging takes place, and it is harder for the rest of the community to monitor the management of the project without interesting themselves substantially in its details. Collective management is in such circumstances a more likely outcome.

Even in the latter case the evident economies of scope between the management and monitoring tasks are to an extent offset by economies of scale; it is senseless to duplicate the management of all the little tasks involved in a landscaping project. Likewise the job of policing a collective agreement to restrict grazing on common land may be worth delegating to employed guards during the night hours, even if it is unnecessary during the daytime because other members can combine the policing task with their own grazing.

The benefits of delegation will also depend on the extent to which the conflicts of interest between the agent and the principals who are the members of the common property resource can be minimized through appropriate remuneration procedures. As the literature on principal-agent problems within firms has emphasized (Jensen and Meckling, 1976), aligning the interests of agents with those of principals is usually restricted by the risk aversion of agents, which makes it very costly for them to bear the full marginal responsibility for their actions. Consequently, the incentives for managing a firm usually consist of a combination of direct financial incentives (like profit-related pay and stockholdings), monitoring by principals, and contingent transfers of control rights to other parties in the event of certain management difficulties, like bankruptcy (Aghion and Bolton,

1992). Recent work in this field has emphasized that for such incentives to be effective, those who have the ability to monitor management must have the *power* to intervene if management acts contrary to principals' interests, and also the *interest* in intervening on behalf of the principals (Dewatripont and Tirole, 1992).

This lesson is nowhere more important than in those circumstances where management of a common property resource has been taken over by the state. The state differs from other agents to whom management of a common property resource might theoretically be delegated in that the chain of delegation is typically longer; citizens delegate to their political representatives who delegate to government ministers who delegate to senior civil servants who delegate to junior civil servants and so on. This long chain of delegation may be unavoidable for non-local commons, but for local commons, shorter chains of delegation are probably feasible. If agents of the state are to be involved in the management of a common resource, they need an incentive to act in the interests of those to whom the resource notionally belongs. Where state management has worked, it has usually been through local involvement and empowerment of those who depend on the resource for their livelihood (see Chopra, Kadekodi and Murty, 1989, for the example of forest resources in the Himalayan foothills). It is not necessarily that their monitoring abilities are superior to those of the state's agents—the latter may be able to call on more sophisticated monitoring technologies—but their interests in the optimal management of the resource may be much greater.

The principal-agent literature has tended to emphasize the problems faced by dispersed principals in monitoring the activities of their agents: in this case, the problem of citizens in monitoring their government. A more realistic approach would recognize that in many principal-agent problems it is those who are notionally the agents who write their own contracts, subject to a greater or lesser degree to the power of veto by their principals. Agents can thereby become entrenched, implementing policies in their own private interests, owing to the costs to dispersed principals of organizing to dislodge them. Nowhere is this more true than when principals are voters and their agents are the many kinds of employees of the modern state. Much of the reaction against state management of local common property resources (whether these are traditional environmental common property resources or others such as industrial enterprises) can be seen as a rewriting by citizens of the terms of their contracts with managing agents, a rewriting that often occurs drastically because the transactions costs between citizens mean that it is forced to take place infrequently.

Conclusion

It can be easy for economists from industrialized countries to disparage developing country management of common property resources, because property rights aren't clear, monitoring arrangements seem very informal, and government agencies are unresponsive to citizens. But of all the professions, economists should perhaps be most sensitive to the fallacy that if the government isn't managing something according to a formal plan, then great inefficiency must be occurring. Likewise, they should be wary of assuming that moving from one situation of imprecise incentives to another with more formal but still somewhat imprecise incentives will always improve efficiency. Local communities have often evolved sophisticated informal methods of managing common property resources. As developing countries move towards greater clarity and enforceability of laws, towards greater reliance on markets, and perhaps towards more democratic government, it is important that these mechanisms not be ignored, disparaged or lost.

Notes

1. In an "open access" problem, as distinguished from the subject of this paper, any agreements governing relations between existing exploiters are vulnerable to free entry by new exploiters from outside. Thus, the problems of common property resources are typically both more complex (since they concern interactions among specific individuals) and potentially more soluble than problems of open access. In the literature, common property resources are sometimes defined more broadly, as resources characterized by difficulty of exclusion as well as by rivalry in consumption (for instance, Berkes, 1989, p. 91). On this view, open access problems are just one kind of common property resource issue, namely one where it is impossible to exclude anybody. Feeny et al. (1990) use the term *communal property* to refer to what are here called common property resources, namely those where some people can be excluded but not others. It is not particularly important which set of definitions is used, so long as each is used consistently, and so long as the issues raised by what are here called common property resources are not confused with those of open access. I have also here avoided use of the term "common pool resources," which may suggest that only the overall stock of the resource matters, whereas I am interested in the more general case where potentially many aspects of the management of a resource can be important.

2. Endangered species have typically been treated in the literature as open access problems. But as Swanson (1993) emphasises, the fact that they are *de facto* open access

should really be treated as endogenous. Governments have the ability to safeguard endangered species by regulating access if they wish to, and their unwillingness to do so is often the symptom of insufficient economic rent generated by the survival of the species in question. Policies to preserve such species are often better addressed to raising the rent appropriable by the parties with the power to control access, than by such currently fashionable means as trade conventions.

3. It is also likely that feelings of altruism and social solidarity, though extremely important, may be more volatile and difficult to promote consciously than perceptions of self-interest. For instance, familiarity and repeated interaction may provoke antipathy instead of sympathy between members of a community. This does not justify ignoring altruism as a social phenomenon, but it may reduce its amenability to systematic analysis. Graham Greene remarks of Scobie in *The Heart of the Matter* that "they had been corrupted by money, and he had been corrupted by sentiment. Sentiment was the more dangerous, because you couldn't name its price. A man open to bribes was to be relied upon below a certain figure, but sentiment might uncoil in the heart at a name, a photograph, even a smell remembered." For a contrary view, see Casson (1992), which develops a theory of leadership as the promotion of cooperative action by the manipulation of people's preferences.

4. More generally, imagine that if both players cooperate, they both receive X. If both defect, both receive 0. If one defects and one cooperates, the player who cooperates receives $-Z$, while the player who defects receives Y. The only restrictions are that $Y > X > 0$, that $2X > Y - Z$ and that $Z > 0$. There is a discount factor g. Then we know that provided $Y - X < gX/(1 - g)$ there exists a retaliation strategy which consists of playing Defect for a finite number of periods in the event that the other player has played Defect after an agreement to cooperate, and which ensures that the other player is no better off from the defection. Let T be the lowest integer such that $Y - X \leq gX + g^2X + \cdots + g^TX$. Then T is the smallest number of periods for which each player must threaten to retaliate in order for the threat credibly to sustain cooperation. If, on the other hand, it happens that $Y - X \geq gX/(1 - g)$, then there exists no finite T, and consequently no retaliatory strategy that can sustain cooperation.

5. See Kreps et al. (1982); the argument is sufficiently well known not to bear repeating in detail here. Dasgupta (1988) provides an application of the reputation model to the problem of building up trust.

6. In the limit, when the complete information game is repeated infinitely often and there is no discounting of the future, the Folk Theorem states that any individually rational payoffs (that is, payments that make continued participation preferable to withdrawing from the game) can be supported as an equilibrium, by a suitable choice of strategies to punish players who deviate from the equilibrium behavior. The Folk Theorem is couched in terms of Nash equilibrium strategies (and may therefore rely on threat strategies that are not credible out of equilibrium). But an extension by Aumann and Shapley (1976) and Rubinstein (1976) shows that any individually rational payoffs can also be supported as a sub-game perfect equilibrium. The idea is to construct strategies that punish players who fail to play their part in punishing those who deviate from equilibrium behavior; the infinite horizon ensures that any player can always be punished for long enough to prevent any deviation from being worthwhile. Unfortunately this result is not necessarily robust in the presence of even very slight discounting of the future, although Fudenberg and Maskin (1986) show that it will be so under certain conditions (namely that the dimension of the space of individually rational payoffs is as great as the number of players). Abreu et al. (1990) prove important and intuitive results for the case of repeated games with discounting and imperfect

monitoring, including the proposition that the equilibrium average value set is monotonic in the discount factor (which means, roughly, that an increased degree of concern for the future always results in increased benefits from cooperation).

7. Dutta and Sundaram (1993) point out that tragedies of the commons can be avoided even in Markovian games where strategies are restricted to being functions of the current state and cannot draw on memory. This is because the stock of the resource can act as a state variable that in some sense embodies a (restricted) memory of past actions. In some equilibria there can even be under-exploitation; however, efficient levels of exploitation cannot be sustained by Markovian strategies.

8. For example, Crawford and Haller (1990) develop a model in which agents in repeated coordination games use past behavior to assist their coordination among multiple equilibria in the future. In their framework, where there are multiple equilibria of each stage game, the choice of past *equilibria* is used to coordinate on future equilibria. If applied to the prisoners' dilemma, players would need to use past *strategies* (which might not have been equilibrium strategies of the one-shot game considered in isolation) to coordinate on future equilibria.

9. Some writers on problems of collective action in developing countries have suggested that these may often be modelled better as a coordination game (sometimes called an assurance game) than a prisoners' dilemma (Runge, 1986; Stevenson, 1991, especially pp. 73–76). In a coordination game, unlike the prisoners' dilemma, it is in the players' interests to cooperate even when they play only once, provided they can be assured that others (or enough others, where multi-person games are in question) will do the same. It is obviously an empirical matter whether particular situations are indeed better modelled as one type of game rather than another. However, one way of viewing the literature on repeated games is as analyzing the circumstances under which the threat of retaliation transforms a prisoners' dilemma in the one-shot game into a supergame whose overall payoff structure is in fact an assurance game.

10. More generally, following the framework from note 4, imagine that it remains true that if both players cooperate, both receive X, and if one cooperates while the other defects, the defector receives Y while the cooperator receives $-Z$. However, if both players defect, it is now true that the player with the property right receives A, while the player without the property right receives $-A$. Assume that $0 < A < X, Z$. This shift may be enough to prevent Player 2 from credibly threatening a retaliation sufficiently costly to Player 1 to enforce the cooperative outcome. To see this, note that even if there exists a T such that

$$Y - X \leq gX + g^2X + \cdots + g^TX \tag{1}$$

which is the condition for there to exist a cooperative equilibrium of the infinite repetition of the game in Figure 12.1, there may exist no T^* such that

$$Y - X \leq g(X - A) + g^2(X - A) + \cdots + g^{T^*}(X - A) \tag{2}$$

which is the analogous condition for Figure 12.2. Indeed, given the value of T, for T^* to exist requires (by manipulation of (1) and (2)):

$$(1 - g^{T^*})/(1 - g^T) \geq X/(X - A) \tag{3}$$

and for any G there evidently exist values of A sufficiently close to X such that (3) is not satisfied. Notice that the shift in bargaining power has made *both* players worse off (not just player 1), since now their discounted equilibrium payoffs are $gA(1 - g)$ and $gA(g - 1)$ respectively, which by assumption are less than those of the cooperative equilibrium.

11. This has striking affinities with the argument in Hirshman (1970). According to him, members of an organization may resort to the options of "exit" or "voice" if the organization is not being run as they would wish; but the exercise of voice typically generates positive externalities for members of the organization, and excessive ease of exit may therefore result in inadequate use of voice. Similar arguments underlie some people's opposition to easy divorce laws.

12. Using the notation in footnote 4, assume that Player 1 (who moves first) represents a worker or tenant who must decide whether to make a relationship-specific investment, while player 2 decides whether or not to reward this. Cooperation will be an equilibrium if $Y - X < gX/(1 - g)$. What difference does it make if the owner now has the opportunity to sell out instead of deciding whether or not to reward the investment? Clearly the owner will sell if the price P received is greater than or equal to the value of continuing to own the asset, i.e. if $P \geq X/(1 - g)$. How much would a new owner be prepared to bid if she were intending to breach the implicit contract? The first period payoff would be Y, then there would be a period of retaliation for the minimum necessary T periods, and only then would be benefits of cooperation resume. So the value V to the new owner is $Y = g^{T+1}X/(1 - g)$. Into this expression we can substitute the equation defining T in footnote 4, to yield that $V < X/(1 - g)$ and consequently that V is always less than P. This shows that any owner who would honor implicit contracts cannot receive a price greater than or equal to the continuation value of the firm from an owner who would not.

References

Aghion, P., and P. Bolton, "An Incomplete Contract Approach to Financial Contracting," *Review of Economic Studies*, July 1992, *59*, 473–94.

Abreu, D., D. Pearce, and E. Stacchetti, "Toward a Theory of Discounted Repeated Games with Imperfect Monitoring," *Econometrica*, September 1990, *58*:5, 1041–63.

Aumann, R., and L. Shapley, "Long-Term Competition and Game-Theoretic Analysis," mimeo, 1976.

Benoit, J-P., and V. Krishna, "Finitely Repeated Games," *Econometrica*, July 1985, *53*:4, 905–22.

Berkes, F., "Local-level Management and the Commons Problem: A Comparative Study of Turkish Coastal Fisheries," *Marine Policy*, 1986, 10, 215–29.

Berkes, F., *Common Property Resources*. London: Belhaven Press, 1989.

Casson, M., *The Economics of Business Culture*. Oxford: Clarendon Press, 1992.

Chopra, K., G. Kadekodi, and M. Murty, "People's Participation and Common Property Resources," *Economic and Political Weekly*, November 23–30, 1989, 24, A-189–95.

Crawford, V., and H. Haller, "Learning How to Cooperate: Optimal Play in Repeated Coordination Games," *Econometrica*, May 1990, 571–96.

Dasgupta, P., "Trust as a Commodity." In Gambetta, D., ed., *Trust*. Cambridge, U.K.: Cambridge University Press, 1988, 42–72.

DeAngelo, H., "Competition and Unanimity," *American Economic Review*, March 1981, *71*:1, 18–27.

Dewatripont, M., and J. Tirole, "A Theory of Debt and Equity: Diversity of Securities and Manager-Shareholder Congruence," IDEI, University of Toulouse, mimeo, 1992.

Dutta, P., and R. Sundaram, "The Tragedy of the Commons?," *Economic Theory*, 1993, 3, 413–26.

Feeny, D., F. Berkes, B. McCay, and J. Acheson, "The Tragedy of the Commons: Twenty-Two Years Later," *Human Ecology*, March 1990, 18, 1–19.

Fraysse, J., and M. Moreaux, "Collusive Equilibria in Oligopolies with Finite Lives," *European Economic Review*, February 1985, 27:1, 45–55.

Friedman, J., "Cooperative Equilibria in Finite Horizon NonCooperative Supergames," *Journal of Economic Theory*, April 1985, 35:2, 390–8.

Fudenberg, D., and E. Maskin, "The Folk Theorem in Repeated Games with Discounting or with Incomplete Information," *Econometrica*, May 1986, 54:3, 533–54.

Grossman, S., and O. Hart, "Takeover Bids, the Free-rider Problem and the Theory of the Corporation," *Bell Journal of Economics*, Spring 1980, 11:1, 42–64.

Hardin, G., "The Tragedy of the Commons," *Science*, December 13, 1968, 162:3859, 1243–48.

Hirshman, A., *Exit, Voice & Loyalty*. Cambridge: Harvard University Press, 1970.

Jensen, M., and W. H. Meckling, "Theory of the Firm: Managerial Behavior, Agency Costs and Ownership Structure," *Journal of Financial Economists*, October 1976, 3:4, 305–60.

Kreps, D., "Corporate Culture and Economic Theory." In Alt, J., and K. Shepsle, eds., *Perspectives on Positive Political Economy*. Cambridge, U.K.: Cambridge University Press, 1990, 90–143.

Kreps, D., P. Milgrom, J. Roberts, and R. Wilson, "Rational Co-operation in the Finitely Repeated Prisoners' Dilemma," *Journal of Economic Theory*, August 1982, 27:2, 245–52.

McCloskey, Donald, "English Open Fields as Behavior Towards Risk," *Research in Economic History*, Fall 1976, 1, 124–70.

Milne, F., "Corporate Investment and Finance Theory in Competitive Equilibrium," *Economic Record*, December 1974, 50:132, 511–33.

Radner, Roy, "Collusive Behavior in Noncooperative Epsilon-Equilibria of Oligopolies with Long but Finite Lives," *Journal of Economic Theory*, April 1980, 22:2, 136–54.

Rubinstein, A., "Equilibrium in Super-Game," discussion paper, Centre for mathematical Economics and Game Theory, Hebrew University of Jerusalem, 1976.

Runge, C., "Common Property and Collective Action in Economic Development," *World Development*, May 1986, 14:5, 623–35.

Sabourian, H., "Repeated Games: A Survey," In Hahn, F., ed., *The Economics of Missing Markets, Information and Games*. Oxford, Clarendon Press, 1990, 62–105.

Seabright, P., "Is Cooperation Habit-Forming?" In Dasgupta, P., and K.-G. Maler, eds., *The Environment and Emerging Development Issues*. Oxford, Clarendon Press, forthcoming.

Shleifer, A., and L. Summers, "Breaches of Trust in Hostile Takeovers." In Auerbach, A., ed., *Corporate Takeovers: Cause and Consequences.* Chicago, University of Chicago Press, 1988, 33–56.

Stevenson, G., *Common Property Economics—A General Theory and Land Use Applications.* Cambridge, U.K.: Cambridge University Press, 1991.

Swanson, T., "Regulating Endangered Species," *Economic Policy*, April 1993, *16*, 183–205.

Tirole, J., "A Theory of Collective Reputations, With Applications to the Persistence of Corruption and to Firm Quality," IDEI, University of Toulouse, mimeo, 1993.

Weitzman, M., "Prices vs. Quantities," *Review of Economic Studies*, October 1974, *41*:4, 447–91.

Sources

1. Pranab Bardhan, "Economics of Development and the Development of Economics," *Journal of Economic Perspectives* 7 (1993): 129–142.

2. Nirvikar Singh, "Theories of Sharecropping," in *The Economic Theory of Agrarian Institutions*, ed. P. Bardhan (Oxford: Clarendon Press, 1989), 33–72.

3. Kaushik Basu and Clive Bell, "Fragmented Duopoly: Theory and Applications to Backward Agriculture," *Journal of Development Economics* 36 (1991): 145–165.

4. Abhijit V. Banerjee and Andrew F. Newman, "Occupational Choice and the Process of Development," *Journal of Political Economy* 101 (1993): 274–298.

5. Lars Ljungqvist, "Economic Underdevelopment: The Case of a Missing Market for Human Capital," *Journal of Development Economics* 40: 219–239.

6. Abhijit V. Banerjee, Timothy Besley, and Timothy W. Guinnane, "Thy Neighbor's Keeper: The Design of a Credit Cooperative with Theory and a Test," *Quarterly Journal of Economics* 109 (1994): 491–515.

7. Kevin M. Murphy, Andrei Shleifer, and Robert W. Vishny, "Industrialization and the Big Push," *Journal of Political Economy* 97 (1989): 1003–1026.

8. Kiminori Matsuyama, "Complementarities and Cumulative Processes in Models of Monopolistic Competition," *Journal of Economic Literature* 33 (1995): 701–729.

9. Robert E. Lucas, Jr., "Making a Miracle," *Econometrica* 61 (1993): 251–272.

10. Diego Puga and Anthony J. Venables, "Agglomeration and Economic Development: Import Substitution vs. Trade Liberalisation," *Economic Journal* 109 (1999): 292–311.

11. Brian R. Copeland and M. Scott Taylor, "North-South Trade and the Environment," *Quarterly Journal of Economics* 109 (1994): 755–787.

12. Paul Seabright, "Managing Local Commons: Theoretical Issues in Incentive Design," *Journal of Economic Perspectives* 7 (1993): 113–134.

Subject Index

Author Index